SE

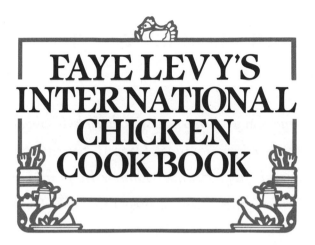

FAYE LEVY'S INTERNATIONAL CHICKEN COOKBOOK

OTHER BOOKS BY FAYE LEVY

Faye Levy's International Jewish Cookbook
Fresh from France: Dessert Sensations
Fresh from France: Dinner Inspirations
Fresh from France: Vegetable Creations
Sensational Pasta
Faye Levy's Chocolate Sensations
Classic Cooking Techniques
La Cuisine du Poisson (in French, with Fernand Chambrette)
Faye Levy's Favorite Recipes (in Hebrew)
French Cooking Without Meat (in Hebrew)
French Desserts (in Hebrew)
French Cakes, Pastries and Cookies (in Hebrew)
The La Varenne Tour Book

FAYE LEVY'S
INTERNATIONAL
CHICKEN
COOKBOOK

Faye Levy

WARNER BOOKS

A Time Warner Company

For my teachers and my students

Warner Books, Inc., 1271 Avenue of the Americas, New York, NY 10020

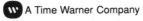 A Time Warner Company

Printed in the United States of America
First printing: September 1992
10 9 8 7 6 5 4 3 2 1

Library of Congress Cataloging-in-Publication Data

Levy, Faye.
  [International chicken cookbook]
  Faye Levy's international chicken cookbook / Faye Levy.
    p.   cm.
  Includes index.
  ISBN 0-446-51569-8
  1. Cookery (Chicken)   2. Cookery, International.   I. Title.
TX750.5.C45L52   1992
641.6′65—dc20   92-54097
                                                          CIP

Book design by Giorgetta Bell McRee

Instructional illustrations by Stephanie Osser

CONTENTS

ACKNOWLEDGMENTS

I would like to express my gratitude to Liv Blumer, my editor, for encouraging me to produce an even better book than I thought I could, for her imaginative suggestions and creative editorial ideas, and for her friendship.

I am thankful to several teachers who taught me many delicious poultry dishes over a period of nearly six years and inspired me with their passion for delectable food. Many thanks to master chefs Fernand Chambrette and Claude Vauguet and to cookbook author Anne Willan, for making the years I studied and worked with them at La Varenne Cooking School in Paris so enlightening and enjoyable.

I am grateful to many colleagues and friends who shared their expertise in cuisines around the globe and gave me excellent recipes. I would especially like to thank cooking teacher Steven Raichlen for his Caribbean chicken recipes; cooking teacher Neelam Batra for her recipes and tips on the cooking of her native India; and chef Michel Ohayon for sharing his knowledge of Moroccan cooking and food customs.

For a stimulating introduction to the Oriental cuisines, I wish to thank two talented teachers: Chinese cooking expert Nina Simonds of Boston, and Thai chef Somchit Singchalee of Bangkok.

When I lived in the Middle East, I savored some of the best chicken dishes in the world. I thank my many relatives in Israel for enthusiastically teaching me how to prepare their favorite chicken dishes.

In Los Angeles, I enjoyed working with the creative team of photographers at De Gennaro Associates on the photographs in the book. Thanks also to Annie Horenn for food styling, to Teri Appleton for helping us cook for the photographs, and to Zero Minus Plus in Santa Monica for providing us with beautiful serving plates for the photographs. Thanks also to Mary Boon for the cover photograph.

I am grateful to Harvey-Jane Kowal at Warner Books for ensuring a smooth and accurate path to publication and to Stephanie Osser for illustrating the techniques for cutting poultry.

Thanks to my mother, Pauline Kahn Luria, for serving wonderful chicken soup and tasty roast chicken every Friday night.

And thanks to my husband Yakir, who helped me in every aspect of producing this book—from research to writing to interviewing to testing and tasting.

INTRODUCTION

In recent years the popularity of poultry has grown dramatically. Chicken has overtaken beef as the most frequently served meat on American tables. Turkey is no longer reserved exclusively for Thanksgiving, but is enjoyed by many families year-round. There are several reasons why chicken and turkey are the meat of choice of so many people. They are low in fat and calories, especially their white meat; they are inexpensive; and they appeal to almost everyone's taste.

In response to the growing demand, supermarkets have been expanding their poultry sections. There is more to choose from than ever before. Ducks, geese, and Cornish hens are increasingly available. Chickens and turkeys can now be purchased conveniently packaged ground or in parts—breasts, legs, thighs, drumsticks, wings, and drummettes. Breasts and thighs are also offered boneless and skinless. A variety of new poultry products fills the shelves at the store—chicken ravioli, chicken pizza, chicken burritos, chicken or turkey Italian sausages, turkey kielbasa, turkey pastrami, and even turkey bacon.

Beyond our own borders, poultry is widely used in every cuisine, from Oriental to European to Mediterranean. Around the globe a myriad of flavorful chicken preparations has

ix

been developed. Every region has its unique poultry specialties. I have savored chicken stir-fries with ginger and soy sauce in the Far East, chicken stews with tomatoes and olives in the Middle East, and chicken sautés with wine, vegetables, and herbs in France and Italy.

Chicken has always been my favorite meat. It was only natural that I particularly enjoyed teaching classes and writing articles on cooking chicken and other poultry. I was pleased to see what a great demand there was for classes on such subjects as ''Mediterranean chicken,'' ''French chicken,'' and others focusing on international recipes for poultry.

For this book I have cooked countless chicken dishes from every major region of the world. From the most delicious recipes, I have selected those that are practical for cooking in the American kitchen, with readily available ingredients. I have given preference to light dishes, and I have always opted for recipes that owe their excellence to their flavor combinations rather than to complex procedures.

I hope you will find this book a great source for tasty chicken dishes that you and your family will enjoy for many years.

1

Cooking Poultry
Around the World

The cooking of most countries is not homogenous, and even relatively small countries have regional and personal variations of the national cuisine. Contributing to the diversity is the migration of ethnic groups throughout history, eventually creating "melting pot" cuisines in many areas of the world. Each of these ethnic mixes is unique and has its own culinary culture. New waves of immigrants lead to the creation of new dishes.

Today ingredients travel more easily than ever before, adding to the array of available seasonings. Still, each area possesses its own assortment of favorite foodstuffs and its own flavor. There are fundamental differences between regions in cooking in general, and specifically in cooking poultry.

Here is a brief overview of the basic seasonings and techniques that have been developed for cooking poultry in different regions of the world.

1

EUROPE

Old-fashioned European chicken dishes are delicate. Poultry is often lightly seasoned and cooked in its own juices to emphasize its natural flavor. Roast chicken and turkey with meat or bread stuffing is popular in much of the continent, and so are chicken soups and stews. Chicken is frequently sautéed or braised with domestic and wild mushrooms as well as seasonal vegetables such as baby carrots, new potatoes, green peas, or asparagus. Breading and frying chicken and turkey breasts is a preferred cooking technique in Austria and European parts of the former Soviet Union. Duck, geese, and game birds are considered delicacies throughout the region, and are usually served roasted, often with a tangy accompaniment such as sauerkraut or with a fruity sauce.

Although Europeans like their poultry to be subtly seasoned, they do not want it bland. Many feel that seasonings should highlight the taste of poultry rather than dominate the dish. When chicken is braised, it is moistened with white or red wine, beer, cider, or chicken stock and flavored with onions, shallots, carrots, a discreet amount of garlic, and such herbs as dill, tarragon, chives, chervil, parsley, marjoram, thyme, or bay leaves. By skillfully combining a few ingredients, cooks have created wonderful dishes such as the Burgundian coq au vin and chicken velouté soup.

Sweet-and-sour dishes are favorites in much of the region, often prepared by cooking poultry with prunes or raisins and finishing the sauce with vinegar and sugar. Mustard and horseradish are used to flavor sauces and are served as condiments. In Hungary, peppers and hot and sweet paprika add zest to many poultry dishes. Variations of Hungary's famous chicken stew with paprika are prepared in Austria, Bulgaria, and Yugoslavia.

For sautéing chicken, butter and vegetable oil are popular everywhere, while goose fat is favored in central Europe and parts of France. Lard, and to a lesser extent, chicken fat, are used for the same purpose by many people. Sauces are often enriched with tangy crème fraîche in France, with sour cream in Germany, Hungary, Poland, and Russia, and with sweet cream in Scandinavia.

In classic French cuisine, which influences European cooking considerably, chicken dishes are classified in two types: white dishes, made with white wine and cream, and brown dishes, made with red wine and brown sauce and for which the chicken is browned thoroughly.

THE MEDITERRANEAN

During the last decade a healthful diet and a Mediterranean way of eating have practically become synonymous. Poultry fits in well with the Mediterranean diet recommended by many nutritionists—a generous amount of vegetables and grains and relatively little saturated fat.

In Mediterranean cooking, olive oil is used rather than the classic northern European staples of butter, cream, and lard. This style has become so fashionable that it is a major source of inspiration for chefs at the forefront of California cuisine and other American regional cuisines.

Garlic is a beloved partner for chicken throughout the region. Herbs are used lavishly. Dill, rosemary, sage, and oregano are matched with chicken in the northern Mediterranean countries, cilantro (fresh coriander) in the south, and mint and Italian parsley in most areas. Spices such as saffron, ground red pepper, ginger, cinnamon, and cumin add an exotic touch to some dishes, especially those of Morocco and other North African countries.

For ages grilling has been a technique of choice for preparing chicken in the Mediterranean region. Cooks in each country have developed wonderful seasoning blends and marinades—some spicy, some tangy, and some delicate—that produce succulent, flavorful grilled chicken. Roast chicken and turkey are also popular, either flavored with rosemary and garlic as in Italy, accompanied by fresh tomato sauce as in Provence, or served with a sherry deglazing sauce as in Spain.

Braised chicken dishes are time-honored favorites. Best known are the aromatic Moroccan tajines of chicken stewed with vegetables or fruits flavored with saffron, cinnamon, and sometimes honey, or with cumin, garlic, and hot pepper, served with couscous. But throughout the Mediterranean area, from Greece to Spain to North Africa, chicken is braised or stewed gently with tomatoes, garlic, onions, herbs, and sometimes spices or olives.

Chicken specialties in the style of the Mediterranean countries have such great taste appeal in America because they are vibrant, richly flavored, aromatic, and occasionally exotic, but rarely strange or "crazy." To our palates, the flavors are well balanced and "make sense."

THE MIDDLE EAST AND INDIA

Since the Middle East begins at the eastern end of the Mediterranean, it's not surprising that the chicken specialties of both regions have much in common. Many of the same flavorings are used, especially garlic, onions, lemon juice, cilantro (fresh coriander), mint, dill, cumin, turmeric, cinnamon, and in some areas, hot peppers. In much of the Middle East, especially in Lebanon, Syria, and the Arabian Peninsula, there is a fondness for hearty chicken dishes such as stews with garbanzo beans, soups with vegetables and rice, and braised chicken dishes with tomato-garlic sauces and zucchini, green beans, okra, or other vegetables. Grilled chicken, in pieces and as kabobs, is a favorite, especially with a tangy garlic-lemon marinade.

Farther east, Iranians often combine several different herbs, such as mint, dill, and cilantro, in a single chicken dish for an aromatic result; they also enjoy stews of chicken with split peas or lentils. The most famous Iranian chicken specialty is a rich, exotic-tasting stew with pomegranate juice and walnuts (Chicken Fesanjan, or Iranian Chicken in Walnut Pomegranate Sauce, page 239) and is also loved in Armenia and Azerbaijan.

Pita bread and bulgur wheat are strongly associated with the Middle East because of their popularity in the region but in fact rice is the accompaniment of choice for poultry in this area, as in the neighboring subcontinent to the east—India.

Since chickens are believed to have been first domesticated in India, cooks there have had a long history of using them. They make use of the full range of spices and herbs to complement poultry in a great variety of dishes. The best known to us are stews of robust flavors, which we refer to as curries, and grilled marinated tandoori chicken. Many of the spices used in the Indian kitchen, such as nutmeg, cinnamon, cloves, and saffron, are ingredients we associate with European cooking, but in India they are combined with the fresh ginger of the Far East. Garlic, onions, hot peppers, and cilantro are used liberally, as are cumin and coriander seeds, the dominant "curry" spices. Marinades, often based on yogurt mixed with spices, are important for grilled and roasted chicken, and impart a rich and slightly tangy flavor. With the main courses aromatic Basmati rice or flat Indian bread is served, and so are salads called raitas made with yogurt for their cooling effect. India has distinct regional cuisines, with an Arab influence in the north and in Pakistan, where the preferred cooking fat is *ghee*, or clarified butter. In southern India, chicken dishes are hotter and are cooked with vegetable oil or coconut milk.

THE ORIENT

Chicken soups are loved throughout the Orient. They might be embellished with wheat or rice noodles, bean threads or rice. Usually they are delicate, containing perhaps a few strips of chicken, mushrooms, a green vegetable such as asparagus, spinach or bok choy leaves, and often chopped green onion or cilantro (fresh coriander). Chicken stock is the base for many other soups as well, even if the main ingredient is fish, pork, or vegetables.

For chicken dishes other than soup, rice is the usual accompaniment. Noodles are combined with strips of chicken, vegetables, and seasonings as a main dish or one of several dishes, rather than served plain as an accompaniment.

The Chinese cooking method of stir-frying chicken and seasoning it with soy sauce, ginger, garlic, sesame oil, and rice wine is very familiar in the West, and the basic ingredients are widely available. Red-cooked chicken, an aromatic form of poached chicken flavored with soy sauce, ginger, and green onions, is another popular technique. Barbecued, braised, and smoked duck are favorite Chinese specialties.

But poultry is prepared and seasoned in the Far East in numerous other ways. In the hot and spicy Sichuan style of western China, dried chilies, chili paste with garlic, chili oil, Sichuan peppercorns, generous quantities of ginger, and sometimes dried tangerine peel are used to flavor chicken. Scallions and garlic are the flavorings of choice in the northern region. The sweet-and-sour combination is said to have originated in that area, although the Cantonese in the south are credited with popularizing it. Both southern and eastern Chinese cooking are marked by subtle use of seasonings.

Vietnamese cooking shares much with Chinese but is often lighter because steaming and poaching are more widely used than frying. Preferred flavorings for chicken are lemongrass, ginger, fish sauce (*nuoc mam*), cilantro, and garlic.

Koreans like the taste of sesame, and often season chicken with a mixture of sesame oil, sesame seeds, garlic, soy sauce, and green onions. Grilling is a favorite technique.

In Japan chicken is often marinated, before being grilled, sautéed, or fried, with sweet-and-pungent mixtures such as teriyaki sauce made of soy sauce, sweet rice wine called mirin, garlic, and sometimes ginger. Small pieces of chicken are braised with vegetables, mushrooms, and noodles in stock with soy sauce, mirin, and sugar, to make one-pot meals. Chicken is frequently combined with seafood and noodles in salads and soups.

Cooking in the Philippines is a blend of Chinese and Spanish styles, sometimes resulting in such dishes as the traditional chicken adobo, a Spanish-named dish of chicken simmered with vinegar and garlic, but with a Chinese touch—soy sauce. Some versions are enriched with coconut milk as well, reflecting the Malay influence on Filipino cuisine.

Located roughly between India and China, Thailand boasts a distinctive cuisine that could be described as a mixture of both. Thus, it's not surprising that the best-loved chicken dishes are stir-fries and curries. Thai chicken stir-fries often feature hot peppers and soy sauce as well as fresh mint or basil leaves. Thai curries are usually based on coconut milk and often are seasoned with lemongrass, Thai basil, fish sauce, a special kind of ginger, copious amounts of hot peppers, and many of the Indian curry spices. There are green curries prepared with green chilies, cilantro, and other fresh green flavorings; red curries made with red chilies; and "Moslem" curries flavored with cumin and ground coriander and bearing a certain resemblance to northern Indian curries.

Spicy chicken curries enriched with coconut milk are also central to the cuisines of Indonesia and Malaysia. Grilled skewered chicken called satay is the Indonesian poultry dish best known to us. It is accompanied by peanut sauce seasoned with chilies, soy sauce, and coconut.

SOUTH AND CENTRAL AMERICA

Many of Latin America's poultry dishes have benefited from the blending of the cooking of the Indians (the Aztecs and the Mayans in Mexico, and the Incas in Peru) and the Spanish settlers. The Indian influence dominates the cuisine in countries such as Mexico, where there is a large Indian population, but is present throughout the continent. Until the Spaniards came to the continent and brought pigs, Latin American Indians did not have fat for cooking, so only then did the technique of frying enter their cuisines.

Chilies add zest to chicken specialties in most parts of Latin America, but on the whole the hottest cooking is done in Mexico, where a great selection of chilies—varying from very hot to mild, in fresh, dried and powdered forms—is available. Cumin and cilantro (fresh coriander) are other well-liked flavorings in the region, as are onions, garlic, and tomatoes, both red and green (tomatillos). Chicken is usually stewed, sometimes served with sauces called *moles*, which contain chilies and often a great number of other ingredients, such as ground nuts, sesame seeds, cinnamon, and cloves, as in the famous *mole poblano*. Other simpler sauces for chicken are the various types of salsa cruda, basically a mixture of chopped chilies, tomatoes, and onions, and guacamole, made of mashed or pureed avocado. Hot tortillas are the favorite Mexican accompaniment, and are also used as wrappers to make enchiladas and burritos, often with chicken or turkey fillings. The Mexican Indians had turkeys before the Spaniards arrived, but not chickens.

Brazilian cooking is a mixture of Portuguese, West African, and some native Indian ingredients. Chicken dishes are spicy, and might come with peanut or coconut sauces flavored with ginger and cilantro. As in Africa, sometimes chicken is stewed with okra. The most common cooking oil is palm oil, also called dende oil, which colors the dishes bright yellow-orange.

In other areas of the continent chicken is often braised in the Spanish style with garlic, onions, and tomatoes, or occasionally with citrus juices or wine. Paella-inspired chicken cooked with rice is loved throughout the region, and a variation is made with duck. In Argentina and southern Brazil, barbecuing is very popular. Frequent accompaniments for poultry are corn, beans, rice, and plantains, or potatoes in Peru, where they originated.

THE CARIBBEAN

The Caribbean Islands are best known for their hot peppery cuisine, although this is more true of certain islands such as Jamaica than of others. Fiery hot sauces are a favorite flavoring for chicken, as well as a table accompaniment, a legacy of the African taste for highly seasoned foods. People of West African origin have the most significant influence on Caribbean menus. Originally brought to the islands as slaves, they are now the dominant population.

Among the various Caribbean Islands, there are differences in cuisine depending on which European country controlled the island and for how long. Thus, the cooking on Spanish-speaking islands such as Cuba and Puerto Rico has much in common with that of Spain. Chicken is often cooked with capers, olives, garlic, oregano, and sherry and is not particularly hot. Stews often begin with a flavoring mixture called *sofrito*, made from annatto oil, sautéed onions, green peppers, garlic, cilantro (fresh coriander), and tomatoes, which is related to the sofrito used in Spain.

French chicken dishes with herbs and creamy sauces are served in many restaurants in the French West Indies. Workers from East India also had a profound influence on Caribbean food, and curry has become one of the favorite island seasonings for chicken. In the Dutch islands, there are Indonesian-style dishes. As in Louisiana, often the word *Creole* is used to describe Caribbean cuisine, denoting a mixture of African and European influences.

In the Caribbean, chicken is often stewed or cooked as soup. Roasting is not a tradition because ovens were not available. The island love for barbecued food is considered a contribution of the native Indians. Favorite ingredients for flavoring chicken, besides chilies and curry powder, are peanuts, avocados, lime juice, oregano, allspice, ginger, nutmeg, cloves, cinnamon, onions, garlic, and tomatoes. Popular accompaniments are beans with rice, fried plantains, and stewed okra. Tropical fruits like mangoes, papayas, pineapples, and guavas are plentiful in the Caribbean Islands. Chefs often combine them with poultry to create new, exotic dishes.

NORTH AMERICA

To a certain extent, chicken specialties in both the United States and Canada reflect the British and French cooking heritage of the early settlers. Many dishes, however, were modified with the availability of unfamiliar ingredients that the Pilgrims found in the New World, such as turkey, corn, cranberries, and sweet potatoes. In spite of the changes in some dishes, the favorite North American poultry dishes reflect a European culinary connection, especially in areas where the majority of the population has its roots in Europe. Some examples of popular, old-fashioned American dishes that originated in Europe are chicken pie, shepherd's pie, chicken salad with mayonnaise, and roast chicken with bread stuffing.

Many American chicken dishes began as an ethnic or regional specialty but have entered the mainstream of American cooking. A good example is chicken chili. Traditionally a flavorful meat sauce or stew, with tomatoes, onions, hot pepper, and usually cumin, its flavoring is Mexican. Yet chili is really an American dish and is not made in Mexico. Its origin is usually ascribed to Texas, and thus it is often called a Tex-Mex dish. Chili used to be prepared mainly with beef and pork, but today it is made with chicken and turkey as well.

As a result of the meeting of people from different areas, other regional styles of American cooking have developed over time. The Cajun-Creole cooking of Louisiana is a blend of French, Spanish, American Indian, and African. Cooks in that southern state have created exciting poultry dishes such as chicken jambalaya, a meal-in-one dish made of rice, chicken, ham, and aromatic vegetables, somewhat like a spicy version of the Spanish paella.

California is known for culinary creativity. The state's great ethnic diversity leads to an abundance of exotic ingredients and a stimulating interaction among the various cultures. In many regions of the country ethnic chicken specialties and cooking techniques have become an integral part of the diet. Many Americans are familiar with Italian chicken cacciatora, Japanese teriyaki chicken, and Chinese chicken with almonds.

Americans borrow freely from other cuisines. Often, however, they incorporate the dishes learned into an American-style menu rather than serving them as they would be served in their country of origin. Pasta, for example, is often served as a main course in America rather than as a first course, as in Italy. Therefore Americans tend to combine chicken with pasta as a meal-in-one-dish, while Italians do not.

At home, people love to stir-fry chicken, or to bake chicken with Italian sauces. Other ethnic styles of cooking in vogue today are the spicy cuisines. These include Thai, Chinese, Mexican, Caribbean, and Indian, all of which have had an impact on the new American cuisine. (See "Cross-Cultural Cooking," following section.)

For many people, highly flavored dishes are a welcome change from the previous blandness of much of the Anglo-Saxon American food. The current enthusiasm for spicy cuisines is also due in part to the fact that strongly seasoned food can be low in fat and still be tasty.

CROSS-CULTURAL COOKING

An interesting trend in today's cooking is a studied blending of tastes, ingredients, and techniques of Western dishes with those of other cuisines. An offshoot of nouvelle cuisine that began in France in the 1970s, this trend was a natural expansion of the conscious effort to add foreign ingredients and cooking methods to French dishes, with the emphasis on creativity. In addition to mixing culinary influences in single dishes, chefs might offer specialties from different parts of the world on the same menu. In sharp contrast to the pre-nouvelle era, chefs are now expected and even required to have a "personal twist" in their dishes in order to attract sophisticated diners.

Light and healthful food is important in this contemporary style of cooking, and so poultry, especially skinless chicken breast, is featured often in appetizers and as main courses.

This style and variations on the theme are known today by many names—combination cuisine, cross-cultural cuisine, fusion cuisine, eclectic cooking, East meets West, Franco-Japanese, Chinois, or Pacific Rim cooking. At a recent culinary conference in Beverly Hills, one of the panelists, a top California chef and proponent of this innovative style, added yet another label—"mish-mash cuisine." In one form or another, this type of imaginative cooking has gained recognition in major cities all over the world, from Hong Kong to New York to Paris to Jerusalem.

In North America, cooks in various areas put different accents on European and American food. In Miami, for example, classically trained chefs are incorporating flavors of the Caribbean and the American South into their dishes. With very large Hispanic and Oriental populations and a wealth of foreign foodstuffs, Los Angeles is a mecca for the cross-cultural style. Local culinary experts come up with such innovations as pizza topped with Peking duck, or chicken salad with French vinaigrette seasoned with fresh ginger and Oriental sesame oil.

2

Pairing Wine with Poultry

 Many people think that white wine is the only right choice for poultry, but in fact poultry is good with a variety of wines. At a course in marrying wine and food at the Académie du Vin in Paris over a decade ago, I learned that poultry has always had a greater degree of flexibility for matching with wines than any other entree. Certainly this is true today when even the most traditional rules have been relaxed, and most people simply drink the wine they prefer with the dishes they like.

The most general guideline is to serve white wine with white meat and red wine with dark meat. This makes it easy to select a wine for dark-meat birds like duck and goose—a mature Bordeaux, a French Burgundy, or a California Cabernet Sauvignon is perfect.

Game birds were traditionally served with red wine because wild game has an assertive flavor. Today the ''game birds'' available at the markets are domestically raised, and their flavor is more delicate. Thus, the same wines that are good with chicken or turkey also marry well with game birds.

Since chicken and turkey have both white and dark meat, both white and red wines

11

complement them. The classic view is that mild, creamy poultry dishes are best with white wine, and more robust entrees call for a heavier red.

If there is already white or red wine in the sauce, then a wine of the same color and a similar character is the best accompaniment for the poultry. I do not necessarily choose the same wine I use in cooking, however; the best wines are generally saved for drinking, and a less expensive wine is used for cooking.

Grilled poultry, because of its bold flavor, tends to go best with a full-bodied red wine like a California Cabernet Sauvignon or a French Côtes du Rhône. Roasted or other simply prepared chicken or turkey is also good with these wines, as well as with lighter red wines like Beaujolais and rich-tasting white wines like California Chardonnay.

With spicy poultry dishes from such cuisines as Thai, Indian, or Mexican, many people prefer rather spicy white wines like Alsatian Gewürtztraminer, zesty red wines like California Zinfandel or French Côtes de Provence, or crisp dry wines like French Chablis or California Sauvignon Blanc. The delicate nuances of flavor of a fine wine would be lost if served with very hot and spicy food. For many tastes, beer is a better choice with these cuisines.

French, Italian, and Californian wines all can be wonderful with poultry. I enjoy matching the wine to the region of origin or inspiration of the dish. For example, a turkey daube from southern France is nice with a Côtes du Rhône, and chicken in sun-dried tomato cream sauce on a bed of fettuccine is very fine with a California Chardonnay.

3

Chicken and Turkey Appetizers

Whether broiled, barbecued, or roasted, poultry served as an appetizer is usually highly flavored. For the seasoning, an important inspiration is the cuisines of the Far East, with its spicy, tangy, and sweet-and-sour themes. These finger-food appetizers can be served on their own or accompanied by dipping sauces. A well-known appetizer of this type is the Indonesian chicken satay with spicy peanut dipping sauce, which turns the familiar peanut butter into an exotic preparation. Chicken wings or drummettes can be broiled with soy-based Chinese marinades, baked with orange juice and honey, or for a Mediterranean delight, grilled and served with garlic oil. With these dishes you can be generous with the spices, since they are eaten in small amounts.

Chicken appetizers are made of the smaller pieces, especially wings and drummettes, which are small drumsticks made from the larger wing piece. Skewered chicken cubes, of either thigh or breast meat, served as brochettes or kabobs, have universal appeal as festive appetizers or party fare.

From Mexican chicken enchiladas flavored with chilies, cilantro, and tomatoes to French

13

Grilled Chicken Drummettes with Garlic Oil
Orange Roasted Drummettes
Sweet-and-Sour Wings
Broiled Chicken Wings with Ginger
and Plum Sauce
Chicken Satays
Niçoise Chicken Liver Pâté with Thyme
and White Wine
Smoked Chicken and Goat Cheese Canapés
Sesame Chicken Crepes with Shiitake
Mushrooms and Leeks
Chicken and Porcini Crepes
Chicken Enchiladas with Tomatoes, Chilies,
and Cilantro
Two-Minute Turkey Pâté with Provençal Herbs
Smoked Turkey and Cabbage Crepes
Zesty Turkey-Bean Burritos

crepes with chicken and mushrooms in a velouté sauce, appetizers of "wrapped" poultry are loved around the world. Although the envelope may differ, the goal is the same: to obtain a delicate wrapper with a richly flavored chicken or turkey filling.

For everyday or spur-of-the-moment entertaining, burritos and enchiladas are a good choice. Since you can buy the tortillas, making these dishes is a snap. Chicken Bruschetta, an Italian open-faced sandwich, is another easy and delicious appetizer (page 285).

A quick pâté or spread is probably the simplest poultry appetizer to make. Blend cooked and smoked chicken or turkey with herbs, and you will have a great appetizer to serve with crusty bread or crackers. Chicken livers require just brief sautéing and seasoning to become a luscious European-style pâté. To accompany these pâtés, you can serve an assortment of crackers or crisp breads.

Chicken and turkey salads served in small quantities make great appetizers, too. They are described in the "salad" chapter (pages 47–74).

OTHER RECIPES THAT CAN BE SERVED AS APPETIZERS

Served in small portions, these dishes can also make delicious appetizers.

Pies and Pastries

Lebanese Chicken Pizza (page 34)
Moroccan Chicken Rolls with Raisins and Walnuts (page 35)
Moroccan Chicken Pie with Cinnamon and Saffron (Bastilla)
(page 40)
Baked Turkey Empanadas (page 41)
Smoked Turkey and Vegetable Tart (page 44)

Salads

Soups

Pasta and Rice Dishes

Other Dishes

GRILLED CHICKEN DRUMMETTES WITH GARLIC OIL

This Lebanese appetizer is a must for garlic lovers, since the garlic oil plays a double role: it flavors the marinade for the chicken and it becomes a tasty dipping sauce.

Drummettes, the large part of the wing, are one of the easiest cuts to grill or broil. They cook faster than drumsticks or thighs and thus don't tend to burn easily, yet their meat is moister than breast meat and their skin becomes crisp.

These drummettes make a great opening for a spicy meal. I also like them as a main course accompanied by fresh corn on the cob, which also tastes good with the garlic oil.

Garlic Oil (page 361)
2 tablespoons plus 2 teaspoons
  strained fresh lemon juice
dash of ground cinnamon
½ teaspoon freshly ground black
  pepper
½ teaspoon dried thyme, crumbled

1 bay leaf
1 tablespoon olive oil
1½ pounds chicken drummettes
  (largest section of the wing)
½ small onion, sliced thin
salt
pinch of cayenne pepper

To make marinade, stir Garlic Oil, measure 1 tablespoon including some garlic pieces, and put in a bowl. Add 2 tablespoons lemon juice, cinnamon, pepper, thyme, bay leaf, and olive oil. Put chicken in shallow dish, add marinade, and toss well. Add onion slices and toss again. Cover and marinate chicken in refrigerator 2 to 6 hours, turning pieces occasionally.

Remove onion from marinade and reserve. Discard marinade. Sprinkle chicken with salt on both sides. Grill over glowing coals or broil about 5 to 6 inches from heat source for about 25 minutes, turning every 8 or 10 minutes.

Add onion from marinade to broiler if desired, and broil about 4 minutes or until slightly charred.

Add 2 teaspoons lemon juice and pinch of cayenne to remaining garlic oil. Serve it with grilled drummettes.

Makes 4 appetizer or 2 main-course servings

ORANGE ROASTED DRUMMETTES

Chicken cooked with orange juice is popular in Spain, Latin America, and Israel. This recipe is from an Israeli friend, Bruria Hadad. The savory chicken glazed with oranges, honey, and garlic has a delicate sweet-and-sour flavor with a hint of spiciness.

Honey and garlic tend to burn, so the drummettes are roasted covered, to allow the flavors to permeate them. At the end of the roasting time, the dish is uncovered to brown the drummettes. To help them brown, it is best to use a roasting pan in which they are not crowded, so that once uncovered, they roast rather than steam.

1¼ pounds chicken wing drummettes
   (largest section of the wing)
¼ teaspoon salt
⅓ cup strained fresh orange juice
½ teaspoon paprika
¼ teaspoon hot red pepper flakes, or a
   few shakes of cayenne pepper

¼ teaspoon turmeric
1 tablespoon liquid honey
1 large garlic clove, finely minced
1 teaspoon strained fresh lemon or
   lime juice

Preheat the oven to 350°F. Sprinkle chicken with salt. Mix all remaining ingredients and toss with chicken in a 10 × 15-inch roasting pan. Place pieces so they don't touch each other. Cover with foil and bake 30 minutes. Uncover, baste, and bake 20 to 25 more minutes, turning chicken twice and basting, or until chicken is tender and golden brown and most of the juices have evaporated. During the last 5 minutes, shake pan a few times so juices don't burn. Serve hot.

Makes 4 to 6 appetizer servings

SWEET-AND-SOUR WINGS

Chicken wings glazed with a Chinese sweet-and-sour sauce have become one of the best-loved American appetizers. The wings are briefly roasted, then brushed with the sauce and baked. You can prepare teriyaki wings the same way; simply substitute the ingredients of the teriyaki sauce (see Teriyaki Turkey, page 278) for the sweet-and-sour sauce. SEE PHOTOGRAPH.

2 pounds chicken wings (10 wings)
salt and ground white pepper
Chinese Sweet-and-Sour Sauce
  (page 372)

green onion fans, for garnish (see
  Note)
orange slices (optional garnish)

Preheat the oven to 400°F. Cut off wing tips; reserve for stock. Leave wings whole; or cut them apart at joints. Lightly oil a roasting pan, then put wings in pan in one layer. Sprinkle with salt and white pepper on both sides. Roast 30 minutes or until meat is no longer pink; cut into thickest part to check.

Set sauce nearby.

Drain off fat from pan of wings, then brush wings lightly with sauce. Roast 5 minutes, turn wings over and brush with sauce, and roast 5 to 10 minutes more or until glazed and browned. Serve hot, on a plate garnished with green onion fans and orange slices. Accompany with remaining sauce for dipping.

Makes 4 or 5 appetizer or 2 main-course servings

NOTE: To make green onion fans, cut off root and all but 3 inches of the white part of a green onion. Make several parallel, lengthwise cuts outward from the center of the 3-inch piece, beginning 1 inch up from the bottom. Put in ice water in refrigerator for about an hour. Ends will curl.

BROILED CHICKEN WINGS
WITH GINGER AND PLUM SAUCE

If you taste the marinade for these Chinese-seasoned wings on its own, it will seem very pungent from the soy sauce and sherry, but it seasons the wings perfectly and gives them an appetizing brown color. I like to add Chinese plum sauce to the marinade since it adds both sweetness and spiciness, but if you don't have it, you can use plum jelly, apricot jam, or honey.

2 medium garlic cloves, minced
1 tablespoon finely minced peeled
  fresh ginger
1 tablespoon plus 1 teaspoon soy sauce
2 teaspoons plum sauce

1 teaspoon dry sherry
¼ teaspoon ground white pepper
1 teaspoon vegetable oil
10 whole chicken wings

Mix garlic with ginger, soy sauce, plum sauce, sherry, pepper, and oil. Rub wings all over with the mixture, put in a shallow dish such as a gratin dish, cover, and refrigerate 30 minutes to 2 hours, turning once or twice.

Preheat the broiler with rack 4 inches from heat. Tuck wing tips underneath so wings lie flat. Put wings on broiler rack, discarding marinade remaining in dish. Broil 15 minutes, turn over, and broil 10 minutes more or until meat is no longer pink; cut in thickest part to check. Serve hot.

Makes 5 appetizer or 2 or 3 main-course servings

CHICKEN SATAYS

Of Indonesian origin, chicken satays—or grilled marinated chicken on skewers—are frequently featured on Thai menus as well. The charm of these appetizers is the accompanying peanut dipping sauce, which is slightly sweet and sour and slightly hot. Serve the satays on a platter garnished with cucumber and onion slices, with the peanut sauce in a small dish for dipping.

1½ pounds boneless chicken breasts, skin removed

Indonesian Satay Marinade (page 349)

Peanut Sauce

1 tablespoon vegetable oil
½ cup minced onion
4 medium garlic cloves, minced
¾ cup canned unsweetened coconut milk, chicken broth, or water
½ teaspoon hot red pepper flakes, or more to taste
½ cup smooth or chunky peanut butter

1 to 2 tablespoons soy sauce
1 teaspoon brown sugar, or more to taste
1 teaspoon strained fresh lemon juice, or more to taste
1½ teaspoons grated, peeled fresh ginger

sliced cucumbers and onions, for accompaniment

Cut chicken in thin strips, about ¾ to 1 inch wide and about 2 inches long. Put in a bowl, add marinade, cover, and marinate 1 or 2 hours in refrigerator. If using bamboo skewers, soak them in cold water for 30 minutes so they won't burn.

For peanut sauce, heat oil in a medium saucepan over medium heat. Add onion and sauté about 7 minutes or until softened. Add garlic and sauté ½ minute. Add coconut milk and red pepper flakes and bring to a boil. Remove pan from heat. Add peanut butter in 4 portions, whisking after each addition. Bring to a simmer. If sauce is too thin, simmer 2 to 3 minutes or until thickened; if it is too thick, stir in 1 or 2 tablespoons water. Add soy sauce, sugar, lemon juice, and ginger and stir. Taste and adjust seasoning, adding more sugar or lemon juice if needed.

Thread the chicken on skewers and brush with marinade. If using bamboo skewers, put foil on ends to prevent burning.

Reheat sauce over low heat, cover, and keep warm. Preheat broiler or prepare grill. Put skewered chicken on lightly oiled broiler rack set about 4 inches from heat or on lightly oiled grill above glowing coals. Grill or broil about 6 minutes, turning often. To check, cut into a large piece—chicken should be white inside, not pink.

Serve on a platter, with small bowls of peanut sauce, and with sliced cucumbers and onions.

Makes 4 to 6 appetizer servings

NIÇOISE CHICKEN LIVER PÂTÉ WITH THYME AND WHITE WINE

This pâté is rich, but a little goes a long way. Serve it as an appetizer in ramekins or other small, deep dishes with thin slices of baguette or other fresh or lightly toasted bread; or spread the pâté on bread as canapés, garnish with a small piece of roasted pepper, gherkin, or sun-dried tomato, and serve as hors d'oeuvres.

8 ounces chicken livers
1 tablespoon Cognac or brandy
¼ cup dry white wine
1 teaspoon dried thyme, crumbled
1 bay leaf
pinch of grated nutmeg

3 tablespoons olive oil
salt and freshly ground pepper
4 medium shallots, chopped
1 medium garlic clove, chopped
5 to 6 tablespoons (¾ stick) butter, softened

Marinate the livers in a mixture of Cognac, wine, ½ teaspoon thyme, bay leaf, and nutmeg for 1 or 2 hours in refrigerator. Turn livers from time to time. Remove livers to paper towels; discard marinade.

Heat 3 tablespoons oil in a skillet over medium-high heat. Add livers, salt, and pepper and sauté 2 minutes. Add shallots and garlic and sauté over medium heat 1 minute more or until livers are browned and just pink inside (but no longer red); cut a large piece to check.

Transfer contents of skillet to a bowl and cool slightly. Puree in a food processor until smooth. Add remaining thyme and 5 tablespoons butter and process until well blended. Taste, adjust seasoning, and blend in remaining butter if desired.

Spoon into ramekins and refrigerate at least 1 hour before serving. *Can be kept, covered, 4 days in refrigerator.*

Makes about 6 appetizer servings

SMOKED CHICKEN AND GOAT CHEESE CANAPÉS

These colorful party appetizers disappear in no time and are very easy to prepare. They make use of a French herb-accented goat cheese spread, which is topped with thin slices of smoked chicken and garnished with roasted red peppers or tomato slices.

¼ pound creamy goat cheese, such as Montrachet, at room temperature
3 to 4 tablespoons heavy cream, crème fraîche, or sour cream
3 tablespoons minced fresh parsley
1 tablespoon snipped chives
2 teaspoons chopped fresh tarragon, or ¾ teaspoon dried, crumbled

salt (optional) and freshly ground pepper
8 to 10 thin slices French bread or good-quality white bread
8 to 10 thin slices smoked chicken breast
1 roasted red bell pepper (page 408), or 2 plum tomatoes

Using a wooden spoon, beat the cheese with 2 tablespoons cream until smooth. Stir in enough remaining cream to obtain a spreading consistency. Stir in parsley, chives, and tarragon. Add a pinch of pepper. Taste spread before adding salt. Cover and refrigerate overnight so that flavors blend.

Using a round 3-inch cutter, cut bread and smoked chicken in rounds. Spread bread with goat cheese mixture and set smoked chicken slice on top. Cut bell pepper in strips, or tomato in thin slices, and use to garnish canapés.

Makes 8 to 10 canapés

SESAME CHICKEN CREPES WITH SHIITAKE MUSHROOMS AND LEEKS

Oriental sesame oil and fresh ginger lend zip to the chicken, leek, and mushroom filling of these French crepes, for a delicious East meets West style appetizer or main course. If serving it as a first course, follow it with a simple main course, such as roast beef or lamb with a green vegetable.

1 ounce dried shiitake mushrooms (about 8 mushrooms)

1 pound leeks (white and light green parts only), halved lengthwise and root removed, rinsed and cut in ¼-inch slices

2 tablespoons (¼ stick) butter

salt and freshly ground pepper

2 tablespoons vegetable oil

½ pound white mushrooms, halved and cut in ⅛-inch slices

2 tablespoons plus 1 teaspoon Oriental sesame oil

1 tablespoon minced garlic

1 tablespoon minced peeled fresh ginger

¼ cup dry white wine

1½ cups shredded cooked chicken

12 crepes (page 393), at room temperature

2 tablespoons sesame seeds, toasted (page 409)

Soak mushrooms in enough hot water to cover them for 30 minutes. Drain mushrooms, discarding liquid. Cut off and discard stems. Halve caps lengthwise and cut them crosswise in thin strips about ⅛ inch wide.

Soak sliced leeks in cold water for 5 minutes to remove any sand. Lift into a colander, rinse, and drain well. Melt butter in heavy medium skillet over medium heat. Add leeks, salt, and pepper. Cook, stirring often, until leeks are soft but not brown, about 10 minutes. If any liquid remains in pan, cook leeks over medium-high heat, stirring, until it evaporates. Transfer leeks to a large bowl.

Wipe skillet clean. Add vegetable oil and heat over medium-high heat. Add white mushrooms, salt, and pepper and sauté, stirring often, about 6 minutes or until they begin to brown and any liquid has evaporated. Add shiitake mushrooms and sauté until any liquid that escapes into pan evaporates. Add 1 teaspoon sesame oil, quickly stir in garlic and ginger, and sauté ½ minute. Add wine and boil over high heat, stirring, until it is completely absorbed by the mushroom mixture.

Transfer the mushrooms to the bowl of leeks. Add chicken and mix well. Stir in 1 tablespoon sesame oil and a pinch of pepper. Taste and adjust seasoning.

Lightly oil 2 medium baking dishes. Spoon 3 tablespoons filling onto less attractive side of each crepe, across lower third. Roll up in cigar shape, beginning at edge with filling. Arrange crepes seam side down in one layer in oiled dish. Brush them with remaining 1 tablespoon sesame oil. Sprinkle with toasted sesame seeds. *Crepes can be kept, covered, 1 day in refrigerator. Bring to room temperature before continuing.*

Preheat the oven to 400°F. Bake crepes until filling is hot, about 12 minutes. Serve immediately.

Makes 6 appetizer servings

CHICKEN AND PORCINI CREPES

This luscious European appetizer of crepes with a creamy filling of chicken fillets and porcini mushrooms can be a quick and easy one as well, if you keep crepes on hand in the freezer or if you purchase them. Fresh crepes are now available in many supermarkets. If chicken fillets are not available, use boneless skinless chicken breasts and cut them in strips about ½ inch thick.

½ ounce dried porcini mushrooms
1½ cups chicken stock or broth
1 pound chicken fillets (tender strip of boned breast; see page 396)
½ teaspoon dried thyme, crumbled
salt and freshly ground pepper
3 tablespoons sherry or Madeira

4 tablespoons (½ stick) butter
3 tablespoons all-purpose flour
¾ cup heavy cream
1 tablespoon snipped chives or minced fresh parsley
8 crepes (page 393), at room temperature

Soak the mushrooms in enough hot water to cover them for 30 minutes. Rinse mushrooms and drain well. Cut large mushrooms in 2 or 3 pieces.

Bring the stock to a simmer in a medium saucepan. Add the chicken, thyme, salt, and pepper. Cover and poach chicken over low heat until it changes color throughout, about 4 minutes. Transfer chicken with slotted spoon to bowl, reserving liquid. Dice chicken.

Add mushrooms and 1 tablespoon sherry to chicken cooking liquid, cover, and cook over low heat 10 minutes. Remove mushrooms with slotted spoon, reserving liquid.

Melt butter in a heavy, medium saucepan over low heat. Transfer 1 tablespoon melted butter to a small cup. Whisk flour into butter in saucepan. Cook over low heat, whisking, until mixture turns light beige, about 2 minutes. Remove from heat. Gradually whisk in mushroom cooking liquid. Bring to boil, whisking. Whisk in 1 tablespoon sherry, followed by cream, and return to boil, whisking. Return mushrooms to sauce and simmer uncovered over low heat, stirring occasionally, until sauce heavily coats a spoon, about 7 minutes. Remove from heat. Leave mushrooms in sauce. Set aside 1 cup sauce for serving separately.

For filling, stir chicken into remaining sauce. Stir in 2 teaspoons chives. Taste and adjust seasoning.

Butter a shallow baking dish. Spoon 3 tablespoons filling onto less attractive side of each crepe, across lower third of crepe. Roll up in cigar shape, beginning at edge with filling. Arrange crepes in a single layer in buttered dish. Brush crepes with reserved tablespoon of melted butter. *Crepes can be kept, covered, 1 day in refrigerator; sauce should be reserved, covered, in separate bowl. Bring crepes to room temperature before continuing.*

Preheat the oven to 425°F. Bake crepes until hot, about 10 minutes. Bring sauce just to boil in small saucepan. Remove from heat and stir in remaining tablespoon sherry. Season to taste with salt and pepper. Spoon a little sauce over each crepe when serving and sprinkle with remaining chives.

Makes 8 appetizer or 4 main-course servings

CHICKEN ENCHILADAS WITH TOMATOES, CHILIES, AND CILANTRO

Tortillas, chilies, and other Latin American ingredients are increasingly available in supermarkets and can be used in many ways to enhance chicken dishes. Tortillas need heating so they are flexible before a filling is added for such Mexican specialties as enchiladas and soft tacos. Many enchilada recipes call for frying the tortillas before filling them, but I like to steam them in the oven instead, for a lighter result.

These chicken enchiladas are rich and satisfying because of the tasty filling. They are hot and spicy but not fiery. Serve them as an appetizer, a party buffet dish, or a main course. For those who always like to add more heat to their plate, serve jalapeño-seasoned Fresh Tomato Salsa (page 362). You can also provide bowls of chopped green onions, cilantro, and sour cream for accompaniment.

Mexican Chicken with Chilies and
  Cilantro-Tomato Sauce (page 251)
2 tablespoons chopped cilantro (fresh
  coriander)
salt to taste

cayenne pepper to taste
20 to 22 corn tortillas
1½ cups shredded Monterey Jack
  cheese

To make filling, remove skin, bones, and visible fat from the prepared chicken. Shred chicken and put in a bowl. With a slotted spoon, add 1 cup sauce from chicken; this way you are adding thicker part of sauce. Add cilantro, then season to taste with salt and cayenne pepper.

Preheat the oven to 350°F. Layer tortillas in 2 stacks in baking dish, sprinkle each stack with about 1 teaspoon water, cover, and bake 8 minutes. Leave oven on.

Put the remaining sauce in a sauté pan, bring to a boil, and remove from heat.

To assemble, dip a tortilla in sauce on both sides, then put on a plate. Spoon 3 tablespoons filling in a strip near one end of a tortilla and roll up tightly. Arrange side by side in a shallow baking dish. Sprinkle with cheese. Bake for 10 minutes. Serve with more heated sauce. (Some sauce will be left over. Serve it with rice and vegetables at another meal.)

Makes 10 appetizer or 5 or 6 main-course servings

NOTE: If you already have 3 cups cooked chicken or turkey, you can use it for the filling. Prepare the sauce as on page 251, cooking it only 15 minutes and omitting the chicken broth.

TWO-MINUTE TURKEY PÂTÉ WITH PROVENÇAL HERBS

Many pâtés require hours of baking and contain large amounts of meat fat. This pâté, however, based on cooked turkey and smoked turkey, is ready in a few minutes and is lighter than classic pâtés.

1 cup diced smoked turkey
1 cup diced cooked turkey
4 tablespoons (½ stick) butter, slightly
   softened
4 tablespoons extra-virgin olive oil
1 tablespoon chopped fresh thyme, or
   1½ teaspoons dried, crumbled

2 tablespoons chopped fresh basil
1 teaspoon grated lemon rind
salt and freshly ground pepper
strips of roasted red pepper from a jar,
   basil sprigs, and black olives, for
   garnish

Grind the smoked turkey in a food processor. Add the cooked turkey, butter, and olive oil and process until blended. Transfer to bowl and stir in thyme, basil, lemon rind, and salt and pepper to taste. Refrigerate 1 hour before serving. *Pâté can be kept, covered, 2 days in refrigerator.*

Serve in ramekins or spread on French bread. Garnish with red pepper, basil, and black olives.

Makes about 8 appetizer servings

SMOKED TURKEY AND CABBAGE CREPES

Smoked turkey, sautéed cabbage, and onions make a flavorful filling in the central European style for these crepes. Sour cream is the traditional topping, but you can substitute plain yogurt if you wish.

½ head green cabbage (about 1¼ pounds), cored and rinsed
4 ounces sliced smoked turkey or chicken
4 tablespoons (½ stick) butter
2 tablespoons vegetable oil
2 large onions, minced
1 teaspoon paprika, plus a pinch for garnish

1 medium garlic clove, minced
salt and freshly ground pepper
⅔ cup sour cream, at room temperature, plus about ½ cup sour cream for serving
8 to 12 crepes (page 393), at room temperature
1 tablespoon melted butter
1 tablespoon chopped fresh parsley

To make filling, shred cabbage finely, using a food processor fitted with shredding disk. Cut smoked turkey in ½-inch squares.

Heat 2 tablespoons butter and 1 tablespoon oil in large skillet over low heat. Add onions and cook, stirring occasionally, until very soft but not browned, about 15 minutes. Add paprika and garlic and stir ½ minute over low heat. Add smoked turkey and stir over low heat another ½ minute. Remove mixture to large bowl.

Wipe skillet clean. Add remaining butter and oil and heat over medium heat. Stir in cabbage and a pinch of salt and pepper. Cook, stirring often, until very tender, about 15 minutes. Mix cabbage with smoked turkey mixture. Cool to room temperature. Stir in ⅔ cup sour cream and pinch of pepper. Taste and adjust seasoning.

Butter a shallow baking dish. Spoon 3 tablespoons filling onto less attractive side of each crepe, across lower third of crepe. Roll up in cigar shape, beginning at edge with filling.

Arrange crepes seam side down in a single layer in buttered dish. Brush with melted butter. *Crepes can be kept, covered, 1 day in refrigerator. Bring to room temperature before continuing.*
   Preheat the oven to 425°F. Bake crepes until hot, about 10 minutes. Serve topped with sour cream and sprinkled with paprika and parsley.

Makes 6 appetizer servings

ZESTY TURKEY-BEAN BURRITOS

Leftover turkey and beans are transformed here into a filling with lots of punch. They are simply rolled inside warmed tortillas to make the northern Mexican specialty, burritos. You can use roasted, poached, or braised turkey or chicken. The roasted jalapeño peppers make the filling pretty hot, but for extra zip, it is flavored with and accompanied by a spicy salsa. I like to make my own salsa because I love its fresh taste, but if you're in a hurry you can buy either mild or hot salsa.

For a dish that is low in fat but still high in flavor, use cooked turkey or chicken breast in the filling and omit the cheese. For a party, you might like to serve the burritos with Guacamole (page 365) and sour cream or yogurt.

2 to 3 tablespoons vegetable oil
1 medium onion, chopped
2 medium garlic cloves, chopped
2 jalapeño peppers, roasted, peeled (page 408), and chopped
3 ripe fresh or canned plum tomatoes, or 1 large tomato, chopped
1 cup cooked or canned beans—pinto, black, or navy

1½ cups shredded cooked turkey or chicken
salt and freshly ground pepper
6 flour tortillas
1½ cups Fresh Tomato Salsa (see page 362), or packaged
¾ cup grated Monterey Jack cheese (optional)

Heat oil in a skillet, add onion, and sauté over medium heat until tender and beginning to brown, about 7 minutes. Add garlic, jalapeño peppers, and tomato and cook 1 minute. Add beans, turkey, salt, and pepper and heat through. Taste and adjust seasoning. *Filling can be kept, covered, 1 day in refrigerator and reheated.*
   Heat an ungreased skillet over medium heat. Add a tortilla and heat about 30 seconds per side. Transfer to a plate and cover. Repeat with remaining tortillas, stacking them.
   Preheat the oven to 350°F. Spoon ½ cup filling into center of each tortilla and top with 1 tablespoon Fresh Tomato Salsa. Sprinkle on 2 tablespoons cheese, if desired. Fold 2 edges

of tortilla, to your left and right, over filling. Then roll up away from you to enclose filling completely.

Put burritos in an oiled shallow baking dish and heat in oven 10 minutes. Serve hot, with more salsa.

Makes 6 appetizer or 2 or 3 main-course servings

NOTE: Instead of heating the tortillas one by one, you can put them all in a baking dish, sprinkle with 1 teaspoon water, cover, and heat 10 minutes in a 300°F oven. This is easier if you're doubling the recipe or heating a fairly large number of tortillas.

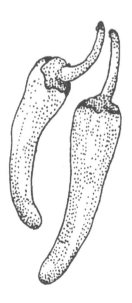

Lebanese Chicken Pizza
Moroccan Chicken Rolls with Raisins
and Walnuts
Chicken Pot Pie
Chicken Pie with Leeks and Wild Mushrooms
Moroccan Chicken Pie with Cinnamon
and Saffron (*Bastilla*)
Baked Turkey Empanadas
Turkey Shepherd's Pie
Smoked Turkey and Vegetable Tart

4

Chicken and Turkey Pies and Pastries

 Pastry turns chicken and turkey into party dishes in many cuisines. Small pastries, like South American Baked Turkey Empanadas (page 41) or Moroccan Chicken Rolls with Raisins and Walnuts (page 35), make delightful appetizers. More substantial dishes, such as Chicken Pot Pie (page 37) or Chicken Pie with Leeks and Wild Mushrooms (page 38), are perfect as festive main courses for entertaining. Depending on the size of the portion, such poultry-in-pastry treats as Smoked Turkey and Vegetable Tart (page 44) or Lebanese Chicken Pizza with pine nuts (page 34) can serve either purpose.

Making these delicacies is easier than you might think. Today many pastries of good quality can be purchased, leaving you to make only the filling. Chinese won-ton wrappers are perfect for making Moroccan chicken rolls; sheets of puff pastry make a delicious topping for chicken, leek, and mushroom pie; and packaged filo dough is the basis for the exotic Moroccan Chicken Bastilla (page 40). Other pastries, such as the yeast dough for the Lebanese Chicken Pizza, the cream cheese dough for Turkey Empanadas, and the pie doughs for the Chicken Pot Pie and Smoked Turkey and Vegetable Tart, can be quickly and easily made in a food processor.

LEBANESE CHICKEN PIZZA

Crisp, thin-crusted individual pizzas make terrific party food or a change-of-pace main course for supper. This is a chicken version of lahmajune, *an Armenian and Lebanese favorite available at restaurants and bakeries. It is usually made with lamb, but I prefer this lighter rendition with chicken and a generous amount of fresh flavoring ingredients—onion, garlic, tomatoes, and parsley.*

The dough is a snap to prepare in the food processor. Now that ground chicken is easily available, the filling is simple to make, too.

Pizza Dough

1 envelope (¼ ounce) active dry yeast
   or 1 fresh cake
¾ cup lukewarm water

2 cups all-purpose flour
1 teaspoon salt
1 tablespoon plus 1 teaspoon olive oil

Topping

½ pound ground chicken (1 cup)
½ pound ripe tomatoes, peeled,
   seeded, and finely chopped
¾ cup finely chopped fresh parsley
1 medium onion, minced
2 medium garlic cloves, minced

1 to 2 tablespoons olive oil, for
   sprinkling

¼ to ½ teaspoon salt
½ teaspoon freshly ground pepper
½ teaspoon freshly grated nutmeg
½ teaspoon paprika
¼ cup pine nuts

To make the dough in a food processor, sprinkle the yeast over ¼ cup lukewarm water in a cup or small bowl and let stand for 10 minutes. Stir until smooth. In food processor with dough blade or metal blade, process flour and salt briefly to mix them. Add remaining water and oil to yeast mixture. With blades of processor turning, gradually pour in yeast mixture. If dough is too dry to come together, add 1 tablespoon water and process again. Process about 1 minute to knead dough. (See Note to make dough by hand.)

Lightly oil a medium bowl. Add dough and turn to coat entire surface. Cover with plastic wrap or lightly dampened towel. Let dough rise in a warm, draft-free area about 1 hour or until doubled in volume.

For topping, thoroughly mix chicken with remaining topping ingredients (but not oil). Broil a teaspoon of mixture on a piece of foil until cooked through and taste it for seasoning. If desired, add more salt and pepper to topping mixture.

Divide dough into 4 pieces. Roll each to a 7- or 8-inch round slightly over ⅛ inch thick. Put on a lightly oiled baking sheet. Spread topping evenly but gently over each pizza with the back of a spoon, leaving a ½-inch border. Press lightly so topping adheres and sprinkle lightly with oil.

Preheat the oven to 400°F. Let pizzas rise for about 15 minutes, while oven is heating. Bake for 18 to 20 minutes or until dough is golden brown and firm. Serve hot.

Makes 4 servings

NOTE: To make dough by hand, sift flour into a bowl and make a well in center. Sprinkle dry yeast or crumble fresh yeast into well. Pour ¼ cup water over yeast and let stand for 10 minutes. Stir until smooth. Add remaining water, oil, and salt and mix with ingredients in middle of well. Stir in flour and mix well to obtain a fairly soft dough. If dough is dry, add 1 tablespoon water. Knead dough vigorously, slapping it on a work surface, until it is smooth and elastic, about 5 minutes. If it is very sticky, flour it occasionally while kneading. Continue as above.

MOROCCAN CHICKEN ROLLS WITH RAISINS AND WALNUTS

The fried Moroccan appetizers are called ''cigars'' because of their shape, and are served on festive occasions like weddings. They can have either a spicy meat filling or a delicate chicken filling with a hint of sweetness, like this one. Traditionally they are made using wrappers made specially for this purpose, but a Moroccan friend visiting the United States found that won-ton wrappers, which are available in many supermarkets, work perfectly. The pastries come out smaller but are the perfect size for hors d'oeuvres, and they come out crisp as if by magic! They're delicious and very easy to make.

Usually Moroccan cigars are not served with a dipping sauce, but I find these pastries do taste good with Chinese Sweet-and-Sour Sauce (page 372) or with a Chinese plum sauce. SEE PHOTOGRAPH.

2 tablespoons raisins
¾ cup diced cooked chicken (dark meat)
¼ cup diced walnuts
¼ teaspoon ground cinnamon
¼ teaspoon sugar

salt and freshly ground pepper
1 egg white
½ (12-ounce) package rectangular won-ton wrappers
oil for frying, about 1 inch deep

Soak the raisins in hot water for 5 minutes to plump, and drain. Put chicken in food processor with raisins and nuts and chop together. Leave a few pieces; the filling should not be a puree. Season with cinnamon, sugar, salt, and pepper and mix well. Add 1½ teaspoons egg white to moisten lightly.

Remove 1 won-ton wrapper from package. Take 1 slightly rounded teaspoon filling and put it along the longer side of wrapper, ¼ inch from edge nearest you, leaving ½ inch of pastry free at each side. Press to compact filling in finger shape. Fold 2 pastry edges, at left and right, over filling. Brush edge of dough farthest from you with remaining egg white. Roll up dough with filling, from edge nearest you to opposite edge, to form a cigar shape. Press to stick to egg-brushed dough.

In a deep heavy saucepan, heat oil to 340–350°F. on a frying thermometer. Fry pastries in batches 2 or 2½ minutes or until golden brown. Transfer to paper towels. Serve hot. *Pastries can be arranged on a plate in one layer, covered, and refrigerated. Reheat uncovered at 350°F. about 5 to 7 minutes.*

Makes 24 small hors d'oeuvres

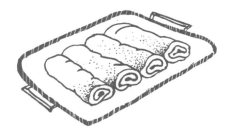

CHICKEN POT PIE

Chicken pot pie is an American favorite made in different versions in various regions of the United States. Unlike other pies, pot pies are often baked in a fairly deep dish, under a pie crust as in the recipe below, or a topping of biscuit dough. Some versions have a double crust, but most have a crust only on top, probably because a bottom crust tends to become soggy under the substantial filling of chicken and sauce. (Pennsylvania Dutch chicken pot pie is completely different, as it doesn't have a pastry crust; it consists of homemade square noodles poached in chicken broth, along with chicken pieces and vegetables.)

For this pot pie, poached chicken is combined with mushrooms, carrots, and a luscious sauce flavored with sautéed onions, green onions, celery, and thyme, then topped with a flaky, golden brown pie crust. If you like, you can substitute 4 cups diced cooked turkey for the chicken.

2 medium onions
4 celery stalks
3 to 3½ pounds chicken pieces
salt and freshly ground pepper
3 cups water
1 bay leaf
2 large carrots, peeled and diced
  (about ½ pound)
5 tablespoons butter
6 tablespoons all-purpose flour

½ teaspoon paprika
8 ounces mushrooms, quartered
½ cup whole milk, half-and-half, or
  heavy cream
1 teaspoon dried thyme, crumbled
¼ cup chopped green onions
¼ cup chopped fresh parsley
Pie Dough (page 394)
1 egg, beaten, for glaze

Cut half of 1 onion in thick slices and put in a heavy casserole. Cut 2 celery stalks in a few pieces and add. Add chicken, salt, pepper, water, and bay leaf. Bring to a boil. Cover and simmer over low heat about 45 minutes or until just tender. Discard chicken skin, remove meat from bones, and discard bones. Pull meat into large chunks and reserve. Strain cooking liquid and discard solids; skim off fat. Add diced carrots to cooking liquid and simmer 10 to 15 minutes or until tender. Remove carrots and reserve with chicken pieces. Measure and reserve 2½ cups broth.

Dice the remaining celery. Chop remaining onion. Melt butter in heavy, medium saucepan. Add onion and remaining celery and sauté over medium heat, stirring often, until softened but not browned, about 7 minutes. Sprinkle with flour and paprika and cook over low heat 2 minutes. Gradually stir in reserved chicken broth and bring to a boil, stirring. Add mushrooms. Simmer, uncovered, 5 minutes, stirring often, until mushrooms are just tender. Stir in milk and simmer 5 minutes or until sauce thickens. Off the heat, stir in thyme, green onions, and parsley. Remove 1 cup sauce and set aside. Stir cooked chicken and carrots into remaining sauce. Season to taste with salt and pepper.

Butter a 9½- to 10-inch square baking dish, about 2 inches deep. Spoon filling into dish. Let cool. *Filling can be kept, covered, 2 days in refrigerator.*

Preheat the oven to 425°F. Roll out pastry on a lightly floured surface to a square less than ¼ inch thick and about 1 inch larger on all sides than dish. Brush edge of dish with egg. Fold dough in half and unfold it over dish to cover filling. Press to stick pastry to edges of dish. Cut off excess dough. Make a few slits in pastry so steam can escape. Brush top with egg. Roll pastry scraps and use a small, round fluted cutter to make ovals; score ovals with knife to make pastry leaves. Or just use ovals and crescents as decorations. Put them on pie, and brush them with egg. Refrigerate pie 10 minutes.

Bake pie about 30 minutes or until golden brown. Reheat reserved sauce, stirring; thin it, if necessary, with a few tablespoons chicken broth, cream, or milk. Serve pie with a large spoon. Serve sauce separately.

Makes 6 servings

CHICKEN PIE
WITH LEEKS AND WILD MUSHROOMS

Americans learned to love chicken pies from the English, who prepare a variety of poultry, meat, and game pies. For this festive version, the chicken is combined with exotic mushrooms, sautéed leeks, and corn in a tarragon-scented sauce. A puff pastry crust lends elegance to the pie but is actually the easiest topping to make, using purchased pastry sheets.

½ to 1 ounce dried
    mushrooms—porcini, morels,
    shiitake, or Polish
2 pounds chicken thighs, poached and
    liquid reserved (page 391)
1 tablespoon vegetable oil
4 tablespoons (½ stick) butter
1 pound (2 large) leeks, white and
    light green parts, cleaned (page
    408), sliced thin
salt and freshly ground pepper
4 tablespoons plus 1 teaspoon all-
    purpose flour

1½ cups chicken stock, or broth (from
    poaching chicken thighs)
½ cup whole milk, half-and-half, or
    heavy cream
1 tablespoon chopped fresh tarragon,
    or 1 teaspoon dried, crumbled
2 tablespoons chopped fresh parsley
1 cup cooked fresh or frozen corn
    kernels
1 frozen puff pastry sheet (half a 17½-
    ounce package)
1 egg, beaten, for glaze

Soak mushrooms in hot water for 30 minutes. Remove from water. If using shiitake mushrooms, discard stems. Slice mushrooms. Remove skin and bones from poached chicken. Cut meat in chunks.

Heat oil and 1 tablespoon butter in a large, deep skillet and add leeks and a little salt and pepper. Cover and cook over low heat, stirring occasionally, 10 minutes or until tender but not brown.

Melt the remaining 3 tablespoons butter in heavy casserole. Add flour and cook over low heat 2 minutes. Gradually stir in chicken broth and bring to a boil, stirring. Add mushrooms. Simmer over low heat 5 minutes, stirring often. Stir in milk. Simmer 2 minutes or until thickened. Stir in tarragon, parsley, chicken, corn, and leeks. Season to taste with salt and pepper. *Filling can be kept, covered, 2 days in refrigerator.*

Preheat the oven to 425°F. with 2 racks, one in upper third of oven. Lightly butter a 9-inch pie pan.

Spread filling evenly in pan, mounding it slightly in center. Roll out puff pastry sheet to enlarge it to a 10-inch square. Brush edge of pie pan with egg. Set pastry over filling and press to stick it to edge of dish. Cut off excess pastry and reserve it. Brush top of pie with egg. To make pastry decorations from excess pastry, cut circles and crescents with a small round cutter (2 inches or less). Set them on the pie and brush them with egg. Refrigerate pie 10 minutes.

Set pie on upper oven rack and put a baking sheet on shelf below to catch any drips. Bake pie 20 minutes. Reduce oven temperature to 350°F. and bake 10 minutes or until crust is golden brown. To serve, cut through crust with a knife, and serve filling with a large spoon.

Makes 6 servings

MOROCCAN CHICKEN PIE WITH CINNAMON AND SAFFRON (*BASTILLA*)

This exotic pastry enclosing saffron- and cinnamon-scented chicken and roasted almonds is a chicken dish I adore. What is unusual is the touch of sweetness—just before serving, the pie is sprinkled with sugar and cinnamon. You will find it on Moroccan menus under several names—bastilla, bastella, pastilla, bestila. Classically prepared with squab, it is today often made with chicken and is usually served as a first course.

I have enjoyed this wonderful pie at many occasions and in different places. When I lived in Paris, the best bastilla I had was served at Timgad, my favorite Moroccan restaurant in France, where the pie is made with flaky Moroccan pastry sheets called ouarka. *The version I love most of all, however, is served in Los Angeles, at Michel Ohayon's Moroccan restaurant Koutoubia. Chef Ohayon shared his recipe with me and showed me how he prepares his specialty. It is made with filo dough, which is thinner and more delicate than* ouarka. *Unlike many bastilla recipes that include large amounts of butter, this one uses very little, and is light and delicious. The pie is not complicated to prepare at home, and the filling can be made ahead.* SEE PHOTOGRAPH.

1 cup minced onion
½ cup minced fresh parsley
½ cup minced (cilantro) fresh
  coriander
1 bay leaf
a 3-pound chicken
salt and freshly ground pepper to taste
½ teaspoon ground cinnamon
3 tablespoons granulated sugar

¼ cup water
8 eggs
¼ teaspoon saffron powder
1¼ cups whole blanched almonds (6
  ounces)
4 sheets filo dough
2 tablespoons (¼ stick) butter, melted
confectioner's sugar and ground
  cinnamon, for sprinkling

In a heavy casserole or Dutch oven, put onion, parsley, coriander, and bay leaf. Place chicken on top of mixture. Sprinkle with salt, pepper, cinnamon, and 1 tablespoon sugar. Heat over medium-high heat until sizzling. Reduce heat to low, cover, and cook 30 minutes. Turn chicken over, add water to pan, cover, and cook about 30 minutes or until tender. Remove cooked chicken and let cool; reserve broth. Discard bay leaf.

Discard chicken skin and bones. Pull meat into small thin pieces and put aside.

Beat eggs lightly. Return casserole to low heat and heat broth, chicken pieces, and saffron until sizzling. Add beaten eggs and cook over low heat, stirring, until set, like dry scrambled eggs. Taste and adjust seasoning. *Filling can be kept, covered, overnight in refrigerator.*

Preheat the oven to 350°F. Toast the almonds in oven for 10 minutes until golden brown.

Transfer to a plate. Cool completely. Finely chop almonds in a food processor with remaining 2 tablespoons sugar, leaving a few chunks.

About 30 minutes before assembling pie, remove filo dough from refrigerator; leave it wrapped until ready to use. Handle dough gently; it tears easily.

Preheat the oven to 375°F. Brush bottom and sides of two 9-inch pie pans lightly with butter. For each pie, lay 2 filo sheets in pan, overlapping in center and allowing about half of each sheet to hang over pan's edge, so there is about 6 to 8 inches of pastry around outside of pan. Sprinkle about ⅓ cup chopped almonds in each pan, and add half the chicken filling to each, crumbling it with your fingers. Sprinkle remaining almonds on top (about ½ cup for each pan). Fold overhanging pastry over filling, lifting it with both hands, and gathering it lightly in center; it naturally forms soft pleats. Brush with remaining melted butter.

Bake pies for 20 to 25 minutes or until tops are golden brown. (If tops brown after 15 minutes, reduce heat to 350°F. and bake 10 more minutes, to be sure the filling becomes thoroughly heated.)

Either slide each pie onto a round serving platter or serve it from the pan. Sprinkle with confectioner's sugar and cinnamon just before serving. Serve hot.

Makes 8 appetizer or 4 or 5 main-course servings

BAKED TURKEY EMPANADAS

Empanadas, or pastry turnovers with savory fillings, are a Latin American specialty also loved in the Caribbean. In their country of origin, Spain, the terminology is slightly different; there an empanada is a savory pie, and individual turnover versions are called empanadillas.

Fillings for Latin American empanadas are most often made with ground meat picadillo, which can be spicy or slightly sweet. The most popular version, which I make with turkey, is flavored with olives and capers, and with a touch of sweetness from raisins. Empanadas can be fried or baked. In South America the pastry is frequently made with lard, but some cooks use a cream cheese dough like this one, which I prefer. It is delicious, wonderfully flaky, and easy to handle, since it does not crack or tear when you roll it out. SEE PHOTOGRAPH.

10 ounces cream cheese
13 ounces (3 sticks plus 2 tablespoons) cold unsalted butter
3⅓ cups all-purpose flour
½ teaspoon salt

5 to 7 tablespoons ice water
Turkey Picadillo (page 280)
1 egg, beaten, for glaze
sesame seeds for sprinkling (optional)

To make dough, cut cream cheese into tablespoon-size pieces and let soften to room temperature. Cut butter into small pieces of about ½ tablespoon and keep cold until ready to use.

In a food processor combine flour and salt and process briefly to blend. Add butter and process with on/off turns until mixture resembles coarse meal. Add cream cheese, distributing it fairly evenly over mixture. Sprinkle with 3 tablespoons ice water. Process with on/off turns until dough just holds together. Add more water by teaspoons if necessary. Wrap dough, press together into a ball, and flatten to a disk. Refrigerate for at least 4 hours. *Dough can be kept in refrigerator for up to 2 days.*

Refrigerate the Turkey Picadillo for about 15 minutes or overnight.

Use one-fourth of dough at a time, keeping remaining dough refrigerated. Roll dough out about ⅛ inch thick. Cut 3-inch circles with a plain or fluted cookie cutter. Put a teaspoon of filling in center of each circle. Brush half the edge with egg and fold over other half to make a half-moon shape. Press edges together. Press edge with tines of fork dipped in flour to seal, then brush with egg. Sprinkle with sesame seeds if desired. Put on a buttered baking sheet. Refrigerate while shaping remaining empanadas from remaining dough. Refrigerate scraps about 1 hour, roll them, and shape more empanadas. Refrigerate all empanadas at least 30 minutes or up to 1 day.

Preheat the oven to 400°F. Bake empanadas 15 to 20 minutes or until golden brown. If placing baking sheets one above the other, switch their positions about half-way through baking time. Serve warm.

Makes 40 to 42 appetizer pastries; about 20 servings

TURKEY SHEPHERD'S PIE

The name of this dish doesn't intend to suggest it was created for guardians of turkeys! This is a turkey version of the old-fashioned English pie of meat topped with mashed potatoes, which was originally made with mutton and subsequently with beef. Anyone who has lived in France on a student's budget has made the acquaintance of shepherd's pie's French relative, hachis parmentier, *or "Parmentier's hash," made of diced cooked meat mixed with sautéed onions, covered with mashed potatoes, sprinkled with cheese, and browned.*

With ground turkey and chicken easily available, this is an easy way to turn them into a satisfying winter supper dish. I prefer to use poultry rather than beef, so I can take advantage of the fat saved and enjoy the buttery mashed potato topping!

2 pounds boiling potatoes
4 to 5 tablespoons butter
½ cup milk
salt and ground white pepper
freshly grated nutmeg (optional)
3 tablespoons vegetable oil
1 large onion, chopped
⅓ cup chopped celery
1 medium carrot, finely diced
3 medium garlic cloves, chopped
1½ pounds ground turkey or chicken
2 to 3 tablespoons tomato paste or
    puree

½ cup dry white wine
1 cup chicken stock or broth
4 teaspoons cornstarch dissolved in 3
    tablespoons water
1 teaspoon dried thyme, crumbled
1 teaspoon dried marjoram, crumbled
¼ cup chopped fresh parsley
freshly ground pepper
2 to 3 tablespoons grated Cheddar or
    Parmesan cheese (optional)

Cook the potatoes in their skins in water to cover about 30 to 35 minutes or until tender. Peel them, return to saucepan, and mash them. With a wooden spoon, beat in butter and milk over low heat. Season to taste with salt, white pepper, and nutmeg.

In a large, deep skillet, heat oil over medium heat. Add onion, celery, and carrot and sauté about 7 minutes or until softened. Stir in garlic, then turkey and sauté, stirring to separate meat particles, about 7 minutes. Stir in 2 tablespoons tomato paste, wine, and stock. Simmer over low heat 5 minutes. Mix cornstarch solution and stir into sauce. Bring to a boil and simmer 5 minutes, stirring often, until thick. Add thyme, marjoram, and parsley. Add more tomato paste if desired. Season to taste with salt and pepper.

Spoon turkey mixture into a 2½- to 3-quart shallow baking dish. Gently spoon potatoes in spoonfuls on top. Spread potatoes lightly to completely cover turkey mixture. Lightly make decorative lines in potatoes with tines of a fork. Sprinkle with cheese if desired. *Dish can be kept, covered, overnight in refrigerator.*

Preheat the oven to 375°F. Set baking dish on a baking sheet. Bake about 40 minutes or until lightly browned.

Makes 4 to 6 servings

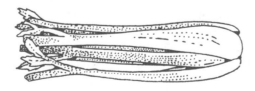

SMOKED TURKEY AND VEGETABLE TART

I learned to prepare savory tarts like this in Paris from Chef Albert Jorant, the head pastry chef of La Varenne Cooking School. Chef Jorant prepares the dough by hand in no time, but for the rest of us, the quickest way is to use a food processor. In France this type of tart made with a yeast dough is known as a country-style tart. Fillings often are composed of smoked meat, especially ham or bacon, along with a little custard and sometimes a vegetable, such as onions or leeks. I like to use smoked turkey along with a colorful mixture of vegetables, as in this recipe. Serve it in small portions as a delectable appetizer, or in larger wedges as a rich main course.

Yeast Dough for Tarts

1 envelope (¼ ounce) active dry yeast
¼ cup warm water (105°–115°F.)
1¾ cups all-purpose flour, preferably
   unbleached
¾ teaspoon salt

2 large eggs, at room temperature
4 tablespoons (½ stick) unsalted
   butter, at room temperature, cut into
   8 pieces

Smoked Turkey and Vegetable Filling

2 medium carrots, peeled
2 large leeks, white and light green
   parts, cleaned (page 408)
2 small zucchini
3 ounces smoked turkey or chicken,
   thinly sliced
3 tablespoons butter

salt and freshly ground pepper
6 ounces mushrooms, halved and cut
   in thin slices
2 large eggs
½ cup milk or heavy cream
freshly grated white pepper
freshly grated nutmeg

To make dough in a food processor, sprinkle yeast over warm water in a small bowl and let stand 10 minutes. Combine flour and salt in a food processor fitted with dough blade or metal blade. Process briefly to blend. Add eggs. With blades of processor turning, quickly pour in yeast mixture. Process 1 minute to knead dough. Add butter and process just until it is absorbed. Dough will be soft and sticky. (To make dough with a mixer, see Note.)

Lightly oil a medium bowl. Add dough, turning to coat entire surface. Cover with plastic wrap or with lightly dampened towel. Let dough rise in a warm, draft-free area about 1 hour, or until doubled in volume.

For filling, cut carrots, leeks, and zucchini in pieces about 1½ inches long. Cut each piece in thin lengthwise slices, and each slice in thin lengthwise strips. Cut smoked turkey in thin strips also.

In a large skillet, melt 2 tablespoons butter over low heat. Add carrots, leeks, salt, and pepper. Cover and cook, stirring often, 15 minutes. Add zucchini and cook, uncovered, until all vegetables are tender, about 3 minutes. Remove from heat. Stir in turkey strips and transfer to a plate.

Melt the remaining tablespoon butter in a skillet over medium heat. Add mushrooms, salt, and pepper and sauté, stirring often, until tender, about 3 minutes.

In a medium bowl whisk eggs and milk until blended. Add salt, white pepper, and nutmeg to taste.

Position a rack in center of oven and preheat oven to 400°F. Butter a 9-inch round fluted tart pan with removable bottom. Lift dough and let it fall into bowl a few times to knock out air. Transfer dough to tart pan with a rubber spatula. With oiled knuckles, push dough from center toward rim, to line pan. With oiled fingers, push dough against rim of pan so tart has border about ½ inch thick at top edge. Set pan on a baking sheet.

Scatter mushrooms over dough and top with smoked turkey mixture. Ladle milk mixture carefully over filling. Let tart rise in warm draft-free area 10 minutes.

Bake about 40 to 45 minutes, or until dough browns and filling sets. Cool on a rack for 15 minutes. Remove tart pan rim by setting pan on an overturned bowl. *Tart can be baked up to 2 hours ahead and kept at room temperature; it can also be frozen. Heat in 300°F. oven before serving.* Serve tart warm or at room temperature.

Makes about 6 servings

NOTE: To make the dough in a mixer with a dough hook, combine yeast and warm water in small bowl and leave 10 minutes. Stir with fork. Sift 1½ cups flour into the bowl of a heavy-duty mixer fitted with dough hook. Add yeast mixture, eggs, and salt and mix at medium-low speed, scraping dough down occasionally from bowl and hook, about 7 minutes, or until dough just begins to cling to hook. Dough will be soft. (If dough seems too wet, beat in remaining flour 1 tablespoon at a time.) Knead by mixing at medium speed, scraping down twice, about 5 minutes or until dough is smooth, clings to hook, and almost cleans sides of bowl. Scrape down from hook. Add half the butter pieces and mix at medium-low speed until thoroughly blended, about 3 minutes. Add remaining butter and mix again until blended, 3 more minutes. Dough will be soft and sticky.

5

Chicken and Turkey Salads

Mention chicken salad or turkey salad and most people think of a bland mixture of cold poultry and mayonnaise. This was the version I grew up with, and I must admit I still enjoy it once in a while. But moving to Europe and then to California taught me many more ways for turning chicken and turkey into colorful, fresh, flavorful salads.

Living in Paris fifteen years ago, at the height of the nouvelle cuisine revolution, I witnessed the rise of a new type of salad—morsels of choice meats like sliced roast duck or chicken fillets on a bed of glistening, perfectly seasoned greens. These innovative salads were so different from our salads of iceberg lettuce tossed with a random assortment of meats, cheeses, fruit, and vegetables and topped with thick, sometimes sweet, dressings.

Inspired by these luxurious salads from France, American chefs, too, have developed elegant salads using poultry. As a result, we have changed our own salads in style, temperature, and presentation. We devote more thought and better ingredients to salads.

In addition to our familiar cool chicken and turkey salads, there's a whole new category of light poultry salads, served warm. For these salads, chicken is usually grilled, sliced, and

47

Warm Chicken Salad with Peppers, Asparagus,
and Fresh Rosemary-Sage Vinaigrette
Chicken Salad with Enoki Mushrooms
and Oriental Vinaigrette
Warm Chicken Salad with Oyster Mushrooms
and Pepper-Caper Vinaigrette
Grilled Chicken Salad with Potatoes, Roquefort,
and Walnuts
Creamy Chicken Salad with Jerusalem Artichokes
Mango, Chicken, and Pasta Salad with Ginger
Creamy Chicken-Noodle Salad with Broccoli
and Toasted Nuts
Hawaiian Chicken and Somen Salad
with Seafood
Chicken, Kiwi, and Rice Salad with Papaya
Chicken Salad with Rice, Chickpeas,
and Sesame Seeds

Tomatoes Stuffed with Chicken-Rice Salad
and Toasted Pecans
Chicken Salad with Asparagus
and Orange Vinaigrette
Summer Chicken Salad with Cherries
and Mint Vinaigrette
Fresh and Smoked Chicken Salad with Potatoes
and Watercress
Zesty Chicken and Black Bean Salad
Chicken Salad with Mustard-Caper Vinaigrette
and Vegetable Julienne
Roast Chicken Salad with Tomato-Garlic Salsa
Chicken Salad with Harissa Vinaigrette
Turkey Tapenade Salad
Turkey Salad with Zesty Cilantro Dressing
Smoked Turkey and Couscous Salad
with Red Pepper and Eggplant
Turkey Tabbouleh

set on mixed lettuces. Frequently these salads are served on individual plates or on a platter, rather than in bowls. Boneless breasts are preferred because they are easy to cut in neat, attractive pieces. The rest is whatever you like—raw or sautéed mushroom slices, sun-dried tomato strips, black olives, marinated artichokes, or even thin fruit wedges.

The dressing of choice for hot salads is vinaigrette, and lately it has superseded mayonnaise in many cold chicken and turkey salads as well. Vinaigrette is lighter and thinner, so less dressing is needed, and the salad ends up lower in fat. There's another advantage to vinaigrette: it shows off the salad's colors beautifully.

To create exciting salads, whether hot or cold, you can choose classic ingredient combinations from different cuisines. For a Mexican-inspired salad, you might toss cooked chicken or turkey with avocado, corn, cilantro, and chilies. Water chestnuts, bean sprouts, and lightly cooked snow peas, with a little soy sauce and sesame oil added to the dressing, give chicken salad an Oriental character. A chicken salad with grilled red bell peppers, rosemary, and sage boldly announces its Italian connection.

Pasta and grains are excellent partners for chicken or turkey in salads, as is almost any cooked vegetable, from sautéed eggplant to blanched carrot strips to canned baby corn. Raw vegetables are good, too, as in Turkey Tabbouleh, for which I have added cooked turkey to the traditional Middle Eastern medley of diced tomatoes, cucumbers, bulgur wheat, fresh mint, and parsley.

The fashion of arranging salad ingredients on baby greens in fine restaurants in France led to the appearance of mélanges of exotic salad greens, already washed, in Paris markets, and now our best markets carry them, too. Such tasty greens as butter lettuce, arugula, radicchio, and green leaf lettuce provide a fresh background for new and familiar poultry salads.

On warm days nothing is more tempting to eat or easier to prepare than a light, refreshing salad. Even shopping is quick—only a few fine-quality, fresh ingredients are required. For cold salads, you can cook chicken or turkey a day or two ahead, or buy some roast chicken or turkey from a deli.

From a recipe for using up leftovers, chicken and turkey salads have evolved into glamorous entrees that are practical as well. As a meal in one dish, the only accompaniment required is good, fresh crisp-crusted bread. All that is needed to complete the meal is ripe fruit, or perhaps a scoop of sorbet or ice cream.

TIPS

✗ If using large leaves for salads, it's best to tear them so they are easy to eat.

✗ A salad is always more enticing if the greens are lightly moistened with vinaigrette. This makes them an integral part of the salad, rather than being left on the plate as mere decoration.

✗ Many people assume that salads must be served as cold as possible. Chilling does keep the greens crisp, but chicken, potatoes, and other cooked vegetables taste better hot or cool and not straight out of the refrigerator.

✗ Cooked green vegetables, such as snow peas, sugar-snap peas, and green beans, lose their bright color after prolonged contact with vinaigrette and therefore are best added just before serving time. Salad greens are also added at the last moment so they remain crisp.

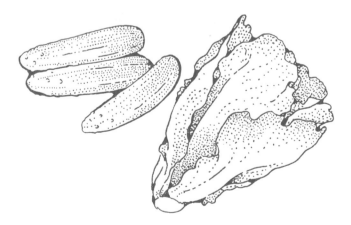

WARM CHICKEN SALAD WITH PEPPERS, ASPARAGUS, AND FRESH ROSEMARY-SAGE VINAIGRETTE

Chicken breasts, either grilled or broiled, are delicious and festive served as a warm salad, with fresh greens, asparagus, corn kernels, sautéed red peppers, and an Italian-style dressing. This type of chicken salad is popular in new Italian, French, and California cooking styles. To save time, you can use roasted red peppers from a jar and frozen asparagus tips. SEE PHOTOGRAPH.

1 pound medium-width asparagus, peeled, ends trimmed, cut in 2-inch lengths

1 tablespoon olive oil, plus 1 to 2 teaspoons for brushing chicken

2 red bell peppers, cut in thin strips

4 boneless chicken breast halves, with skin (total about 1½ pounds)

salt and freshly ground pepper

1⅓ cups fresh or frozen corn kernels, cooked

Fresh Rosemary-Sage Vinaigrette (page 356)

6 cups mixed lettuces, such as romaine, red leaf lettuce, and arugula

Cook asparagus in a medium saucepan of boiling salted water, uncovered over high heat, about 3 minutes or until crisp-tender. Drain, rinse with cold water, and drain well. Heat oil in a large skillet over medium heat. Add red peppers and sauté until crisp-tender, about 8 minutes.

Sprinkle both sides of chicken with salt and pepper. Brush lightly with oil. Broil about 4 inches from heat, or grill above glowing coals about 7 minutes per side or until tender and no longer pink when cut. Remove to a board, cut in 3 or 4 diagonal slices, and keep warm.

Set aside 8 asparagus tips. Add corn, pepper strips, remaining asparagus, and ¼ cup vinaigrette to greens and toss until coated. Taste and adjust seasoning. Divide among plates, spooning corn from bottom of bowl onto each. Set chicken slices on salad mixture and asparagus tips on top. Spoon remaining vinaigrette over chicken. Serve immediately.

Makes 4 appetizer or light main-course servings

CHICKEN SALAD WITH ENOKI MUSHROOMS AND ORIENTAL VINAIGRETTE

In this typical cross-cultural dish, combining ingredients and techniques of East and West, Oriental flavorings season the Western-style vinaigrette dressing. Japanese enoki mushrooms garnish the salad of a warm grilled chicken breast on a bed of spinach.

Theories and trends aside, this salad looks elegant, tastes delicious, uses very little oil, and is ready in minutes!

1 tablespoon plus 1 teaspoon vegetable oil
½ teaspoon Oriental sesame oil
1½ teaspoons rice vinegar
1 teaspoon soy sauce
a few drops of chili oil, bottled hot pepper sauce, or cayenne pepper to taste
2 cups spinach leaves, rinsed and patted dry

1 ounce (⅓ package) enoki mushrooms, bases trimmed, rinsed
2 boneless and skinless chicken breast halves (total about ¾ pound)
salt and freshly ground pepper
1 or 2 thin half-slices red onion, divided in half-rings

For dressing, whisk together 1 tablespoon vegetable oil, sesame oil, vinegar, soy sauce, and chili oil.

Make a bed of spinach leaves on each plate. Near edge of each plate, set mushrooms in 3 bunches on spinach. Sprinkle each salad with 1 teaspoon dressing.

Sprinkle chicken with salt and pepper and rub lightly with remaining oil. Put on broiler rack about 4 inches from heat. Broil about 7 minutes per side or until white inside; cut into thickest part to check.

Cut chicken in thin slices and set on spinach in center of each plate. Scatter onions around chicken. Sprinkle salad with remaining dressing and serve.

Makes 2 light main-course servings

WARM CHICKEN SALAD WITH OYSTER MUSHROOMS AND PEPPER-CAPER VINAIGRETTE

This is representative of the elegant, modern salads so popular in fashionable restaurants serving European and American cuisines. Here the seasonings are Mediterranean—the famous balsamic vinegar of Italy, olive oil, capers, and diced roasted red peppers. The result is a fresh, appealing, yet easy-to-prepare main course, a perfect summer lunch.

I use extra-virgin olive oil for the dressing and pure olive oil for sautéing the mushrooms and rubbing on the chicken, but if you keep only one kind of olive oil in the kitchen, use it for both purposes.

2 teaspoons balsamic vinegar
3 tablespoons olive oil, plus a little for
  rubbing on chicken
salt and freshly ground pepper
2 tablespoons diced roasted red
  peppers (from a jar, or see page 408)
2 teaspoons capers, rinsed

4 cups butter lettuce (Boston lettuce),
  rinsed and dried well
½ pound oyster mushrooms
1 pound boneless and skinless chicken
  breasts or fillets (tender strip of
  boned breast; see page 396)

Whisk vinegar, 2 tablespoons olive oil, salt, and pepper in a small bowl. Stir in red peppers and capers. Line 2 or 4 plates with lettuce leaves.

Gently rinse mushrooms and cut in bite-size pieces. Cut stems in thin diagonal slices or halve them lengthwise. Heat 1 tablespoon olive oil in a large skillet over high heat. Add mushrooms, salt, and pepper and sauté about 4 minutes or until lightly browned and any liquid that escapes has evaporated. Reserve in pan.

Rub chicken lightly with olive oil. Sprinkle with salt and pepper. Grill on stovetop grill over medium-high heat about 5 minutes per side for breasts or about 3 minutes per side for fillets, pressing occasionally on chicken with slotted spatula to mark it with stripes.

To serve, reheat mushrooms. Slice chicken breasts in 5 or 6 diagonal slices but keep them together to show striped pattern. Set chicken on lettuce. Spoon mushrooms around chicken. Stir dressing, spoon it over chicken, and serve.

Makes 4 appetizer or 2 main-course servings

GRILLED CHICKEN SALAD WITH POTATOES, ROQUEFORT, AND WALNUTS

For me this salad always brings back memories of Paris café lunches, where my husband and I often ordered the salade auvergnate *of greens, potatoes, Roquefort or Cantal cheese, and walnuts. In this chicken adaptation, an assortment of colorful lettuces is topped by slices of grilled chicken breast, quartered baby potatoes, chunks of Roquefort, and toasted walnuts. You can either toss the chicken and potatoes together for a rustic look, or arrange each on the greens separately, side by side.*

The walnut oil vinaigrette lends a lovely flavor, but be sure to use fresh, fine-quality oil. After you open a bottle of walnut oil, keep it in the refrigerator to prevent it from quickly going rancid. If mâche *(lamb's lettuce) is available, add 1 or 2 cups after rinsing the delicate leaves thoroughly.*

For this salad the chicken is marinated in the vinaigrette after being grilled and is served cool, but you can serve it right away, while still hot, if you prefer.

⅔ cup walnut pieces

Vinaigrette

3 tablespoons white wine vinegar or
  herb vinegar
salt and freshly ground pepper
½ cup plus 1 tablespoon French
  walnut oil

1 tablespoon minced fresh thyme
  leaves, or 1 teaspoon dried,
  crumbled

1½ pounds boneless chicken breast,
  with skin on, patted dry
1 tablespoon vegetable oil
½ teaspoon dried thyme, crumbled
salt and freshly ground pepper
1 pound baby red potatoes

4 cups romaine lettuce leaves, loosely
  packed
4 radicchio leaves
3 cups red or green leaf lettuce, loosely
  packed
3 ounces Roquefort cheese, coarsely
  crumbled (about ½ cup)

Preheat the oven or toaster oven to 350°F. Toast walnuts on a small cookie sheet, stirring once or twice, until lightly browned, about 5 minutes. Transfer to a plate and let cool.

For the vinaigrette, whisk vinegar with salt and pepper in a medium bowl. Whisk in oil. Stir in thyme. Taste and adjust seasoning.

Heat a ridged stovetop grill pan over medium-high heat, preheat broiler, or prepare charcoal grill. Rub meat side of chicken with vegetable oil and sprinkle it with thyme and a pinch of salt and pepper. Lightly oil the ridged grill pan or rack. Set chicken, skin side down, on pan or rack and grill about 7 minutes per side, pressing occasionally on thickest part of chicken with a spatula. To check whether chicken is done, cut into thickest part with tip of a sharp knife; color should no longer be pink, but white.

Transfer chicken to a plate, cool, and discard any juices that escape. Remove skin. Cut chicken in ⅜-inch slices crosswise, slightly on the diagonal, and put in a bowl. Whisk vinaigrette, add ¼ cup to chicken, and toss. Cover and refrigerate, turning pieces over occasionally, about 1 hour.

Cook potatoes in a saucepan of salted water, covered, about 25 minutes or until tender enough so that knife pierces center of largest potato easily. Drain potatoes in colander and quarter them. Put potatoes in bowl. Rewhisk vinaigrette until blended, pour 3 tablespoons over potatoes, and toss gently. Cool to room temperature. *Chicken, potatoes, and vinaigrette can be refrigerated, covered, 1 day.*

Rinse and thoroughly dry salad greens, tear each leaf in 2 or 3 pieces, and put them in a large bowl.

To serve, toss greens with enough of remaining vinaigrette to moisten. Taste and adjust seasoning. Divide among 4 plates. Taste potatoes and chicken for seasoning and add more vinaigrette to each if desired. Top greens with chicken and potatoes, either mixed together or arranged side by side. Sprinkle with crumbled Roquefort and walnuts.

Makes 4 main-course servings

CREAMY CHICKEN SALAD WITH JERUSALEM ARTICHOKES

Wine-poached chicken breasts are wonderful in creamy chicken salads like this one, prepared with mayonnaise in the traditional American style. The dressing benefits from being flavored with a sharp ingredient, such as mustard, and the salad tastes best when something crunchy, such as Jerusalem artichokes, is added for textural contrast.

In spite of their name, Jerusalem artichokes originated in North America and were used by the Indians. Although it is part of our culinary heritage from the days of the pioneers, for many of us this vegetable, which is also called sunchokes, is new and exotic.

1½ pounds chicken breast halves with bone
½ cup dry white wine
¼ cup water
1 fresh thyme sprig, or ¼ teaspoon dried leaves
1 medium garlic clove, crushed
salt and freshly ground pepper

1 cup mayonnaise
1 tablespoon Dijon mustard
1 pound Jerusalem artichokes (sunchokes), scrubbed
¼ cup thinly sliced green onions
¼ cup coarsely grated carrot
thin slices of green part of green onions, for garnish

Put chicken pieces with wine, water, thyme, garlic, salt, and pepper in a medium sauté pan. Bring to a boil. Cover and cook over low heat, turning twice, for 22 to 25 minutes or until chicken is tender when pierced at its thickest point with a knife. Remove chicken, reserving cooking liquid. Pull off chicken skin and remove bones. Cut meat in strips of about 1½ × ⅜ × ⅜ inch.

Boil chicken cooking liquid until reduced to ¼ cup. Remove thyme sprigs and garlic, pour reduced liquid into a bowl, and cool to room temperature. Whisk 2 tablespoons of reduced cooking liquid into mayonnaise. Whisk in mustard and taste for seasoning.

Peel Jerusalem artichokes with a paring knife. Put each as it is peeled into a bowl of water. Cut each in thin strips, of about 1½ × ³⁄₁₆ × ³⁄₁₆ inch, and return strips to water. Rinse them in a colander, drain them well, and pat dry.

Combine chicken, Jerusalem artichokes, and dressing in a bowl and toss until blended. Add sliced green onions and carrot, toss, and taste salad for seasoning. *Salad can be kept, covered, 1 day in refrigerator.* Serve it garnished with thinly sliced green onion.

Makes 4 light main-course servings

MANGO, CHICKEN, AND PASTA SALAD WITH GINGER

Lime juice, along with the mango and ginger, adds an exotic, Caribbean touch to this light salad of grilled soy-and-ginger-marinated chicken. The chicken slices are tossed with fedelini, a long, thin flat type of pasta. The salad is ideal for summer, when mangoes are plentiful and at their best.

1 pound boneless chicken breast halves, skin removed
Ginger-Lime Marinade (page 350)
3 ripe medium mangoes
2 tablespoons finely grated, peeled fresh ginger
1 large shallot, minced
1 teaspoon finely grated lime zest

1 teaspoon soy sauce
freshly ground pepper to taste
8 ounces fedelini, spaghettini, or vermicelli
1 tablespoon vegetable oil
¼ cup thin slices green part of green onion
a few strips of lime zest, for garnish

Put chicken on a plate and rub with 3 tablespoons of marinade, setting aside rest for dressing. Cover chicken and refrigerate 30 minutes to 1 hour.

Preheat broiler or grill with rack about 4 inches from heat source; or heat stovetop ridged grill over medium-high heat. Lightly oil grill or broiler rack. Set chicken breast on broiler rack or grill beginning with skin side facing heat source. Broil or grill about 5 minutes per side, pressing occasionally on thickest part of chicken with spatula, or until meat in thickest part is no longer pink when cut. Cool to room temperature and discard any juices that escape. Cut in lengthwise diagonal strips about ¼ inch wide.

Peel each mango by first slitting skin around fruit twice, so skin is slit in quarters, then pull skin off. Cut pulp from most attractive mango in large chunks; be careful because mango is slippery. Cut mango chunks in slices about ¼ inch thick. Set aside for garnish. Coarsely chop the other 2 mangoes. Reserve for dressing.

Make mango dressing. To the bowl of reserved marinade add the ginger, shallot, lime zest, soy sauce, and pepper. Whisk until blended. Stir in chopped mangoes.

Cook pasta in a large pot of boiling salted water 6 to 7 minutes or until tender but firm to the bite. Drain, rinse with cold water, and drain well. Transfer to a bowl and toss it with the oil, then with dressing. Taste and adjust seasoning.

Reserve a few chicken strips for garnish. Add remaining strips and green onion slices to pasta and toss. Spoon salad onto 4 plates. Garnish with mango slices, chicken strips, and lime zest strips and serve. *Salad is best when freshly made but can be kept up to 8 hours in refrigerator; if making ahead, mix all of chicken and mango slices into salad.*

Makes 4 main-course servings

CREAMY CHICKEN-NOODLE SALAD WITH BROCCOLI AND TOASTED NUTS

For this delicate main-course salad, chicken fillets—the tender strip of meat at the bottom of the breast—are gently cooked in white wine, which is then used to flavor the Russian-style creamy dill dressing. If you are serving the dish for a party, you can provide bowls of assorted toasted nuts— pistachios, almonds, peanuts, and macadamias—for sprinkling on the salad. Sliced cooked beets with vinaigrette make a fitting accompaniment.

2 tablespoons vegetable oil
1½ pounds boneless chicken fillets
 (tender strip of boned breast; see
 page 396) or breast, skin removed,
 patted dry

salt and freshly ground pepper to taste
1 medium shallot, minced
⅓ cup dry white wine

Dill Dressing

⅔ cup sour cream or yogurt
½ cup heavy cream

3 to 4 tablespoons snipped fresh dill
salt and freshly ground pepper to taste

1½ pounds broccoli
8 ounces wide egg noodles (about 5⅔
 cups)
1 to 2 teaspoons strained fresh lemon
 juice (optional)

2 teaspoons snipped fresh dill
½ to ¾ cup toasted pistachios,
 macadamia nuts, almonds, peanuts,
 or assorted nuts, coarsely chopped
 (page 409)

Heat oil in a large skillet over medium heat. Sprinkle chicken with salt and pepper. Add about one-third of chicken to skillet and sauté until outer surface turns white, about 1 minute per side for fillets or about 2 minutes per side for chicken breast. Remove with a slotted spoon. Sauté remaining chicken in 2 batches.

Return all of chicken to skillet. Add shallot and wine, stir well, and bring just to simmer. Cover and cook over low heat, turning once, about 5 minutes for fillets or about 7 minutes for larger breast pieces, or until meat in thickest part is no longer pink when cut. Transfer chicken to a plate with slotted spoon. Boil juices until reduced to 3 or 4 tablespoons. Pour juices into a small bowl and reserve for dressing.

If using chicken breast halves, cut them diagonally in about 2 × ⅜ × ⅜-inch strips.

Make dill dressing: Spoon sour cream or yogurt into a small bowl and whisk in cream. Whisk in 3 tablespoons reserved chicken juices. Stir in dill, salt, and pepper.

Divide broccoli into small florets with 1-inch stems; pare large stalks, remove tough ends and cut pared stalks in 2 × ¼ × ¼-inch sticks. Cook florets and sticks in a large saucepan of boiling salted water, uncovered, over high heat about 2 minutes or until crisp-tender. Drain, rinse with cold water, and drain again gently to avoid bruising florets.

Cook pasta, uncovered, in a large pot of boiling salted water over high heat, stirring occasionally, about 5 minutes or until tender but firm to the bite. Drain, rinse with cold water, and drain well.

Toss pasta with chicken and about half of dressing. Reserve about 2 cups broccoli florets for garnish. Add remaining broccoli to salad and toss. *Salad can be kept, covered, 1 day in refrigerator. Keep remaining dressing and broccoli in separate containers. Let stand about 15 minutes at room temperature before serving.*

Add remaining dressing to salad and toss. Taste, and add lemon juice if desired. To serve, sprinkle salad with snipped dill. Garnish with remaining broccoli in a ring around edge of salad and sprinkle 1 or 2 tablespoons chopped nuts on center. Serve remaining nuts in a separate bowl.

Makes 4 main-course servings

HAWAIIAN CHICKEN AND SOMEN SALAD WITH SEAFOOD

My friend Patsy Allen, owner of Crème de la Crème catering in Los Angeles, taught me how to prepare this salad of poached chicken, Japanese somen noodles, and a sesame-soy-rice-vinegar dressing. Ms. Allen includes this salad on picnic menus, to add an exotic note. Sometimes she serves it as part of a Hawaiian buffet, which might also include Kahlua pork, Hawaiian sweet potatoes, lomi-lomi salmon (salted salmon with onions and tomatoes), steamed rice, clams, and for dessert, coconut cake and fresh pineapple.

The somen noodles and the Japanese fish cake called for in the salad are available in Japanese markets and can be found in the refrigerated section of many supermarkets. In my neighborhood supermarket in Santa Monica, the fish cakes come in three varieties. If you can't find them, substitute ¼ pound cooked small shrimp. Ms. Allen also stirs in Chinese omelet strips (page 392), for additional color and good flavor.

2 (9-ounce) packages Japanese somen noodles (very thin white noodles)
1 to 2 tablespoons Oriental sesame oil, to taste
1 package *kamaboko* (Japanese fish cake), or ¼ pound cooked small shrimp

1 pound boned chicken breasts, poached (page 391), shredded
½ pound crabmeat (optional)
5 green onions, finely chopped
1½ cups watercress leaves
1 small head iceberg lettuce, shredded
Sesame-Soy Dressing (page 359)

Cook noodles in a large pot of boiling salted water, stirring often with chopsticks or fork, about 1½ minutes or until just tender. Rinse with cold water and drain well. Transfer noodles to a large bowl and toss with 1 or 2 tablespoons sesame oil.

Cut fish cake in thin slices, then cut slices in strips. Combine noodles with fish cake strips or shrimp, chicken, and remaining salad ingredients. Add dressing to salad, and toss. Taste and adjust seasoning.

Makes 4 main-course servings

CHICKEN, KIWI, AND RICE SALAD WITH PAPAYA

Kiwis give this chicken salad a new accent and a New Zealand flavor. Kiwis are probably that country's best-known export, and the New Zealanders use the fruit to great advantage in a variety of dishes. This colorful salad, which also includes papaya and toasted macadamia nuts, evolved from an idea I got from a relative who lives in ''Kiwi land.''

5 cups water
salt
1½ pounds chicken thighs or drumsticks
2 tablespoons plus 2 teaspoons red wine vinegar
6 tablespoons vegetable oil
salt and freshly ground pepper
1 tablespoon grated fresh ginger, or ½ teaspoon ground ginger

1½ cups long-grain white rice
4 kiwi fruits
1 small ripe papaya, mango, or orange
⅓ cup chopped green onions
3 tablespoons toasted macadamia nuts or almonds, coarsely chopped (optional)

Bring water to a boil and add salt. Add chicken, cover, and poach over low heat about 30 minutes or until tender. Discard chicken skin and bones. Cut meat in strips. Measure 3 cups chicken cooking liquid to cook rice; let cool to room temperature.

Whisk together vinegar, oil, salt, pepper, and ginger. Add 3 tablespoons of this dressing to chicken.

Rinse rice, combine with cooled stock in a heavy, medium saucepan, and bring to a boil. Cover and cook over low heat about 12 to 14 minutes or until just tender. Transfer to a large bowl, fluff with fork, and cool.

Peel and cut 2 kiwis in thin slices. Leave 3 whole slices for garnish, and cut remaining slices in half. Peel and slice 2 other kiwis and quarter the slices. Peel and dice papaya.

Toss chicken with rice, green onions, and remaining dressing. Taste and adjust seasoning. Add papaya and small kiwi pieces. Sprinkle with nuts if desired. Garnish with kiwi slices, placing 3 whole slices in center and a ring of half kiwis around salad.

Makes 6 appetizer servings

CHICKEN SALAD WITH RICE, CHICKPEAS, AND SESAME SEEDS

Toasted sesame seeds, ground toasted chickpeas, and dried marjoram are the major ingredients of the popular Middle Eastern seasoning mixture called zaatar, *which is sprinkled over pastries and cheeses and which I also like in chicken salads. The flavor combination provides the inspiration for this easy-to-make salad, which also includes green onions and a touch of olive oil and lemon juice. I usually serve the salad on a bed of lettuce or spinach. Marinated red peppers and black olives make a natural accompaniment. If you can get* zaatar, *which is sold at some Middle Eastern grocery stores, follow the variation (see Note).*

1 cup long-grain white rice
½ cup cooked chickpeas (garbanzo beans), or 1 (8¾-ounce) can, drained and rinsed
3 cups diced cooked chicken or turkey
3 green onions, chopped (½ cup)
2 tablespoons extra-virgin olive oil

1 tablespoon strained fresh lemon juice
salt and freshly ground pepper
1 teaspoon dried marjoram, crumbled
1 teaspoon dried oregano, crumbled
2 tablespoons sesame seeds, toasted (page 409)
lettuce or spinach leaves (optional)

Cook the rice in a large pan of boiling salted water, uncovered, about 14 minutes or until just tender but still firm. Drain, rinse with cold water, and drain well. Mix rice with chickpeas, chicken, and green onions.

In a small bowl whisk oil, lemon juice, salt, and pepper. Add to salad. Sprinkle with herbs and fold in. Taste and adjust seasoning. *Salad can be kept, covered, overnight in refrigerator.*

Just before serving, fold in about two-thirds of the sesame seeds. Sprinkle the rest on top. Serve, if desired, on a bed of lettuce or spinach leaves.

Makes 3 or 4 main-course servings

NOTE: If you have *zaatar*, omit marjoram, oregano, and sesame seeds. Add 4 teaspoons *zaatar* to salad, or to taste.

TOMATOES STUFFED WITH CHICKEN-RICE SALAD AND TOASTED PECANS

Combining the regional favorites of pecans and rice with chicken, then seasoning the salad with a lively vinaigrette dressing marks it as typical of the cooking style of the American South. Summer is the best time to prepare this cool appetizer, when the tomatoes are beautiful and perfectly ripe. At other times of the year, you can serve the tasty, easy-to-make chicken-rice salad with its cilantro-caper dressing on a bed of lettuce instead.

1¼ cups long-grain white rice
2 celery stalks, peeled and diced
1½ cups diced cooked chicken or turkey
¾ cup pitted black olives, quartered lengthwise
4 tablespoons chopped cilantro (fresh coriander)

1 tablespoon chopped fresh parsley
2 teaspoons drained capers
3 tablespoons white wine vinegar
½ cup plus 1 tablespoon olive oil
salt and freshly ground pepper
6 large tomatoes
⅓ cup pecan halves, toasted (page 409)

Cook rice in a large pan of boiling salted water, uncovered, about 14 minutes or until just tender but still firm. Drain, rinse with cold water, and drain well. Mix rice with celery, chicken, olives, cilantro, parsley, and capers in a large bowl.

Make vinaigrette dressing by combining vinegar, oil, salt, and pepper to taste in a small bowl; whisk thoroughly. Add to rice mixture; mix gently. Taste for seasoning. Cover and refrigerate at least 1 hour or up to 2 days.

Halve tomatoes horizontally. Remove interior with a teaspoon, leaving a layer of pulp attached to skin to form a shell. Turn tomatoes over on a plate and leave to drain about 30 minutes.

Halve pecans lengthwise, then crosswise. Set aside 12 pecan pieces. Stir remaining pecan pieces into salad mixture. Fill tomato halves with salad, mounding filling. Set a pecan piece on each one. Serve within 1 hour.

Makes 6 appetizer servings

CHICKEN SALAD WITH ASPARAGUS AND ORANGE VINAIGRETTE

Asparagus and orange-flavored sauce are traditional partners in the classic European kitchen. When cooked chicken is seasoned with the orange vinaigrette and added to the asparagus, as in this warm salad, the classic gets even better.

1½ pounds medium asparagus, peeled if over ¼ inch thick
2 medium carrots, peeled

3 cups shredded cooked chicken
Orange Marinade/Vinaigrette (page 350)

Cut off asparagus tips. Cut stems in 3 pieces, discarding tough ends. Cut carrots in thin strips, about 1½ inches long. Boil carrots, uncovered, in medium saucepan of boiling salted water 3 minutes. Add asparagus and boil until it is just tender when pierced with a small sharp knife, about 2 or 3 minutes. Drain vegetables together well.

Combine asparagus, carrots, and chicken in a bowl and toss with dressing. Taste and adjust seasoning. Serve warm.

Makes 4 to 6 appetizer servings

SUMMER CHICKEN SALAD WITH CHERRIES AND MINT VINAIGRETTE

The tastes of chicken and fruit go very well together in salads, especially with a mint dressing. This flavor combination is new, but is based on traditional techniques I learned in France. To balance the sweetness of the cherries, the vinaigrette has more vinegar than in the classic proportions. The result is a lighter salad with less oil. Other summer fruit, such as peaches, nectarines, or berries, can be substituted for the cherries in this fresh-tasting salad.

1 tablespoon plus 1 teaspoon white
   wine vinegar
2 tablespoons plus 2 teaspoons
   vegetable oil
salt and freshly ground pepper
2 tablespoons plus 2 teaspoons
   chopped fresh mint

2 cups diced cooked chicken or turkey
14 large sweet dark cherries, pitted
   and halved (about ⅔ cup)
lettuce leaves (optional)

For vinaigrette, combine vinegar, oil, salt, and pepper in a bowl and whisk until blended. Add 1 tablespoon mint. Add chicken and toss to coat it. Taste and adjust seasoning.

   Just before serving, add remaining mint and cherries and toss lightly. Serve on a bed of lettuce, if desired.

Makes 2 light main-course servings

FRESH AND SMOKED CHICKEN SALAD WITH POTATOES AND WATERCRESS

Mustard, watercress, and potatoes turn chicken into a hearty northern European salad that is good at any season. In the winter, serve it warm with a grated carrot or beet salad; in the summer, serve it cool on a bed of baby greens and accompany it with sliced ripe tomatoes.

1 pound red-skinned potatoes of
   uniform size, scrubbed but not
   peeled
Mustard-Wine Vinaigrette (page 360)
2 cups diced cooked chicken
¾ cup diced smoked chicken breast
   (from thin slices)

½ cup minced red onion
1 cup watercress leaves
1 hard-boiled egg, chopped (optional)
⅓ cup black olives, for garnish

Put potatoes in a saucepan, cover with water, and add salt. Bring to boil. Cover and simmer over low heat about 25 to 30 minutes or until tender enough so that knife pierces center of largest potato easily.

Drain potatoes in colander and peel while hot. Halve potatoes lengthwise, put them cut side downward, halve again lengthwise, and quickly cut them in ⅜-inch crosswise slices.

Put potatoes in a bowl. Rewhisk vinaigrette and pour half of it over potatoes. Toss or fold gently to mix thoroughly. Cool to room temperature. Add 1 tablespoon vinaigrette to cooked chicken, refrigerate, and marinate while potatoes are cooling.

Whisk remaining vinaigrette again until blended. Add to potato salad and fold it in gently using rubber spatula. Add marinated chicken, smoked chicken, onion, watercress, and egg and fold gently. *Salad can be prepared 1 day ahead, covered and refrigerated.* Taste and adjust seasoning. Let stand about 15 minutes at room temperature before serving. Serve garnished with olives.

Makes 4 appetizer servings

ZESTY CHICKEN AND BLACK BEAN SALAD

Lime juice, cilantro, jalapeño peppers, and black beans lend a Latin American note to this colorful, flavorful salad, which is also popular in the Caribbean. Serve it with country bread for a delicious lunch or supper. It makes a terrific party dish and if you use canned beans, it can be made in no time.

1 cup dried black beans; or 2 (15- or 16-ounce) cans, drained and rinsed
6 cups water
3½ cups diced cooked chicken
2 tablespoons fresh lime juice
6 tablespoons vegetable oil
salt

3 or 4 jalapeño peppers, seeded, minced
¾ cup coarsely chopped cilantro (fresh coriander)
6 plum tomatoes, diced
1⅓ cups thin red onion slivers (see Note)

Sort beans and discard any stones. Soak beans overnight in 5 cups cold water. Rinse and drain. Put beans in pan with 6 cups water. Bring to boil, skim foam, cover, and simmer over low heat 1½ to 2 hours or until tender. Drain. Transfer to large bowl and add chicken.

Whisk lime juice in a bowl with oil and salt. Stir in peppers and add to chicken-bean mixture. Add cilantro, tomatoes, and onion. Taste and adjust seasoning. *Salad can be kept, covered, 2 days in refrigerator.*

Makes 6 appetizer or 4 main-course servings

NOTE: To make red onion slivers, halve the onion lengthwise (from top to root end), put it cut side down, and cut in half again lengthwise. Holding the two halves together, cut in thin slices crosswise. They will be quarter slices. Separate them into their natural divisions; they will be in thin slivers.

CHICKEN SALAD
WITH MUSTARD-CAPER VINAIGRETTE
AND VEGETABLE JULIENNE

This is a California-style transformation of an old-fashioned French beef salad. Instead of poached beef, it's made with roast chicken. Rather than being mixed with just potatoes, it comes with a crisp colorful julienne of sautéed vegetables: snow peas, yellow squash, and carrots. The zesty Dijon mustard vinaigrette with capers keeps its original Gallic flavor and has become a favorite in new American cuisine.

2 pounds fairly small round potatoes
salt
Mustard-Caper Vinaigrette (page 357)
2 tablespoons dry white wine
1 large carrot
2 small yellow crookneck or yellow
   summer squash

4 ounces snow peas
2 tablespoons vegetable oil
3½- to 4-pound chicken, roasted; or 3
   to 4 cups cooked chicken strips
freshly ground pepper
12 romaine lettuce leaves

Put potatoes in medium saucepan, cover with water, and add salt. Bring to boil. Cover, reduce heat, and simmer about 25 minutes or until tender enough so that knife pierces center of largest potato easily. Drain potatoes in colander and slice them in rounds about ¼ inch thick. Put potatoes in large shallow bowl. Rewhisk vinaigrette until blended. Combine wine with 6 tablespoons vinaigrette and pour over potatoes. Toss or fold gently. Cool to room temperature.

Peel carrot and cut in thin strips, about 2 × ¼ × ⅛ inch. Cut squash in strips of about same size as carrot. Remove ends from snow peas and cut diagonally in strips about ¼ inch wide.

In a large skillet heat oil over medium-high heat. Add carrot and sauté, stirring, 2 minutes. Add squash and snow peas and sauté 2 minutes or until crisp-tender. Transfer to a bowl.

Discard chicken skin and bones. Cut meat in strips. Transfer to a bowl. Whisk remaining vinaigrette, add to chicken, and toss. *Potatoes, chicken, and vegetables can be kept in separate containers, covered, 1 day in refrigerator.*

Add sautéed vegetables to chicken and toss. Taste and adjust seasoning. Taste potatoes and adjust seasoning. Make a bed of lettuce on each of 4 plates. Arrange a ring of potato slices near outer edge of lettuce. Mound chicken salad in center.

Makes 4 main-course servings

ROAST CHICKEN SALAD
WITH TOMATO-GARLIC SALSA

Salsa, the popular Mexican uncooked vegetable sauce, is good for more than just tortilla-based dishes. Chicken salad, for example, gains a boost in flavor from this zesty, low-calorie Mexican-inspired dressing. The salsa is also delicious as an alternative to the chutney in Chicken Burgers with Pine Nuts and Jalapeño-Garlic Chutney (page 366).

1 pound ripe tomatoes, peeled, seeded, diced
2 large garlic cloves, minced
1 fresh hot pepper (jalapeño or serrano), seeded, ribs removed, minced
3 tablespoons minced green onion

1 tablespoon olive oil
1 teaspoon strained fresh lime juice (optional)
salt and freshly ground pepper
romaine or butter lettuce leaves, torn in pieces
12 slices roast chicken or turkey

Combine tomatoes, garlic, hot pepper, green onion, oil, lime juice, salt, and pepper in a small bowl and stir. Let stand about 30 minutes at room temperature or up to 4 hours in refrigerator. Bring to room temperature for serving.

Make bed of lettuce on each plate and top with chicken or turkey slices. Spoon a little salsa over chicken. Serve remaining salsa separately.

Makes 4 to 6 main-course servings

CHICKEN SALAD
WITH HARISSA VINAIGRETTE

The North African hot pepper sauce called harissa *flavors this easy chicken salad, but it doesn't have to be fiery unless you want it to be. I use just enough harissa to give the dressing a little zip. It's best to add it gradually, as different brands of harissa, like other hot sauces, vary in hotness. Marinating the chicken in the dressing makes it hotter.*

For a quick lunch or supper when there's not much time to prepare the ingredients, frozen vegetables are a big help. In this salad I like to use a blend of frozen vegetables that includes sliced carrots, corn, and green beans. The cooked vegetables and chicken make a colorful mélange, which gains freshness by being accented by lettuce, tomato slices, and radish sprouts.

2 teaspoons strained fresh lemon juice
2 tablespoons extra-virgin olive oil
½ to 1 teaspoon Harissa (page 366) or bottled hot pepper sauce, or more to taste
salt and freshly ground pepper
2 cups coarsely shredded roast chicken

2 cups mixed diced fresh or frozen vegetables (such as corn, carrots and beans), cooked, drained, rinsed
2 tablespoons chopped fresh parsley
leaves of butter lettuce or Boston lettuce
1 ripe tomato, cut in half slices
a few radish sprouts (optional)

Combine lemon juice, oil, Harissa, salt, and pepper in a bowl and whisk to blend.

Mix chicken with dressing. Let stand 5 to 10 minutes, or refrigerate about 30 minutes. Mix in cooked vegetables and parsley. Taste and adjust seasoning. Serve on a bed of lettuce; garnish plate with tomato slices and radish sprouts.

Makes 2 light main-course servings

TURKEY TAPENADE SALAD

Tapenade is a black olive spread from Provence that is flavored with capers and anchovies. For this turkey salad I have used the tapenade theme as an inspiration for the dressing. Rather than pureeing the olives and capers, I kept them in distinct pieces, and then I tossed the mixture with the turkey, potatoes, and green beans.

2 cups diced cooked turkey or chicken
Tapenade Dressing (page 360)
1 pound small new potatoes
**½ cup halved thinly sliced red onion,
  separated in half rings**
⅓ cup chopped fresh parsley

**½ pound green beans, cut in 1½-inch
  pieces**
3 ripe plum tomatoes, sliced
1 tablespoon capers, for garnish
6 to 8 black olives, for garnish

Mix turkey with 2 tablespoons dressing. Cook, halve, and slice potatoes. Mix them gently with 3 tablespoons dressing. Let cool. Lightly mix in turkey, onion and parsley. *Salad can be kept, covered, 1 day in refrigerator.*

Cook green beans, uncovered, in a saucepan of boiling salted water about 7 minutes or until crisp-tender. Rinse with cold water and drain well.

Add green beans, tomatoes, and remaining dressing to salad. Taste and adjust seasoning, adding more olive oil and lemon juice if you like. Sprinkle with capers and garnish with whole olives.

Makes 6 appetizer or 3 or 4 light main-course servings

TURKEY SALAD
WITH CREAMY CILANTRO DRESSING

With the addition of avocado, fresh mushrooms, tomatoes, and olives, roast turkey is turned into a colorful entree, perfect for hot weather. The Mexican-inspired dressing adds zip to the meat yet is not overly hot.

3 large white mushrooms (4 ounces)
1 ripe avocado, preferably Haas
12 leaves red leaf lettuce
12 to 16 thin slices roast turkey

2 small tomatoes, cut in wedges
12 to 16 fine-quality black olives, such
 as Kalamata
Creamy Cilantro Dressing (page 356)

Cut mushrooms in thin slices. Peel and halve avocado, remove pit, and cut in thin crosswise slices. On each plate make a bed of red leaf lettuce. Arrange rows of slices of turkey, mushroom, and avocado on lettuce, overlapping them. Garnish with tomato wedges and olives. Serve dressing separately.

Makes 4 main-course servings

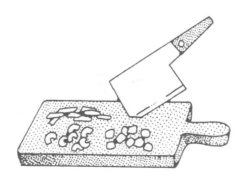

SMOKED TURKEY AND COUSCOUS SALAD WITH RED PEPPER AND EGGPLANT

Moroccan couscous, teamed up with a refreshing Greek yogurt-mint-garlic dressing and toasted pine nuts, gives this colorful salad its Mediterranean flair. For best results buy a piece of smoked turkey breast rather than sliced pressed turkey. If you wish, you can use the whole wheat couscous available at health food stores, but cook it according to the package directions.

½ cup extra-virgin olive oil
salt and freshly ground pepper
3 tablespoons strained fresh lemon
   juice, more if desired
1 large red bell pepper, cut in 2 × ¼-
   inch strips
1⅓ cups couscous
1¼ cups boiling water
1 fairly small eggplant (about ¾
   pound)

2 tablespoons vegetable oil
8 ounces smoked turkey breast
¼ cup chopped fresh mint
3 tablespoons chopped fresh parsley
2 tablespoons chopped green onion
12 leaves butter lettuce or Boston
   lettuce
Yogurt, Mint, and Garlic Dressing
   (page 359)
¼ cup pine nuts, toasted (page 409)

In a small bowl whisk 6 tablespoons olive oil with salt, pepper, and 3 tablespoons lemon juice. Set aside.

Heat remaining 2 tablespoons olive oil in a large skillet over medium-low heat. Add pepper strips and cook, stirring often, about 6 minutes or until softened. Remove from heat. Add couscous and a pinch of salt and pepper. Shake skillet to spread couscous in an even layer. Pour boiling water evenly over couscous, immediately cover tightly, and let stand 5 minutes. Whisk reserved oil and lemon dressing and drizzle 3 tablespoons of it over couscous. Cover and let stand 2 minutes. Transfer couscous to a bowl and break up any lumps with a fork. Cool completely.

Cut eggplant in ¾-inch dice. Heat vegetable oil in a large skillet over medium heat. Add eggplant, salt, and pepper and sauté about 3 minutes. Cover and cook over medium-low heat about 7 minutes or until eggplant is tender. Remove to a plate. Cool.

Cut turkey in ½ × ½ × ¼-inch dice. Whisk remaining oil and lemon dressing, drizzle it over couscous, and toss gently with a fork. Add turkey, eggplant, mint, parsley, and green onion and toss salad gently. Taste and adjust seasoning. Add more lemon juice if desired. *Salad can be kept, covered, 1 day in refrigerator.*

To serve, make a bed of lettuce on each of 4 plates and spoon couscous salad on lettuce. Spoon a little Yogurt, Mint, and Garlic Dressing on center of couscous mixture and sprinkle with pine nuts. Serve remaining yogurt dressing separately.

Makes 4 appetizer or light main-course servings

TURKEY TABBOULEH

This Mediterranean dish makes an enticing, colorful buffet salad. Some chefs now use the traditional, vegetarian tabbouleh recipe and add other ingredients, such as seafood, to it. I find tabbouleh's refreshing flavors of mint, green onions, and lemon, together with the richness of olive oil, perfect as the basis for a turkey salad. The combination of cracked wheat and turkey makes for a light but satisfying main course.

Bulgur wheat can be found at Middle Eastern and/or Mediterranean shops, health food stores, and some supermarkets. The bulgur grains have a more distinct texture when soaked, as in the recipe, but if you are in a rush you can cook the bulgur instead, as in the variation. If you can't find bulgur wheat, substitute couscous—that's what French chefs use to make tabbouleh. Prepare it according to the package instructions, omitting any butter or oil specified.

1 cup bulgur wheat
3 cups boiling water
2 cups diced cooked turkey
3 tablespoons lemon juice, or more to taste
salt and freshly ground black pepper
cayenne pepper to taste
6 tablespoons extra-virgin olive oil

5 plum tomatoes
½ long (European) cucumber, or 1 medium cucumber, peeled
3 green onions
⅔ cup chopped fresh parsley, preferably Italian
¾ cup chopped fresh mint
lettuce leaves (optional)

Put bulgur wheat in a large bowl. Pour boiling water over wheat and let stand until it is completely cool and tender, about 1 hour.

Meanwhile, combine turkey, 1 tablespoon lemon juice, salt, pepper, cayenne, and 3 tablespoons oil in a bowl. Cover and refrigerate while preparing remaining ingredients.

Drain wheat in a colander. Gently squeeze out excess water and return wheat to large bowl.

Dice tomatoes and cucumbers very small. Cut green onions in thin slices. Gently mix diced cucumbers with green onions, herbs, and wheat and add turkey mixture. Gently fold in tomatoes and add remaining oil and lemon juice. Taste and adjust seasoning, adding more lemon juice, oil, and cayenne if desired. *Salad can be kept, covered, 1 day in refrigerator.* Serve on a lettuce-lined platter, either cold or cool.

Makes 12 cups; about 8 appetizer or 5 or 6 main-course servings

VARIATION: **Quick Turkey Tabbouleh**
In a medium saucepan, combine bulgur wheat and 2¼ cups boiling water. Cover and cook over low heat 15 minutes or until tender. Turn out into a large bowl and let cool. Continue as above.

6

Chicken and Turkey Soups

Our image of chicken soup is of a delicate broth to be enjoyed occasionally in winter, usually as a first course. It might contain a few noodles, rice grains, or chicken strips and maybe a vegetable or two.

Yet chicken soup plays a major part as a light main course year-round in menus in much of the world. In the Orient, chicken soup with noodles is the favorite lunch. For millions of people in China, Japan, and Thailand, it is as common as a lunchtime sandwich is here. The noodles can be of wheat or rice, and there will frequently be a few herbs, vegetables, or strips of chicken or other meats. Hearty, satisfying, with plenty of noodles and often accented with soy sauce and hot pepper, it is designed to give enough energy to last through the day. Thai Chicken Noodle Soup with Roasted Peanuts (page 78) is this kind of soup. It has a variety of Oriental vegetables and rice noodles and makes a light yet satisfying main course.

On the other side of the globe, pasta in brodo—or pasta in a clear soup—is one of the most popular Italian ways of serving tortellini, ravioli, and other stuffed and plain pastas. The soup is often chicken soup, and is used to showcase the pasta as a first course.

75

Thai Chicken Noodle Soup with Roasted Peanuts
Main-Course Minestrone
Chicken Soup with Lentils and Lemon
Chicken Vegetable Soup with Mint and Basil
Golden Chicken Soup with Orzo and Garlic
Chicken Soup with Split Peas and Cilantro
Chicken Garlic Soup with Broccoli
Iranian Chicken Soup with Plums and Mint
Springtime Chicken Soup
Near Eastern Chicken Soup
with Chickpeas, Rice, and Spinach
Hearty Chicken Soup with Zucchini, Tomatoes,
and Lima Beans
Chicken Soup with Osso Buco and Fine Noodles
Chinese Chicken Soup with Asparagus
and Mushrooms
Chicken Velouté Soup
with Leeks and Fresh Herbs
Turkey Soup with Spinach Tortellini
and Mushrooms
Avocado-Turkey Chowder
Korean Turkey Soup with Spinach

Wonderful chicken soups turn up in unexpected places. One of the best chicken soups I ever tasted was served at a Cuban restaurant. It had a flavorful tomato-scented broth with a touch of hot pepper sauce but otherwise there was nothing unusual about the components: strips of chicken, sliced carrots and diced potatoes. It was simply cooked and seasoned very well. In fact I should not have been surprised. Chicken soup is loved and served often throughout the Caribbean and Latin America.

One advantage of serving chicken soup as either a first or main course is that it is naturally low in fat. The chicken is poached in liquid, and then the fat is skimmed from the soup. Yet there is no feeling of deprivation when chicken soup is on the menu. For many people a bowl of homemade chicken soup is the ultimate comfort food.

I usually make soup from meaty chicken pieces and lots of vegetables, and serve the soup as a light main course. What vegetables to put in the pot is up to you. In addition to the traditional onion and carrot, I often add celery, mushrooms, zucchini, cubes of winter squash, and tomatoes. To give the soup substance, I alternate among potatoes, rice, and different shapes of pasta. Even fruit is sometimes added to chicken soup, as in Iranian Chicken Soup with Plums and Mint (page 86), a refreshing summer soup.

Dried beans are delicious additions to chicken soup. Occasionally I add them with other vegetables to make chicken minestrone or a Middle Eastern chicken soup with chickpeas and spinach. When I have less time, I add chicken pieces and sliced fresh vegetables to one of the many packaged dried bean soups now available and cook them together. For a finishing touch, I stir in fresh dill, cilantro, or parsley. This makes a warming, colorful main-course soup with very little effort.

Basic chicken soup or stock is usually delicate, even in the culinary repertoires of nations who love spicy cooking. Chicken stock or broth is the basis for most Chinese soups and for many Western soups as well. The Chinese version is subtly flavored with fresh ginger and green onion, while European and American versions might have thyme, bay leaves, onion, and carrots. In the Middle East well-liked flavorings include cilantro, cumin, and garlic.

Making good-tasting chicken soup is very easy. You can use whole chickens, chicken pieces, or chicken legs, thighs, backs, or wings. Turkey wings, legs, and thighs make flavorful turkey soup. Breast pieces are best for other uses, as they do not give as rich-tasting a broth as the other cuts, and they're more expensive anyway. Necks and gizzards can be added to other pieces but if they are used on their own, the taste of the broth is too strong.

Clear strained soup with a few vegetables makes a superb appetizer, like the elegant Chinese Chicken Soup with Asparagus and Mushrooms (page 91). Smooth, creamy French-style chicken velouté soups, Provençal chicken bourride, and rich American-style chicken or turkey chowders are best served in small quantities as first courses.

You don't need much else to serve with soup. Country-style French or Italian bread are classic accompaniments and so are croutons and breadsticks. Bagel crisps, pita crisps, or any form of toasted bread are also good with chicken soup.

Chicken soup does take an hour and a half or two to become well flavored, but you can use shortcuts to enjoy quick soup. Simmer diced chicken or turkey breasts in canned chicken broth (I prefer the low-salt versions) or reconstituted frozen chicken stock base with some quick-cooking vegetables, and you'll have chicken soup in a hurry. Or cook some frozen vegetables in the stock and stir in cubes or strips of roasted chicken or turkey.

TIP

✖ Because chicken gives off fat as it cooks, the broth should be skimmed thoroughly before being served. The simplest way is to chill it first, so the fat solidifies and can be easily removed. Otherwise, skim the fat from the surface of the soup several times with a spoon. Remember, the cooler the broth is, the easier it is to skim off the fat.

THAI CHICKEN NOODLE SOUP WITH ROASTED PEANUTS

When I lived in Paris I spent some wonderful weekends learning about Thai cuisine from my friend Somchit Singchalee, a Thai chef. One simple dish she taught me was this noodle soup. It begins like any chicken soup—the meat is cooked with onions, carrots, celery, and leeks to a light stock. Then rice noodles, bok choy, and bean sprouts are added. Finally it is sprinkled with peanuts and served with soy sauce, sesame oil, and a touch of vinegar and sugar. There are also hot red pepper flakes— lots of them! Somchit always insisted she made the dish only ''baby hot'' for me, the way they make it in Thailand for babies, whose delicate palates aren't used to all those hot peppers.

Although each condiment is served separately in Thailand, I mix them together as a seasoning sauce for easier serving. Thai cooks also add 1 or 2 tablespoons fish sauce (nam pla) to the sauce for a salty flavor but it's not easily available and the soup has enough flavor without it. SEE PHOTOGRAPH.

1 medium leek, split, cleaned (page 408)
2 pounds chicken pieces, all dark meat or white and dark
2 medium carrots, sliced
2 medium celery stalks, sliced

1 medium onion, halved, sliced
pinch of salt
2 quarts water
½ pound dried rice noodles or rice sticks

Pepper-Soy-Vinegar Seasoning Sauce

2 teaspoons hot red pepper flakes
4 tablespoons soy sauce
2 tablespoons plus 2 teaspoons rice vinegar

2 teaspoons sugar
2 teaspoons Oriental sesame oil

4 large bok choy leaves, green part only, rinsed, cut in bite-size pieces
2 tablespoons soy sauce
2 to 2½ cups bean sprouts, rinsed, ends removed

¼ cup coarsely chopped cilantro (fresh coriander), green onion, or both
½ cup chopped toasted peanuts

Use white, light green, and 2 inches of dark green of leek. Slice and put in large pot. Add chicken, carrots, celery, onion, salt, and water. Bring to a simmer and skim foam. Cover and cook over low heat 1 hour. Discard chicken skin and bones; shred meat. *Soup can be kept, covered, 2 days in refrigerator; reserve chicken separately.*

Meanwhile, put rice noodles in a large bowl, cover with hot water, and let soak 10 minutes. Remove noodles and rinse in a colander. Add them to a saucepan of boiling water and simmer, lifting strands often with tongs, 1 minute or until just tender. Drain and rinse with hot water and drain again.

For seasoning sauce, mix pepper flakes, soy sauce, vinegar, sugar, and sesame oil.

Skim fat from soup. Bring soup to simmer, add bok choy, and cook, uncovered, 2 minutes. Add chicken and reheat gently 1 minute. Stir in soy sauce.

Put noodles and bean sprouts in soup bowls. Ladle soup into bowls. Add 1 teaspoon seasoning sauce to each bowl. Sprinkle each bowl with cilantro and 1 tablespoon peanuts. Serve remaining sauce and more peanuts separately.

Makes 4 or 5 main-course servings

MAIN-COURSE MINESTRONE

Although we are most familiar with minestrone made solely of vegetables, meat is added in some regions of Italy. I find minestrone makes a delicious and colorful chicken-noodle soup. Vary the vegetables according to the seasons—the soup might include green beans, pumpkin, winter squash, spinach, or a small amount of turnip.

Pesto is not always added to minestrone in Italy, and in this soup the chicken adds enough richness and flavor so the soup is good without it. Of course, if you do add pesto, it will perk up the soup's flavor, especially if the pesto was freshly made at home.

½ cup dried white beans, such as
   Great Northern
3 quarts water
2 tablespoons olive oil
2 medium onions, chopped
2 medium celery stalks, cut in thin
   slices
1 pound tomatoes, peeled, seeded, and
   chopped; or 1 (28-ounce) can plum
   tomatoes, drained and chopped
½ teaspoon dried thyme, crumbled
2 pounds chicken pieces
2 small carrots, peeled and diced

1 large potato, peeled and diced
4 Swiss chard leaves, cut in thin strips
   (optional)
salt and freshly ground pepper
4 small zucchini (about 1 pound), cut
   in cubes
½ pound peas, shelled, or ½ cup
   frozen peas
1 cup medium noodles
Pesto (page 363) or ⅓ to ½ cup
   packaged pesto (optional)
grated Parmesan cheese, for serving

Pick over beans, discarding any pebbles or broken or discolored beans. Rinse beans, drain, and place in a large bowl; add 3 cups water. Cover and let stand for at least 8 hours or overnight. Or, to shorten soaking period, place beans in a medium saucepan with 1 quart water; boil uncovered for 2 minutes, remove from heat, cover, and let stand 1 hour.

Drain beans, discarding soaking liquid, and rinse. Put beans in a large saucepan with 5 cups water. Bring to boil, cover, and simmer for 1 hour, adding hot water occasionally so beans remain covered. Drain beans, reserving ¾ cup liquid. Pour reserved liquid over beans.

Heat oil in large saucepan over low heat, add onions, and sauté about 10 minutes. Add celery, tomatoes, and thyme and cook over medium heat, stirring, 5 minutes.

Add chicken, carrots, potato, chard, beans in their reserved liquid, remaining 1 quart water, and a pinch of salt and pepper and bring to boil. Cover and cook over low heat 30 minutes. Add zucchini and simmer until chicken is tender, about 20 minutes. Remove chicken, discard skin and bones, and return meat to pot.

Add peas and noodles to soup and simmer until just tender, about 10 minutes. Remove from heat, ladle into a tureen, and stir in pesto, if using. Taste, and add salt and pepper if needed. Serve immediately. Serve grated cheese separately.

Makes 8 to 10 appetizer or 6 main-course servings

NOTE: If you like, substitute a 15-ounce can cooked white beans, drained, for dried beans, and add ¾ cup more water to soup.

CHICKEN SOUP
WITH LENTILS AND LEMON

Unlike some lentil soups, this one is not thick or sticky, but light and fresh tasting. Seasoned in the Lebanese fashion with garlic, parsley, and lemon, it is very simple to make. Serve the soup with bowls of rice or with crusty country bread or pita.

3 pounds chicken pieces
2 medium onions, sliced
2 large carrots, cut in thick slices
    (about ⅜ inch)
10 cups water
1 bay leaf
salt and freshly ground pepper

2 small dried hot peppers, such as
    chiles arbol or *chiles japones* (optional)
1½ cups lentils
4 medium garlic cloves, chopped
½ cup chopped fresh parsley or
    cilantro (fresh coriander)
lemon wedges, for serving

Put chicken in large pot with onions, carrots, water, bay leaf, salt, pepper, and hot peppers and bring to a boil. Skim foam and fat. Simmer 30 minutes.

Pick over lentils and discard any stones. Rinse lentils and add to soup. Add garlic. Cover and simmer over low heat 1 hour or until lentils are tender. Discard bay leaf and hot peppers. Either leave chicken in pieces, or remove it from bone, dice it, and return to soup; or reserve chicken for other uses.

Skim fat from surface of soup. Taste and adjust seasoning. Add parsley. Serve with lemon wedges.

Makes 6 main-course servings

CHICKEN VEGETABLE SOUP WITH MINT AND BASIL

The taste of fresh herbs dominates this light, refreshing chicken vegetable soup from North Africa. Serve it with Italian sesame bread or pita for a savory Mediterranean-style lunch, or as a first course.

2½ to 3 pounds chicken pieces
2 medium onions, sliced
2 quarts water
salt
2 medium carrots, peeled, cut in large dice
3 medium garlic cloves, chopped (optional)
1 pound boiling potatoes, peeled, cut in large dice
½ pound zucchini, cut in large dice

½ pound crookneck squash, yellow summer squash, or patty pan squash, cut in large dice
3 ripe medium tomatoes, peeled and diced; or 1 (14- or 16-ounce) can plum tomatoes, drained and diced
8 ounces mushrooms, quartered
7 tablespoons chopped fresh mint
¾ cup chopped fresh basil
freshly ground pepper
a few drops lemon juice (optional)

Put chicken and onions in large pot, cover with water, add salt, and bring to a boil. Reduce heat to low. Skim foam and fat from surface. Cover and cook 30 minutes. Add carrots, garlic, and potatoes and cook 30 minutes. Add zucchini, crookneck squash, tomatoes and mushrooms, and cook 20 to 30 minutes or until vegetables are tender. *Soup can be kept, covered, 2 days in refrigerator.*

Skim fat and reheat soup if necessary. Add ¼ cup mint and simmer 2 minutes. Add ½ cup basil. Season with salt, pepper, and lemon juice, if desired. When serving, sprinkle with remaining mint and basil.

Makes 4 or 5 main-course servings

GOLDEN CHICKEN SOUP WITH ORZO AND GARLIC

Garlic-flavored orzo, or rice-shaped pasta, lends interest to this colorful North African-inspired chicken soup with vegetables. It is simple to prepare, does not require many ingredients, and makes a great party soup in winter. Instead of being simmered in the pot of soup, the orzo is made into a pilaf with some of the soup, and is served on the side so it keeps its texture.

2 pounds chicken legs or thighs
1 medium onion, sliced
8 medium garlic cloves, chopped
salt and freshly ground pepper
½ teaspoon turmeric
10 cups water

3 medium carrots, sliced ½ inch thick
2 tablespoons vegetable or olive oil
2 cups orzo or riso (rice-shaped pasta)
2 medium zucchini, halved and sliced
2 tablespoons chopped fresh Italian or
    curly parsley

Combine chicken with onion, 3 garlic cloves, salt, pepper, and turmeric in large saucepan and add water. Bring to a boil. Skim foam from surface. Cover and simmer 45 minutes. Add carrots and simmer 20 minutes or until tender. Skim fat from soup.

In a medium saucepan heat oil, add remaining garlic and the orzo and sauté over low heat, stirring often, for 3 minutes. Add salt, pepper, and 4 cups soup (without chicken or vegetables). Stir and bring to a boil. Cover and cook over low heat about 12 minutes or until orzo is just tender. Fluff with fork. *Soup and orzo can be kept in separate containers, covered, 2 days in refrigerator. Reheat orzo with ½ cup hot soup.*

Remove chicken from bones if desired; discard skin. Meanwhile, add zucchini slices to remaining soup, bring to simmer, cover, and cook over low heat about 10 minutes or until just tender. Return chicken to soup. Taste and adjust seasoning. Stir in parsley. Ladle soup into bowls and add a spoonful of orzo to each. Serve remaining orzo separately.

Makes 4 or 5 main-course servings

CHICKEN SOUP
WITH SPLIT PEAS AND CILANTRO

This Persian soup is very different from our familiar split pea soups that are thick purees. Here each ingredient—strips of chicken, peas, and rice—retains its individuality and the tastes are bold and fresh from the garlic and plenty of herbs. The soup has a warm golden color and is perfect for winter.

⅔ cup split peas
1½ pounds chicken drumsticks or
  thighs
1 medium onion, sliced
9 cups water
salt and freshly ground pepper

1 teaspoon turmeric
7 to 8 tablespoons chopped cilantro
  (fresh coriander) or parsley
4 medium garlic cloves, chopped
⅔ cup long-grain rice, preferably
  Basmati

Sort through peas to remove dirt and pebbles. Put in bowl or saucepan, cover with water by 2 inches, and soak overnight. Drain and rinse.

In large saucepan cook chicken with peas, onion, and 7 cups water for 1 hour and 15 minutes or until peas are tender. Skim fat from surface. Season soup with salt and pepper. Remove chicken pieces and discard skin and bones. Pull off chicken from bones in large pieces and return to pan.

Add remaining water, turmeric, 6 tablespoons cilantro or parsley, and garlic. Bring to simmer. Add rice and bring to simmer again. Cover and simmer 15 minutes until rice is tender. Sprinkle remaining cilantro or parsley when serving. *If soup is made ahead, it thickens; add a little water when reheating.*

Makes 4 main-course servings

CHICKEN GARLIC SOUP WITH BROCCOLI

Bourride, or garlic soup, is traditionally a fish soup-stew that is creamy in consistency because of the addition of the zesty Provençal garlic sauce, aïoli. The first time I tasted bourride was in a small restaurant in Marseille, in the area where the famous garlic soup originated. Since then I have enjoyed many versions of the soup, with different types of seafood and vegetables. Eventually I tried it with chicken and found it was also delicious, as the garlic taste blends beautifully with the flavor of chicken soup.

2 pounds chicken drumsticks or thighs
1 quart chicken stock, thoroughly
   skimmed of fat (page 389)
1 medium onion, sliced
1 medium celery stalk, broken in 2
   pieces

1 large sprig fresh thyme, or ½
   teaspoon dried leaves, crumbled
1 bay leaf
salt and freshly ground pepper

Aïoli

4 large garlic cloves, chopped
4 egg yolks
1 teaspoon strained fresh lemon juice

½ cup extra-virgin olive oil
pinch of salt and freshly ground
   pepper

1½ pounds broccoli, divided in small
   florets

Put chicken pieces in a heavy, medium saucepan. Add stock, onion, celery, thyme, bay leaf, salt, and pepper. Bring to simmer. Cover and poach over low heat, skimming foam occasionally, until chicken is tender when pierced in thickest parts with point of a knife, about 30 minutes. Remove chicken and leave until cool enough to handle.

Pour broth into bowl, cool to lukewarm, and chill to skim fat. Meanwhile pull off chicken skin. Remove meat from bones in as large pieces as possible. Cut large pieces of meat in ½-inch dice, removing any fat and cartilage. Combine dice with remaining smaller pieces in a bowl. *Soup can be kept, covered, 1 day in refrigerator; cover chicken pieces and refrigerate separately.*

For aïoli, drop garlic cloves through feed tube of a food processor fitted with metal blade, with motor running, and process until finely chopped. Add egg yolks, lemon juice, 1 tablespoon oil, and a little salt and pepper and process until very thoroughly blended, scraping bottom and sides of container several times. With motor running, gradually pour in remaining oil in a thin trickle. After adding ¼ cup, oil can be poured in a little faster, in a fine stream. *Aïoli can be kept, covered, 1 day in refrigerator.*

In a large saucepan of boiling salted water, cook broccoli for 2 minutes, or until just tender.

Drain, rinse under cold water, and drain well. Handle broccoli gently to avoid bruising florets.

Skim fat thoroughly from soup. Bring to a boil in heavy medium saucepan. Discard celery, thyme sprigs, and bay leaf. Add chicken and broccoli to soup and cook over low heat 1 minute to heat through. Remove from heat. Using slotted spoon, remove chicken and broccoli to large strainer set over bowl; pour any soup that goes through into bowl back into pan.

Spoon aïoli into a heavy medium bowl. Gradually whisk about 2 cups hot soup into aïoli. With saucepan of soup off heat, gradually whisk mixture into remaining soup. Return soup to low heat and heat, whisking constantly, 4 or 5 minutes; do not let it come near a boil. Remove from heat and gently stir in broccoli and chicken. Taste and adjust seasoning. Serve immediately.

Makes 6 appetizer or 4 main-course servings

IRANIAN CHICKEN SOUP WITH PLUMS AND MINT

This may seem a soup of surprising tastes, but actually, tart flavors are a favorite in soups in many countries, from French sorrel soup to Greek lemon soups to Chinese hot and sour soup. Here fresh plums add a delicately tart flavor to the refreshing soup and make an attractive bright red garnish as well. Serve with individual bowls of rice for spooning into the soup, and don't forget to warn your family or guests that the plums have pits. Grilled lamb chops or kabobs would make a good main course, served with ''chopped salad'' of tomatoes, cucumbers, and red onions.

½ cup split peas
1½ pounds chicken drumsticks or
   thighs
1 medium onion, sliced
6 cups water
salt and freshly ground pepper

1 pound small whole red plums
1 teaspoon ground cinnamon
2 teaspoons sugar
2 tablespoons chopped fresh parsley
⅔ cup plus 2 tablespoons chopped
   fresh mint

Sort through peas. Put in bowl or saucepan, cover with water by 2 inches, and soak overnight. Drain and rinse.

Cook chicken with peas, onion, and water for 1 hour and 15 minutes or until peas are tender. Skim fat from surface. Season soup with salt and pepper. Remove chicken pieces and discard skin and bones. Shred or dice meat and return to soup.

Just before serving, add red plums, cinnamon, sugar, parsley, and ⅔ cup chopped mint. Cook over low heat about 8 minutes or until plums are just tender. Taste and adjust seasoning. Sprinkle with remaining mint and serve.

Makes 6 first-course servings

SPRINGTIME CHICKEN SOUP

The delights of spring—asparagus, new potatoes, fresh carrots, and spring onions—combine with chicken to make this light, colorful European-style soup. I like to use a whole chicken to make the soup and serve the meat in the soup as a casual main course, but you can reserve all or some of the meat for a chicken salad and serve this as a first-course soup instead.

3½-pound chicken, or 2½ to 3 pounds
   chicken pieces
salt and freshly ground pepper
1 large onion, whole or sliced
1 bay leaf
about 2 quarts water
12 small new potatoes
4 medium (¾ pound) carrots, peeled
   and cut in 2-inch lengths

2 medium garlic cloves, chopped
1 pound medium-width asparagus,
   peeled and cut in 2-inch lengths
1 pound fresh peas, shelled, or 1 cup
   frozen peas (optional)
⅓ cup chopped green onions
2 tablespoons chopped fresh parsley

Remove fat from chicken. Put chicken in a large casserole or pot. If chicken giblets are available, add neck and giblets, except liver. Sprinkle with salt and pepper. Add onion and bay leaf and cover ingredients generously with water. Bring to a boil. Skim excess foam from surface. Cover and cook over low heat 1 hour.

Peel potatoes. Add potatoes, carrots, and garlic to casserole, cover, and cook over low heat 45 minutes. Discard bay leaf. Skim off fat. (This is easier to do when soup is cold.) Remove skin from chicken, remove meat from bones, and cut in strips; return chicken to soup. *Soup can be kept, covered, 3 days in refrigerator.*

Reheat soup, add asparagus and peas, and cook about 10 minutes or until just tender. Stir in green onions. Taste and adjust seasoning. Sprinkle with parsley when serving.

Makes 4 to 6 main-course servings

NEAR EASTERN CHICKEN SOUP WITH CHICKPEAS, RICE, AND SPINACH

Our images of the food of the lands of the eastern Mediterranean and the Middle East are usually associated with summer. But in this region there are many wonderful winter dishes as well, like this thick, satisfying chicken soup, which is a meal in one dish. The chickpeas (also called garbanzo beans) and rice give it substance, while spinach and dill enliven it by adding a fresh touch.

To save time, you can use canned chickpeas. If you like, you can use brown rice rather than white; simmer it 45 minutes or until it is tender. Sometimes fine vermicelli pasta is served with this soup instead of rice.

1½ cups dried chickpeas (garbanzo beans) (about 10 ounces, see Note)
2 medium onions, sliced
3½-pound chicken, with neck and gizzard, fat and liver removed
4 medium garlic cloves, chopped
½ teaspoon turmeric
10 cups water
salt and freshly ground pepper

¼ to ½ teaspoon hot red pepper flakes, or cayenne pepper to taste
¾ cup long-grain white rice
1 bunch spinach (¾ pound), rinsed, stems removed, cut in bite-size pieces
½ cup chopped fresh parsley
¼ cup snipped or chopped fresh dill

Sort chickpeas, discarding any broken ones and any stones. In a large bowl soak peas in cold water to cover generously overnight. Or, for a quicker method, cover peas with 2 quarts water in a large saucepan, bring to a boil, and boil 2 minutes; cover and let stand off heat 1 hour.

Drain peas and rinse. In large pot or Dutch oven combine peas, onions, chicken, garlic, turmeric, and 10 cups water and bring to a boil. Skim foam from surface. Cover and cook over low heat 1 hour, skimming occasionally. Add salt, pepper, and hot pepper flakes and cook 30 minutes. Remove chicken. If necessary, cook another 30 minutes or until chickpeas are tender.

Add rice to soup, stir once, cover, and cook over low heat 20 minutes or until rice is tender. Discard chicken skin and bones. Dice or shred meat in fairly large pieces and return to soup. *Soup can be kept, covered, 2 days in refrigerator. It thickens on standing, so add a little water when reheating it.*

Skim fat from soup. Bring soup to simmer. Add spinach and bring to boil. Cook 2 minutes or until wilted. Add parsley and 2 tablespoons dill. Taste and adjust seasoning. Sprinkle with remaining dill when serving.

Makes 8 appetizer or 4 to 6 main-course servings

NOTE: Four cups cooked chickpeas or 3 (15- or 16-ounce) cans, drained and rinsed, can be substituted for dried ones. Add them after chicken is tender.

HEARTY CHICKEN SOUP WITH ZUCCHINI, TOMATOES, AND LIMA BEANS

In the Middle East, cooks use fava beans in this soup, but for most of us it's easier to find and quicker to use frozen lima beans. You can serve this in several ways—family or peasant style, in shallow bowls with the chicken portions in the soup; or in a more elegant setting, with the meat removed from the bones, diced, and returned to the soup, in which case it can be a first or main course. When the soup is a main course, rice is a good accompaniment, for each person to spoon into his or her soup bowl. SEE PHOTOGRAPH.

3-pound chicken, or 2½ to 3 pounds
   chicken pieces
salt and freshly ground pepper
1 tablespoon ground cumin
1 teaspoon turmeric
1 large onion, sliced
2 or 3 dried hot red peppers (optional)
about 3 quarts water

6 or 7 plum tomatoes (about ¾ pound)
4 to 6 medium round boiling potatoes
   (about 1¼ pounds)
4 large garlic cloves, coarsely chopped
1¼ cups frozen lima beans
6 medium zucchini, cut in 1-inch
   lengths (about 1¼ pounds)
⅓ cup chopped green onions

Remove fat from chicken. Put chicken in a large casserole or pot. Add neck and other giblets, if available, except liver. Sprinkle with salt, pepper, and spices on both sides.

Add onion and hot peppers, if using, and cover ingredients with water. Bring to a simmer. Skim foam from surface. Add 2 tomatoes and cook about 10 seconds. Remove them and put in a bowl of cold water. Peel the blanched tomatoes, chop, and add to soup. Cover and cook over low heat 30 minutes.

Peel and halve potatoes and add to pot. Add garlic, cover, and cook over low heat 45 minutes. Add lima beans and cook 5 minutes. Add zucchini and bring to a simmer. Cover and cook over low heat 15 to 20 minutes or until vegetables are tender. Discard hot peppers. Skim off fat. (This is easier to do when soup is cold.) Taste and adjust seasoning. If desired, remove skin from chicken and cut meat from bones; return chicken to soup. *Soup can be kept, covered, 3 days in refrigerator.*

Cut remaining tomatoes in small dice, add to soup, and simmer 3 minutes. Serve soup in fairly shallow bowls with chicken and vegetables. Add green onions to each bowl when serving.

Makes 8 first-course or 4 to 6 main-course servings

CHICKEN SOUP WITH OSSO BUCO AND FINE NOODLES

Chicken and veal are classic partners for making a fine stock and are also delicious when combined in a soup, like in this Mediterranean-style dish flavored with sage and garlic. This is an easy way to cook both chicken and osso buco, since no browning of the meat is necessary. Serve the osso buco and chicken wings with noodles, vegetables, and some of the broth as a main course. You'll have extra broth to serve another time as a flavorful first course.

1½ pounds chicken wings
4 slices (2 pounds total) veal shanks
   (osso buco)
salt and freshly ground pepper
9 to 10 cups water
1 medium onion, sliced
1 celery stalk, diced
1 medium carrot, diced

3 medium garlic cloves, chopped
¾ pound ripe tomatoes, peeled and
   diced
4 ounces small mushrooms, quartered
2 medium zucchini, diced
3 tablespoons thin slivers fresh sage,
   or 2 teaspoons dried leaves
2 cups thin noodles for soup

Put chicken wings and veal in a heavy casserole or Dutch oven, season with salt and pepper, cover with water, and bring to a boil. Skim foam. Add onion, celery, and carrot. Cover and cook over low heat 2 hours or until veal is tender.

Add garlic, tomatoes, mushrooms, zucchini, and sage. Bring to a simmer. Add noodles and cook uncovered over medium heat, stirring occasionally, about 8 to 10 minutes or until noodles are tender. Taste and adjust seasoning. Serve in shallow soup bowls.

Makes 4 main-course servings

NOTE: The tomatoes can be made easier to peel by blanching them in the soup for 10 seconds. There's no need to boil extra water.

CHINESE CHICKEN SOUP
WITH ASPARAGUS AND MUSHROOMS

Oriental flavorings quickly turn simple chicken stock into a light and refreshing first course. If asparagus is not in season, thin strips of leeks, celery, or zucchini can be cooked in the soup instead. If you like, sprinkle each serving with chopped green onions.

5 cups chicken stock or broth (page 389)
10 small dried shiitake mushrooms
3 green onions, halved crosswise
3 slices (about ¼ inch thick) peeled fresh ginger

salt and freshly ground pepper
12 thin asparagus spears (total about 7 ounces)
1 tablespoon plus 2 teaspoons Chinese rice wine or dry sherry

Skim any fat from surface of stock. Soak mushrooms in warm water to cover until caps are soft, about 30 minutes. Rinse and drain thoroughly. Cut off stems and discard. Cut caps in quarters.

Combine chicken stock, green onions, ginger, and a pinch of salt and pepper in a large saucepan. Bring to boil, reduce heat to low, and simmer uncovered for 30 minutes. Add mushrooms and simmer for 15 minutes. *Soup can be kept, covered, up to 2 days in refrigerator.*

Peel asparagus and cut off white bases. Cut stalks in 1-inch pieces and leave tips whole.

Reheat soup if necessary. Discard green onions and ginger, using a slotted spoon. Add asparagus to soup, cover, and simmer over low heat until tender, about 7 minutes. Stir in sherry. Taste, and add salt and pepper if needed. Serve hot.

Makes 4 appetizer servings

CHICKEN VELOUTÉ SOUP
WITH LEEKS AND FRESH HERBS

*The first time I tasted a creamy velouté soup, demonstrated by Parisian Chef Fernand Chambrette,
I was impressed that such a delicious soup could be so easy to make. The velouté is a French class of
soups that owe their silky texture to a roux of butter and flour cooked together. Because the soups
contain flour, it is important to cook them in a heavy saucepan to prevent sticking. A whisk is most
practical for stirring this type of soup, and it should be stirred often to ensure that it remains smooth.*

*Velouté in French means ''velvety,'' and the soup is enriched with cream to ensure its luxurious
texture. Traditionally the soup is thickened with egg yolks as well, but today they are often omitted
in the interest of lightness and to make the soup easy to reheat.*

In this festive appetizer soup, which features the time-honored French herb mélange of fines
herbes—*chives, tarragon, and parsley—you can use just one of the herbs instead of all three, or
substitute dill or cilantro. If you would like a more substantial soup, you can add ½ to 1 cup cooked
diced chicken or small shrimp.*

2 medium leeks, cleaned (page 408)
¼ cup (½ stick) butter (see Note)
3 tablespoons all-purpose flour
3¼ cups chicken stock or broth (page
    389)

salt and freshly ground pepper
½ cup heavy cream or milk
1 tablespoon chopped fresh tarragon
1 tablespoon thinly sliced chives
1 tablespoon chopped fresh parsley

Finely chop white part of leeks; reserve green part for stock or other use.

Melt butter in a heavy medium saucepan over low heat. Add leeks and cook, stirring,
until soft, about 5 minutes. Whisk in flour. Cook over low heat, whisking, until mixture
turns light beige, about 3 minutes. Remove from heat.

Gradually ladle stock into flour mixture, whisking. Bring to boil over medium-high heat,
whisking. Add pinch of salt and pepper. Reduce heat to medium-low and simmer, uncovered,
whisking often, for 5 minutes. *Soup can be kept, covered, up to 1 day in refrigerator.*

Bring soup to simmer in a heavy medium saucepan over medium-low heat, whisking.
Stir in cream and simmer, whisking occasionally, until soup thickens slightly. Remove from
heat.

Stir in tarragon, chives, and parsley. Taste and adjust seasoning. Serve hot.

Makes 4 appetizer servings

NOTE: If you like, substitute 2 tablespoons butter and 2 tablespoons vegetable oil for the
butter, or substitute ¼ cup margarine.

TURKEY SOUP WITH SPINACH TORTELLINI AND MUSHROOMS

Tortellini in brodo, or tortellini in broth, *usually is just that—tortellini served in a clear soup as a first course. For a light and easy main course for supper, I prepare this heartier version of the Italian classic, which also includes vegetables and cooked turkey. I like to use small spinach tortellini with a cheese filling in this delicate soup. The bright green pasta looks especially pretty in the golden chicken broth dotted with diced tomatoes, zucchini, mushrooms, and turkey. If you wish, serve the soup with grated Parmesan cheese.* SEE PHOTOGRAPH.

1 quart chicken stock or broth (page 389)
1½ cups water
4 ounces small mushrooms, cut in thin slices
1 medium celery stalk, cut in thin slices
½ teaspoon dried thyme
salt (optional) and freshly ground pepper

1 (8- to 10-ounce) package fresh spinach tortellini, agnolotti, or ravioli
1 small zucchini, cut in thin strips
1 large tomato, diced small
1 to 1½ cups shredded cooked turkey or chicken
2 tablespoons chopped cilantro (fresh coriander) or parsley

In a medium saucepan combine stock, water, mushrooms, celery, thyme, and a pinch of pepper. Add salt if using unsalted homemade stock. Bring to a simmer.

Add pasta and zucchini and bring to a boil. Cook, uncovered, over medium heat, stirring occasionally, about 6 minutes or until pasta is just tender but still firm to the bite; cut off a piece of pasta to check. Add tomato and turkey and heat for about 1 minute. Add cilantro. Taste, adjust seasoning, and serve.

Makes 4 or 5 appetizer or 2 or 3 main-course servings

AVOCADO-TURKEY CHOWDER

This soup begins like a French velouté soup, but in character it owes more to the American Southwest, with avocado, corn, green onions, and cayenne pepper complementing the turkey.

2 cups turkey or chicken stock or
   broth (page 391, 389)
1 cup fresh or frozen corn kernels
1 tablespoon butter or margarine
1 tablespoon all-purpose flour
salt and freshly ground pepper
1¼ cups milk, whole or skim
2 ripe medium avocados (total 1¼
   pounds), preferably Haas

¼ teaspoon dried thyme, crumbled
1 tablespoon minced green onion
cayenne pepper to taste
1½ cups diced cooked turkey or
   chicken
½ teaspoon fresh lemon juice, or more
   to taste
⅓ cup sour cream or yogurt, at room
   temperature, stirred until smooth

In a medium saucepan bring stock to a boil. Add corn, cover, and simmer over low heat for 2 to 4 minutes, or until just tender. Transfer corn to a bowl with a slotted spoon, draining it thoroughly, and reserve stock separately.

In a heavy, medium saucepan melt butter over low heat, whisk in flour, and cook mixture, whisking, for 2 minutes, or until foaming but not browned. Gradually whisk in 1 cup of the reserved stock. Bring to a boil, whisking. Add salt and pepper and simmer over low heat for 5 minutes, whisking occasionally. Whisk in milk and bring to a simmer.

Halve the avocados lengthwise, remove pits, and scoop out pulp of all but one-fourth of 1 avocado. Reserve that avocado portion for garnish and cover it tightly with plastic wrap.

In a food processor or blender puree avocado pulp with thyme and green onion until nearly smooth. Gradually add remaining cup of stock while processing. Whisk avocado mixture into soup. *Soup may be made 1 hour in advance and kept covered tightly and chilled; corn and turkey should be reserved separately.*

A short time before serving, cut reserved avocado section into small dice (about ¼ inch) for garnish. Heat soup, whisking, just until it is hot. Season it to taste with salt, pepper, and cayenne. Stir in any liquid that escaped from corn. Add turkey and corn and heat through, stirring often, for 2 minutes. Add lemon juice. Taste and adjust seasoning, adding more lemon juice if desired. Ladle soup into bowls. Spoon a small dollop of sour cream or yogurt into center of each bowl. Sprinkle soup with diced avocado.

Makes 4 appetizer servings

KOREAN TURKEY SOUP WITH SPINACH

Oriental sesame oil lends a pleasant flavor and richness to this easy soup that needs only ten minutes of cooking. Usually made with ground beef, it's also excellent with ground turkey or chicken. Instead of ground poultry, you can use 1 or 2 cups diced roast turkey or chicken. Simply sauté it briefly as below, then add the spinach together with the liquid.

6 ounces fresh spinach leaves (6 cups
  packed)
1 tablespoon vegetable oil
1 tablespoon Oriental sesame oil
½ pound ground turkey
1 large garlic clove, minced

salt and freshly ground pepper
2 teaspoons soy sauce
2 cups rich chicken stock or broth
  (page 389)
2 cups water
1 green onion, chopped

Rinse spinach leaves and remove any thick stems. Heat vegetable oil and sesame oil in a large saucepan over medium heat. Add ground turkey and sauté, stirring to separate the particles, for 3 minutes. Add garlic, salt, and pepper and stir-fry 30 seconds. Add soy sauce, then stock and water. Bring to boil. Cover and simmer over low heat 5 minutes. Add spinach and return to a simmer. Cover and cook 5 minutes. Taste and adjust seasoning. Add green onion. Serve hot.

Makes 4 appetizer servings

7

Chicken and Turkey with Pasta and Grains

 Home cooks and chefs throughout the world discovered long ago that chicken is excellent with pasta and grains.

Moroccan chefs serve chicken and a zesty broth with couscous, their "national" pasta. Indian-style chicken in spicy sauces requires Basmati or other good-quality rice as an accompaniment.

There also are casseroles of chicken and rice cooked together. Paella, the national dish of Spain, often features chicken with rice, saffron, and seafood. *Arroz con pollo*, or rice with chicken, is a traditional favorite in Latin America as well as Spain and usually is flavored with peppers, garlic, cumin, and sometimes saffron. The similar sounding *poulet au riz*, or chicken with rice, has long been popular in France and has a completely different character, combining the delicate flavors of mushrooms and herbs.

There is a third way of pairing pasta or grains with poultry, which is a boon to those of us with busy schedules. Pasta and quick-cooking grains like rice, bulgur wheat, or buckwheat can be mixed with cooked chicken or turkey to create wonderful, "meal-in-one-dish" entrees. Whether the rice is simply cooked in water or made into pilaf or risotto, cooked

Tortellini with Chicken, Peppers,
and Lemon-Sage Butter
Singapore Chicken and Noodles
Chicken in Sun-Dried Tomato Cream Sauce
on a Bed of Fettuccine
Chinese Noodles with Chicken, Ginger,
and Chives
Lasagne with Chicken, Spinach, and Tomatoes
Fettuccine with Basil-Scented
Chicken Bolognese Sauce
Greek Mostaccioli and Chicken Casserole
with Kefalotiri Cheese
Spaghetti with Spicy Chicken Sausage Sauce
Braised Chicken with Tomatoes, Cumin,
and Couscous
Curried Chicken with Couscous and Zucchini
Risotto with Chicken and Mushrooms
Creamy Rice Pilaf with Chicken, Asparagus,
and Herbs

Paella with Chicken, Shrimp, and Artichokes
Spanish Rice with Chicken (Arroz con Pollo)
Cuban Chicken with Yellow Rice
Chicken and Sausage Jambalaya
Zucchini with Chicken-Rice Stuffing
Bulgur Wheat with Chicken and Green Onions
Chicken with Kasha and Bowtie Pasta
Pasta with Mexican Turkey Picadillo Sauce
Vermicelli with Smoked Turkey and Broccoli
Orzo with Smoked Turkey
and Chinese Seasonings
Corsican Rice with Turkey Sausage, Black Olives,
and Thyme
Brown Rice Pilaf with Turkey and Zucchini
Acorn Squash Stuffed with Turkey
and Wild Rice

diced chicken turns it into a satisfying main course. You can use roasted, poached, or even grilled chicken or turkey. Simply shred the meat and heat it briefly with the cooked pasta or grains of your choice. Then, for color and nutritional balance, add quick-cooking vegetables or just stir in some diced tomatoes and cucumbers. For a festive touch, sprinkle the dish with toasted nuts or sunflower seeds.

I like to cook extra chicken or turkey to have on hand for making these types of dishes. If you don't happen to have cooked chicken or turkey, you can buy them roasted, smoked, or as sausages and prepare such dishes as Linguine with Smoked Turkey and Spicy Mushrooms (page 279) or Corsican Rice with Turkey Sausage, Black Olives, and Thyme (page 125).

Italian- and Chinese-style pasta sauces that are usually made with ground beef or pork are leaner when made with ground chicken or turkey. I find ground chicken delicious in a basil-scented bolognese sauce and in a Greek red wine sauce for pasta (in Greek Mostaccioli and Chicken Casserole, page 107. Both sauces are good with fettuccine, ravioli, or rice. Chicken and turkey sausages can also be used to create quick and easy sauces for pasta or rice, as in Spaghetti with Spicy Chicken Sausage Sauce, seasoned in the Indian style (page 109).

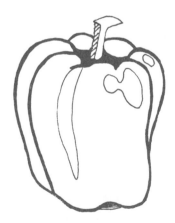

TORTELLINI WITH CHICKEN, PEPPERS, AND LEMON-SAGE BUTTER

Lemon, sage, and tortellini turn leftover cooked chicken into an easy, delightful northern Italian dish. I love the taste of the butter, since it reminds me of pastas with sage butter that I savored in Italy, but olive oil can be substituted. To save time, you can use roasted peppers from a jar.

1 red bell pepper, roasted and peeled (page 408)
salt
8 to 10 ounces chicken- or cheese-filled tortellini, fresh or frozen
2 tablespoons extra-virgin olive oil
4 thin slices smoked chicken, cut in thin strips (optional)
2 tablespoons (¼ stick) butter

2 tablespoons thin strips of sage leaves
1½ to 2 cups thin strips cooked chicken or turkey
freshly ground pepper
1½ teaspoons grated lemon rind
2 tablespoons strained fresh lemon juice
2 tablespoons chopped fresh parsley

Halve the pepper lengthwise and discard seeds and ribs. Pat dry. Halve pepper pieces crosswise; cut each half in thin lengthwise strips about ¼ inch wide.

In a large pot of boiling salted water cook pasta uncovered over medium-high heat, stirring occasionally, about 8 minutes or according to package directions or until tender. Drain well. Transfer to a large bowl. Add 1 tablespoon olive oil, pepper strips, and smoked chicken and toss to combine.

Heat butter and remaining oil in a medium skillet over medium heat. Add sage, cooked chicken, salt, and pepper and heat through. Remove from heat and add lemon rind and 1 tablespoon juice. Add mixture to pasta and toss. Add remaining lemon juice and parsley. Season to taste with salt and pepper. Serve hot.

Makes 4 to 6 first-course or 3 main-course servings

SINGAPORE CHICKEN AND NOODLES

The first time I tasted this colorful dish of fine noodles with chicken strips, shrimp, green and red peppers, bean sprouts, and a peppery curry seasoning was in Hong Kong. It was part of an amazing menu that included Southeast Asian, Chinese, French, and Italian specialties, as well as items that combined elements from different cuisines.

You can prepare this dish with Oriental rice noodles or any other thin noodles. Some versions of this dish feature Chinese omelet strips (page 392). SEE PHOTOGRAPH.

7 ounces thin dried rice noodles, rice sticks, or rice vermicelli
¾ pound chicken fillets (tender strip of boned breast; see page 396) or boneless skinless breasts, patted dry
2 teaspoons ground cumin
1 teaspoon ground coriander
½ teaspoon turmeric
5 tablespoons vegetable oil
½ green bell pepper, cut in thin strips
½ red bell pepper, cut in thin strips

½ pound medium shrimp, shelled, rinsed, patted dry
salt and freshly ground pepper to taste
2 large garlic cloves, minced
1 or 2 jalapeño peppers, minced
¾ cup chicken stock
hot red pepper flakes or cayenne pepper to taste
½ cup minced green onions
1 cup bean sprouts

Put noodles in a large bowl, cover generously with hot water, and soak 10 minutes. Drain well.

If using boneless chicken breasts rather than fillets, cut each in 4 or 5 lengthwise strips. Mix cumin, coriander, and turmeric. Heat 1 tablespoon oil in a large deep skillet over medium heat. Add bell peppers and sauté about 7 minutes or until crisp-tender. Remove from skillet. Add 2 tablespoons oil and heat over medium heat. Add shrimp, salt, and pepper and sauté, tossing often, 1½ to 2 minutes or until shrimp are pink. Transfer to a platter. Add 2 tablespoons oil and heat. Add garlic, jalapeño pepper, chicken, salt, and spice mixture and sauté, stirring, about 2 minutes or until chicken changes color throughout. Remove to a plate.

Pour stock into skillet, add noodles, and cook over medium-high heat about 2 minutes or until stock is absorbed and noodles are tender but slightly firm to bite.

Return shrimp, chicken, and peppers to skillet containing noodles and toss lightly over low heat. Add hot pepper flakes, green onions, and bean sprouts; taste and adjust seasoning. Serve hot.

Makes 4 main-course servings

CHICKEN IN SUN-DRIED TOMATO CREAM SAUCE ON A BED OF FETTUCCINE

In my cooking classes I occasionally teach this California-style dish, and no matter what other dishes are on the program, this one is usually the favorite. For the rich-tasting cream reduction sauce, I use the inexpensive form of sun-dried tomatoes, packaged without olive oil. The tomatoes cook in chicken stock and turn it into a delicious, quick, and easy way to make sauce for the chicken breasts. The flavor they contribute to the sauce is entirely different from that of fresh tomatoes. This sauce is also wonderful for heating up strips of already-cooked chicken or turkey, for serving on a bed of pasta or rice.

½ cup dry-packed sun-dried tomatoes
1 tablespoon butter
1 medium garlic clove, minced
1 cup chicken stock or low-salt broth
1 cup heavy cream
1 pound boneless and skinless chicken
  breast halves

salt and freshly ground pepper to taste
2 tablespoons vegetable oil
2 tablespoons chopped fresh basil, or 2
  teaspoons dried, crumbled
8 ounces fettuccine

Snip tomatoes into bite-size pieces. Melt butter in a small saucepan over low heat, add garlic, and cook ½ minute. Add ¾ cup stock and tomatoes and bring to boil. Simmer, uncovered, over medium heat about 10 minutes or until tomatoes are tender. Add cream and bring to a boil, stirring. Simmer over medium heat until sauce is thick enough to lightly coat a spoon. *Sauce can be kept, covered, 1 day in refrigerator.* Reheat over low heat.

Sprinkle chicken with salt and pepper on both sides. Heat oil in a large, heavy skillet over medium-high heat. Add chicken and sauté, pressing on chicken occasionally with slotted spatula, about 4 minutes per side or until meat feels springy and is no longer pink inside; cut to check. Transfer to a board, cover, and keep warm.

Discard fat from skillet. Add remaining stock and bring to a boil, stirring and scraping up pan juices. Boil to reduce slightly; then add to sauce. Stir in basil; taste and adjust seasoning.

Meanwhile, cook pasta, uncovered, in a large pot of boiling salted water over high heat, stirring occasionally, about 1 to 2 minutes for fresh or 3 to 5 minutes for dried fettuccine, or until tender but firm to the bite. Drain, transfer to a bowl, and toss with 3 or 4 tablespoons sauce.

Cut each chicken breast into 2 or 3 diagonal slices. Reheat gently in sauce if needed. Transfer pasta to plates, top with chicken, and coat with sauce.

Makes 4 main-course servings

CHINESE NOODLES
WITH CHICKEN, GINGER, AND CHIVES

I learned to make this tasty dish in a class taught by Chinese cooking teacher Lucy Lo in Hong Kong. Chinese omelet strips add good flavor and texture, but they are optional.

8 ounces Chinese egg noodles or
  spaghetti
salt
½ pound boneless and skinless
  chicken breast or thighs
2 tablespoons soy sauce
1 teaspoon Oriental sesame oil
1½ teaspoons cornstarch

5 tablespoons vegetable oil
1 tablespoon minced peeled fresh
  ginger
1½ cups bean sprouts
Chinese omelet strips (optional, page
  392)
1 tablespoon snipped chives

Cook noodles in a large pan of boiling salted water until just tender, or al dente. Drain, rinse, and drain well.

Cut chicken into thin slices crosswise, then into thin strips. Mix with 1 tablespoon soy sauce, ½ teaspoon sesame oil, and cornstarch and marinate for 15 or 20 minutes.

Heat 2 tablespoons vegetable oil in a wok or deep skillet over medium heat. Add noodles and toss until heated. Add remaining soy sauce and sesame oil and toss. Transfer to a platter.

Heat remaining 3 tablespoons vegetable oil in a wok or deep skillet over medium-high heat. Add ginger, then chicken and sauté, tossing, about 2 minutes or until chicken changes color. Add bean sprouts and heat about ½ minute. Remove from heat. Add omelet pieces, if using, and chives; spoon over noodles and serve.

Makes 3 or 4 main-course servings

LASAGNE WITH CHICKEN, SPINACH, AND TOMATOES

This light version of lasagne in inspired by a creamy pasta dish my husband and I enjoyed in Valle d'Aosta in northern Italy. Layers of chicken in a delicate white wine velouté sauce alternate with the lasagne noodles, fresh tomato sauce, and nutmeg-scented spinach.

Chicken in Velouté Sauce

½ cup dry white wine
2½ cups chicken stock or broth
½ teaspoon dried thyme, crumbled
1 bay leaf
salt and freshly ground pepper
2 pounds chicken breast halves, with
   skin and bones

¼ cup water
3 tablespoons butter
3 tablespoons all-purpose flour
¼ cup heavy cream
cayenne pepper to taste

2 pounds fresh spinach, stems
   removed, leaves rinsed thoroughly
2 tablespoons (¼ stick) butter
½ cup plus 3 tablespoons heavy cream
salt and freshly ground pepper
freshly grated nutmeg

¾ pound thin lasagne noodles
2 cups Fresh Tomato Sauce (page 369)
cayenne pepper to taste
¼ to ⅓ cup freshly grated Parmesan
   cheese

For chicken in velouté sauce, combine wine, stock, thyme, bay leaf, salt and pepper in a large saucepan and bring to a boil. Add chicken and enough water to barely cover it. Bring to a simmer, cover, and poach chicken over low heat, turning once, for 20 minutes or until tender. Remove chicken, reserving cooking liquid. Boil liquid until reduced to 1½ cups. Discard chicken skin and bones. Dice meat in ½-inch cubes. Strain liquid and skim off excess fat.

Melt butter in a heavy, medium saucepan over low heat. Add flour and cook, whisking, 2 minutes or until foaming but not browned. Remove from heat. Whisk in chicken cooking liquid. Bring to a boil, whisking. Simmer over low heat, whisking often, 5 minutes. Whisk in ¼ cup cream and bring to a boil. Reserve ½ cup sauce for topping. Gently stir remaining sauce into diced chicken and add salt, pepper, and cayenne to taste; season generously.

For spinach layer, cook spinach uncovered in a large saucepan of boiling salted water over high heat about 2 minutes or until wilted. Drain, rinse with cold water, and drain well. Squeeze out as much liquid as possible. Chop spinach. Melt butter in a saucepan, add spinach, and cook over low heat 1 minute. Stir in 3 tablespoons cream and cook until it is absorbed. Season to taste with salt, pepper, and nutmeg. *Chicken mixture, sauce and spinach can be kept, covered, overnight in refrigerator.*

Cook lasagne, a few pieces at a time, in a large pot of boiling salted water, according to package instructions or until flexible. Transfer them gently with a slotted spoon to a large bowl of cold water. Remove them and spread them out in one layer on towels to drain.

Simmer tomato sauce until very thick; reserve. In a small saucepan bring ½ cup reserved chicken sauce to a boil, whisking. Add ½ cup cream and simmer over medium heat, whisking often, until sauce is reduced to about ¾ cup. Taste and adjust seasoning, adding cayenne pepper if needed.

Arrange one layer of lasagne noodles in a buttered 8-inch baking dish, cutting them to fit if necessary, and top with half of chicken mixture. Top with another layer of noodles, then with tomato sauce, then another layer of noodles, and remaining chicken mixture. Add another noodle layer and top with spinach mixture. Cover with a layer of noodles and pour the cream sauce over it. Sprinkle with cheese. *Lasagne can be kept, covered, overnight in refrigerator.*

Preheat oven to 400°F. Bake about 30 to 40 minutes or until top is golden brown and inside is hot. Serve from baking dish.

Makes 4 main-course servings

FETTUCCINE WITH BASIL-SCENTED CHICKEN BOLOGNESE SAUCE

Classic Bolognese sauce is usually made with beef or pork in northern Italy, but this is a lighter version made with chicken or turkey, and seasoned liberally with fresh basil and a healthy punch of garlic. If you like, accompany the pasta with a bowl of freshly grated Parmesan cheese.

2 tablespoons olive oil
2 tablespoons (¼ stick) butter
1 large onion, minced
1 small carrot, diced
1 large celery stalk, sliced
1 pound ground chicken or turkey
4 medium garlic cloves, peeled
1½ pounds ripe tomatoes, peeled and
    seeded; or 1 (28-ounce) can plum
    tomatoes, drained

1 bay leaf
1 teaspoon dried thyme, crumbled
freshly grated nutmeg to taste
salt and freshly ground pepper
1 pound fettuccine
2 to 3 tablespoons chopped fresh basil
3 tablespoons finely shredded fresh
    basil

Heat oil and butter in a heavy, medium casserole over medium heat. Add onion, carrot, and celery and cook, stirring, 10 minutes or until onion is soft but not brown. Add chicken and sauté over medium heat, crumbling with a fork, until it changes color.

Puree the garlic and tomatoes in a food processor and add to casserole. Add bay leaf, thyme, nutmeg, salt, and pepper and bring to a boil, stirring. Cover and cook over low heat, stirring occasionally, 30 minutes or until well flavored. Discard bay leaf. *Sauce can be kept, covered, 2 days in refrigerator; or it can be frozen.*

Cook pasta uncovered in a large pot of boiling salted water over high heat, stirring occasionally, about 1 to 2 minutes for fresh or 3 to 5 minutes for dried fettuccine, or until tender but firm to the bite. Meanwhile reheat sauce in a covered saucepan over medium-low heat, stirring occasionally.

Drain pasta well and transfer to a large heated bowl. Add sauce and toss. Add chopped basil and toss lightly. Taste and adjust seasoning. Sprinkle with shredded basil and serve.

Makes 6 to 8 first-course or 4 or 5 main-course servings

GREEK MOSTACCIOLI AND CHICKEN CASSEROLE WITH KEFALOTIRI CHEESE

In this rich and meaty party dish, the cheesy pasta alternates with layers of chicken sauce accented with red wine, cinnamon, and oregano.

Chicken Sauce with Red Wine

5 tablespoons olive oil, vegetable oil,
  or butter
1 large onion, minced
1½ pounds ground chicken
¾ cup dry red wine
salt and freshly ground pepper to taste

½ teaspoon ground cinnamon
1 bay leaf
1½ teaspoons dried oregano, crumbled
3 tablespoons tomato paste
3 tablespoons water

1 pound mostaccioli or penne
  (diagonal-cut macaroni)
1¼ cups finely grated kefalotiri,
  Parmesan, or kashkaval cheese
  (about 4 ounces)

salt and freshly ground pepper to taste

Béchamel Sauce

3 tablespoons butter
3 tablespoons all-purpose flour
2 cups milk

salt and freshly ground white pepper
   to taste
freshly grated nutmeg to taste

For chicken sauce, heat 3 tablespoons oil in a medium saucepan over medium-low heat. Add onion and sauté about 10 minutes. Add chicken and cook over medium heat, crumbling with a fork, until it changes color, about 7 minutes. Add wine, salt, pepper, cinnamon, bay leaf, and oregano and bring to a simmer. Add tomato paste and water and mix well. Cover and cook over low heat 30 minutes. Uncover and cook over medium heat 10 minutes or until mixture is fairly dry. Discard bay leaf. Taste and adjust seasoning.

Cook pasta, uncovered, in a large pot of boiling salted water over high heat, stirring occasionally, about 6 minutes or until tender but still firm to the bite. Drain, rinse with cold water and drain well. Transfer to a large bowl. Toss with remaining oil or butter, then with ½ cup grated cheese. Season with salt and pepper.

Butter a 13 × 9 × 2-inch baking dish. Put half the pasta in prepared dish. Spread chicken sauce on top. Sprinkle with ½ cup cheese. Top with remaining pasta.

For béchamel sauce, melt butter in a heavy, medium saucepan over low heat. Whisk in flour and cook, whisking, 2 minutes or until foaming but not browned. Remove from heat. Whisk in milk. Cook over medium-high heat, whisking, until sauce thickens and comes to a boil. Add a pinch of salt, white pepper, and nutmeg. Simmer sauce over low heat, whisking often, 10 minutes. Taste and adjust seasoning. Pour sauce over top layer of pasta and spread evenly with spatula. Sprinkle with remaining cheese. *Dish can be kept, covered, 1 day in refrigerator.*

Preheat oven to 350°F. Bake casserole about 40 to 45 minutes or until golden and bubbling. Let stand about 10 minutes before serving. Serve from baking dish.

Makes 6 to 8 main-course servings

SPAGHETTI WITH SPICY CHICKEN SAUSAGE SAUCE

Spices loved in the eastern Mediterranean and in India—cumin, turmeric, fresh ginger, hot peppers, and garlic—add zest and a warm orange hue to this pasta dish, which makes use of hot chicken sausages as the basis for the sauce. Although spicy, it is not too hot. For an easy menu for casual entertaining, serve it with a salad and follow it with fruit or ice cream.

12 ounces hot Italian chicken sausage
   or other fresh chicken sausage meat
   (1½ cups)
5 tablespoons olive oil
2 medium onions, minced
1 cup chopped celery
2 serrano peppers, ribs and seeds
   removed, minced (see Note)
salt and freshly ground pepper to taste
2 tablespoons minced fresh ginger

4 medium garlic cloves, minced
1 tablespoon ground cumin
1 teaspoon turmeric
1 cup chicken stock or broth, Fresh
   Tomato Sauce (page 369), or
   packaged sauce
12 ounces spaghetti
¼ cup chopped fresh parsley
3 tablespoons chopped green onion

Cook sausage in a large, heavy skillet over medium-high heat, breaking up meat with a wooden spoon, until it is no longer pink, about 8 minutes. Transfer to a strainer above a bowl and drain, reserving drippings.

Return 1 tablespoon drippings to skillet. Add 3 tablespoons oil and heat over medium heat. Add onions, celery, peppers, and a pinch of salt and pepper. Cook, stirring occasionally, about 10 minutes or until onions are soft but not brown. Add ginger and cook 2 minutes. Add cooked sausage, garlic, cumin, and turmeric and cook, stirring, 1 minute. Add stock or tomato sauce and simmer 5 minutes; with stock, sauce will be bright orange, and with tomato sauce it will be red. *Sausage mixture can be kept, covered, 2 days in refrigerator. Reheat before continuing.*

Cook spaghetti uncovered in a large pot of boiling salted water over high heat, lifting occasionally with tongs, for 8 to 9 minutes or until tender but firm to the bite. Meanwhile, reheat sausage mixture over medium heat, stirring.

Drain spaghetti well and transfer it to a large heated bowl. Toss with remaining 2 tablespoons oil. Add sausage mixture, parsley, and green onion and toss lightly until blended. Taste and adjust seasoning. Bring some of sausage mixture to top for serving. Serve immediately.

Makes 4 main-course servings

NOTE: Wear gloves when handling hot peppers.

BRAISED CHICKEN WITH TOMATOES, CUMIN, AND COUSCOUS

Chicken couscous is one of the classics of the North African kitchen. But this fine dish can be very time-consuming, with repeated steamings of the couscous above a chicken soup. For this easy version, the chicken is braised with the traditional flavorings of tomatoes, garlic, cumin, as well as zucchini and chickpeas, and is served with quick-cooking couscous.

The accompaniment de rigueur is fiery harissa, which is quite simple to make or can be purchased in Middle Eastern shops. Although the taste will be different, you can substitute any hot sauce you want—Mexican, Oriental, or Louisiana style.

3 pounds chicken pieces
salt and freshly ground pepper
2 tablespoons olive or vegetable oil
1 large onion, cut in thin slices
4 medium garlic cloves, chopped
1½ teaspoons ground cumin
1 pound ripe tomatoes, peeled, seeded, and chopped; or 1 (28-ounce) can whole plum tomatoes, drained and chopped

⅔ cup chicken stock or broth
¼ to ½ teaspoon hot red pepper flakes
2 small zucchini, diced
1 (15-ounce) can chickpeas (garbanzo beans), rinsed and drained
2 tablespoons tomato paste
2 tablespoons chopped cilantro (fresh coriander) or parsley

Quick Couscous

1¼ cups hot chicken stock or broth
1 tablespoon butter or olive oil
1¼ cups couscous

Harissa (page 366) or bottled harissa
  or other hot sauce

Season chicken lightly with salt and pepper. Heat oil in a large, wide casserole or Dutch oven. Add chicken in batches and brown lightly on all sides. Remove to a plate.

Add onion to casserole and cook over low heat until soft but not brown. Add garlic and cook about ½ minute. Stir in cumin and tomatoes and cook for 2 or 3 minutes, stirring often. Return chicken to pan and add stock and pepper flakes. Cover and simmer over low heat 15 minutes. Add zucchini and simmer 20 to 25 minutes or until chicken and zucchini are tender. Stir in chickpeas, tomato paste, and 1 tablespoon cilantro and heat briefly. *Chicken can be kept, covered, 1 day in refrigerator.*

For quick couscous, bring stock and butter to a boil in a heavy small saucepan. Add couscous, stir, and cover. Turn off heat and leave for 5 minutes. Fluff gently with a fork. Taste and adjust seasoning.

Spoon couscous onto center of a large platter. Arrange chicken and zucchini around it and moisten them with sauce. Sprinkle them with chopped cilantro. Serve remaining sauce and Harissa separately.

Makes 4 main-course servings

CURRIED CHICKEN WITH COUSCOUS AND ZUCCHINI

Cutting chicken in strips and sautéing them makes them cook quickly, and although we associate this technique with Oriental cuisines, it is very convenient for European and American-style dishes as well. This is a ''combination cuisine'' dish, with the quick-sautéed chicken and zucchini strips moistened with a modern French-style curry sauce, made by reducing stock and cream. The chicken and zucchini are served in a ring of couscous, but if you don't have couscous, they could instead be served on a bed of noodles or rice.

3 tablespoons butter
1 large onion, minced
¾ pound boneless and skinless
   chicken breast halves
2 to 3 tablespoons vegetable oil
2 small zucchini, cut in 2 × ¼ ×
   ¼-inch strips
2 large garlic cloves, minced

2 teaspoons curry powder
2¼ cups chicken stock or low-salt
   broth
½ cup heavy cream
1¼ cups couscous
salt and freshly ground pepper
2 tablespoons plus 1 teaspoon coarsely
   chopped cilantro (fresh coriander)

Melt 2 tablespoons butter in a large, heavy skillet, add onion, and cook over low heat, stirring often, 10 minutes or until soft but not brown.

Cut chicken crosswise in diagonal strips, about 2½ × ½ × ½ inch. In a second large, heavy skillet heat 2 tablespoons oil over medium-high heat, add chicken strips in batches, and sauté, tossing often, for 3 minutes, or until brown on both sides and just tender; transfer them as they are cooked with a slotted spoon to a platter. Add oil to skillet if necessary, and heat it. Add zucchini strips and sauté over medium heat for 2 minutes, or until barely tender. Transfer to a bowl.

Add ½ cup cooked onion to second skillet and heat through. Add garlic and 1 teaspoon curry powder and cook over low heat, stirring, 1 minute. Stir in 1 cup stock and boil until reduced to about ½ cup. Add cream and cook sauce until it is thick enough to coat a spoon.

Reheat onion remaining in first skillet. Add remaining curry powder and cook over low heat, stirring, for 1 minute. Add remaining butter and heat until melted. Add couscous, salt, and pepper and stir with a fork. Remove from heat and shake skillet to spread couscous in an even layer. In a small saucepan bring remaining stock to a boil, pour it evenly over couscous, immediately cover skillet tightly, and let couscous stand for 5 minutes.

Meanwhile, reheat sauce, add chicken and zucchini with a slotted spoon, and reheat briefly over low heat. Taste and adjust seasoning. Fluff couscous with a fork, add 2 table-spoons cilantro, and taste for seasoning. To serve, mound couscous on a platter, make a large hollow in center, and spoon chicken mixture into it. Sprinkle chicken with remaining cilantro.

Makes 3 main-course servings

RISOTTO
WITH CHICKEN AND MUSHROOMS

This is a re-creation of a lovely dish that I relished at a restaurant in Portofino, a picturesque fishing port on the Italian Riviera.

Chicken and sautéed mushrooms lend this risotto a good flavor, which is heightened by white wine, chicken broth, red pepper flakes, and Parmesan. I find that risotto's reputation as being hard to make is not deserved. It does require adding the broth in two or three batches and stirring after each, but there is no need to stir continuously. Because risotto is rich, it is best served in small portions as a first course.

4 tablespoons olive oil
8 ounces white mushrooms, quartered
salt and freshly ground pepper
½ cup chopped onion
2 large garlic cloves, minced
1½ cups Arborio or other round risotto
  rice
½ cup dry white wine
¼ teaspoon hot red pepper flakes

3½ cups hot chicken stock or broth
2 cups shredded or diced cooked
  chicken
freshly grated nutmeg to taste
1 tablespoon butter (optional)
⅓ cup chopped fresh parsley
¼ cup grated Parmesan cheese, plus
  more for serving

Heat 2 tablespoons oil in a heavy, medium saucepan over medium-high heat. Add mushrooms, salt, and pepper and sauté 7 minutes or until light brown. Transfer mushrooms and any liquid in pan to a bowl.

Add remaining 2 tablespoons oil to pan and heat over medium heat. Add onion and sauté 5 minutes or until soft but not brown. Add garlic and rice and stir 2 minutes until coated. Add wine and stir. Simmer over medium heat 1 or 2 minutes until wine evaporates.

Add pepper flakes and 2 cups hot chicken broth and stir. Simmer uncovered, stirring occasionally, 9 to 10 minutes or until liquid is absorbed. Add remaining broth, stir, and cook 5 minutes. Add chicken and mushrooms with their liquid and simmer 3 minutes or until rice is al dente and chicken is hot. Remove from heat. Add pepper and nutmeg. Let stand 2 or 3 minutes. Add butter, parsley, and ¼ cup Parmesan. Serve in deep dishes, with more Parmesan.

Makes 6 appetizer or 3 main-course servings

CREAMY RICE PILAF
WITH CHICKEN, ASPARAGUS, AND HERBS

When I studied French cooking at La Varenne in Paris, we prepared a variety of creamy pilafs like this one—sometimes with shellfish like mussels or shrimp, sometimes with poultry, like poached chicken or roast turkey, and occasionally with poultry and shellfish together. Ideally, the rice is cooked with chicken poaching liquid or homemade stock, but to save time you can use canned or frozen chicken stock. We always finished the pilaf with chopped fresh herbs. Tarragon and chives were favorites at the school, but I also love this dish with fresh dill or cilantro.

14 asparagus spears (5 or 6 ounces),
   peeled
3 tablespoons butter or vegetable oil
½ cup minced onion
1¼ cups long-grain white rice
2½ cups hot chicken stock, broth, or
   water
½ teaspoon dried thyme, crumbled

1 bay leaf
salt and freshly ground pepper to taste
1½ to 2 cups diced cooked chicken
3 or 4 tablespoons heavy cream, at
   room temperature
2 tablespoons minced fresh tarragon,
   chives, dill, or cilantro (fresh
   coriander)

Cut 2½-inch-long asparagus tips from stems. Cut stems in about 1½-inch pieces, discarding tough ends.

Heat 2 tablespoons butter or oil in a large sauté pan or deep skillet over medium heat. Add onion and cook until soft but not brown, about 7 minutes. Add rice and sauté, stirring, until grains begin to turn white, about 3 minutes. Pour hot stock over rice and stir once. Add thyme, bay leaf, salt, and pepper. Bring to boil. Cover tightly and simmer over low heat, without stirring, 12 minutes. Add chicken, cover, and simmer 6 minutes, or until rice is tender and liquid is absorbed.

Put asparagus stems in saucepan of boiling salted water and cook uncovered 2 minutes. Add tips and cook until just tender when pierced with a small sharp knife, about 2 minutes. Drain, rinse with cold water, and drain well.

When rice is cooked, pour cream quickly and evenly over it; do not stir. Cover and let stand 5 minutes, or just until cream is absorbed.

Melt 1 tablespoon butter in a large skillet over medium heat. Add asparagus and sauté just until hot, about 1 minute. Fluff rice with fork and gently stir in chopped herbs and asparagus. Discard bay leaf. Taste and adjust seasoning. Serve hot.

Makes 2 or 3 main-course servings

PAELLA WITH CHICKEN, SHRIMP, AND ARTICHOKES

When my husband and I took a month-long vacation driving around Spain, we tasted paella in several regions. It was always different—the only thing you could count on having was rice, chicken, and olive oil. It might or might not be flavored with saffron, garlic, tomatoes, or peppers. Most versions we tasted also had at least some seafood, usually shrimp and occasionally squid or mussels. Sometimes there was ham, bacon, or even beef. We had excellent paella in surprising places, like a truck stop on the road between Valencia and Alicante.

There were also paella-like dishes by other names, such as Arroz a la Murciana, *which was made of saffron rice, chicken, tomato, red and green peppers, and peas.*

The lesson we learned was that you could make paella with chicken combined with almost any other meat or seafood. The rice gains a wonderful taste from being cooked together with the chicken. There are special paella pans but a large skillet or wide casserole works fine.

Paella is a practical main dish because it's a whole meal. Even at restaurants, we only began with a few small hors d'oeuvres, usually green olives and perhaps a salad or a refreshing bowl of gazpacho.

3 cups chicken stock or broth
½ teaspoon crushed saffron threads
4 tablespoons olive oil
2 to 2½ pounds chicken drummettes
  (largest section of the wing)
salt and freshly ground pepper
½ pound chicken Italian sausages
1 medium onion, chopped
1 small red bell pepper, cut in ¼-inch-
  wide strips
1½ cups white rice, preferably short-
  grain

1 ripe medium tomato, peeled, seeded,
  and chopped
3 medium garlic cloves, minced
8 ounces medium shrimp, shelled
3 fresh artichoke hearts, cooked (page
  408) and quartered, or 12 frozen
  artichoke pieces, cooked
1 to 2 tablespoons chopped fresh
  parsley

Bring stock to a simmer in a medium saucepan. Crush saffron threads in a small bowl and pour hot stock over them. Cover and let mixture stand about 20 minutes, or while continuing next step.

Heat 2 tablespoons oil in a large, deep, heavy skillet or sauté pan over medium-high heat. Add chicken in batches, sprinkle with salt and pepper and brown the pieces. Transfer to a plate. Add sausages to skillet and brown them, then cut them in chunks.

Add remaining oil to skillet and heat over low heat. Add onion and bell pepper and cook, stirring often, about 10 minutes or until softened. Add rice and sauté over low heat, stirring, 2 minutes. Stir in hot stock, tomato, and garlic. Add chicken and sausages and bring to a simmer. Sprinkle with salt and pepper. Reduce heat to low, cover, and cook 20 minutes. *Paella can be kept, covered, 1 day in refrigerator. To reheat, pour ½ cup additional hot stock over paella, cover, and reheat without stirring over low heat.* Scatter shrimp and cooked artichokes over top, cover, and cook about 5 more minutes or until chicken and rice are tender and liquid is absorbed. Sprinkle with parsley and serve.

Makes 4 main-course servings

SPANISH RICE WITH CHICKEN (*ARROZ CON POLLO*)

A simpler and less expensive cousin of paella popular in Spain and Latin America, arroz con pollo *is usually spiced with cumin rather than saffron and does not contain shellfish. Still, it is simple to prepare, flavorful, and colorful and makes a good dish for entertaining.*

2 tablespoons olive or vegetable oil
3 pounds chicken pieces, patted dry
salt and freshly ground pepper
1 large onion, thinly sliced
1 red bell pepper, cut in thin strips
3 large garlic cloves, minced
1 jalapeño pepper, minced
1½ cups white rice, preferably short-
    grain

1 teaspoon ground cumin
3 ripe fresh or 3 canned plum
    tomatoes, peeled, seeded, and
    chopped
3 cups hot chicken stock or broth
¼ cup chopped cilantro (fresh
    coriander)

Heat oil in a large, deep, heavy skillet or wide casserole. Add chicken leg and thigh pieces, sprinkle with salt and pepper, and brown them on all sides over medium-low heat for about 15 minutes. Remove them and brown white meat chicken pieces for 5 minutes; remove.

Add onion and bell pepper to skillet and cook over low heat, stirring often, about 7 minutes. Add garlic, jalapeño pepper, rice, and cumin and sauté over low heat, stirring, 2 minutes. Stir in tomatoes, hot stock, and half the cilantro and bring to a simmer. Add chicken pieces, putting in leg and thigh pieces first to be sure they are close to base of pan.

Return to a simmer. Reduce heat to very low and cook, covered tightly, about 30 to 40 minutes or until chicken and rice are tender and liquid is absorbed. Serve sprinkled with remaining cilantro. *Chicken and rice can be kept, covered, 1 day in refrigerator. To reheat, pour ½ cup additional hot stock over dish, cover, and heat without stirring over low heat.*

Makes 4 main-course servings

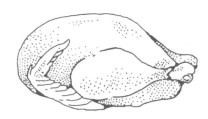

CUBAN CHICKEN WITH YELLOW RICE

My friend Steven Raichlen, an expert on Caribbean cuisine and a great cooking teacher, gave me his recipe for Cuban-style arroz con pollo. *One of the glories of the island's rich culinary tradition, the dish is made of chicken marinated with cumin and oregano, then sautéed with a* sofrito, *or mixture of aromatic vegetables—onions, garlic, bell peppers, and cilantro. The oil used for sautéing often is annatto oil, made by soaking annatto seeds in oil to give it a reddish-orange hue. Next the chicken is braised with wine, beer, and saffron. The savory chicken finally simmers with Valencia-style rice, a short-grain rice similar to Italian Arborio. Look for this type of rice at Hispanic grocery stores or the ethnic food section of supermarkets, or substitute Arborio rice. Fried plantains (see Colombian Chicken, page 250) are a traditional accompaniment for this chicken.*

4 large chicken breast halves, with the bone in	1 teaspoon ground cumin
1 teaspoon dried oregano	½ teaspoon fresh white pepper
	1 tablespoon lime juice

Sofrito

3 tablespoons olive or annatto oil	3 medium garlic cloves, minced
1 small onion, finely chopped	3 tablespoons chopped cilantro (fresh coriander)
1 small red bell pepper, cored, seeded, and finely chopped	1 small tomato, seeded and diced
3 cups water	salt and freshly ground black pepper
1 cup dry white wine	1 pound Valencia-style rice, Arborio rice, or other short-grain rice
1½ cups beer	
¼ teaspoon saffron	½ cup cooked peas
1 tablespoon tomato paste	2 red pimientos (from a jar), diced
¼ cup green olives, pitted	

Place chicken in a glass bowl and sprinkle with oregano, cumin, pepper, and lime juice. Let marinate for 15 minutes.

For the sofrito, heat oil in a large casserole. Add onion, pepper, garlic, and cilantro and cook over medium heat for 1 minute. Add tomato and cook another minute.

Add chicken breasts to sofrito and sauté lightly on both sides. Add any marinade remaining from chicken. Add water, wine, beer, saffron, tomato paste, olives, salt, and pepper. Bring to a boil. Reduce heat and simmer chicken for 30 minutes. *Chicken can be kept, covered, overnight in refrigerator.*

Place rice in a bowl with cold water to cover by several inches. Swirl it with your fingers and pour off the water. Continue adding water and swirling and draining the rice until the water runs clear.

Thirty minutes before serving, bring chicken mixture to a boil. Stir in rice, reduce the heat, cover the pan, and gently simmer for 20 to 25 minutes, or until rice is tender. If rice becomes dry but is not yet tender, add more water. If mixture looks too soupy, remove cover during last 5 minutes of cooking.

Just before the rice is done, stir in half the peas and pimientos. Use the remainder to garnish the top and serve at once.

Makes 4 main-course servings

CHICKEN AND SAUSAGE JAMBALAYA

The classic Cajun meat and rice stew, jambalaya is the perfect dinner in one pot. It is made in many versions—some with seafood, others with a variety of meats—but the combination of chicken and sausage remains one of the best loved.

My first taste of chicken and sausage jambalaya was at an outdoor cooking feast in Lafayette, Louisiana. The food was cooked by a club of local men, who get together regularly to prepare Louisiana specialties. Their jambalaya was such a scorcher that I could eat only a minute amount, and had to wash it down with several glasses of water. When I'm serving jambalaya, I spice it moderately with cayenne and put a bottle of Louisiana hot sauce on the table, so everyone can adjust the hotness to his or her taste.

2½-pound chicken, cut in small pieces
4 tablespoons vegetable oil
1 large onion, chopped
1 green bell pepper, chopped
½ cup chopped celery
2 medium garlic cloves, minced
1 cup smooth tomato sauce, homemade (page 369) or purchased
1 teaspoon dried thyme, crumbled
1 bay leaf

3 cups chicken stock or broth
1½ cups diced smoked turkey sausage, preferably a spicy variety
2 cups long- or medium-grain white rice
salt and freshly ground pepper
½ teaspoon cayenne pepper, or to taste, or bottled hot pepper sauce
4 tablespoons chopped fresh parsley

Pat chicken dry. Heat oil in a large, deep skillet over medium-high heat. Add chicken pieces, brown them well on all sides, and remove. Add onion, bell pepper, and celery and sauté over medium heat, stirring, 7 minutes. Add garlic, tomato sauce, thyme, bay leaf, chicken stock, and sausage. Cover and cook 20 minutes.

Bring mixture to a boil and stir in rice. Return chicken to pan. Add salt, pepper, cayenne, and 3 tablespoons parsley. Cover and cook over low heat 30 to 40 minutes, or until chicken and rice are tender. Do not stir much, to avoid crushing rice. Remove bay leaf. *Jambalaya can be kept, covered, 1 day in refrigerator. To reheat, pour ½ cup additional hot stock over jambalaya, cover, and reheat without stirring over low heat.* Sprinkle with remaining parsley and serve.

Makes 6 main-course servings

ZUCCHINI WITH CHICKEN-RICE STUFFING

Vegetables with a meat and rice stuffing are a Mediterranean favorite. Traditionally the meat used is lamb or beef, but I love a lighter chicken or turkey stuffing. Now that ground chicken and turkey are both widely available, the stuffing is easy to make. In this dish the stuffing is seasoned in the Provençal style, with Parmesan cheese, garlic, and herbs.

3 tablespoons olive oil
6 ounces ground chicken or turkey
  (about ¾ cup)
1½ teaspoons chopped fresh thyme, or
  ½ teaspoon dried thyme, crumbled
½ cup long-grain white rice
2 cups water
salt and freshly ground pepper

4 tablespoons grated Parmesan cheese
2 large garlic cloves, finely chopped
2 tablespoons chopped fresh basil or
  parsley
2 eggs
6 small zucchini (total 1¾ to 2 pounds)
2 cups Fresh Tomato Sauce (page 369)
  or packaged

For the stuffing, heat 2 tablespoons oil in a medium skillet, add chicken and thyme, and sauté over medium heat, stirring, about 5 minutes or until meat changes color. In a saucepan cook rice with boiling salted water for about 14 minutes or until just tender. Drain, rinse with cold running water, and drain thoroughly. Mix rice with chicken, 2 tablespoons cheese, garlic, 1 tablespoon basil, and eggs. Knead briefly to mix thoroughly. Add pepper and taste for seasoning.

Preheat oven to 400°F. Halve each zucchini lengthwise and use tip of a vegetable peeler to remove center containing seeds, leaving a boat-shaped container. Put zucchini in an oiled, large shallow baking dish. Fill each half with stuffing. Sprinkle with remaining oil and bake 15 minutes.

Meanwhile, heat tomato sauce. Reduce oven temperature to 350°F. Spoon sauce over zucchini, sprinkle with remaining cheese, and bake 15 more minutes or until very tender. Sprinkle with remaining basil and serve hot.

Makes 6 main-course servings

BULGUR WHEAT WITH CHICKEN AND GREEN ONIONS

Flavors of the Near East are dominant in this zesty dish. Bulgur wheat, sometimes called cracked wheat, takes only about 15 minutes to cook and becomes an easy and satisfying main course or appetizer with the addition of cooked or smoked chicken or turkey. A handful of green onions gives the bulgur a zesty taste, and chicken broth contributes flavor. With smoked poultry or turkey pastrami, it's best to use unsalted or low-salt broth for cooking the bulgur.

To complete the regional theme, serve this dish with a Mediterranean salad of diced tomato, cucumber, bell pepper, olive oil, and lemon juice.

3 tablespoons vegetable or olive oil
1 small onion, minced
¼ pound mushrooms, diced
salt and freshly ground pepper
cayenne pepper to taste
2 medium garlic cloves, minced

1 cup bulgur wheat
2 cups chicken stock or broth, or broth
   mixed with water
1¼ cups finely diced roasted or
   smoked chicken or turkey
3 green onions, minced (about ½ cup)

Heat oil in a heavy, medium skillet over medium heat. Add onion and sauté, stirring often, about 5 minutes or until softened. Add mushrooms, salt, and cayenne and sauté 3 minutes. Add garlic and bulgur and sauté, stirring, 2 minutes. Add stock, salt, and pepper and bring to boil. Reduce heat to low, cover, and cook about 15 minutes or until liquid is absorbed. *Pilaf can be kept warm, covered, 15 minutes.*

Gently stir chicken into bulgur using a fork. Cover and heat 2 minutes over low heat. Stir in green onions. Taste and adjust seasoning. Serve hot.

Makes 4 light main-course servings

CHICKEN WITH KASHA AND BOWTIE PASTA

In the cuisines of Russia and Poland, kasha, or buckwheat groats, often mixed with bowtie pasta is a popular accompaniment for chicken. Here the quick-cooking grain is combined with cooked chicken, pasta, and vegetables for a hearty main course. If you like, serve it with sour cream or yogurt mixed with a little chopped dill and with a cucumber salad.

3 or 4 tablespoons vegetable oil or butter
½ medium onion, chopped
4 ounces mushrooms, halved and sliced
1 cup medium-grain kasha (buckwheat groats)
1 egg, beaten with pinch of salt
2 cups hot chicken broth, or broth mixed with water
2 medium carrots, halved lengthwise, sliced thin

2 medium zucchini, coarsely grated
2 cups shredded or diced cooked chicken
1 (7- or 8-ounce) package bowtie pasta
salt and freshly ground pepper
2 tablespoons chopped fresh parsley (optional)
2 tablespoons chopped fresh dill, or 2 teaspoons dried

Heat 2 tablespoons oil or butter in a heavy skillet, add onion, and sauté over medium heat 7 minutes or until softened. Add mushrooms and sauté 5 minutes or until lightly browned. Remove from skillet.

Combine kasha with beaten egg in a wide bowl and stir with a fork until grains are thoroughly coated. Add to skillet and heat over medium heat about 3 minutes, stirring to keep grains separate. Add hot chicken broth and stir. Add carrots. Cover and cook over low heat 5 minutes. Add zucchini and chicken. Cook, covered, 10 minutes or until broth is absorbed. Stir with a fork to fluff. Add sautéed mushroom mixture.

Meanwhile, cook pasta in a large pan of boiling salted water about 6 to 8 minutes or until just tender. Drain well, transfer to a large bowl, and mix with 1 or 2 tablespoons oil or butter. Mix lightly with kasha mixture. Taste and adjust seasoning. Stir in parsley and dill and serve.

Makes 4 main-course servings

PASTA WITH MEXICAN TURKEY PICADILLO SAUCE

Sweet and savory turkey picadillo, flavored with raisins and olives, is best known as a pastry filling. Like chili, it is versatile, and I find it makes an enticing, change-of-pace spaghetti sauce. Here it gains extra flavor from jalapeño peppers and garlic, and is moistened with tomato sauce.

Choose a thin type of pasta so the sauce clings well to it, such as Mexican fideos, *which are similar to angel hair pasta.*

2 to 3 tablespoons vegetable or olive
   oil
2 jalapeño peppers, seeded and
   chopped
4 medium garlic cloves, chopped
Turkey Picadillo (page 280)
⅓ to ½ cup tomato sauce or tomato
   puree; or ¼ cup tomato
   paste mixed with ¼ cup water

½ pound *fideos*, angel hair pasta,
   vermicelli, or spaghettini
salt
½ cup chopped green onions

Heat 2 tablespoons oil in a large saucepan, add jalapeño peppers and garlic, and sauté about ½ minute. Add picadillo and tomato sauce and simmer 4 to 5 minutes until heated and thickened. Add a few tablespoons water if sauce is too thick. Taste and adjust seasoning.

Cook pasta in a large pot of boiling salted water until just tender, al dente. Drain pasta and transfer to a bowl. Toss with 1 tablespoon oil if desired, then with ⅓ cup chopped green onions and half the sauce. Top with remaining sauce, sprinkle with remaining green onions, and serve.

Makes 4 main-course servings

VERMICELLI WITH SMOKED TURKEY AND BROCCOLI

Inspired by a southern Italian specialty of spaghetti with a sauce of broccoli, olive oil, and grated Parmesan cheese, this is one of the fastest dishes possible. The pasta and broccoli are cooked together in the same pot, while the sauce ingredients—strips of smoked turkey, diced tomatoes, olive oil, and basil—are simply mixed in the serving bowl. All you need to do when the pasta and broccoli are cooked is toss everything together.

2 ripe fresh medium or 4 canned plum
    tomatoes, diced
3 tablespoons extra-virgin olive oil
salt and freshly ground pepper
1 tablespoon fresh basil strips, or 1
    teaspoon dried basil, crumbled
8 ounces vermicelli or spaghettini

1 pound broccoli, divided into
    medium florets
3 or 4 thin slices turkey pastrami or
    smoked turkey, cut in thin strips
freshly grated Parmesan cheese, for
    serving

In large bowl, combine tomatoes, oil, salt, pepper, and dried basil, if using. Let stand while cooking pasta.

    Cook pasta in a large pot of boiling salted water uncovered over high heat, lifting occasionally with tongs, 2 minutes. Add broccoli and cook together 5 minutes or until pasta is tender but firm to the bite. Drain both together. Add to bowl of tomato mixture. Add turkey. Toss well. Add fresh basil if using. Serve with grated Parmesan.

Makes 2 main-course servings

ORZO WITH SMOKED TURKEY AND CHINESE SEASONINGS

This dish looks and tastes Oriental but makes use of orzo, the rice-shaped pasta popular in Greece and Italy. Together with smoked turkey and plenty of fresh vegetables, it makes a quick, easy, colorful, and tasty main course. You can substitute smoked chicken for the turkey, or instead add 2 cups shredded or diced roast chicken or turkey.

1½ cups rice-shaped pasta (orzo or riso)
2 medium carrots, cut in sticks about ¼ inch thick
6 to 8 medium asparagus spears, peeled, cut in 3, bases discarded
6 ounces mushrooms, quartered
2 medium zucchini, cut in sticks about same size as carrot sticks

6 ounces smoked turkey breast, cut in sticks
2 green onions, chopped
2 tablespoons vegetable oil
1 tablespoon Oriental sesame oil
1 tablespoon soy sauce
¼ teaspoon hot pepper sauce
salt and freshly ground pepper

Bring a large pan of water to a boil. Add orzo and carrots and cook 7 minutes. Add asparagus, mushrooms, and zucchini and cook 4 minutes or until orzo and vegetables are tender. Remove from heat, add turkey, and drain all together in strainer. Transfer orzo mixture to a large bowl. Add green onions, vegetable oil, sesame oil, soy sauce, and hot pepper sauce. Stir well. Add salt and pepper to taste. Serve hot or warm.

Makes 3 main-course servings

CORSICAN RICE WITH TURKEY SAUSAGE, BLACK OLIVES, AND THYME

For this tasty Mediterranean pilaf, the light sausages add flavor to the rice as they cook together. A refreshing salad of diced cucumbers, tomatoes, and green onion is a fine accompaniment.

3 tablespoons olive oil
2 medium onions, halved and sliced thin
2 medium garlic cloves, chopped
6 ounces turkey frankfurters or other small cooked turkey or chicken sausages, sliced or diced
1½ cups long-grain white rice
3 cups hot water

1 teaspoon dried thyme
1 bay leaf
1 cup halved pitted black olives, preferably Greek style
1 roasted red pepper, diced, or ¾ cup diced bottled roasted red pepper (optional; see Note)
salt (optional) and freshly ground pepper to taste

Heat oil in a medium sauté pan or deep skillet, add onions, and sauté over medium heat about 10 minutes or until softened. Stir in garlic, then add frankfurters and rice and sauté together, stirring, 3 minutes, until grains begin to turn white.

Add water, thyme, and bay leaf; stir once and bring to a boil. Cover and cook over low heat, without stirring, 15 minutes. Sprinkle olives and red pepper over top, cover, and cook 3 to 5 more minutes or until rice is tender. Discard bay leaf. Add black pepper; toss lightly with a fork to blend ingredients. Taste and adjust seasoning; salt may not be needed, depending on saltiness of olives and sausages.

Makes 2 or 3 main-course servings

NOTE: If you don't have roasted red peppers, you can add diced oil-packed sun-dried tomatoes or fresh tomatoes.

BROWN RICE PILAF WITH TURKEY AND ZUCCHINI

As rice pilaf entered the cuisines of various nations during the course of history, traveling from Persia to the Mediterranean and the rest of Europe, it was combined with different ingredients to suit local tastes and gave rise to such diverse dishes as sumptuous Indian pilaus and Spanish paellas, combining vegetables and chicken or other meats with rice. In traditional dishes the rice is white, but I find that brown rice makes delicious pilafs as well, as in this adaptation of a simple Turkish-style pilaf.

From a nutritional standpoint, combining nutrient-rich brown rice with a small amount of lean turkey is a sensible choice for a main course. To enhance the dish by adding color and freshness, I like to add one or more cooked vegetables—asparagus, artichokes, or peas in spring, peeled red and green peppers or sautéed eggplant in summer, and diced carrots, zucchini strips, cauliflower or broccoli florets, or sautéed mushrooms all year.

3 tablespoons olive oil or butter
¾ pound boneless and skinless turkey breasts, chicken breasts, or chicken thighs, diced
salt and freshly ground pepper to taste
2 or 3 small zucchini, cut in thin sticks about 1½ inches long
½ cup minced onion

2 medium garlic cloves, minced
1¼ cups long-grain brown rice
2½ cups hot chicken stock, broth, or water
½ teaspoon dried thyme, crumbled
2 tablespoons minced fresh parsley or cilantro (fresh coriander)

Heat 2 tablespoons oil or butter in a large sauté pan or deep skillet over medium-high heat. Add turkey, salt, and pepper and sauté about 3 minutes for turkey or 5 minutes for chicken, tossing often. Remove with a slotted spatula. Add zucchini sticks, salt, and pepper to pan and sauté about 2 minutes. Remove with slotted spoon.

Add 1 tablespoon oil or butter to pan. Add onion and cook over medium heat until soft but not brown, about 7 minutes. Add garlic and rice and sauté, stirring, until grains begin to turn white, about 3 minutes.

Pour hot stock over rice and stir once. Add thyme, salt, and pepper. Bring to boil. Cover tightly and simmer over low heat, without stirring, 40 minutes. Scatter turkey and zucchini over top. Cover and simmer 3 to 5 minutes or until rice is tender and liquid is absorbed. Fluff rice gently with a fork. Add parsley or cilantro. Taste, adjust seasoning, and serve.

Makes 2 or 3 main-course servings

ACORN SQUASH STUFFED WITH TURKEY AND WILD RICE

This festive dish features typical American ingredients—wild rice, pecans, acorn squash, and turkey—and is perfect for using up leftover Thanksgiving turkey. It's prettiest with small acorn squashes so you can serve them whole, but medium acorn squashes work well, too. If you choose stock rather than butter or oil to spoon over the stuffing to moisten it before baking, the dish will be low in fat. The stuffing is also good in bell peppers, as in the variation.

4 small acorn squashes, each about ¾
  pound, or 2 larger ones of 1¼ to 1½
  pounds
½ cup wild rice
salt and freshly ground pepper
1½ cups boiling water
2 tablespoons vegetable oil or butter
1 medium onion, chopped

1 medium celery stalk, finely diced
1½ cups diced cooked turkey or
  chicken
¼ cup pecans or walnuts, toasted
  (page 409) and chopped
4 tablespoons chicken stock, vegetable
  oil, or butter

Preheat the oven to 350°F. Cut a thin slice from bottom of each acorn squash, if necessary, so they stand straight. Place in a nonstick or foil-lined pan. Bake small squashes about 1 hour, larger squashes about 1½ hours or until tender.

Add wild rice and a pinch of salt to a medium saucepan with boiling water. Cover and cook over low heat about 45 minutes or until tender. Drain rice. Measure 1½ cups cooked rice.

In the same saucepan, heat oil or butter. Add onion and celery and sauté over medium heat until onion is soft but not browned, about 7 minutes. Stir in turkey or chicken and measured rice and heat through. Add nuts. Season to taste with salt and pepper.

If using small squash, cut off the top quarter of each squash to form a hat; reserve the slice. If using larger squash, cut each in half horizontally to make two boat-shaped pieces. Gently scoop out seeds from squashes; do not pierce shells. Sprinkle squashes with salt and pepper. Fill small squashes or large squash halves generously with turkey mixture. Replace hat on small squashes. Cover with foil. *Stuffed squashes can be kept, covered, overnight in refrigerator.*

Preheat oven to 350°F. Remove hats from squashes; spoon 1 tablespoon stock, oil, or melted butter over stuffing in each squash or squash half; replace squash hats. Cover and heat squashes about 20 minutes if warm, or about 40 minutes if they were cold, or until filling is hot. If desired, combine any remaining stuffing with any remaining cooked rice and heat, covered, in a lightly oiled saucepan. Serve it separately.

Makes 2 to 4 main-course servings

VARIATION: **Bell Peppers Stuffed with Turkey and Wild Rice**

Halve 3 green or red bell peppers lengthwise; remove ribs and seeds. Put peppers cut side up in oiled baking dish. Sprinkle with salt. Bake at 350°F., uncovered, 20 minutes. Cover and bake 15 minutes or until tender. Cool slightly; if there is liquid inside the peppers, pour it out. Mound stuffing slightly in peppers. *Stuffed peppers can be kept, covered, 1 day in refrigerator.* Spoon 1 tablespoon chicken stock, vegetable oil, or melted butter over stuffing in each pepper. Cover peppers and bake at 350°F. for 20 minutes if they are warm, or about 30 minutes if they are cold.

Makes 6 appetizer or 3 main-course servings

Braised Chicken with Artichokes, Tomatoes, and Dill
Springtime Chicken Sauté with Asparagus and Carrots
Stewed Chicken with Celery, Potatoes, Cumin,
and Cilantro
Mediterranean Chicken with Okra, Jalapeño
Peppers, and Tomatoes
Moroccan Chicken Tajine
with Tomatoes, Cilantro, and Zucchini
Braised Drumsticks with Potatoes, Green Beans,
and Red Onion
Chicken Cassoulet with Roast Duck
and Turkey Sausages
Casserole-Roasted Chicken with Leeks and Potatoes
Chicken Potée with Winter Vegetables
Chicken and Vegetables with Korean Sesame Sauce
Quick and Spicy Chicken Meatballs with
Mushrooms and Peppers
Turkey Breast Slices with Summer Vegetables
Turkey Breasts with Pesto and Potatoes
Turkey Hash with Vegetables and Rosemary
African Turkey and Peanut Stew with Eggplant
and Okra

8

Chicken and Turkey
with Vegetables

 If you peek into saucepans in Hong Kong, Los Angeles, or Paris, you will come to the conclusion that chicken and vegetables are universally recognized as natural partners. The chicken contributes rich taste and the vegetables provide lightness, color, and crisp texture. This chapter contains chicken and turkey dishes that include enough vegetables to complete the main course. Here the amounts of vegetables are generous so that you don't have to prepare additional vegetable accompaniments.

Delicious chicken-and-vegetable combinations vary from Chinese stir-fried dishes to Thai curries to Moroccan tajines to French ragouts. Turkey, being an American bird, is rarely cooked in Oriental cuisines, but it too can be used in all these types of dishes.

Vegetables are cooked with chicken or turkey for two purposes: as aromatic vegetables and as accompaniments. Aromatic vegetables simmer with braised or poached poultry to lend flavor and fragrance to the sauce or cooking liquid. Members of the onion family—onions, leeks, shallots, and garlic—head the list of vegetables in this category, and are cooked with poultry in every cuisine. In European and American cuisines carrots and celery are also added to the pot for the same purpose.

Mushrooms and tomatoes could belong to both categories of vegetables. Popular in fresh, dried, and canned forms, they are used in much of the world to lend their flavor to sauces and to be served as a vegetable.

Most other vegetables are paired with chicken or turkey to balance the menu. Naturally, any vegetable can be cooked separately and served with the bird. But for many meals, it is much more convenient to cook the chicken or turkey and vegetable in the same pot.

Although vegetables can be added to poultry cooked by any method, the most suitable techniques for cooking plenty of vegetables along with chicken or turkey are braising and poaching. The poultry cooks over gentle heat, and the vegetables are added part way through the cooking time. This is true, for example, of Moroccan Chicken Tajine with Tomatoes, Cilantro, and Zucchini (page 135).

Many cooks prefer to briefly cook green vegetables separately in water and to add them to chicken or turkey for the last few minutes of cooking. This way they keep their vivid color and texture but still absorb flavor from the bird's juices. Other vegetables, like peppers, mushrooms, or eggplant, are often sautéed or grilled before being cooked with chicken.

In some styles of cooking the vegetable's bright color is not important. In the Middle East, for example, green beans might be braised in a chicken stew until they are very tender. At this point they are no longer bright green, but their flavor is rich from the long gentle simmering with the chicken.

Cooked dried beans are often combined with chicken as a casserole. This method is especially prevalent in Mediterranean countries. Often the chicken and beans begin cooking separately, as in chicken cassoulet, then bake or simmer together so the chicken flavors the beans.

TIP

✗ To make a quick tasty dish out of leftover chicken or turkey cooked by any method, I like to combine it with plenty of vegetables. First I remove all the skin, bones, and any visible fat from the chicken. Next I pull the meat into long shreds or cut it in dice or strips with a knife. Then I cook or sauté whatever vegetables I happen to have. If I have leftover sauce or gravy, I gently heat the chicken in a little of it and add the vegetables. If I don't have sauce, I either sauté the chicken or heat it in a little chicken stock or canned broth. I then add the vegetables and serve the dish over rice or pasta.

BRAISED CHICKEN WITH ARTICHOKES, TOMATOES, AND DILL

Artichokes are best known as a first course, but they make a tasty partner for chicken in a main course. When fresh artichokes are not in season or when you are busy, frozen artichoke hearts can be substituted. In this Greek-style dish, white wine and tomatoes give the sauce a tangy flavor that complements the chicken's richness. Serve the chicken with white rice.

3½ pounds chicken pieces, patted dry
salt and freshly ground pepper
2 tablespoons olive oil
1 fairly small onion, chopped
2 medium garlic cloves, chopped
½ cup dry white wine
¾ pound ripe tomatoes, peeled, seeded, and chopped; or 1 (16-ounce) can whole tomatoes, drained and chopped

1 bay leaf
4 tablespoons minced fresh dill
4 fresh artichokes, or 1 (9-ounce) package frozen artichoke hearts

If chicken breast is in one piece, cut it in half lengthwise along the breastbone. Sprinkle chicken pieces with salt and pepper. Heat oil in a large skillet or sauté pan over medium-high heat and brown chicken pieces, taking about 10 minutes for leg pieces and about 7 minutes for breast pieces. Remove with tongs.

Discard all but 1 or 2 tablespoons fat. Add onion and sauté 7 minutes, stirring often. Stir in garlic, then add wine, tomatoes, and bay leaf. Bring to a boil. Simmer uncovered 5 minutes. Stir in 2 tablespoons dill. Add chicken, placing leg pieces in pan first so they are in contact with base. Cover and cook 15 minutes. Turn pieces over and simmer about 10 minutes or until breast pieces are tender. Remove them and continue simmering leg pieces until tender, about 5 more minutes. Discard bay leaf. Return breast pieces to pan. *Chicken can be kept, covered, overnight in refrigerator. Before continuing, bring to simmer, covered.*

If using fresh artichokes, prepare artichoke hearts and cook them (see page 408). Cut each in 4 pieces. Or cook frozen artichokes according to package directions.

Gently stir artichoke pieces into stew and heat 2 or 3 minutes. Stir in remaining 2 tablespoons dill. Taste and adjust seasoning.

Makes 4 servings

SPRINGTIME CHICKEN SAUTÉ
WITH ASPARAGUS AND CARROTS

This beautiful French entree, ideal for an elegant spring dinner, was the star recipe of my article on Chicken Sautés in Bon Appétit, *and appeared as the cover photo of the magazine. The colorful dish, which is enhanced by a Madeira sauce, needs no accompaniments because it already contains a generous amount of vegetables.*

3 pounds chicken pieces, patted dry
salt and freshly ground pepper
1 tablespoon vegetable oil
1 tablespoon butter
3 medium carrots (about 10 ounces),
　peeled, cut in 2-inch lengths

1¼ pounds medium-width asparagus,
　peeled
½ cup Madeira
½ cup heavy cream (optional; see
　Note)

Sprinkle chicken lightly with salt and pepper on all sides. Heat oil and butter in large, heavy skillet over medium heat. Add chicken leg and thigh pieces and brown lightly on all sides. Set on a plate, using slotted spoon. Lightly brown breast and wing pieces.

Return leg and thigh pieces to skillet. If pieces don't fit in one layer, arrange breast and wing pieces on top. Add chicken juices from plate. Cover and cook over low heat about 15 minutes or until breast pieces are tender. Transfer them to a platter, cover, and keep them warm. Continue cooking remaining pieces another 10 minutes or until tender. Add them to platter.

Meanwhile, quarter the thick carrot pieces lengthwise; halve thin pieces lengthwise. Put carrots in medium saucepan, cover with water, and add salt. Bring to a boil. Cover and simmer 15 minutes.

Trim asparagus and cut off tough ends. Reserve tips. Cut stems in 2 or 3 pieces. Add stem pieces to pan of carrots and simmer together 7 minutes or until tender. Drain cooking liquid into a measuring cup. Reserve 1 cup. Cover pan to keep vegetables warm.

Skim as much fat as possible from chicken juices in skillet. Reheat juices until very hot. Add reserved vegetable cooking liquid and boil, stirring, until reduced to about ¼ cup. Add Madeira and bring to a boil. Add cream and simmer over medium heat, stirring often, until thick enough to coat a spoon.

Cook asparagus tips uncovered in a saucepan of boiling salted water over high heat about 3 minutes or until just tender. Drain and reserve for garnish. Add carrots and asparagus stems to sauce and heat 2 or 3 minutes. Taste for seasoning.

Drain any fat from platter and wipe clean with paper towel. Spoon carrot mixture over chicken in platter. Spoon sauce over all. Arrange asparagus tips in small piles around chicken. Serve immediately.

Makes 4 servings

NOTE: If you would like to omit the cream but prefer a thickened sauce, mix ¾ teaspoon potato starch or cornstarch with 2 teaspoons water in a small cup, then whisk the mixture into the simmering sauce over medium heat. Cook 1 or 2 minutes or until thickened.

STEWED CHICKEN WITH CELERY, POTATOES, CUMIN, AND CILANTRO

A friend of mine who was born in the Arabian Peninsula showed me how she prepares this dish, in which the flavorful cumin- and cilantro-scented chicken and its juices add a zesty taste to the potatoes. She serves the chicken with rice and with a tomato salad, or with zucchini or okra cooked in tomato sauce.

The chicken is browned slowly with the spices so they add color and flavor to the oil but don't burn. Wash your hands right after rubbing the chicken with the spices, so your fingers won't be colored orange.

2½ teaspoons ground cumin
½ teaspoon turmeric
3 pounds chicken pieces
salt and freshly ground pepper
6 large celery stalks

1¼ pounds boiling potatoes
2 tablespoons vegetable oil
1¼ cups water
2 to 3 tablespoons chopped cilantro
   (fresh coriander) or parsley

Mix cumin and turmeric. Season chicken with salt, pepper, and spice mixture. Let stand while preparing vegetables.

Peel and halve celery stalks and cut in 3-inch lengths. Peel potatoes and cut into ⅜-inch slices.

Heat oil in a large, deep casserole over medium heat and lightly brown chicken pieces in batches, taking about 7 minutes per batch. Remove to plate.

Add potato slices and sauté lightly, stirring, 2 minutes. Add celery and stir. Return chicken to pan, with any juices from plate, making sure leg pieces are at bottom of pan. Add water and bring to simmer. Cover and cook over low heat, turning pieces over once or twice and pushing potatoes into liquid, about 45 minutes, or until chicken pieces are tender. *Stew can be kept, covered, overnight in refrigerator.* Before *continuing, bring to simmer, covered.* Remove chicken. Continue simmering vegetables 5 minutes or until tender.

If desired, remove vegetables carefully and boil juices briefly to reduce; then return ingredients to pan and reheat gently. Stir in half the cilantro. Taste and adjust seasoning. Sprinkle chicken with remaining cilantro when serving.

Makes 4 servings

MEDITERRANEAN CHICKEN WITH OKRA, JALAPEÑO PEPPERS, AND TOMATOES

For this Tunisian recipe, the chicken is braised in a sauce flavored with both jalapeño peppers and harissa, but in place of harissa, you can use whatever hot sauce you like, whether from Mexico, Louisiana, or the Far East. Even Chinese chili paste with garlic is good, although it gives the dish a different character. The jalapeño peppers are left whole and served as a spicy garnish. For best texture, choose small okra, about 3 inches long or less, so they will be tender. Serve with couscous or rice.

2 tablespoons vegetable oil
3½-pound chicken, cut in pieces,
    patted dry
2 teaspoons ground coriander
salt and freshly ground pepper
1 large onion, sliced
1 red bell pepper, cut in ¾-inch dice
1 pound tomatoes, peeled, seeded, and
    chopped; or 1 (28-ounce) can,
    drained, halved, drained again, and
    chopped

1 large garlic clove, chopped
1 to 2 teaspoons Harissa (page 366) or
    bottled hot pepper sauce
1½ teaspoons paprika
½ cup water
¾ pound okra
4 whole jalapeño peppers

Heat oil over medium-high heat in large casserole. Season chicken with coriander, salt, and pepper and sauté in oil in batches until lightly browned. Remove from pan.

Add onion and sauté over medium heat 5 minutes. Add salt, bell pepper, tomatoes, garlic, Harissa or hot sauce, and paprika, and mix well. Add water. Bring to a boil. Add chicken, putting breast pieces on top. Cover and cook over low heat, stirring from time to time and turning pieces occasionally. Remove breasts and wings when tender, after about 30 minutes. Cook legs and thighs 15 to 20 minutes more. Remove from pan.

Rinse okra. Cut stem ends off. Add okra and whole hot peppers to casserole. Cover and simmer without stirring 20 to 25 minutes or until tender. Remove okra and cover them. Boil sauce uncovered about 5 minutes or until thickened and well flavored. Taste and adjust seasoning, adding more hot sauce if desired. Reheat chicken in sauce, covered. Put chicken on serving dish, spoon sauce and okra around it, top meat with hot peppers, and serve.

Makes 4 servings

MOROCCAN CHICKEN TAJINE WITH TOMATOES, CILANTRO, AND ZUCCHINI

Moroccan tajines like this one are made by a variation of the poaching technique. The chicken pieces are not browned as in braised chicken. Instead, before any liquid is added, they are heated gently with the spices and sliced onions. I have often seen women from the Middle East cooking chicken by this relaxed, easy method. It is a pleasure to prepare chicken this way, as there is no need to worry about splattering oil.

A generous amount of cilantro gives this chicken stew a fresh, aromatic character. The herb simmers with the chicken to give depth of flavor to the sauce, and then more is added just before serving for a fresh finishing touch. Cumin, ginger, and hot pepper flakes enhance the sauce rather than dominate it, so that the flavor of the chicken and tomatoes comes through. Serve the chicken with rice or couscous, and if you like, with Harissa (page 366) on the side.

2 large onions, halved and cut in thin slices (half-moons)
2 medium garlic cloves, coarsely chopped
6 tablespoons chopped cilantro (fresh coriander)
1 teaspoon ground cumin
1 teaspoon ground ginger
½ teaspoon hot red pepper flakes
½ teaspoon paprika
2 tablespoons olive oil
3½-pound chicken, quartered
salt and freshly ground black pepper
¼ cup water
1½ pounds tomatoes, peeled, seeded, and chopped; or 3 (14-ounce) cans tomatoes, drained, and chopped
¾ pound zucchini, cut in ½-inch slices

In a large casserole or Dutch oven mix onions, garlic, 2 tablespoons cilantro, spices, and oil. Add chicken, sprinkle with salt and pepper, and warm over low heat about 5 minutes, turning a few times, to flavor well with spices.

Push most of onions to base of pan. Add water and bring to a boil. Reduce heat to low, cover, and simmer 15 minutes. Add tomatoes and simmer 15 minutes. Turn chicken pieces over and cook 15 minutes or until breast pieces are tender; remove breast pieces. Add zucchini, sprinkle with salt and pepper, and simmer until remaining chicken pieces and zucchini are tender, about 15 minutes.

If you would like a thicker sauce, remove pieces and boil sauce a few minutes to thicken. *Chicken can be kept, covered, 2 days in refrigerator.* Reheat over low heat. Stir in 3 tablespoons cilantro. Taste and adjust seasoning. When serving, sprinkle with remaining tablespoon cilantro.

Makes 4 servings

BRAISED DRUMSTICKS WITH POTATOES, GREEN BEANS, AND RED ONION

This simple recipe of braised chicken with onions and potatoes makes the most of the inherent character of each ingredient and is popular throughout Europe. The browned onion and chicken flavor each other, and each contributes its taste to the potatoes. The chicken cooks in its own juices, and only at the end a little water is added to cook the potatoes.

To this basic preparation, I like to add blanched green beans, sliced mushrooms, red onions, and plenty of parsley to finish. This is the kind of recipe that home cooks everywhere vary according to what's available in the market. You can use other quick-cooking vegetables like crookneck squash, zucchini, or turnips, and other herbs like thyme, tarragon, oregano, or cilantro. Serve the chicken with a salad of diced tomato, cucumber, and green onion.

2 tablespoons vegetable oil
2 pounds chicken thighs or drumsticks
salt and freshly ground pepper
1 large yellow onion, chopped
4 to 6 ounces green beans, cut in 2 or
    3 pieces, or 1 cup frozen "Frenched"
    green beans

1 to 1¼ pounds boiling potatoes,
    peeled and cut in ¾-inch cubes
¾ cup water
4 ounces mushrooms, sliced
½ cup chopped red onion
¼ cup chopped fresh parsley

Heat oil in a large casserole or Dutch oven over medium heat, add chicken pieces in batches, sprinkle with salt and pepper, and brown on both sides. Remove to a plate. Add yellow onion and sauté until it begins to turn golden, about 10 minutes.

Meanwhile, cook fresh green beans (but not frozen) in a saucepan of boiling salted water uncovered about 5 minutes. Rinse with cold water and drain.

Return chicken to casserole. Cover and cook over low heat, shaking pan and turning pieces occasionally, 30 minutes. Add potato cubes, sprinkle with salt, and push under chicken. Add water and bring to boil. Simmer about 20 minutes. Add fresh parboiled or frozen green beans and mushrooms and simmer 5 to 10 minutes or until chicken and vegetables are tender. Add red onion and parsley. Taste and adjust seasoning. Serve hot.

Makes 3 or 4 servings

CHICKEN CASSOULET WITH ROAST DUCK AND TURKEY SAUSAGES

Cassoulet, a casserole of beans and meats, is a symbol of French regional cooking. This robust dish of peasant origin, most loved and esteemed in France, has survived all the various cooking trends and is one of the favorites in both home and restaurant kitchens.

Like many good country dishes, cassoulet developed out of the simple need to use the products at hand. The beans were combined with any available meats, from sausages to pork to game when it was in season. As usual with traditional dishes, recipes vary from one village to the next and from one cook to another. Some cooks add bacon; some like a strong tomato flavor while others do not put in any tomato at all. There are people who prefer their cassoulet to be very moist and almost soupy, and others who want theirs relatively dry.

The versions of cassoulet that I prefer feature several kinds of poultry: chicken thighs braised with tomatoes and onions, to flavor the sauce for the beans; roast duck or goose; and turkey rather than pork sausages. Although leaner than most meat versions, poultry cassoulet is still hearty, wonderfully rich and delicious, a perfect winter dish.

Serve the cassoulet with fresh crusty French bread, a green salad, and, for dessert, crisp apples or a simple French fruit dessert like pears poached in red wine.

1 pound dried white beans, such as
  Great Northern (about 2⅓ cups)
1 medium onion, peeled and studded
  with 2 whole cloves
1 medium carrot, peeled
2 bay leaves
5 medium garlic cloves, peeled
1 teaspoon dried thyme, crumbled
4½- to 5-pound duck, thawed (if
  frozen), patted dry
salt and freshly ground pepper
8 to 10 ounces small boiling onions or
  pearl onions

2 tablespoons olive oil (optional)
1 pound ripe tomatoes, peeled, seeded,
  and chopped; or 1 (28-ounce) can
  whole plum tomatoes, drained and
  chopped
2½ pounds chicken thighs
¾ cup chicken stock, broth, or water
2 tablespoons chopped fresh basil, or 2
  teaspoons dried, crumbled
½ pound smoked turkey Polish
  sausages or other sausages
¼ cup unseasoned bread crumbs

Sort beans, discarding broken ones and any stones. In a large bowl soak beans in 7 cups cold water overnight. For a quicker method, cover beans with 7 cups water in a large saucepan, boil 2 minutes, and let stand off heat for 1 hour.

Rinse and drain beans and put them in a large saucepan. Add enough water to cover them by at least 2 inches. Add clove-studded onion and carrot and push them into liquid. Tie 1 bay leaf and 2 garlic cloves in a piece of cheesecloth and add to pan. Add ½ teaspoon thyme. Cover and bring to a boil over medium heat. Simmer over low heat for 1½ hours or until just tender, adding hot water if necessary so beans remain covered. Keep beans in their cooking liquid. *Beans can be cooked 1 day ahead and refrigerated.*

Preheat oven to 400°F. Pull out fat from inside duck. Sprinkle duck inside and out with salt and pepper. Using trussing needle or skewer, pierce skin all over at intervals of about ½ inch; do not pierce meat. Roast duck on a rack in a roasting pan for 1 hour. Cut it into 8 pieces. Reserve 2 tablespoons fat from pan for sauce if desired.

Cook baby onions in boiling water for 1 minute. Rinse, drain, and peel. Heat oil or 2 tablespoons fat from duck in a large, heavy casserole over medium heat. Add baby onions and brown lightly. Remove them with slotted spoon. Chop remaining garlic, add to pan, and cook ½ minute. Stir in tomatoes and cook 2 minutes. Add chicken, stock, and remaining thyme and bay leaf. Cover and simmer 15 minutes. Turn chicken pieces, add baby onions, and cook 30 minutes more or until chicken is tender. Discard bay leaf. Add basil. Taste sauce and adjust seasoning. Skim off excess fat. Discard chicken skin. Remove meat from bones in large pieces.

Put sausages in a pan, cover with water, and bring just to a simmer. Cook over low heat for 15 minutes. Drain and slice.

Discard onion, carrot, and cheesecloth bag from beans. With a slotted spoon, put half the beans in a 10-cup gratin dish in an even layer. Arrange chicken and duck pieces and sausage slices on beans. With slotted spoon, add baby onions. Spoon remaining beans on top. Reserve remaining bean liquid. Ladle chicken sauce over beans; add enough of reserved bean cooking liquid to come nearly to top of beans. *Cassoulet can be kept, covered, 2 days in refrigerator.*

Preheat oven to 375°F. Sprinkle cassoulet with bread crumbs and bake about 35 minutes (or 50 minutes if it was cold) or until hot and golden brown. Serve from baking dish.

Makes 6 to 8 servings

CASSEROLE-ROASTED CHICKEN WITH LEEKS AND POTATOES

Leeks and potatoes are a classic pair in French soups, but they are also marvelous when cooked with a chicken roasted en cocotte, *a favorite technique throughout France, and flavored with the chicken's buttery juices.*

3½-pound frying chicken, patted dry
salt and freshly ground pepper
2 tablespoons vegetable oil
1 tablespoon butter
2 large leeks (total about 1 pound),
   white and light green parts only,
   split and rinsed (page 408)

6 medium oval potatoes (total about
   1½ pounds)
2 teaspoons fresh thyme leaves, or ¾
   teaspoon dried, crumbled
¼ cup dry white wine
¼ cup chicken stock
1 tablespoon chopped fresh parsley

Preheat oven to 400°F. Truss chicken if desired, for more attractive shape. Sprinkle chicken evenly with salt and pepper.

Heat oil and butter in heavy, oval, enamel-lined casserole over medium-high heat. Set chicken in casserole on its side, so leg is in contact with fat. Cover with large splatter screen and brown side of chicken. Using 2 wooden spoons and standing back to avoid splatters, turn chicken onto its breast and brown it. Brown other side, then brown chicken back. If oil begins to turn dark brown, reduce heat to medium.

Leave chicken on its back. Baste chicken with pan juices. Cover and bake until juices run clear when thickest part of leg is pierced with thin skewer, about 45 minutes; if juices are pink, bake a few more minutes and test again. Discard any trussing strings. *Chicken can be kept warm in casserole, covered, for 15 minutes.*

Cut leeks into 2-inch pieces, press to flatten them, and cut into ¼-inch lengthwise slices; separate slices in strips if they remain joined at root end.

Peel potatoes and halve them lengthwise. Trim each half to an oval shape, using paring knife, and put in large saucepan of cold water. Bring to boil. Add salt, cover, and simmer over medium heat until nearly tender, about 10 minutes. Drain thoroughly.

When chicken is tender, transfer it to platter, reserving juices in casserole. Cover chicken with foil and keep it warm.

Bring chicken juices to a boil. Reduce heat to low. Add potatoes, half the thyme, salt, and pepper. Cook, carefully turning potatoes often, until lightly browned and just tender, about 10 minutes. Remove with slotted spoon and keep warm.

Add leeks to casserole and sprinkle with salt and pepper. Cover and cook over low heat, stirring occasionally, until just tender, about 5 minutes. Discard any juices that escaped from chicken. Remove leeks with slotted spoon and arrange around chicken.

Skim as much fat as possible from juices in casserole. Bring juices to boil. Add wine and bring to boil, stirring and scraping in any browned bits. Add stock and boil 1 or 2 minutes to reduce lightly. Add remaining thyme. Taste and adjust seasoning.

To serve, arrange potatoes on leeks around chicken. Sprinkle potatoes with chopped parsley. Serve juices separately.

Makes 4 servings

CHICKEN POTÉE WITH WINTER VEGETABLES

A staple of country cooking in many regions of France, poule au pot, *or chicken in the pot, features a whole chicken poached with herbs and a variety of vegetables—carrots, turnips, leeks, celery, and sometimes cabbage. A traditional Sunday family meal, it is served in two courses—first the broth, with noodles or crusty French bread, then a large platter of the chicken and vegetables, accompanied by coarse salt or shallot-herb vinaigrette. Potée is a similar dish made of pork and sausages poached with the vegetables and accompanied by mustard. This recipe is a combination of the two classics, with chicken sausages added to the chicken.*

For poule au pot *often the chicken is filled with a garlic- and herb-flavored stuffing, such as Orzo, Garlic, and Walnut Stuffing (page 339) or Rosemary Stuffing (page 336). I find it easier to bake the stuffing separately to avoid having to truss the chicken.*

For a Mediterranean touch, serve the chicken with Italian Green Sauce (page 160), which is a popular accompaniment in Provence for poached chicken.

For a double-rich broth, use chicken stock instead of all of or part of the water for poaching the chicken.

3½-to 4½-pound frying or roasting chicken

salt and freshly ground pepper

1 large onion, whole

1 bay leaf

4 fresh thyme sprigs, or 1 teaspoon dried thyme, crumbled

about 2 quarts water, or mixed chicken stock and water

½ small green cabbage, cored and cut in half (optional)

6 medium carrots, peeled and cut in 2-inch lengths

4 small leeks, white and light green parts, cleaned, cut in 2-inch lengths

6 medium celery stalks, cut in 2-inch lengths

3 small turnips, quartered

2 medium garlic cloves, chopped

½ to ¾ pound chicken or turkey sausages

2 tablespoons chopped fresh parsley

Dijon mustard, coarse salt, or Shallot-Herb Vinaigrette (optional, page 358)

Remove fat from chicken. Put chicken in a large casserole or pot. Add neck and giblets, except liver. Sprinkle with salt and pepper. Add onion, bay leaf, and thyme sprigs and cover ingredients generously with water or stock. Bring to a boil. Skim excess foam from surface. Cover and cook over low heat 45 minutes.

Meanwhile, add cabbage to a large pot of boiling salted water and boil 5 minutes. Drain, rinse with cold water, and drain well. Cut each piece in 4 pieces.

After chicken has cooked 45 minutes, add carrots and cabbage and cook 15 minutes. Add leeks, celery, turnips, and garlic and cook over low heat 15 to 20 minutes or until vegetables are tender. Discard bay leaf and thyme sprigs. Skim fat from soup. Cut chicken in pieces, discarding skin. *Soup can be kept, covered, 2 days in refrigerator.*

Put sausages in a pan, cover with water, and bring just to a simmer. Cook over low heat for 15 minutes. Drain.

Reheat soup and add parsley. Taste and adjust seasoning. To serve as one course, slice sausages and serve them with chicken pieces and vegetables in soup. To serve in 2 courses, dice a few of the vegetables, add to soup, and serve as first course; then serve chicken pieces with sausages and remaining vegetables as main course, accompanied by coarse salt, mustard, or vinaigrette.

Makes about 6 servings

CHICKEN AND VEGETABLES
WITH KOREAN SESAME SAUCE

By adding fresh vegetables and a flavorful sauce to leftover roast chicken or turkey, you have an entirely new dish. The Korean sauce features sesame in two ways—aromatic sesame oil and a sprinkling of toasted sesame seeds—and is a wonderful complement to the chicken. You can make it mild or hot, according to the amount of chili sauce you like to add. The sauce is simple to prepare— you just mix the ingredients together.

For this dish I sauté exotic mushrooms, like oyster mushrooms or shiitakes, with other vegetables I have on hand—often carrots, zucchini, celery, and canned baby corn. Of course, you can use regular mushrooms, too. I add the chicken and sauce and serve this easy, colorful dish over steamed rice.

1 tablespoon sesame seeds
¾ cup sliced or diced carrot
2 tablespoons plus 2 teaspoons soy
  sauce
2 teaspoons Oriental sesame oil
2 tablespoons rice wine or dry sherry
½ to 1 teaspoon chili paste with garlic
  or hot sauce
2 medium garlic cloves, minced
1 tablespoon finely chopped green
  onion
1 teaspoon sugar

½ pound fresh shiitake or oyster
  mushrooms
2 tablespoons vegetable oil
2 medium zucchini, halved and cut in
  thin slices
¾ cup thinly sliced celery
2 cups coarsely shredded cooked
  chicken
10 ears canned baby corn, drained,
  rinsed
salt to taste
hot cooked rice

In a small skillet toast sesame seeds over medium heat 2 or 3 minutes or until lightly browned. Transfer to a plate.

Put carrot in a saucepan with water to cover, bring to a boil, and cook 5 minutes. Reserve 1 tablespoon cooking liquid and let cool. Drain carrot.

Combine soy sauce, sesame oil, rice wine, chili paste, garlic, green onion, sugar, and reserved tablespoon carrot cooking liquid. Mix well.

If using shiitake mushrooms, discard stems. Cut mushrooms in bite-size pieces. Heat 1 tablespoon oil in a skillet over high heat. Add mushrooms and sauté 3 minutes. Remove. Heat another tablespoon oil, add zucchini and celery, and sauté 2 minutes. Add chicken and corn and sprinkle with salt. Toss briefly over heat. Add sauce and remaining vegetables and heat until bubbling. Toss well. Spoon over rice. Sprinkle with toasted sesame seeds.

Makes 3 servings

QUICK AND SPICY CHICKEN MEATBALLS WITH MUSHROOMS AND PEPPERS

These chicken meatballs, spiced in the Middle Eastern style, are easy to make with ground chicken, which is becoming more available. Diced green peppers and sliced mushrooms give the tomato sauce an interesting flavor, color, and texture but you can vary the vegetables as you like. For example, if you add peas, diced red pepper, and cubes of cooked potato, the dish becomes albondigas a la andaluza, *or Andalusian meatballs, which I enjoyed in Granada, in southern Spain.* SEE PHOTO-GRAPH.

1 tablespoon unseasoned bread crumbs
4 medium garlic cloves, minced
¼ teaspoon cayenne pepper, plus a
   pinch for sauce
¼ teaspoon turmeric
1 teaspoon ground cumin
¼ to ½ teaspoon salt

10 ounces ground chicken (1⅓ cups)
2 tablespoons olive oil
½ green bell pepper, diced
8 ounces mushrooms, sliced
1 cup Fresh Tomato Sauce (page 369)
   or packaged

Mix bread crumbs with garlic, spices, and ¼ to ½ teaspoon salt, depending on whether you like food lightly or generously salted. Add to chicken and mix well. Make walnut-size balls, using 1 tablespoon mixture for each. Put on plate. Refrigerate 5 minutes.

Heat oil in skillet over medium-high heat. Add meatballs and brown them on all sides, taking 5 minutes. Transfer to paper towels with slotted spoon. Add green pepper to oil and sauté 2 minutes over medium heat. Add mushrooms and sauté 3 minutes.

Heat tomato sauce in medium saucepan; if it is very thick, dilute with 2 or 3 tablespoons water. Add meatballs, cover, and cook over low heat 5 minutes. Add vegetables, cover, and cook 5 more minutes. Season sauce to taste with cayenne pepper.

Makes 2 or 3 servings

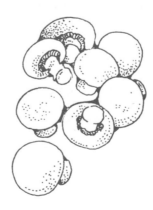

TURKEY BREAST SLICES WITH SUMMER VEGETABLES

The time-honored Mediterranean trio of eggplant, zucchini, and peppers makes a lively accompaniment for sautéed turkey breast slices. For this easy dish no sauce is needed, just a finishing touch à la provençale of garlic and fresh herbs.

1 small eggplant (about ¾ pound)
3 small zucchini (about ¾ pound)
1 large red bell pepper
5 to 6 tablespoons olive oil
salt and freshly ground pepper
cayenne pepper to taste
2 teaspoons chopped fresh thyme
　leaves, or ¾ teaspoon dried

1 pound turkey breast slices, ¼ inch
　thick, patted dry
1 large ripe tomato, cut in small dice
1 medium garlic clove, very finely
　minced
½ teaspoon dried oregano, crumbled
2 tablespoons chopped fresh parsley

Cut eggplant in ¾-inch dice. Slice zucchini in rounds about ¼ inch thick. Core pepper and cut in lengthwise strips about ¼ inch wide.

　Heat 2 tablespoons oil in a large, heavy skillet or sauté pan over medium heat. Add eggplant, salt, and pepper and sauté, stirring, about 3 or 4 minutes. Sprinkle with cayenne and half the thyme. Cover and cook over medium-low heat, stirring often, 7 to 10 minutes or until eggplant is tender. Transfer to a bowl.

　Add 1 tablespoon oil to skillet. Add zucchini, sprinkle with salt and pepper, and sauté over medium-high heat about 1 or 2 minutes per side or until tender. Remove with slotted spoon. Add 1 tablespoon oil if skillet is dry. Add red bell pepper and sauté about 5 minutes or until tender. Return eggplant and zucchini to skillet and cover.

　Heat 2 tablespoons oil in large, heavy skillet over high heat. Add turkey, in batches if necessary, sprinkle with salt and pepper, and sauté about 1 minute per side or until lightly browned and just tender. Transfer to a platter, cover, and keep warm in 250°F oven. Reserve oil in pan.

　Reheat vegetables. Remove from heat and add diced tomato and remaining thyme. Taste and adjust seasoning.

　Place turkey slices on plates, with vegetables alongside. Reheat skillet from turkey, add garlic and oregano, and pour over turkey. Sprinkle with parsley.

Makes 4 servings

TURKEY BREASTS
WITH PESTO AND POTATOES

When I was in the northern Italian port city of Genoa, I tasted the classic Genoese pasta al pesto, which contains potato slices mixed with the pasta, and I have loved the combination of potatoes and pesto ever since. Pesto is also wonderful with turkey and chicken, both in cold salads and in hot dishes like this one, in which sautéed turkey breast slices are coated with pesto and served with potatoes and zucchini. If you use red-skinned potatoes and yellow summer squash, this dish will be especially attractive. Serve this summery entree with ripe cherry tomatoes.

1½ to 2 pounds red-skinned potatoes,
   unpeeled
salt and freshly ground pepper
1 pound turkey breast slices (about ¼
   inch thick), patted dry

3 tablespoons olive or vegetable oil
1 pound yellow summer squash or
   green zucchini, sliced ¼ inch thick
Pesto (page 363)
sprigs of fresh basil, for garnish

Cover potatoes with water in a saucepan, add salt, and bring to a boil. Simmer until just tender, about 25 minutes. Remove. Cut in thick slices. Cover and keep warm.

Cut each turkey slice in 6 or 8 pieces, each with about 1½- or 2-inch sides. Put on paper towel-lined plate. Heat oil in a large, heavy skillet over medium-high heat. Sprinkle turkey with salt and pepper. Add half the turkey to pan and sauté, stirring often, about 1 minute per side, just until color changes throughout; cut a piece to check. Transfer turkey to bowl and keep warm. Repeat with remaining turkey. Add squash slices to pan, sprinkle with salt and pepper, and sauté 3 minutes or until just tender.

Add ¼ cup pesto to turkey and mix gently. Serve with potatoes and zucchini. Serve remaining pesto separately, for spooning on vegetables. Garnish with basil sprigs.

Makes 4 servings

TURKEY HASH
WITH VEGETABLES AND ROSEMARY

Hash is a casual, homey dish, made of diced cooked poultry or meat, usually combined with potato cubes and other vegetables and moistened with gravy or with a creamy sauce. It is a great way to put turkey leftovers to good use. An American favorite, it is also prepared in European countries, such as France, where it is called hachis. *Some serve this for breakfast or brunch.*

4 tablespoons (½ stick) butter, or 2 tablespoons vegetable oil and 2 tablespoons (¼ stick) butter
1 small onion, chopped
1 medium garlic clove, chopped
¼ cup all-purpose flour
2 cups turkey or chicken stock or broth
¼ cup dry sherry
¼ cup heavy cream, half-and-half, or milk (whole or skim)
2 teaspoons chopped fresh rosemary, or ¾ teaspoon dried

3 cups diced cooked turkey
1½ cups diced cooked potatoes
½ cup cooked or frozen peas, or mixed peas and carrots
½ cup cooked or frozen corn
1 cup diced smoked turkey
1 to 2 teaspoons Worcestershire sauce (optional)
Tabasco or other hot pepper sauce, or cayenne pepper to taste
salt and freshly ground pepper
⅓ cup chopped fresh parsley

Melt butter in a large skillet, add onion, and sauté 5 minutes or until softened. Stir in garlic, then flour and cook over low heat 2 minutes, stirring. Off the heat, stir in stock and sherry. Bring to a boil, stirring. Add cream and rosemary and bring to a simmer. If you prefer a thicker sauce, simmer it to desired thickness. Add cooked turkey, potatoes, peas, and corn and simmer, stirring often, 5 minutes. Stir in smoked turkey and heat 1 minute. If sauce is too thick at this point, stir in 1 or 2 tablespoons stock, milk, or water. Season to taste with Worcestershire and hot pepper sauce, salt, and pepper. Stir in parsley and serve.

Makes 4 to 6 servings

AFRICAN TURKEY AND PEANUT STEW WITH EGGPLANT AND OKRA

In West Africa this hearty dish is called groundnut stew. It is often made with chicken or with a mixture of chicken and beef, but it's also delicious with turkey. Generally it's served fiery hot. This version is moderately hot, but if you want a real scorcher, you can double the number of hot peppers and leave in the seeds. I prefer to simply serve hot sauce on the side for whoever wants some. The peanut butter, which is used to thicken the sauce, makes it smooth textured and rich tasting.

2 large onions
3 pounds turkey thighs (2 thighs)
1 quart water
salt and freshly ground pepper
4 medium slices fresh ginger, about ¼ inch thick
2 large carrots, peeled and cut in 2 or 3 pieces
2 tablespoons peanut or vegetable oil
6 to 8 jalapeño or serrano chilies, chopped

1 pound ripe tomatoes, chopped, or 1 (14- to 16-ounce) can plum tomatoes, drained and chopped
¼ cup tomato paste
1½ pounds boiling potatoes (4 potatoes)
1 medium eggplant (about 1 pound)
¾ pound fresh or frozen okra
½ cup chunk-style peanut butter, preferably unsweetened
cayenne pepper to taste

Cut ½ onion in 2 pieces and put in large casserole. Add turkey, water, salt, pepper, and ginger. Bring to a boil. Cover and simmer 30 minutes. Add carrots, immerse them in liquid, and simmer 30 more minutes. Remove carrots and turkey and reserve them. Discard onion and ginger. Pour broth from casserole and reserve. Skim fat from broth.

Chop remaining 1½ onions. Heat oil in casserole, add chopped onions, and sauté about 7 minutes over medium heat. Add chilies and sauté 2 minutes. Add tomatoes and tomato paste and cook 5 minutes, stirring often. Add 2 cups reserved turkey broth, salt, and pepper; return turkey to casserole. Cook 1 hour, turning once, or until turkey is tender.

Remove turkey. Remove skin with the aid of a paring knife. Discard bones, cartilage, and visible fat from turkey. Pull or cut meat into strips. Dice carrots. Skim fat from tomato sauce. Add 1¼ cups remaining turkey broth.

Peel and cut potatoes and eggplant in ¾- to 1-inch dice. If using fresh okra, trim stem ends. Bring tomato sauce to a simmer. Add potatoes, cover, and cook 10 minutes. Add eggplant and okra, cover, and cook, gently stirring occasionally, about 20 minutes or until vegetables are tender. Mix peanut butter with 1 cup of the sauce. Gently stir into casserole and bring to a simmer.

Stir turkey and carrots into sauce. If stew is too thick, add about ¼ cup broth. Cover and heat gently 10 minutes. Taste and adjust seasoning. Add cayenne if you would like a hotter sauce. *Stew can be kept, covered, 2 days in refrigerator. It thickens on standing; add a little more broth when reheating it.*

Makes 6 servings

—9—

Grilled and Broiled Chicken and Turkey

 Lately, grilled and barbecued poultry have become the best-selling menu items of many restaurants. The appetizing aroma and flavor of chicken grilled over an open fire cannot be duplicated by any other cooking method. A much quicker technique than braising or stewing, grilling has another advantage—of cooking almost entirely without fat. Grilling over charcoal or over a wood fire adds a smoky taste that complements the rich flavor and texture of the meat.

Grilling enhances the qualities of poultry—the skin turns into a crisp and attractive brown crust, the interior remains moist and succulent, and much of the fat melts and drips away. Fortunately, grilled poultry is easy to prepare at home. Chicken legs, thighs, and wings can be grilled with little effort; they just need to be turned about halfway through the cooking time. If you are grilling or broiling lean cuts of poultry, such as chicken or turkey breasts or game birds, you need to take extra care to prevent them from becoming too dry by using oil-based marinades, by basting, and by making sure not to overcook them. Still, these cuts have an important plus—a short cooking time—which makes grilled chicken breasts a frequent choice for speedy meals.

149

Grilled Chicken Breasts with
Garlic-Lemon Marinade
Grilled Chicken Breasts with Fresh Salsa
Grilled Chicken with Mushrooms
and Hot Herb Vinaigrette
Provençal Grilled Chicken with
Fresh Tomato Sauce and Green Beans
Grilled Chicken Breasts
with Easy Barbecue Sauce
Grilled Chicken Breasts with Garlic Puree
Grilled Chicken Breasts with Lemon-Herb Butter
Chicken Fajitas
Grilled Chicken with Italian Green Sauce
Middle Eastern Chicken Brochettes with Peppers
Mustard-Broiled Chicken
Turkish Broiled Chicken with Walnut-Garlic Sauce
Citrus Marinated Chicken
Grilled Chicken Breasts with Roquefort Sauce
Grilled Chicken Thighs with
Coriander-Cumin Marinade
Creole Grilled Turkey
Easy Broiled Turkey with Middle Eastern Marinade

To further add interest to grilled foods, you can prepare marinades in a variety of flavors, from the simple olive oil and lemon juice mixtures preferred in southern Europe and the eastern Mediterranean to the spicy blends of India to the soy-based marinades of the Far East. Please see the marinades in Chapter 17.

There is no point in preparing a delicate sauce to serve with barbecued poultry, since its taste would be overwhelmed. The smoky flavor of the grilled meat calls for assertive partners. These can be spicy barbecue sauces for marinating and basting, fiery salsas, pungent sweet-and-sour sauces, or boldly flavored chutneys for accompaniment. For these sauces garlic, rosemary, mint, herb vinegar, peppers, ginger, hot Dijon mustard, and other robust flavorings are ideal.

Besides being served on its own, grilled poultry is valuable as an ingredient in other dishes, such as grain and pasta entrees and salads. The grilled meat imparts a distinctive flavor accent to these types of dishes, and not as much meat is needed as when it is served as a main course. This makes possible more economical entrees, as well as nutritionally balanced menus with less meat and more vegetables and grains. In fact, this idea is time tested: Chinese cooks have been adding barbecued duck to soups and to rice and pasta dishes for ages, and barbecued or broiled chicken and turkey can be used the same way.

A useful piece of equipment to have in your *batterie de cuisine* is the ridged stovetop grill. These come in nonstick versions and are excellent for quickly preparing grilled poultry, especially thin boneless chicken breasts and thighs. The food is as easy to cook as if it were in a frying pan, yet can be cooked with no added fat. It's also easier to control the cooking with this type of pan than with a charcoal barbecue, and for this reason I prefer it for cooking turkey breast slices, which overcook easily. Moreover, this type of grill becomes hot in just a few minutes and is simpler to handle, because you're not leaning over extremely hot, smoky coals.

Charcoal grilling receives so much emphasis these days that it seems the broiler is being somewhat ignored. During most of the year the broiler and the stovetop grill are much more practical alternatives. They give similar results, though without the smoky flavor, and enable us to cook delicious chicken and turkey quickly and easily.

TIPS

✗ Chicken drumsticks, thighs, and especially legs, which consist of connected thighs and drumsticks, require a longer time than breasts to cook through.

✗ When grilling poultry, allow the coals to burn until they are covered with gray ash before putting the poultry on, and keep it far enough from the coals so the skin doesn't become too charred. About six inches is a good distance.

GRILLED CHICKEN BREASTS WITH GARLIC-LEMON MARINADE

The tangy, eastern Mediterranean marinade with a light garlic taste and a hint of cumin keeps the delicate chicken breast meat from becoming dry and enhances but does not overpower its flavor. This light dish is great for summer barbecues. Alongside the chicken, barbecue some red and green peppers and large mushroom caps and serve them as accompaniments.

6 chicken breast halves, with skin and
 bone (about 3 pounds)
¼ cup olive oil
2 medium garlic cloves, minced
2 tablespoons strained fresh lemon
 juice

1 teaspoon freshly ground black
 pepper
1 teaspoon ground cumin
½ teaspoon salt

Put chicken on plate. Combine remaining ingredients in a small bowl and pour evenly over both sides of chicken. Rub spice mixture into chicken. Let stand at room temperature while heating coals or refrigerate up to 2 hours.

Set chicken on an oiled rack about 5 or 6 inches above glowing coals, or on broiler rack about 4 inches from heat. Grill, covered, or broil about 10 minutes per side, or until thickest part of meat near bone is no longer pink when cut. Serve immediately.

Makes 6 servings

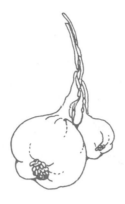

GRILLED CHICKEN BREASTS WITH FRESH SALSA

Mexican salsa cruda, or uncooked salsa, makes a zesty and colorful accompaniment for grilled chicken with no added fat. In keeping with the Mexican theme, the chicken is seasoned with a cumin-oregano mixture before being grilled. If you have time, let the chicken marinate in the seasoning mixture for a half-hour for extra flavor. Serve the chicken with green beans and rice or warm tortillas.

Fresh Tomato Salsa (page 362)
4 boneless chicken breasts, with skin
 (total 1¼ to 1½ pounds)
2 tablespoons olive oil

salt and freshly ground pepper
1 teaspoon ground cumin
1 teaspoon dried oregano, crumbled

Bring salsa to room temperature while preparing chicken. Rub chicken breasts with olive oil and sprinkle them on both sides with salt, pepper, cumin, and oregano. Rub spices into chicken.

Set chicken on oiled rack about 5 or 6 inches above glowing coals, on broiler rack about 4 inches from heat, or on heated ridged stovetop grill pan over medium-high heat. Grill or broil about 6 or 7 minutes per side, or until color is no longer pink; cut in thickest part to check.

Serve hot, with salsa.

Makes 4 servings

GRILLED CHICKEN WITH MUSHROOMS AND HOT HERB VINAIGRETTE

Vinaigrette, the traditional French salad dressing, has plenty of uses in the modern kitchen beyond seasoning lettuce. One new application of the classic dressing, popular in modern American cuisine, is as a marinade for chicken before it is grilled. Another use is as a light sauce to moisten grilled poultry and vegetables. In this recipe it is used both ways.

4 chicken breast halves, with skin and bone (about 2 pounds)
Herb Marinade/Vinaigrette (page 351)
2 red or green bell peppers, quartered (optional)

1 pound large mushroom caps
cilantro (fresh coriander) or parsley sprigs, for garnish

Put chicken on plate. Set aside 3 tablespoons marinade for use as a sauce. Pour all but 1 tablespoon of remaining marinade evenly over both sides of chicken. Rub mixture into chicken. Let stand at room temperature while heating coals or refrigerate up to 2 hours.

Set chicken on oiled rack about 5 to 6 inches above glowing coals or on oiled broiler rack about 5 or 6 inches from heat source. Grill, covered, or broil about 10 minutes per side, or until thickest part of meat near bone is no longer pink when cut. For the last 10 minutes of grilling, add pepper pieces to grill, skin side down, and add mushrooms. Brush vegetables lightly with the tablespoon of remaining marinade. Grill them until tender, about 10 to 12 minutes.

Warm the reserved dressing slightly in a very small saucepan and pour over chicken. Serve immediately, with mushrooms, peppers, and herb sprigs.

Makes 4 servings

PROVENÇAL GRILLED CHICKEN WITH FRESH TOMATO SAUCE AND GREEN BEANS

Both the chicken and the sauce are seasoned liberally with fragrant herbs of the south of France— thyme, rosemary, and basil. The sauce is cooked only a few minutes so it keeps the fresh flavor of ripe tomatoes. If you can get the thin French green beans called haricots verts, *they are perfect with the chicken but any good green or wax beans will be fine. Serve crusty French or Italian bread with the chicken, and a green salad and perhaps some French goat cheese afterwards.*

6 chicken breast halves, with skin and bone (about 3 pounds)
Provençal Garlic and Herb Marinade (page 351)
1¼ to 1½ pounds green beans or *haricots verts*, trimmed
1½ cups Fresh Tomato Sauce (page 369)
1½ teaspoons chopped fresh rosemary, or ½ teaspoon dried, crumbled

1½ teaspoons fresh thyme leaves, or ½ teaspoon dried, crumbled
2 tablespoons chopped fresh basil, or 2 teaspoons dried, crumbled
fresh basil and thyme sprigs, for garnish (optional)

Put chicken on plate. Pour marinade evenly over both sides of chicken and rub into chicken. Let stand at room temperature while heating coals or refrigerate up to 2 hours.

Set chicken on oiled rack about 5 or 6 inches above glowing coals or on oiled broiler rack about 5 or 6 inches from heat source. Grill, covered, or broil about 10 minutes per side, or until thickest part of meat near bone is no longer pink when cut.

Meanwhile, cook beans in a large pan of boiling salted water until just tender, about 5 to 7 minutes. Drain well. In a small saucepan, bring tomato sauce to a boil. Stir in herbs.

Serve chicken with tomato sauce and beans. Garnish with herb sprigs.

Makes 6 servings

GRILLED CHICKEN BREASTS WITH EASY BARBECUE SAUCE

These chicken breasts prepared in the traditional American style are perfect for Fourth of July barbecues. Barbecue some sweet corn, halved Maui onions, and bell peppers at the same time as the chicken, and your accompaniments are all ready. Begin the meal with a simple salad of ripe tomatoes, serve ice cream or brownies for dessert, and you'll have an easy to prepare feast.

4 chicken breast halves, with skin and
  bones (about 2 pounds)
1 tablespoon vegetable or olive oil

salt and freshly ground pepper
cayenne pepper to taste
Easy Barbecue Sauce (page 373)

Preheat broiler with rack about 6 inches from heat source; or prepare grill. Brush chicken with the oil on both sides and sprinkle with salt, pepper, and cayenne pepper.

Put chicken breasts on oiled rack above glowing coals or on hot broiler rack. Grill or broil about 10 to 12 minutes per side; during grilling, quickly brush chicken every few minutes with sauce. Chicken is done when tender when pierced with a thin, sharp knife and when juices are clear, not pink. Serve hot.

Makes 4 servings

GRILLED CHICKEN BREASTS WITH GARLIC PUREE

The first time I tasted garlic puree, it was made by Master Chef Fernand Chambrette, who was my teacher at La Varenne Cooking School in Paris. It was so delicious, I couldn't stop eating it! I find this puree of cooked garlic one of the best partners for grilled chicken. Smooth and flavorful, it stands up well to the taste of the grilled chicken, which is seasoned simply with thyme in the French manner. Since the puree is white, serve colorful accompaniments, such as broccoli, green beans, and sliced tomatoes.

2 medium whole heads garlic
1 tablespoon butter
salt and freshly ground pepper
3 to 4 tablespoons heavy cream
4 boneless chicken breast halves or
  boneless thighs, with skin (total 1¼
  to 1½ pounds)

about 2 teaspoons vegetable oil
¾ teaspoon dried thyme, crumbled

Separate garlic heads into cloves and peel them. Put them in a small heavy saucepan of cold water, bring to a boil, and cook 5 minutes. Drain well. In a heavy, medium saucepan, heat butter over very low heat. Add garlic, salt, and pepper, and cook, stirring often, about 20 minutes, or until nearly all moisture evaporates. Do not let garlic burn.

Puree garlic in a food processor or blender, adding a little cream if necessary; or mash it with a fork. Return it to saucepan. *Garlic puree can be kept, covered, 1 day in refrigerator.*

Prepare a charcoal grill or heat broiler with rack about 4 inches from heat source; or heat a ridged stovetop grill pan over medium-high heat.

Rub chicken with oil. Sprinkle with thyme, salt, and pepper on both sides. Set chicken on an oiled rack above glowing coals, on broiler rack, or on grill, with skin facing down. Grill or broil until meat feels springy, about 5 to 7 minutes per side. To check whether chicken is done, cut into thickest part with tip of a sharp knife; color should be white, not pink.

Reheat garlic puree over low heat, stirring. Gradually stir in 2 or 3 tablespoons cream and heat just until hot. Season to taste with salt and pepper. Serve puree alongside chicken.

Makes 4 servings

GRILLED CHICKEN BREASTS WITH LEMON-HERB BUTTER

Herb-seasoned butter is the classic European and American accompaniment for grilled chicken. As the chicken is removed from the grill, the butter melts into it and gives it a luscious flavor. I prefer using seasoned butters with lean boneless skinless chicken breasts, which I grill quickly on a ridged stovetop grill. It makes an elegant, delicate presentation. Chefs in France usually bring the seasoned butter to room temperature and spoon a little onto the grilled chicken so it melts at once, rather than forming the butter into cylinders, freezing it, and slicing it frozen, and I think they are right.

In addition to the lemon-herb butter, a lemon and thyme marinade flavors this chicken and helps keep it moist during grilling. If you like, grill some mushroom caps and bell peppers as accompaniments, or serve the chicken with crisp-tender sugar-snap peas.

4 boneless chicken breast halves or
   boneless thighs, with skin (total 1¼
   to 1½ pounds)
Lemon and Thyme Marinade (page
   352)

Lemon-Herb Butter

¼ cup (½ stick) butter, softened
1 teaspoon strained fresh lemon juice
½ teaspoon grated lemon rind
2 teaspoons fresh thyme, or ¾
   teaspoon dried, crumbled

1 tablespoon snipped chives (optional)
1 tablespoon chopped fresh parsley
1 small shallot, minced
salt and freshly ground pepper

salt and freshly ground pepper
lemon wedges and thyme or parsley
   sprigs, for garnish

Put chicken in a shallow dish large enough to hold pieces in one layer. Add marinade and turn chicken pieces to coat them with marinade. Cover and marinate in refrigerator up to 6 hours, turning from time to time.

For the lemon-herb butter, beat butter in a small bowl until very soft. Beat in lemon juice gradually. Stir in lemon rind, thyme, chives, parsley, and shallot. Season with salt and pepper to taste. Cover and refrigerate 1 or 2 hours so flavors blend, or up to 1 day.

Bring herb butter to room temperature. Prepare a charcoal grill or heat broiler with rack about 4 inches from heat source; or heat a ridged stovetop grill pan over medium-high heat.

Remove chicken from marinade and discard marinade. Sprinkle chicken with salt and pepper on both sides. Set chicken on an oiled rack above glowing coals, or on oiled broiler rack or stovetop grill, with skin facing down. Grill or broil until meat feels springy, about 5 to 8 minutes per side. To check whether chicken is done, cut into thickest part with tip of a sharp knife; color should be white, not pink.

Transfer chicken to plates. Top each piece with about 1 teaspoon herb butter. Garnish with lemon wedges and herb sprigs. Serve immediately, with remaining herb butter.

Makes 4 servings

CHICKEN FAJITAS

Fajitas (pronounced fa-HEE-tas), a Mexican-inspired dish created in Texas, are fun food, really: fun to cook, fun to serve, fun to eat. They are a great way to make use of lean chicken breasts. Chicken fajitas have become so popular in recent years that upscale markets in California sell the chicken mixed with pepper strips and onions as ready-to-cook fajitas.

Although this is a casual sort of dish, it looks elegant when served, with a platter of grilled red and green peppers topped with strips of grilled chicken breast, another platter of hot tortillas, bowls of herb-flecked tomato salsa, and plates of avocado slices.

To save time, serve ready-made salsa instead of homemade. If you wish, you can also serve sour cream as an accompaniment.

2 pounds boneless and skinless
   chicken breasts
Mexican Marinade (page 352)
2 large onions, peeled and cut in
   rounds ¼ to ⅜ inch thick
about 1 tablespoon vegetable oil
salt to taste
2 red and 2 green bell peppers, grilled
   and peeled (page 408), cut in strips
   about ½ inch wide

12 flour tortillas, heated according to
   package instructions
3 ripe avocados, sliced thin; or
   Guacamole (page 365)
1½ cups thick Fresh Tomato Salsa
   (page 369, variation)

Pound the chicken until about ⅜ inch thick. Put in a shallow dish. Pour marinade over chicken, and rub on both sides. Cover and refrigerate 1 hour or up to overnight.

Preheat broiler with rack about 4 inches from heat; or prepare charcoal or ridged stovetop grill. Brush onion slices with oil. Grill or broil them about 5 minutes per side or until done to your taste.

Sprinkle chicken with salt. Grill or broil chicken on oiled rack about 4 inches from heat or on stovetop grill over medium-high heat 3 to 4 minutes per side, brushing once with marinade just after turning over; chicken is done when no longer pink when cut. Transfer to a board and cut each breast crosswise in 5 or 6 strips. Put pepper strips and onions on a platter. Top with chicken slices.

Serve with tortillas, avocado, and salsa. To eat, spoon chicken and grilled vegetables into tortillas, top with avocado and salsa to taste, and roll up.

Makes 6 servings

NOTE: If necessary, broil or grill chicken in 2 batches and keep warm.

GRILLED CHICKEN
WITH ITALIAN GREEN SAUCE

In Italy green sauce is made by pureeing herbs with a little olive oil and garlic, as in making pesto, which itself is a type of green sauce. Traditionally green sauce is served with boiled meats, and is designed to perk up chicken that was cooked for soup. I find its zesty flavor stands up wonderfully to grilled chicken as well. My favorite accompaniment for this chicken in summer is corn on the cob.

Most versions of Italian green sauce use chopped anchovies; for this quick version, I use anchovy paste, but you can omit it and the sauce will still have plenty of flavor from the capers, lemon juice, basil, and garlic.

I like to use a ridged stovetop grill for this chicken but you can also use a broiler or barbecue. If your stovetop grill is small and you have only one, cook the chicken breasts in several batches and keep the cooked ones warm, covered, in the oven.

Italian Green Sauce

1 small garlic clove
½ cup parsley sprigs
1 tablespoon capers, rinsed
¼ cup cubed onion
3 tablespoons plus 1 teaspoon extra-
  virgin olive oil

½ teaspoon anchovy paste
1 or 2 tablespoons chopped fresh basil
1 tablespoon strained fresh lemon
  juice, or more to taste
salt and freshly ground black pepper

4 boneless chicken breast halves, with
  skin (about 1½ pounds)

In a food processor chop garlic, add parsley, and chop fine. Add capers and onion, and chop together with on/off turns. Transfer to a bowl. In a cup, stir 3 tablespoons oil into the anchovy paste until well blended; add to parsley mixture. Stir in basil, lemon juice, and plenty of black pepper. Taste, and add salt and more lemon juice if needed.

Heat 1 large or 2 small ridged stovetop grills over medium-high heat. Add chicken skin side down. Grill 7 minutes, pressing firmly on chicken with slotted spatula a few times. Rub lightly with olive oil and turn over. Grill 7 more minutes or until meat has changed color throughout; cut to check.

Serve chicken with a spoonful of sauce on the side. Serve remaining sauce separately.

Makes 4 servings

MIDDLE EASTERN CHICKEN BROCHETTES WITH PEPPERS

Colorful brochettes or kabobs of skewered chicken with peppers, onions, and mushrooms are a specialty of the Middle East. In Lebanese restaurants, these are served with pita and fresh mint leaves. This dish reminds me of dinners I've enjoyed in Tel Aviv restaurants, where you get long skewers of sizzling grilled chicken and a large flat type of pita that resembles lavosh (Armenian flatbread). The brochettes are served with a hot sauce (such as Jalapeño Garlic Chutney, page 366) for those who want it. On the menu there also is foie gras, or rich duck liver, grilled on skewers, an unforgettable treat.

If you have time, let the chicken sit in the refrigerator with its savory marinade of lemon juice, pepper, oregano, and olive oil for a few hours so it absorbs extra flavor. Either present the chicken skewers on a bed of parsley and mint sprigs, or take the hot cubes of chicken and vegetables off the skewer and put them in a pita, add some fresh mint leaves, and have a wonderful sandwich. Another attractive way to serve these colorful entree skewers is on a bed of rice. SEE PHOTOGRAPH.

1½ pounds boneless chicken breasts,
 turkey tenderloins, or turkey steaks
Mediterranean Marinade (page 353)
1 red or green bell pepper
1 medium onion, red or brown

salt
12 small or medium mushrooms
6 cherry tomatoes (optional)
fresh mint leaves, chopped parsley,
 and pita bread, for serving

Remove skin and cut each chicken breast half in 6 or 7 equal pieces with about 1¼-inch sides. Put in a bowl. Add marinade. Cover and marinate 2 to 6 hours in refrigerator. If using bamboo skewers, soak them in cold water 30 minutes so they won't burn.

Cut pepper in squares of about same size as chicken. Quarter onion lengthwise and cut each piece in 2. Sprinkle chicken with salt. Thread the chicken pieces on skewers with vegetables. Brush chicken and vegetables with marinade. If using bamboo skewers, put foil on ends to prevent burning.

Put in broiler about 4 inches from heat, on oiled rack above glowing coals or on ridged stovetop grill. Grill or broil 10 to 12 minutes, turning often. To check, cut into a large piece; chicken should not be pink inside.

Serve on a platter with mint leaves and chopped parsley. Accompany with pita.

Makes 2 or 3 servings

MUSTARD-BROILED CHICKEN

This is an easy version of the dish the French call poulet à la diable, *or devil's chicken. The reason for this name is that the chicken is coated entirely with hot mustard and cayenne pepper before being grilled.*

1 tablespoon Dijon mustard
2 boneless chicken breast halves
   (about ¾ pound total)
salt and freshly ground pepper

cayenne pepper to taste
about 1½ teaspoons unseasoned bread
   crumbs

Spread mustard on both sides of chicken. Cover and refrigerate 10 minutes to 2 hours.
   Preheat broiler with rack about 4 inches from heat source. Lightly oil a broilerproof pan. Sprinkle chicken with salt, pepper, and cayenne and put in pan, skin side up. Broil 6 minutes per side. Turn skin side up. Sprinkle lightly with bread crumbs and broil 1 or 2 more minutes or until browned. Serve immediately, with juices from pan spooned over chicken.

Makes 2 servings

TURKISH BROILED CHICKEN
WITH WALNUT-GARLIC SAUCE

Chicken with sauces of ground nuts are popular in much of Mediterranean Europe—in southern France, Italy, Turkey, and Spain. Serve this chicken and its rich, garlicky sauce with rice pilaf, a specialty of Turkey, and with a diced tomato, cucumber, and bell pepper salad.

6 chicken breast halves, with skin and
   bone (about 3 pounds)
2 tablespoons vegetable oil
1 tablespoon strained fresh lemon juice

salt and freshly ground pepper
Walnut-Garlic Sauce (page 364)
lemon wedges and parsley sprigs, for
   garnish

Put chicken on a plate. Combine oil and lemon juice in a small bowl and pour evenly over both sides of chicken. Sprinkle chicken with salt and pepper.
   Set chicken on an oiled rack about 5 or 6 inches above glowing coals, or on broiler rack

about 6 inches from heat. Grill, covered, or broil about 10 minutes per side, or until thickest part of meat near bone is no longer pink when cut. Serve immediately, accompanied by sauce, lemon wedges, and parsley sprigs.

Makes 6 servings

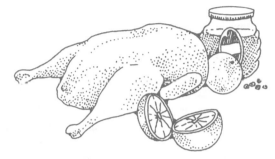

CITRUS MARINATED CHICKEN

A Japanese-inspired marinade of orange and lemon juices, soy sauce, and a touch of spice gives grilled or broiled chicken breasts an intriguing, delicious flavor. I love this chicken garnished with orange slices and green onions, and accompanied by asparagus and white rice. You may want to serve Japanese pickled ginger on the side.

¼ cup soy sauce
¼ cup strained, fresh orange juice
2 tablespoons strained, fresh lemon
  juice
1 tablespoon vegetable oil
1 tablespoon honey
1 teaspoon grated orange rind

½ teaspoon grated lemon rind
1 medium shallot, minced
1 teaspoon ground ginger
¼ teaspoon ground cloves
pinch of pepper
4 chicken breast halves, with skin and
  bones (about 2 pounds)

In a shallow dish mix soy sauce, orange juice, lemon juice, oil, honey, grated orange and lemon rinds, shallot, ginger, cloves, and pepper. Add chicken pieces and turn them over in mixture. Rub mixture thoroughly into chicken. Cover and refrigerate chicken for 2 hours or up to overnight, turning occasionally.

Preheat broiler or grill with rack about 6 inches from heat source. Remove chicken from marinade, reserving marinade, and put chicken on hot broiler rack or oiled rack of grill. Broil chicken, or grill, covered, above glowing coals, turning and brushing twice with marinade, for 10 minutes. Broil or grill about 10 more minutes or until thickest part of meat near bone is no longer pink when cut. Serve immediately.

Makes 4 servings

GRILLED CHICKEN BREASTS WITH ROQUEFORT SAUCE

At Parisian restaurants I've enjoyed sautéed veal with Roquefort sauce, but I find the same sauce is an even better match with grilled chicken. The Roquefort melts easily and smoothly into the sauce, but it's good to reserve a little to sprinkle on top. I like pasta bowties or other pretty shapes as an accompaniment—they taste great with the rich sauce. Keep side dishes simple; crisp-tender broccoli, cauliflower, or zucchini are good choices.

1 tablespoon butter
2 medium shallots, minced
⅓ cup dry white wine
1 cup heavy cream
¾ cup crumbled Roquefort cheese

salt and freshly ground pepper
4 boneless chicken breast halves, with skin (1¼ to 1½ pounds)
1 to 2 tablespoons vegetable oil

Melt butter in a medium saucepan. Add the shallots and cook them over low heat, stirring, for 2 minutes. Add the wine and simmer the mixture, stirring often, until only about 2 tablespoons liquid remain. Stir in the cream and cook over medium-high heat, stirring often, for 7 minutes, or until sauce is thick enough to coat a spoon. Whisk in ½ cup Roquefort cheese and cook sauce over low heat, whisking, just until it is smooth. Add pepper to taste.

Prepare a charcoal grill or heat broiler with rack about 4 inches from heat source; or heat a ridged stovetop grill pan over medium-high heat. Rub chicken with oil and sprinkle with salt and pepper on both sides.

Set chicken on an oiled rack above glowing coals, on broiler rack, or on stovetop grill, with skin facing down. Grill or broil until meat feels springy, about 5 to 7 minutes per side. To check whether chicken is done, cut into thickest part with tip of a sharp knife; color should be white, not pink.

Set chicken on plates and spoon a little sauce over it. Sprinkle with a little more Roquefort. Serve any remaining sauce separately.

Makes 4 servings

GRILLED CHICKEN THIGHS
WITH CORIANDER-CUMIN MARINADE

Garlic, coriander, and cumin lend character to this Egyptian marinade, which is ideal for the dark meat of chicken. Chicken thighs can be grilled or broiled either on the bone, or boneless. For grilling over charcoal, I find meat on the bone comes out more moist and tasty but boneless thighs are delicious in the broiler or on a stovetop grill. Grilled eggplant slices, rice pilaf sprinkled with toasted pine nuts, and a salad of diced tomato, cucumber, and green onion are my favorite accompaniments for this chicken. SEE PHOTOGRAPH.

3 to 3½ pounds chicken legs and
  thighs
¼ cup olive oil
2 tablespoons grated onion

2 teaspoons ground coriander
2 teaspoons ground cumin
½ teaspoon cayenne pepper
¼ teaspoon salt

Put chicken on a plate. Combine remaining ingredients in a small bowl and pour evenly over both sides of chicken. Rub spice mixture into chicken. Let stand at room temperature while heating coals or refrigerate up to 2 hours.

Set chicken on rack about 5 to 6 inches above glowing coals. Cover and grill about 15 to 18 minutes per side for thighs, or 18 to 22 minutes per side for legs with thighs attached, or until thickest part of meat near bone is no longer pink when cut. Serve immediately.

Makes 5 or 6 servings

CREOLE GRILLED TURKEY

This is a turkey take-off on a Creole dish called grillades and grits that I enjoyed for brunch at the Commander's Palace restaurant in New Orleans, where it was prepared with veal. Traditional versions are made with beef as well, and are often fried.

Serve the turkey in the customary manner with Creole Sauce, accompanied by buttered grits or with rice or mashed potatoes. Packages of quick-cooking grits are available at many supermarkets.

1 medium garlic clove, minced
¼ teaspoon cayenne pepper
1 teaspoon paprika
½ teaspoon dried thyme, crumbled

½ teaspoon dried rosemary
2 tablespoons vegetable oil
1 pound turkey breast slices
salt
1½ cups Creole Sauce (page 370)

Combine garlic, cayenne pepper, paprika, thyme, rosemary, and oil. Pour over turkey breast slices in a shallow dish and rub mixture well into the meat. Cover and marinate in refrigerator 2 to 4 hours.

A short time before serving, heat sauce. Cover and keep it warm over low heat.

Heat 1 large or 2 small ridged stovetop grills over medium-high heat; or heat broiler with rack about 3 inches from heat source. Sprinkle turkey slices with salt. Grill or broil turkey about 2 minutes per side or until meat has changed color throughout; cut to check. Serve slices whole, or cut each in thin strips. Spoon some sauce onto each plate and top with turkey. Serve remaining sauce separately.

Makes 4 servings

EASY BROILED TURKEY
WITH MIDDLE EASTERN MARINADE

The lean meat of turkey benefits from being soaked in a savory olive oil marinade before being broiled or grilled, and even though it absorbs a little oil, it remains a low-fat main course. The cumin and olive oil marinade gives turkey a zesty flavor, and makes this quick recipe a perfect choice for dinner in a hurry. It tastes good on its own with just lemon wedges for garnish, but for a more festive entree, top each portion with a small dab of Cilantro Butter or Jalapeño Garlic Chutney. Serve the turkey with sautéed peppers, eggplant, or other vegetables in season and with cooked rice.

For this recipe the easiest cut to use is turkey breast slices. Or you can buy turkey tenderloins— long strips cut from turkey breasts—and use a sharp knife to cut them in diagonal slices. This takes a few extra minutes but results in a tastier dish.

1 to 1¼ pounds turkey breast slices,
  about ¼ to ½ inch thick
Middle Eastern Marinade (page 353)
Cilantro Butter (page 368) or Jalapeño-
  Garlic Chutney (page 366) (optional)

salt and freshly ground pepper
lemon wedges

Put turkey in a shallow dish and pour marinade over it. Rub marinade into slices. Cover and refrigerate at least 15 minutes or up to overnight. If serving Cilantro Butter, bring it to room temperature.

Preheat broiler with rack about 3 inches from heat, or heat ridged stovetop grill. Sprinkle turkey with salt and pepper on both sides. Broil or grill turkey for 3 minutes. Turn over and continue broiling about 2 minutes or until just tender when pierced with a sharp knife; do not overcook or meat will be dry.

Top with a spoonful of Cilantro Butter or a little chutney, if desired. Serve immediately, with lemon wedges.

Makes 4 servings

10

Roasted Chicken and Turkey

ROAST CHICKEN

A golden brown, juicy roast chicken is, in my opinion, one of the best entrees for a weekend family supper or a dinner party. Yet several of my friends told me they don't often roast poultry because they find it is too much trouble, involving frequent basting, bulky handling, and time-consuming carving.

I reminded my friends that even when cooked in the old-fashioned manner, roast chicken has long been one of the easiest main courses to make. When I was growing up, my mother served it every Friday for dinner because she considered it a most convenient dish. She seasoned the chicken and put it in the oven to cook slowly at medium heat, and meanwhile prepared an appetizer and side dishes. The result was a festive main course that required little effort.

What finally enabled me to convince my skeptical friends that roast chicken can fit perfectly into their busy schedules were three tips for shortening the roasting time of chicken that I learned when I studied cooking in France.

169

Roast Chicken with Aromatic Red Wine Sauce
Roast Chicken with Potatoes, Bell Peppers,
and Rosemary
Curry Roasted Chicken with Pineapple
and Apples
Polish Roast Chicken with Dill Bread Stuffing
Spanish Roast Chicken with Sherry
Chicken Seasoned Under the Skin
with Tarragon Butter
Honey-Glazed Roast Chicken
Roast Marinated Chicken with Cilantro
and Garlic
Chicken Stuffed with Figs, Almonds, and Rice
Roast Chicken with Madeira, Asparagus,
and Baby Onions
Lemon-Lime Chicken with Sweet Potatoes

Roast Chicken with Rosemary Stuffing
Casserole-Roasted Chicken with Tarragon
Easy Tandoori Chicken
Baked Chicken with White Beans, Sage,
and Tomato Sauce
Middle Eastern Baked Chicken with Potatoes
and Onions
Chicken with Chickpeas, Garlic, and Cayenne
Roast Turkey with Pepper, Corn,
and Cilantro Stuffing
Roast Turkey with Apple-Apricot Stuffing
Roast Turkey with Herbed Onion Stuffing
Roast Turkey with Hazelnut-Mushroom Stuffing
Roast Turkey Breast with Sage and Thyme
Roast Turkey Breast with Cumin and Peppers

First, a chicken can be roasted faster by simply using high heat. French chefs like this technique, since it produces succulent meat and beautifully browned, delicately crisp skin. Although chefs recommend trussing, or tying the chicken in a neat shape, I skip this step for quick meals.

Second, small chickens cook more quickly than big ones, and so to save time I choose 3- to 3½-pound fryers rather than larger roasting chickens. If you need more servings, you can roast two birds together in the time it takes to roast one.

The third way to shorten a chicken's cooking time is to roast it without stuffing, since the oven's heat takes long to penetrate dense meat- or bread-based stuffing. It's quicker to bake this type of stuffing in a separate casserole.

Basting is not crucial for chicken because its skin provides enough protection as it roasts. But if you're in the kitchen anyway, spooning the pan juices over the breast meat once or twice will further ensure that it does not become dry.

Many Western cooks prefer to season chicken for roasting only lightly, so the natural taste of the chicken comes through. In India, however, tandoori chicken is first marinated with garlic, fresh ginger, and spices, which beautifully complement the chicken and produce a wonderful dish. A Middle Eastern cilantro marinade, or a mixture of cumin and turmeric, also gives roast chicken a deliciously different flavor.

Perfectly roasted chickens and smaller birds are so flavorful they can be served even at a three-star meal in Paris without a sauce. One of the famous specialties of Alain Senderens, chef of one of France's best restaurants, is a roasted squab served simply on a bed of slowly cooked leeks.

For special occasions when you would like a sauce, the delicious pan juices can be easily turned into one. All you do is skim the fat from the roasting pan and then heat the juices with a little wine or chicken broth. This is called "deglazing." (For more about deglazing, see page 300.) Spoon the sauce over any accompanying rice, pasta, or vegetables or serve it with the chicken for extra flavor.

Before carving a roast chicken or any roast bird, cover it loosely and let it stand about 10 to 20 minutes, so it reabsorbs some of its juices. Carving chicken is easy, since it's a small, tender bird. You simply cut off the thighs, with the drumsticks attached, at the joint. Next you cut off the breast and wing portions. Poultry shears make this a very simple task, but it's not difficult to do with a sturdy sharp knife.

From a nutritional standpoint, roast chicken is naturally light. Classic recipes, however, recommend rubbing the chicken with butter before roasting. Diet books go to the other extreme. They require removing the bird's skin before roasting to reduce calories. Recent research indicates that this practice makes no difference in the bird's caloric content compared to roasting and then removing the skin. I prefer a middle-of-the-road approach—I leave the skin on to protect the meat from drying, and I rarely add butter.

Whether to set the chicken on a rack in the roasting pan is a matter of choice. Roasting the bird on a rack permits the heat to circulate more evenly around the bird and keeps it above the fat that escapes, so the bird cooks from the dry oven heat and does not fry in the fat. Most chefs I know, however, prefer to roast chickens directly in the pan, as the contact with the pan produces more flavorful juices to use in a sauce. In either case, a low-sided roasting pan is better than a deep one because it lets the bird brown better.

A special type of roast chicken is casserole-roasted chicken, also known as chicken *en cocotte*. For this technique, the whole chicken is browned in a little oil or butter on top of the stove, then is covered and baked in the oven. The result is a combination of roasting and steaming, which produces wonderfully moist, rich-tasting meat.

Instead of roasting a chicken whole, you can roast chicken pieces. The cooking time is even briefer, and the chicken is easier to serve, as there is no need for carving.

Almost every vegetable goes well with roast chicken, so choose whatever is at the height of its season. Roast or baked potatoes are great with chicken. I love sugar-snap peas or green beans in summer, asparagus in spring, and carrots year-round. A simple green salad also makes a tasty accompaniment, whether the chicken is served hot or cold.

ROAST TURKEY

A whole roast turkey is an impressive main course, and we all enjoy it for Thanksgiving. Now that so many of us are nutrition conscious and appreciate leaner foods, it's a good idea to serve roast turkey for festive occasions or large gatherings throughout the year. In Europe it's popular for other holidays. In France and Italy, for example, a roast turkey, often with a chestnut or sausage stuffing, is a favorite Christmas dinner.

Seasoning the turkey affects mainly the skin. The best way to add flavor to a whole roast turkey is to add a stuffing and serve the slices of turkey with a sauce made from the delicious roasting juices. (For more on stuffings and sauces, see pages 323 and 349). For Thanksgiving, when people are in a nostalgic mood, it's best to stick to familiar, traditional foods. Still, the festive menu is more exciting with one or two new elements, such as Pepper, Corn and Cilantro Stuffing (page 327) or Spicy Sausage Stuffing (page 331), which features an Indian spice mixture. You can always rely on familiar accompaniments to keep the spirit of the holiday.

A quick, easy, and tasty turkey dinner for the holidays might seem an unrealistic expectation, but that is exactly what some of us wish for when turkey season comes around. Today there are alternatives to spending hours roasting and basting the holiday bird. Fast, festive meals can be planned around turkey breasts, which are now easy to find at the supermarket.

Turkey breast roasts are not only much quicker to roast but also easier to handle than a whole bird. Their great advantage is that the breast meat comes out moister because it doesn't have to sit in the oven and wait for the leg meat to cook to the right temperature. And, of course, breast meat is low in fat. Depending on how many people you want to serve, you can buy a whole or half breast.

Turkey breast roasts are available on the bone and boneless, but I prefer to roast the turkey on the bone for moister meat. Boneless turkey breasts are better braised because this technique prevents them from being overly dry.

TIP

✗ A whole chicken is done when its internal temperature is 180°F. To check, insert a regular meat thermometer or instant-read thermometer into the thick part of the thigh next to the body. This method works best with large chickens; in small ones it's difficult to obtain an accurate thermometer reading because the meat is not thick enough. Therefore an average-size chicken (under 4 pounds) is usually checked for doneness by piercing the thick part of the thigh with a trussing needle, skewer or thin knife. If the juices that run from the meat are clear, not red or pink, the chicken is done.

ROAST CHICKEN
WITH AROMATIC RED WINE SAUCE

I have always loved the classic French ways of roasting chicken, in which fresh herbs and roasted onions and carrots lend a subtle taste to both the chicken and the sauce. The dish calls for old-fashioned accompaniments, like French fries or baked potatoes and lightly cooked green beans or the thin French beans, haricots verts.

3½- to 4-pound roasting or frying
   chicken, patted dry
salt and freshly ground pepper
3 fresh thyme sprigs, or 1 teaspoon
   dried leaves, crumbled

1 medium onion, quartered
1 medium carrot, quartered

Red Wine Sauce

¾ cup dry red wine
1 shallot, minced
½ teaspoon dried thyme, crumbled
1 cup chicken stock or broth
1 teaspoon potato starch, arrowroot, or
  cornstarch, dissolved in 2
  tablespoons cold water

2 teaspoons finely snipped chives or
  minced fresh tarragon
2 teaspoons minced fresh parsley
pinch of sugar (optional)

Preheat the oven to 400°F. Reserve chicken neck and giblets. Pull out fat from inside chicken. Sprinkle chicken evenly inside and outside with salt and pepper. Put thyme sprigs inside chicken. Truss chicken if desired.

Set chicken in a roasting pan with neck and giblets (except liver). Add onion and carrot to pan. Roast chicken 50 to 60 minutes or until juices run clear when thickest part of thigh is pierced with thin knife or skewer; if juices are pink, roast a few more minutes and test again. Transfer chicken to a board, cover, and keep warm.

To make sauce, skim fat from juices in pan. Add wine to pan and bring to a simmer, scraping browned bits into wine. Pour wine with vegetables from roasting pan into a medium saucepan. Add shallot and thyme and boil, stirring occasionally, until wine is reduced to about ⅓ cup. Remove vegetables.

Strain wine into a bowl, pressing on shallots. Return to saucepan. Add stock and bring to boil. Boil 1 or 2 minutes to reduce slightly. Whisk potato starch mixture and gradually pour into simmering sauce, whisking constantly. Bring to a boil, whisking. Simmer 1 or 2 minutes until thickened. Remove from heat and stir in herbs. Taste and adjust seasoning; if flavor is too tart, add pinch of sugar.

Carve chicken and serve with sauce.

Makes 4 servings

ROAST CHICKEN WITH POTATOES, BELL PEPPERS, AND ROSEMARY

The roasting juices of chicken lend good flavor to vegetables, and so I often add them to the pan, as in this Italian-style dish, in which the rosemary-accented juices flavor the potatoes and peppers. Since the cooking time of peppers is fairly short, I add them toward the end of the roasting time. Besides having a great taste, this dish is convenient, since the chicken cooks with its accompaniments.

3- to 3½-pound chicken
4 fresh rosemary sprigs
4 tablespoons extra-virgin olive oil
salt and freshly ground pepper
2 pounds small new potatoes or
  medium red potatoes

1 red bell pepper, cored and quartered
  lengthwise
1 green bell pepper, cored and
  quartered lengthwise
fresh rosemary, for garnish (optional)

Preheat the oven to 400°F. Pull out fat from inside chicken. Set chicken in a small roasting pan just large enough to hold it and potatoes in one layer. Stuff chicken with 1 rosemary sprig. Pour 1 tablespoon oil over chicken, sprinkle it with salt and pepper, and rub seasonings into chicken. Add remaining rosemary to pan and tuck it under chicken.

If potatoes are small, peel a strip of peel around center. If potatoes are over 1 inch in diameter, halve them. Put potatoes around chicken and sprinkle with salt, pepper, and remaining oil. Stir to coat potatoes with oil.

Roast chicken uncovered for 30 minutes. Turn potatoes over. Tip pan and baste chicken and potatoes. Add peppers to pan; push them under potatoes and chicken. Roast 30 minutes more, or until potatoes are tender and chicken juices run clear when thickest part of thigh is pierced with a thin knife or skewer. Transfer to board and keep warm. If potatoes are not yet tender, remove chicken and bake potatoes a few more minutes.

Carve chicken into 4 pieces and put on platter or plates. Add peppers and potatoes. Skim excess fat from roasting juices. Taste juices and adjust seasoning. When serving, spoon a little of pan juices over chicken and potatoes. Garnish with fresh rosemary.

Makes 4 servings

CURRY ROASTED CHICKEN WITH PINEAPPLE AND APPLES

I learned to make this dish when I worked at a restaurant called La Ciboulette in Paris. It features a typically European flavor combination of curry-seasoned chicken with fruit. This flavor match probably originated when European chefs began preparing so-called Indian-style dishes by seasoning stews with curry powder and serving them with sliced fruit and grated coconut, accompaniments inspired by Indian chutneys.

At the restaurant the dish was prepared with chicken or guinea hen. The bird was served sprinkled with grated coconut and chopped fresh chervil, and was accompanied by fried zucchini slices.

I find curry powder to be a wonderful seasoning for rubbing on chicken for roasting or grilling, since it gives the chicken and its roasting juices a delicious flavor and an attractive golden color.

3½- to 4-pound chicken
1 tablespoon curry powder
salt and freshly ground pepper
2 tablespoons vegetable oil
2 large tart apples, such as Granny Smith
2 tablespoons (¼ stick) butter, or more if needed

8 slices fresh pineapple, cored and halved
¾ cup chicken stock or broth (optional)
chervil or parsley sprigs, for garnish

Preheat the oven to 400°F. Pull out fat from inside chicken. Mix curry powder, salt, pepper, and oil. Rub chicken all over inside and out with mixture. Set chicken on a rack in a roasting pan. Roast chicken, basting occasionally, about 1 hour or until juices come out clear when a skewer is inserted into thickest part of thigh, about 1 hour. If juices are pink, roast chicken a few more minutes.

Meanwhile, peel apples. Core and cut them in eighths. Heat butter and remaining tablespoon oil in a large skillet over medium heat. Add apples and sauté about 5 minutes on each side, or until lightly browned and tender. Remove from pan. Add more butter if pan is dry. Add pineapple and sauté lightly, about 2 minutes per side.

Transfer chicken to a carving board. Cover loosely and let stand about 10 minutes before serving.

If you would like a sauce, discard excess fat from roasting pan, add stock to pan and boil 1 or 2 minutes, stirring, until well flavored. Season to taste with salt and pepper and strain into a sauce dish.

Reheat fruit if necessary. Serve chicken with sautéed fruit. Garnish with chervil or parsley sprigs.

Makes 4 servings

POLISH ROAST CHICKEN
WITH DILL BREAD STUFFING

This is a traditional central European style of roast chicken that everyone loves. The chicken is delicately seasoned so its natural flavor dominates, and the stuffing is perked up with the gentle taste of fresh dill. If you like, you can season the roasting juices with a little dill, too. Serve the chicken with sautéed mushrooms, baby onions, and glazed carrots.

3½- to 4-pound chicken
¼ teaspoon salt
¼ teaspoon freshly ground pepper
½ teaspoon paprika
2 teaspoons vegetable oil

Dill Stuffing (page 335)
1 to 2 tablespoons butter
¼ to ½ cup chicken stock or broth, for basting
dill sprigs, for garnish

Preheat the oven to 375°F. Pull out fat from inside chicken. Mix salt, pepper, paprika, and oil. Rub chicken all over with mixture. Spoon stuffing lightly into chicken. Fold skin over stuffing; truss or skewer closed, if desired. Set chicken in a roasting pan.

Add a little stock, if necessary, to extra stuffing so that most of bread is very lightly moistened. Grease a baking dish slightly larger than amount of remaining stuffing; spoon stuffing into it. Dot with butter and cover dish.

Roast chicken 45 minutes. Then put extra pan of stuffing in oven and roast both together about 45 minutes, basting chicken occasionally with pan juices and basting stuffing occasionally with a few tablespoons of stock. To check whether chicken is done, insert a skewer into thickest part of thigh; juices that run from chicken should be clear. Also insert a skewer into stuffing inside chicken; it should come out hot.

Transfer chicken to a carving board or platter and remove any trussing strings. Cover loosely and let stand about 10 minutes. Carve chicken and serve hot, with stuffing. Garnish with dill sprigs.

Makes 4 servings

SPANISH ROAST CHICKEN WITH SHERRY

When my husband and I visited the graceful city of Segovia in central Spain, we dined at a restaurant called Candido, which is well known for its impressive roasts. The chef said his philosophy was to keep things simple and let the ingredients speak for themselves. At the restaurant this roast chicken with sherry-flavored roasting juices was served with a small bunch of fresh watercress, some sautéed peppers, and very good fresh bread. Dessert was the perfect summer treat—a bowl of strawberries lightly sprinkled with orange juice and Grand Marnier.

3- to 3½-pound chicken, patted dry
2 tablespoons (¼ stick) butter,
　softened

salt and freshly ground pepper
⅓ cup dry sherry
⅓ cup chicken stock or broth

Preheat the oven to 400°F. Pull out fat from inside chicken. Truss chicken if desired. Rub soft butter over chicken. Sprinkle with salt and pepper.

Set chicken on a rack in a roasting pan. Roast 1 hour, basting occasionally, or until juices run clear when thickest part of thigh is pierced with thin knife or skewer; if juices are pink, roast a few more minutes and test again. Transfer chicken to a platter. Discard any trussing strings. Cover loosely.

Discard excess fat from roasting pan. Heat pan until juices are very hot. Add sherry and stir to dissolve pan juices. Pour into a saucepan. Add stock and bring to a boil. Boil to reduce if desired. Taste and adjust seasoning. Carve chicken. Serve juices separately.

Makes 4 servings

CHICKEN SEASONED UNDER THE SKIN WITH TARRAGON BUTTER

During the last decade, the French technique of seasoning chicken under the skin has gained in importance, simply because many people no longer eat the skin. And so if you spread a seasoning mixture such as tarragon butter on the meat under the skin and roast the bird, the meat will still be flavored, even if you remove the skin before eating it. You can use Pesto (page 363), Cilantro Butter (page 368), or Bajan ''Pesto'' (page 364) the same way.

Please note that the ''stuffing'' melts during roasting, so don't look for any afterwards! It serves simply as a flavoring.

4 tablespoons (½ stick) butter,
  softened
1 teaspoon strained, fresh lemon juice
1½ to 2 tablespoons chopped fresh
  tarragon

salt and freshly ground pepper
3½-pound chicken
tarragon sprigs, for garnish

Preheat the oven to 400°F. Beat butter until soft. Beat in lemon juice. Stir in tarragon. Season to taste with salt and pepper.

Lift skin above one chicken breast carefully from neck end and rub herb butter gently underneath, on breast meat; repeat with other chicken breast. Rub a little herb butter over chicken skin. Put remaining herb butter inside chicken. For a neater appearance, truss chicken, if desired.

Put chicken on a rack and roast about 1 hour or until chicken is tender; when chicken leg is pierced with a thin skewer, juices that come out should be clear. Transfer to a board, cover loosely, and let stand about 10 minutes before carving. Serve hot, garnished with tarragon sprigs.

Makes 4 servings

HONEY-GLAZED ROAST CHICKEN

A honey and soy glaze gives the chicken skin a deep mahogany color that reminds me of the roast ducks in Chinatown restaurants and delis. The flavors of the glaze, delicately spiced with ginger, cinnamon, and pepper, are echoed in the simple sauce made from the pan juices. The roasted vegetables from the pan are also very tasty, and can be served with the chicken, along with rice and a crisp vegetable such as sugar-snap peas. Rice is a good accompaniment or, for a festive touch, serve rice garnished with raisins and toasted almonds.

5½- to 6-pound roasting chicken
3 tablespoons liquid honey, plus 1
   more teaspoon if needed
4 tablespoons soy sauce
1 teaspoon freshly ground black
   pepper

2 teaspoons ground ginger
½ teaspoon ground cinnamon
1 medium onion, quartered
4 medium carrots, quartered
½ cup chicken stock, broth, or water

Position rack in lower third of oven and preheat to 400°F. Mix 3 tablespoons honey, soy sauce, pepper, ginger, and cinnamon in a small bowl. Set aside 1 tablespoon of mixture in a small cup and cover.

Put onion and carrots in roasting pan. Put rack on top, and set chicken on rack. Rub chicken inside and out with remaining honey mixture. Roast 15 minutes. Add 2 tablespoons hot water to pan juices if they brown. Reduce oven temperature to 350°F. Roast chicken 30 minutes. Baste chicken, cover with foil, and roast about 1¼ to 1½ hours more, basting every 30 minutes and adding a few tablespoons water to pan if needed, or until juices that run from thickest part of thigh, when pierced with a skewer, are clear; or thermometer inserted into thickest part of thigh reaches 180°F. Transfer to a board and cover loosely. Remove vegetables. Add ½ cup stock or water to juices and bring to a simmer, scraping.

Strain juices into a saucepan. Skim off fat. Add remaining honey mixture and bring to a simmer. Taste and adjust seasoning. Add another teaspoon honey if you like. Serve with roasted vegetables if desired.

Makes 6 servings

ROAST MARINATED CHICKEN WITH CILANTRO AND GARLIC

This chicken owes its delicious flavor to a Moroccan-style marinade similar to pesto but made with cilantro instead of basil. I like to add white wine to the roasting juices to make a quick sauce, but you can skip this step if you like. Serve the chicken hot with couscous or rice and a Mediterranean-style vegetable like sautéed zucchini or eggplant with red peppers; or serve it cold with tomato, cucumber, and pepper salad.

3½-pound chicken
Moroccan Cilantro Pesto Marinade
   (page 354)
⅓ cup dry white wine

1 tablespoon chopped cilantro (fresh
   coriander)
cilantro sprigs, for garnish
lemon wedges, for serving

Lift skin of chicken breast carefully from neck end and rub herb mixture gently underneath, on breast meat; lift skin of breast at opposite end of chicken and repeat rubbing with marinade. Rub chicken thoroughly, inside and outside, with marinade. Put any remaining marinade inside chicken. For a neater appearance, truss chicken, if desired. Refrigerate chicken and marinate 1 hour.

Preheat the oven to 400°F. Set chicken in roasting pan and roast 20 minutes, basting once. Reduce oven temperature to 375°F. Roast 40 to 45 minutes more or until chicken is tender; when chicken leg is pierced with a thin skewer, juices that come out should be clear.

Remove chicken from roasting pan to platter and cover. Skim fat from roasting pan. Reheat roasting juices in pan. Add wine to pan and bring to boil, stirring. Boil 2 or 3 minutes to reduce slightly. Strain sauce. Add chopped cilantro and taste for seasoning.

Carve chicken. Spoon a little sauce over each serving. Garnish with cilantro sprigs and lemon wedges. Serve any remaining sauce separately.

Makes 4 servings

NOTE: Chicken can be served cold, without sauce.

For an international medley of poultry appetizers, serve **Baked Turkey Empanadas** (page 41) from Latin America, **Easy Tandoori Chicken Drummettes** from India (page 189), **Middle Eastern Chicken Brochettes with Peppers** (page 161), Chinese **Sweet-and-Sour Wings** (page 20), and **Moroccan Chicken Rolls with Raisins and Walnuts** (page 35).

Chicken breasts grilled on a ridged stove-top grill, fresh greens, and crisp vegetables make **Warm Chicken Salad with Peppers, Asparagus, and Rosemary-Sage Vinaigrette** (page 52) a light entree in the style of southern France and California.

Barbecued chicken, a universal favorite, is enhanced with southern Mediterranean seasonings in **Grilled Chicken with Coriander-Cumin Marinade** (page 165). Corn, peppers, squashes, and eggplant grilled alongside the chicken make tasty accompaniments.

Three appealing alternatives to the familiar chicken soup are **Thai Chicken Noodle Soup with Roasted Peanuts** (page 78), Italian-inspired **Turkey Soup with Spinach Tortellini and Mushrooms** (page 93), and **Hearty Chicken Soup with Zucchini, Tomatoes, and Lima Beans** (page 89) in the Middle Eastern style.

A **Roast Turkey with Stuffing** (pages 192-197) is the traditional choice for a Thanksgiving celebration. For an intimate holiday dinner, some would prefer **Roast Duck with Cranberries and Red Wine** (page 306) accompanied by **Hazelnut-Mushroom Stuffing** (page 330), or **Cornish Hens with Chestnuts** (page 316) served with a selection of colorful vegetables.

Exotic **Moroccan Chicken Pie with Cinnamon and Saffron** (*Bastilla*) (page 40) has a luscious chicken and toasted almond filling topped with a light filo-dough crust and a sprinkling of cinnamon and powdered sugar.

A new twist on meatballs and spaghetti is **Quick and Spicy Chicken Meatballs with Mushrooms and Peppers** (page 143) seasoned in the Middle Eastern style, served with **Orzo Pilaf with Garlic and Walnuts** (page 339).

Fast-cooking colorful Oriental chicken dishes range from curry-flavored **Singapore Chicken and Noodles** with shrimp and peppers (page 102) to delicate Chinese **Stir-Fried Chicken with Baby Corn, Snow Peas, and Mushrooms** (page 216), to hot **Thai Chicken Stir-Fry with Mint Leaves and Chilies** (page 219).

CHICKEN STUFFED WITH FIGS, ALMONDS, AND RICE

Aromatic ground coriander flavors this chicken and its Mediterranean-style rice stuffing. I like to prepare it using a roasting chicken, which has a slightly richer flavor than a frying chicken. For the stuffing I prefer to use regular long- or medium-grain rice rather than Basmati, because the latter's delicate grains are easily crushed. Spoon the stuffing lightly into the chicken to avoid squashing the rice.

3 tablespoons olive or vegetable oil
1 small onion, finely chopped
1 cup long-grain rice
2 cups hot water
2 teaspoons ground coriander
salt and freshly ground pepper

½ cup slivered almonds
1 cup dried small dark figs (Mission figs), stems removed, quartered
cayenne pepper to taste
4-pound roasting chicken

Heat 2 tablespoons oil in a deep frying pan over low heat. Add onion and cook, stirring often, until tender, about 5 minutes. Raise heat to medium, add rice, and sauté for 2 minutes. Add water, 1 teaspoon coriander, salt, and pepper and bring to a boil. Reduce heat to low, cover, and cook without stirring for 18 minutes or until just tender.

Preheat the oven to 400°F. Toast almonds in a baking dish in oven, stirring occasionally, until lightly browned, about 5 minutes. Transfer to a bowl and let cool.

Fluff rice with fork. Gently stir in almonds and figs. Add cayenne; taste and season stuffing well. Let cool.

Rub chicken with remaining oil and sprinkle it with coriander, salt, and pepper on all sides. Spoon enough stuffing into chicken to fill it, without packing it tightly; reserve extra stuffing at room temperature.

Set chicken on a rack in a roasting pan and roast until juices come out clear when a skewer is inserted into thickest part of thigh, about 1 hour. If juices are pink, continue roasting chicken a few more minutes. Transfer chicken to a carving board. Cover loosely. Let stand about 10 minutes before serving.

Heat remaining stuffing in a skillet over low heat, stirring with fork. Spoon into a serving dish.

Serve chicken and its stuffing on a platter. Serve remaining rice mixture separately.

Makes 4 servings

ROAST CHICKEN WITH MADEIRA, ASPARAGUS, AND BABY ONIONS

In the traditional French kitchen, the fine flavor of a roast chicken needs no enhancement, and so it is simply seasoned with salt and pepper before being roasted in a hot oven. If you would like to serve a sauce, follow the French practice of putting a quartered onion and carrot in the pan to flavor the juices. Then all you need is a little Madeira to finish the sauce. When asparagus is not in season, green beans, spinach, or carrots are also good accompaniments.

3½- to 4-pound chicken
salt and freshly ground pepper
1 medium onion, quartered
1 medium carrot, quartered
24 baby or pearl onions (about 6 ounces)

1 pound medium-width asparagus spears, peeled
2 tablespoons (¼ stick) butter
¼ cup Madeira
¼ cup chicken stock or broth

Preheat the oven to 400°F. Reserve chicken neck and giblets. Refrigerate liver for another recipe. Pull out fat from inside chicken. Cut off wing tips. Pat chicken dry. Sprinkle chicken evenly inside and out with salt and pepper. Truss chicken if desired.

Put quartered onion, carrot, chicken neck, and giblets in a small roasting pan. Set a rack on top, and set chicken on rack. Roast chicken 50 to 60 minutes or until juices run clear when thickest part of thigh is pierced with thin knife or skewer; if juices are pink, roast a few more minutes and test again.

In a medium saucepan, cover baby onions with water and bring to a boil. Boil 1 minute. Drain, rinse with cold water, and drain well. Peel with aid of a paring knife. Add more water to pan and bring to a boil. Add onions, cover, and simmer over medium heat until just tender, about 10 minutes. Drain well.

Cut asparagus in 2-inch pieces, discarding about 1½ inches of bases. Boil asparagus in a saucepan of boiling salted water for 2 minutes. Drain, rinse with cold water, and drain well.

When chicken is done, transfer it to a platter or carving board. Cover loosely. Let stand about 10 minutes before serving.

Melt butter in a sauté pan or skillet. Add asparagus and baby onions, sprinkle with salt and pepper, and cook over low heat until heated through.

Discard excess fat from roasting pan. Heat pan until juices are very hot. Add Madeira and stir to dissolve pan juices. Strain into a saucepan. Add stock and bring to a boil. Boil to reduce if desired. Taste and adjust seasoning. Discard any trussing strings and carve chicken. Serve with vegetables. Serve juices separately.

Makes 4 servings

LEMON-LIME CHICKEN WITH SWEET POTATOES

My editor, Olivia Blumer, told me about a roast chicken recipe she loves in which the chicken is stuffed with whole lemons. That recipe, from Marcella Hazan's More Classic Italian Cooking, *is the inspiration for this easy entree, in which the limes give the chicken juices a Caribbean aroma.*

Another favorite Caribbean ingredient, sweet potatoes, which bake at the same time as the chicken, make a delicious and convenient partner for the roast bird. I also like to accompany the dish with a salad of diced jicama, tomato, cucumber, and chopped green onion seasoned lightly with hot pepper sauce, salt, and a sprinkling of olive oil.

3½- to 4-pound chicken, patted dry
salt and freshly ground pepper
2 limes, rinsed, dried, and quartered
1 lemon, rinsed, dried, and quartered

3 pounds sweet potatoes or yams, rinsed
fresh lime slices or wedges, for garnish

Preheat the oven to 400°F. with rack in upper third. Pull out fat from inside chicken. Sprinkle chicken evenly inside and outside with salt and pepper. Rub seasonings into chicken. Put lime and lemon quarters inside chicken. Use trussing skewers to close chicken opening; or truss chicken (page 400).

Put sweet potatoes in a foil-lined baking dish in oven on upper or lower rack. Set chicken, breast side down, in a small roasting pan. Roast chicken on upper rack 15 minutes. Turn breast side up. Roast another 50 to 55 minutes or until juices run clear when thickest part of thigh is pierced with thin knife or skewer; if juices are pink, roast a few more minutes and test again. Transfer chicken to a board, cover loosely, and keep warm about 10 minutes before carving. Test sweet potatoes with fork to be sure they are tender, and remove from oven.

Carve chicken, discarding lime and lemon quarters. Spoon carving juices from inside chicken over pieces, or serve juices separately. Serve with sweet potatoes. Garnish with fresh lime slices or wedges.

Makes 4 servings

NOTE: I prefer to bake the sweet potatoes in a separate pan because often their juices caramelize and, if baked alongside the chicken, could cause the chicken's juices to burn.

ROAST CHICKEN WITH ROSEMARY STUFFING

Italian and Provençal cooks discovered chicken's natural affinity for rosemary. In this recipe rosemary flavors the chicken's wine-flavored juices as it roasts, as well as the stuffing, which is enriched by ham or smoked turkey. Serve the chicken with ratatouille or other Mediterranean-style vegetables in summer, or with baked acorn squash in fall or winter.

3- to 3½-pound chicken
6 tablespoons dry white wine
3 tablespoons extra-virgin olive oil
salt and freshly ground pepper

Rosemary Stuffing (page 336)
7 fresh rosemary sprigs, or 1½
  teaspoons dried leaves
¼ to ½ cup chicken stock or broth
1 to 2 tablespoons butter

Preheat the oven to 400°F. Set chicken in a small roasting pan. Pour wine and oil over chicken, sprinkle it with salt and pepper, and rub seasonings into chicken. Spoon stuffing into chicken, packing it gently. Add 3 rosemary sprigs to pan.

Add a little stock to remaining stuffing so that most of bread is very lightly moistened. Butter a casserole of same as or slightly larger volume than extra stuffing and spoon stuffing into it. Dot with butter. Cover casserole.

Roast chicken, basting occasionally with pan juices, about 1 hour. Roast extra stuffing, basting once or twice with stock, about 30 minutes, then uncover and bake 5 minutes more. Chicken is done when juices that run from thigh, when pierced in thickest part with a skewer, are clear. If juices are pink, roast a few more minutes and check again. Check stuffing in bird also; skewer inserted in it should come out hot. Transfer to a board, cover loosely, and let stand about 10 minutes before serving.

Carve chicken and serve with stuffing. Taste pan juices, adjust seasoning, and serve separately. Garnish with fresh rosemary sprigs.

Makes 4 servings

CASSEROLE-ROASTED CHICKEN WITH TARRAGON

Roasting en cocotte, *or in a covered casserole, is a traditional French method for baking whole chickens in the oven. The chicken is first browned on top of the stove, then is covered and baked. Unlike roasting on a rack in an open pan, the bird's skin does not become as brown, but the meat remains moister and the juices become richer because they are in contact with the chicken.*

In this simple recipe, the chicken and juices are flavored with fresh tarragon, but you can substitute other herbs like thyme or cilantro, or you can add flavoring vegetables like onions, shallots, or garlic. Serve the chicken with sautéed chanterelle mushrooms, baby onions, glazed carrots, or any seasonal vegetable, and with crusty French bread or oven-fried potatoes.

9 fresh tarragon sprigs
3½-pound frying chicken, patted dry
salt and freshly ground pepper

2 tablespoons vegetable oil
1 tablespoon butter
1 tablespoon chopped fresh tarragon

Preheat the oven to 400°F. Put 5 tarragon sprigs inside chicken. Truss chicken if desired, for more attractive shape. Sprinkle chicken evenly with salt and pepper.

Heat oil and butter in a heavy oval enamel-lined casserole over medium-high heat. Set chicken in casserole on its side, so that leg is in contact with fat. Cover with large splatter screen and brown side of chicken. Using 2 wooden spoons and standing back to avoid splatters, turn chicken onto its breast and brown it. Brown other side, then brown chicken back. If oil begins to turn dark brown, reduce heat to medium.

Leave chicken on its back. Baste with pan juices. Cover and bake until juices run clear when thickest part of leg is pierced with thin skewer, about 45 minutes; if juices are pink, bake a few more minutes and test again. Discard trussing strings, if used. *Chicken can be kept warm in casserole, covered, for 15 minutes.*

Bring juices to boil. Taste and adjust seasoning. Stir in chopped tarragon. Serve chicken whole and carve it at table, discarding tarragon sprigs from inside. Serve juices separately. Garnish with small fresh tarragon sprigs.

Makes 4 servings

EASY TANDOORI CHICKEN

Indian cooks have developed one of the most flavorful types of roast chicken, which before being roasted is marinated with ginger, garlic, spices, and yogurt. I have savored tandoori chicken in Indian restaurants in London, Paris, and Los Angeles, and I find it the best dish for introducing Indian cuisine to the uninitiated. Spicy but not hot, tandoori chicken fits in perfectly with Western-style menus.

In Indian restaurants it's baked in a clay oven called a tandoor, *which reaches incredibly high temperatures, but it also comes out wonderful roasted in a home oven. Tandoori chicken is delicious broiled as well, as in the variation, or grilled, and cooks faster than in the oven. For this easy version of the recipe, you'll find all the ingredients in the supermarket.*

Classic tandoori chicken is cooked without the skin, and that makes this roasting method even more appealing for low-fat cooking. The yogurt-based marinade, which I make with low-fat yogurt, keeps the meat moist.

Serve the chicken with long-grain white rice, preferably the fragrant Basmati rice from India. I like to roast onion slices in the pan along with the chicken for serving. Occasionally, along with the onion I add a red or green bell pepper that I've cut in six pieces. If you want an additional vegetable, serve peas, green beans, or sautéed eggplant, or a simple green salad.

1 medium onion
1 tablespoon coarsely chopped peeled
   fresh ginger
3 medium garlic cloves, peeled
1 tablespoon strained, fresh lemon
   juice
1 tablespoon vegetable oil
½ cup plain yogurt
1½ teaspoons ground coriander
1 teaspoon ground cumin
½ teaspoon turmeric

¼ teaspoon freshly grated nutmeg
¼ teaspoon ground cinnamon
pinch of cloves
¼ teaspoon freshly ground black
   pepper
¼ teaspoon cayenne
½ teaspoon salt
6 chicken thighs (2 pounds)
lemon wedges, for serving

Dice ¼ onion. Reserve remaining onion. In a food processor, process diced onion, ginger, and garlic until finely chopped. Add lemon juice and oil and process to blend. Transfer to a bowl and stir in yogurt, spices, and salt.

Remove skin and trim excess fat from chicken thighs. Make 2 or 3 small slits in each chicken piece so marinade will penetrate better. Put in a shallow dish. Pour marinade over chicken and turn pieces so both sides are coated. Cover and refrigerate 2 hours to overnight.

Preheat the oven to 400°F. Slice rest of onion in thick slices and put in roasting pan. Put rack on top. Set chicken on rack. Roast until juices come out clear when meat is pricked in thickest part with a thin knife, about 45 minutes. If juices are pink, roast a few more minutes. Serve with lemon wedges and roasted onion slices.

Makes 3 or 4 servings

VARIATIONS:

Broiled Tandoori Chicken

Broil chicken 6 minutes from heat source about 10 to 12 minutes per side. Watch carefully; turn chicken over often during last few minutes so it won't burn. If you like, add sliced onion to broiler for last few minutes to char it lightly.

Easy Tandori Chicken Drummettes

Use 2 pounds drummettes. Leave skin on. Roast about 35 minutes or broil or grill, turning often, about 25 minutes. SEE PHOTOGRAPH.

BAKED CHICKEN WITH WHITE BEANS, SAGE, AND TOMATO SAUCE

In this simple Italian cousin of cassoulet, chicken pieces bake with sage-scented white beans and lend them a wonderful flavor. It is easiest to prepare this casserole in an ovenproof sauté pan. The chicken reheats beautifully and makes a perfect winter party dish; all that is needed to complete the meal is a green salad or perhaps some lightly cooked broccoli or sautéed zucchini, and breadsticks or Italian sesame bread. For dessert, I like to serve a creamy chocolate zuccotto.

1⅓ cups dried white beans (about 8 ounces)
1 bay leaf
1 medium celery stalk (optional)
salt and freshly ground pepper
2 tablespoons olive oil
2 pounds chicken thighs or drumsticks, patted dry
1 medium onion, chopped
1 large garlic clove, chopped

1 to 1¼ pounds ripe tomatoes, peeled, seeded, and chopped; or 1 (28-ounce) can whole tomatoes, drained and chopped
¼ teaspoon hot red pepper flakes, or cayenne pepper to taste
2 tablespoons canned tomato puree or paste (optional)
4 tablespoons chopped fresh sage, or 1 tablespoon dried, crumbled

Sort beans, discarding any broken ones and any stones. In a large bowl soak beans in 4 cups cold water overnight. For a quicker method, cover beans with 4 cups water in a large saucepan, boil 2 minutes, and let stand off heat for 1 hour.

Rinse and drain beans and put them in a large saucepan. Add enough water to cover them by at least 2 inches. Add bay leaf and celery. Cover and bring to a boil over medium heat. Simmer over low heat 45 minutes; add a pinch of salt and cook about 45 minutes more or until just tender, adding hot water if necessary so beans remain covered. Keep beans in their cooking liquid to keep them moist. *Beans can be cooked 1 day ahead and refrigerated.*

Preheat the oven to 375°F. Heat oil in a large sauté pan or deep skillet, preferably oven-proof, over medium-high heat. Add half of chicken pieces, salt, and pepper and brown well on all sides. Remove to plate. Repeat with remaining chicken. Pour off all but 2 tablespoons oil.

Add onion to pan and cook over medium-low heat until softened, about 7 minutes. Stir in garlic, then tomatoes, hot pepper flakes, and a little salt and pepper. Cook over medium heat, stirring often, about 10 minutes or until thick. Add puree if desired and heat to blend. Add 2 tablespoons sage and taste for seasoning. (*To make chicken ahead, see Note.*) Reserve ⅓ cup sauce for spooning over chicken.

Discard bay leaf and celery from beans. With slotted spoon, gently put beans in skillet containing sauce, if it is ovenproof, or put them in a 5- or 6-cup baking dish and add sauce. Reserve bean liquid. Gently mix sauce into beans and taste for seasoning. Arrange chicken pieces on top, and pour juices from plate over them. Spoon reserved sauce over each chicken piece and spread it smooth. Cover and bake 20 minutes. Add 1 or 2 tablespoons bean liquid if mixture looks dry. Bake about 25 minutes more or until chicken is tender. If using fresh sage, stir all but 2 teaspoons into beans. Sprinkle with remaining sage when serving.

Makes 3 or 4 servings

NOTE: To make this dish ahead, add browned chicken pieces to tomato sauce, cover, and simmer about 35 minutes or until just tender. Remove pieces and layer with beans and sauce as in last paragraph. Cover and refrigerate 1 or 2 days. Reheat, covered, about 40 minutes in 350°F. oven.

MIDDLE EASTERN BAKED CHICKEN WITH POTATOES AND ONIONS

My husband's cousin, who was born in Yemen, taught me how to prepare this savory Yemenite dish, which is cooked by a combination of baking and broiling. Baking keeps the chicken pieces juicy; broiling turns them an appetizing golden brown. The spice mixture of cumin, turmeric, and pepper gives the chicken and the potatoes a delicious taste and a golden hue. I like to serve the chicken with Jalapeño-Garlic Chutney (page 366) and with sautéed eggplant flavored with thyme and cayenne pepper.

4 teaspoons ground cumin, freshly
  ground if possible
1 teaspoon ground turmeric
½ teaspoon ground black pepper
3 to 3¼ pounds boiling potatoes,
  peeled and sliced about ⅜ inch thick

salt and freshly ground pepper
3 to 3¼ pounds chicken pieces
1½ pounds onions, halved and sliced

Preheat the oven to 450°F. Mix cumin, turmeric, and ground pepper in a bag. Lightly oil a roasting pan. Add potatoes and sprinkle with salt and freshly ground pepper. Toss so all are coated. Toss chicken pieces in bag with salt and spice mixture. Set on potatoes. Top with sliced onions. Cover with foil and bake 50 to 55 minutes or until chicken is tender; juices should no longer be pink when thickest part of thigh is pierced; potatoes should be tender as well.

Just before serving, uncover and broil 4 inches from heat for about 8 minutes or until browned.

Makes 6 servings

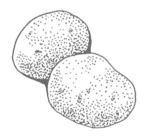

CHICKEN WITH CHICKPEAS, GARLIC, AND CAYENNE

An easy way to enjoy the flavor of roast chicken without having to carve it is to use chicken pieces, as in this simple but tasty Moroccan-style recipe. It makes use of canned chickpeas, which are flavored by the juices of the chicken, together with onion, garlic, and spice. I like to serve this dish with cooked carrots and green beans, and with pasta mixed with sautéed mushrooms, as well as diced Mediterranean salad.

2½ to 3 pounds chicken pieces
salt and freshly ground pepper
1 teaspoon paprika
cayenne pepper
2 large garlic cloves, chopped
about 2 tablespoons plus 1 teaspoon
  olive oil

1 medium onion, halved and sliced
1 (15- or 16-ounce) can chickpeas
  (garbanzo beans), drained and
  rinsed

Preheat the oven to 425°F. Sprinkle chicken with salt, pepper, and paprika on both sides. Sprinkle lightly with cayenne pepper. Put in small roasting pan. Sprinkle garlic in pan. Drizzle chicken lightly with about 1 teaspoon olive oil. Bake uncovered for 20 minutes.

    Heat 2 tablespoons olive oil in a skillet, add onion, and sauté about 7 minutes or until softened. Add onion to chicken, pushing it under pieces. Reduce oven temperature to 350°F. and bake about 30 more minutes or until chicken is tender.

    Add chickpeas to juices in pan and sprinkle with a little paprika and cayenne. Cover and bake 5 minutes. Serve chicken with chickpeas.

Makes 4 servings

ROAST TURKEY WITH PEPPER, CORN, AND CILANTRO STUFFING

Mexican flavors accent the zesty, colorful stuffing of this turkey, as well as the sauce made from the pan juices. The stuffing is a traditional American-style bread stuffing with a new twist, so there is still enough familiarity to make this bird ideal as a festive Thanksgiving centerpiece.

10- to 12-pound fresh or thawed
   frozen turkey
salt and freshly ground pepper
Pepper, Corn, and Cilantro Stuffing
   (page 327)
6 tablespoons (¾ stick) butter,
   softened
¼ cup olive or vegetable oil
3 cups turkey stock (page 390),
   chicken stock (page 389), or broth

½ red bell pepper, diced
1 or 2 jalapeño peppers, chopped
2 tablespoons potato starch, arrowroot,
   or cornstarch
3 tablespoons water
¼ cup chopped cilantro (fresh
   coriander)

Remove top oven rack. Preheat the oven to 425°F. Sprinkle turkey inside and out with salt and pepper. Spoon some stuffing into neck cavity. Fold neck skin under body and fasten with a skewer. Pack body cavity loosely with stuffing and cover opening with a crumpled piece of foil. Truss turkey if desired. Spoon remaining stuffing into a buttered 4- to 6-cup baking dish.

Spread turkey with softened butter and put breast side up on a rack in a large roasting pan. Roast 30 minutes, basting twice. Meanwhile, soak a large double piece of cheesecloth in ¼ cup oil.

Reduce oven temperature to 350°F. Cover turkey breast with oil-soaked cheesecloth. Roast turkey 1½ hours, basting with pan juices every 15 minutes. If pan becomes dry, add ¼ cup of stock.

Put dish of extra stuffing in oven and baste with turkey juices. Cover with foil; bake about 45 minutes. Meanwhile, continue roasting turkey, basting every 15 minutes, until juices run clear when leg is pricked, or thermometer inserted into thickest part of thigh registers 180°F., about 20 to 45 minutes.

Transfer turkey to platter or large board. Discard strings, skewers, and cheesecloth. Baste once with pan juices, and cover turkey.

Pour roasting juices into measuring cup. Pour off fat and reserve it. Return juices to pan. Add ¾ cup stock and bring to a boil, stirring and scraping to dissolve any browned bits in pan. Strain into a bowl.

Heat 2 tablespoons reserved fat in a saucepan over medium-low heat. Add diced pepper and sauté, stirring, until softened. Add jalapeño peppers and sauté ½ minute. Add remaining 2¼ cups stock and liquid used to deglaze roasting pan.

Mix potato starch with water in small bowl until blended. Bring turkey sauce to a simmer. Gradually whisk in about half of potato starch solution and simmer 1 or 2 minutes or until thickened. For a thicker sauce, whisk in remaining solution and simmer until thickened. Add cilantro. Taste and adjust seasoning.

Carve turkey and arrange on platter. Spoon stuffing onto platter or into a serving dish. Reheat sauce briefly. Pour into a sauceboat and serve alongside turkey.

Makes 8 servings

ROAST TURKEY
WITH APPLE-APRICOT STUFFING

A fruit stuffing is a traditional American favorite for the holiday turkey, and is a good complement for the time-honored cranberry sauce. The gravy for this turkey is accented by the French apple brandy, Calvados, to match the flavor of the stuffing. The traditional turkey partners—Brussels sprouts, baby onions, and braised chestnuts—are perfect with this dish.

10- to 12-pound fresh or thawed
   frozen turkey
salt and freshly ground pepper
Apple, Apricot, and Walnut Stuffing
   (page 328)
½ cup (1 stick) butter, softened

2 tablespoons vegetable oil
3 cups turkey stock (page 390),
   chicken stock (page 389), or broth
4 to 5 tablespoons Calvados
¼ cup all-purpose flour

Preheat the oven to 425°F. Remove top rack. Sprinkle turkey inside and out with salt and pepper. Spoon some stuffing into neck cavity. Fold neck skin under body and fasten with a skewer. Pack body cavity loosely with stuffing and cover opening with a crumpled piece of foil. Truss turkey if desired. Spoon remaining stuffing into a buttered 4- to 6-cup baking dish.

Spread turkey with 6 tablespoons softened butter and put breast side up on a rack in a large roasting pan. Roast for 30 minutes, basting twice. Meanwhile, melt remaining 2 tablespoons butter in oil in a medium saucepan and put a large double piece of cheesecloth in saucepan.

Reduce oven temperature to 350°F. Cover turkey breast with butter-soaked cheesecloth. Roast turkey for 1½ hours, basting with pan juices every 15 minutes. If pan becomes dry, add ¼ cup of stock.

Put dish of extra stuffing in oven and baste with turkey juices. Cover with foil; bake about 45 minutes. Meanwhile, continue roasting turkey, basting every 15 minutes, until juices run clear when thigh is pricked, or thermometer inserted into thickest part of thigh registers 180°F., about 20 to 45 minutes.

Transfer turkey to platter or large board. Discard strings, skewers, and cheesecloth. Baste once with pan juices, and cover turkey.

Pour roasting juices into measuring cup. Pour off fat and reserve it. Return juices to pan. Add ¼ cup Calvados and ¾ cup stock and bring to a boil, stirring and scraping to dissolve any browned bits in pan. Strain into a bowl.

Heat ⅓ cup reserved fat in a saucepan over low heat. Add flour and cook over low heat, whisking, about 4 minutes or until bubbling. Add remaining 2¼ cups stock and liquid used to deglaze roasting pan. Bring to a boil, whisking. Simmer, whisking occasionally, about 5 minutes or until thick enough to coat a spoon. Add Calvados to taste. Taste and adjust seasoning.

Carve turkey and arrange on platter. Spoon stuffing onto platter or into a serving dish. Reheat sauce briefly. Pour into a sauceboat and serve alongside turkey.

Makes 8 servings

ROAST TURKEY
WITH HERBED ONION STUFFING

Italian accents—oregano, rosemary, and sage in both the stuffing and the tomato sauce enriched with the turkey roasting juices—make for a delicious Thanksgiving turkey. For a festive but different holiday dinner, serve some Italian-style dishes too, alongside the customary American turkey accompaniments. Fresh fettuccine mixed with sautéed porcini or other mushrooms makes a terrific holiday first course, and nutmeg-scented spinach or lightly cooked broccoli de rabe *(Italian broccoli) is a nice change from Brussels sprouts.* SEE PHOTOGRAPH.

10- to 12-pound fresh or thawed
   frozen turkey
salt and freshly ground pepper
Herbed Onion Stuffing (page 329)
4 tablespoons (½ stick) butter,
   softened
6 tablespoons olive oil
1½ cups turkey stock (page 390),
   chicken stock (page 389), or broth
½ cup dry white wine

2 cups Fresh Tomato Sauce (page 369)
   or purchased
1 tablespoon minced fresh rosemary,
   or 1 teaspoon dried
1 teaspoon dried oregano, crumbled
1 tablespoon minced fresh sage, or 1
   teaspoon dried, crumbled
2 tablespoons tomato paste (optional)
¼ cup chopped fresh Italian or curly
   parsley

Remove top oven rack. Preheat the oven to 425°F. Sprinkle turkey inside and out with salt and pepper. Spoon some stuffing into neck cavity. Fold neck skin under body and fasten with a skewer. Pack body cavity loosely with stuffing and cover opening with a crumpled piece of foil. Truss turkey if desired. Spoon remaining stuffing into a buttered 4- to 6-cup baking dish.

Spread turkey with softened butter and put breast side up on a rack in a large roasting pan. Roast for 30 minutes, basting twice. Meanwhile, soak a large double piece of cheesecloth in olive oil.

Reduce oven temperature to 350°F. Cover turkey breast with oil-soaked cheesecloth. Roast turkey for 1½ hours, basting with pan juices every 15 minutes. If pan becomes dry, add ¼ cup of stock.

Put dish of extra stuffing in oven and baste with a little of turkey juices. Cover with foil; bake about 45 minutes. Meanwhile, continue roasting turkey, basting every 15 minutes, until juices run clear when leg is pricked, or thermometer inserted into thickest part of thigh registers 180°F., about 20 to 45 minutes.

Transfer turkey to platter or large board. Discard strings, skewers, and cheesecloth. Baste once with pan juices, and cover turkey.

Pour roasting juices into measuring cup. Pour off fat and discard it. Return juices to pan. Add wine and bring to a boil, stirring and scraping to dissolve any browned bits in pan. Strain into a saucepan. Add stock and simmer 5 minutes. Add tomato sauce, rosemary, oregano, and sage and simmer 5 more minutes or until thickened to taste. If you would like thicker or redder sauce, add tomato paste. Taste and adjust seasoning.

Carve turkey and arrange on platter. Spoon stuffing onto platter or into a serving dish. Reheat sauce briefly and add parsley. Pour into a sauceboat and serve alongside turkey.

Makes 8 servings

ROAST TURKEY WITH HAZELNUT-MUSHROOM STUFFING

This is a time-honored American Thanksgiving classic—a golden brown turkey with a savory bread stuffing, accented with toasted nuts. The rich gravy is made the old-fashioned way with turkey stock and enhanced by a little white wine. Serve the turkey with homemade mashed potatoes or sweet potatoes, cranberry sauce, and perhaps some glazed carrots or lightly cooked broccoli or Brussels sprouts, and for dessert, pumpkin pie, chocolate pecan pie, or devil's food cake.

The main challenge in roasting turkey is keeping the breast meat moist in the long time required for the bird to cook. Basting often with butter and covering the breast for part of the roasting time help to accomplish this.

14-pound turkey
salt and freshly ground pepper
Hazelnut-Mushroom Stuffing (page 330)
¾ cup (1½ sticks) butter

¼ cup vegetable oil
½ cup dry white wine
3 cups chicken stock or broth
¼ cup all-purpose flour

Remove upper rack from oven. Preheat the oven to 400°F. Sprinkle turkey inside and out with salt and pepper. Spoon some stuffing into neck cavity. Fold neck skin under body and fasten with a skewer. Pack body cavity loosely with stuffing and skewer flaps closed, or cover opening with a crumpled piece of foil. Spoon remaining stuffing into a buttered 4- to 6-cup baking dish.

Spread turkey with ½ cup softened butter and put in an oiled large roasting pan, breast side up. Roast for 30 minutes. Reduce oven temperature to 325°F. Roast turkey for 30 minutes, basting with oil every 15 minutes. Cover turkey loosely with foil. Roast for 1 hour, basting turkey with any remaining oil and with pan juices every 30 minutes. If pan becomes dry, add ¼ cup of the wine. Put dish of extra stuffing in oven. Uncover turkey and continue roasting, basting every 15 minutes, about 1 more hour or until juices run clear when leg is pricked, or meat thermometer inserted into thickest part of thigh registers 180°F.

Transfer turkey carefully to platter or large board, discard skewers, baste once with pan juices, and cover turkey.

Skim fat from juices in pan. Add remaining wine and ½ cup stock to pan and bring to a boil, stirring and scraping to dissolve any browned bits. Boil liquid until reduced to about ½ cup. Strain into a bowl.

Melt remaining ¼ cup butter in a large, heavy saucepan over low heat. Whisk in flour. Cook, whisking constantly, about 3 minutes or until mixture turns light beige. Remove from heat. Gradually add remaining 2½ cups stock, whisking. Bring to a boil over medium-high heat, whisking. Add strained turkey pan juices. Reduce heat to medium-low and simmer, uncovered, whisking often, about 5 minutes or until thick enough to coat a spoon. Taste and adjust seasoning.

Carve turkey and arrange on platter. Spoon stuffing onto platter or into a serving dish. Reheat gravy briefly. Pour into a sauceboat and serve alongside turkey.

Makes 8 to 10 servings

ROAST TURKEY BREAST
WITH SAGE AND THYME

I love roasting turkey breasts because their cooking time is much shorter than that of a whole turkey and so their meat tends to remain moister. Mediterranean flavors give this roast its fine taste. It's simple to prepare, elegant, and suitable for Thanksgiving or for entertaining during most of the year. Green beans, lima beans, and potatoes are good accompaniments, or, for a fall holiday meal, serve braised chestnuts and glazed carrots.

3-pound turkey breast half, with skin
    and bones
1 large onion, quartered
1 large carrot, quartered
20 fresh sage leaves
3 tablespoons olive oil
1 teaspoon dried leaf thyme

salt and freshly ground pepper
½ cup dry white wine
¾ cup chicken stock or broth
1 tablespoon potato starch dissolved in
    2 tablespoons water
1 tablespoon chopped fresh sage
1 tablespoon chopped fresh parsley

Preheat the oven to 400°F. Put turkey breast in a roasting pan with onion and carrot. Slip about 10 sage leaves under turkey skin. Rub turkey with oil. Sprinkle with thyme, salt, and pepper. Put remaining sage leaves in pan under turkey.

Roast turkey 15 minutes. Baste with pan juices. Reduce oven temperature to 350°F. Roast turkey, basting every 20 minutes, about 1¼ hours or until a meat thermometer or instant-read thermometer inserted in thick part of meat, not touching bone, registers 170°F.

Remove turkey to a board, leaving vegetables in pan. Cover turkey. Skim fat from juices. Add wine and bring to a simmer, scraping browned juices into wine. Pour liquid with vegetables into a saucepan. Add stock and simmer 2 or 3 minutes, then strain into a bowl and return to saucepan. Bring to a simmer, then stir potato starch mixture and whisk into simmering broth. Simmer 1 to 2 minutes until thickened. Stir in chopped sage and parsley. Add juices from turkey board. Taste sauce and adjust seasoning. Cut turkey in thin slices and serve with sauce.

Makes 4 servings

ROAST TURKEY BREAST WITH CUMIN AND PEPPERS

A Moroccan-style cumin-garlic seasoning paste gives a delicious flavor to this easy turkey roast as well as to the red peppers and onions that roast alongside it. Serve the turkey and peppers with the zesty roasting juices, and with couscous or rice, cauliflower, and green beans.

2¾- to 3-pound turkey breast half,
  skin on, bone in
2 medium onions, quartered
salt and freshly ground pepper
3 tablespoons olive oil
6 medium garlic cloves, minced

¼ teaspoon cayenne pepper
2 teaspoons ground cumin
1 teaspoon paprika
2 red bell peppers, each cut in 4 or 6
  pieces

Preheat the oven to 400°F. Put turkey breast in a roasting pan, bone side down, with onions. Sprinkle turkey with salt and pepper. Combine olive oil, garlic, cayenne pepper, cumin, and paprika, and rub all over turkey with back of a spoon.

Roast turkey 15 minutes. Reduce oven temperature to 350°F. and roast 30 minutes. Baste turkey; add pepper pieces to pan. Roast 20 minutes, baste turkey, and turn peppers over. Continue roasting about 30 more minutes or until a regular meat thermometer or instant-read thermometer (inserted in thickest part of meat, not touching bone) registers 170°F. Cover turkey if it becomes dark brown.

Carve turkey in thin slices and serve with juices and roasted vegetables.

Makes 4 or 5 servings

11

Sautéed and Fried Chicken and Turkey

When a piece of chicken or turkey comes in contact with hot oil, something delicious happens. The flavor of the poultry along with any seasonings and vegetables being sautéed or fried with it, intensifies as the food is seared. The juices are sealed in too, and the result is a moist, succulent piece of meat that is irresistible.

There are three main ways to use hot oil to cook chicken or turkey: sautéing, frying, and stir-frying. Besides giving a wonderful flavor, these techniques are practical, since the poultry cooks faster than by any other method.

Chicken is fried in oil in kitchens around the world but tastes different in every area, largely because of different seasonings. Garlic, ginger, and sometimes chili paste flavor the stir-fried chicken of China, and often it is coated with a light soy and rice wine sauce. Cumin, hot pepper, and sometimes turmeric are favorite accents for chicken and turkey in the Middle East. In Europe chicken and turkey are flavored with herbs—oregano, sage, and rosemary in the Mediterranean countries; chives and tarragon farther north. Tomatoes, wine, or stock might be added to the pan after the chicken is sautéed to make a light sauce.

Sautéed Chicken Breasts with Tomatoes, Chilies,
and Oregano
Chicken Involtini with Smoked Chicken, Pesto,
and Peppers
Macadamia Chicken
Chicken Paillardes with Porcini Mushrooms
and Shallots
Sautéed Chicken Breasts
with Herbed Mushroom Sauce
Chicken Saltimbocca
Chicken Thigh Sauté with Red Wine, Baby
Onions, and Mushrooms
Spicy Fried Chicken with Capers
Austrian Fried Chicken

Chili-Spiced Fried Chicken
Stir-Fried Chicken with Baby Corn, Snow Peas,
and Mushrooms
Spicy Stir-Fried Chicken with Peppers
and Broccoli
Thai Chicken Stir-Fry with Mint Leaves
and Chilies
Hungarian-Style Chicken Livers with Onions
Savory Chicken Livers with Onions,
Middle Eastern Style
Sautéed Turkey with Shallot Puree and Beets
Tunisian Turkey Slices with Tomato Sauce,
Olives, and Capers
Turkey Breast Slices with Horseradish Sauce

Vegetable and olive oils are ideal for sautéing poultry. Butter imparts a lovely flavor but can burn if used on its own. For recipes in which you want the taste of butter, the solution is to melt it with an equal amount of oil in the skillet. Cooks in some regions of India use a special type of clarified butter called *ghee*, which lends an exotic buttery aroma to the sautéed meat; *ghee* is available at some natural foods stores and Indian specialty shops.

For sautéing, a small amount of oil is used—just enough to cover the bottom of the pan. Chicken and turkey can be sautéed with a coating, which enables them to brown better, helps prevent sticking, and aids in preventing moisture from the meat from splattering upon contact with the hot oil.

Fried chicken or turkey is cooked in enough oil to cover or nearly cover the pieces. The chicken must be coated with either flour or flour, egg, and bread crumbs to protect its flesh from the searing heat.

Chinese stir-frying, when done the classic way, is a combination of sautéing and deep-frying. The chicken is cut in bite-size chunks or strips and is first cooked through in deep oil. Then it is sautéed over high heat with seasonings and vegetables to quickly finish the dish. Today many cooks skip the step of the preliminary frying and simply sauté the chicken over high heat. As its name suggests, the chicken and vegetables are stirred continuously as they are fried to prevent sticking or burning. Turkey is not a traditional meat in China, but the technique can be used for boneless turkey also.

Stir-frying produces delicious results and has been adopted in Thai and other styles of Oriental cuisine. In much of the Western world more and more people stir-fry even when they're not cooking with Oriental flavors. Part of the reason for the appeal of this cooking technique is that each bite-size piece of poultry becomes coated with the flavorings and tastes more seasoned than a big hunk of meat.

Sautéing, stir-frying, and frying are ideal methods for cooking boneless poultry—chicken breasts and thighs and turkey breast slices—because these cuts are thin and tender and cook through rapidly. Turkey breast slices are usually sold in thinner pieces than chicken breasts and so they cook more quickly. Since turkey slices have no skin to protect them, they must be cooked carefully to prevent them from being too dry.

Quickest of all to cook are chicken breast fillets, the tender strip of meat at the bottom of the breast, which are available in some markets. Sometimes labeled "chicken breast tenders," these thin, small chicken strips cook in no time and are perfect for sautéing or stir-frying.

For chicken on the bone, a French-style chicken sauté is preferable. It begins like the usual form of sautéing, with the chicken pieces browned in a skillet, but then the heat is turned down, the pan is covered, and the chicken finishes cooking gently in its own juices. This method enables the heat to penetrate the thicker pieces that contain bones and to cook them thoroughly. It also creates tasty juices, which can be deglazed with wine or stock and made into delectable sauces, as in Chicken Thigh Sauté with Red Wine, Baby Onions, and Mushrooms (page 212) or Springtime Chicken Sauté with Asparagus and Carrots (page 132).

Vegetables are usually added to stir-fried poultry dishes and sometimes to sautéed chicken.

Onions, leeks, peppers, and mushrooms are the most popular, since they can be easily sautéed with the chicken if there is room in the skillet. Other vegetables like carrots, eggplant, or zucchini are often cooked separately, then combined with the chicken to absorb flavor from the juices.

TIPS

✗ For the best results when sautéing, use a heavy skillet large enough so the chicken or turkey has plenty of room. Crowding the pieces in the pan causes them to steam and their coating to become soggy.

✗ The heat for sautéing chicken or turkey should be medium-high. If it is too low, any coatings used absorb too much fat and begin to stick.

✗ Once poultry is coated with either flour or egg and bread crumbs, it should be handled with care. The pieces should not be stacked before cooking, or moisture from the meat will make the coating gummy. Whenever sautéed chicken or turkey is kept warm, the pieces should be placed in the oven on a platter in a single layer and left uncovered, so the coating will not soften.

✗ For recipes calling for boneless chicken breasts, it saves money to buy the breasts with the skin on, since the packaged skinless breasts are more expensive. Pulling the skin off is easy, especially if you grip the skin with a paper towel. You can also buy breasts on the bone and bone them yourself (see page 405).

SAUTÉED CHICKEN BREASTS WITH TOMATOES, CHILIES, AND OREGANO

We associate oregano with Italian cooking but we tend to forget that it is a favorite in Mexican cuisine as well. This flavorful tomato sauce with oregano and chilies, for example, was served to me with sautéed chicken at a restaurant in the Mexican coastal town of Ensenada, south of the California border. Serve the chicken with green beans or peas and with rice, warmed tortillas, or the Mexican-Spanish noodles called fideos.

4 tablespoons olive or vegetable oil
1 or 2 jalapeño peppers, minced
2 medium garlic cloves, minced
2½ pounds ripe tomatoes, peeled, seeded, and chopped; or 2 (28-ounce) canned plum tomatoes, drained and chopped
1 bay leaf

salt and freshly ground pepper
4 boneless chicken breast halves (6 to 7 ounces each), skinned
¼ cup all-purpose flour
⅓ cup chicken stock or broth
1 tablespoon chopped fresh oregano, or 1 teaspoon dried
pinch of sugar (optional)

Heat 1 tablespoon oil in a heavy skillet over medium heat. Add peppers and garlic, and sauté ½ minute. Add tomatoes, bay leaf, salt, and pepper. Cook over medium heat, stirring often, until sauce is thick, about 20 minutes. Discard bay leaf. Puree sauce in a food processor or blender until very smooth.

Trim chicken breast halves of fat, cartilage, and tendons. Pound them one by one between 2 pieces of plastic wrap or wax paper until ¼ inch thick, using a flat meat pounder or rolling pin. Do not pound too forcefully or meat may tear. Carefully peel off wrap or paper.

Spread flour on a plate. Sprinkle chicken with salt and pepper on both sides. Lightly coat 2 chicken pieces with flour on both sides. Tap them to remove excess flour and arrange them side by side on a plate.

Heat remaining oil in a heavy, large skillet over medium-high heat. Add coated chicken. Sauté until browned on bottom, about 2 minutes. Using 2 wide spatulas, turn chicken over carefully. Sauté second side until browned and chicken is tender when pierced with a small sharp knife, about 2 minutes. Transfer chicken to platter, arrange pieces side by side, and keep warm in low oven. Flour and sauté remaining chicken. If oil in pan turns brown, reduce heat.

Discard oil from skillet. Add stock and oregano and bring to a boil, stirring and scraping to dissolve any browned bits in pan. Add tomato sauce and simmer, stirring, until sauce absorbs the stock, about 2 minutes. Taste, and add salt and pepper if needed; if sauce is too acid, add a pinch of sugar. To serve, spoon a little sauce on each of 4 plates and spread it to coat bottom of plate. Set chicken breasts on top, letting sauce show. Serve immediately; serve remaining sauce separately.

Makes 4 servings

CHICKEN INVOLTINI
WITH SMOKED CHICKEN, PESTO,
AND PEPPERS

Involtini are an Italian specialty usually made of a thin slice of veal rolled around a meat stuffing. I love to prepare them with boneless chicken breasts, which I spread with pesto, cover with strips of red pepper and smoked chicken, and roll up. A tomato-mushroom sauce flavored with plenty of fresh basil completes this elegant dish. Pasta spirals or fusilli and sautéed or steamed zucchini are good accompaniments.

4 boneless chicken breasts (about 1½ pounds), skin removed
salt and freshly ground pepper
¼ cup Pesto (page 363) or purchased
4 thin slices smoked chicken
1 roasted red bell pepper (page 408) or from a jar, patted dry and quartered
2 tablespoons olive oil

about ¼ cup all-purpose flour
4 ounces mushrooms, halved and sliced
2 teaspoons minced garlic
¼ cup dry white wine
1 cup Smooth Tomato Sauce (page 369) or purchased
2 tablespoons chopped fresh basil

Pound chicken breasts between sheets of wax paper to thickness of ¼ inch. Sprinkle chicken with salt and pepper. Spread each chicken breast with about 1 tablespoon pesto. Top with a slice of smoked chicken, then with ¼ roasted pepper. Starting at one long side of chicken breast, roll up tightly. Tie with 2 pieces of kitchen string to hold in place. Refrigerate 10 minutes.

Heat oil in heavy, large skillet over medium-high heat. Sprinkle chicken with salt and pepper. Dredge in flour and shake off excess. Put chicken in oil seam side down and sauté until golden brown on all sides, carefully turning with 2 spatulas, about 4 or 5 minutes. Put seam side down again. Cover and cook over low heat about 10 minutes or until chicken is cooked through. Remove chicken. Cover and keep warm.

Add mushrooms to skillet and sauté over medium heat 3 minutes. Stir in garlic and sauté

½ minute. Add wine to skillet and boil 1 or 2 minutes. Add tomato sauce and simmer until sauce is of desired thickness. Discard strings from chicken. Return chicken to sauce and heat through. Add basil. Taste sauce, adjust seasoning, and serve over chicken.

Makes 4 servings

MACADAMIA CHICKEN

When I was developing dishes for my article on macadamia nuts for Gourmet *magazine, I discovered that ground macadamia nuts could be used instead of breading to form a delicious, delicately crunchy crust on sautéed chicken breasts. The chicken can be topped with macadamia nut butter, for an extra festive touch. Dishes such as these are being developed as part of the ''new Hawaiian cuisine,'' making use of the islands' wonderful nuts. In fact, almonds, hazelnuts, or pecans can be used this way too. Nutmeg-accented spinach is a good accompaniment for the chicken.*

Macadamia Nut Butter (page 367, optional)
1 cup (about 4½ ounces) raw or dry-roasted macadamia nuts
2 boneless and skinless chicken breast halves (each about 5 ounces)
salt and freshly ground black pepper

⅓ cup all-purpose flour
1 egg, lightly beaten
¼ cup vegetable oil
2 tablespoons (¼ stick) butter
half-slices of a zested lime, for optional garnish

Bring Macadamia Nut Butter to room temperature. Transfer to a pastry bag fitted with a small star tip.

Grind macadamia nuts fine in a food processor. Pound chicken breasts between 2 sheets of wax paper until about ¼ inch thick. Sprinkle chicken lightly with salt and pepper on both sides, dredge it in flour, tapping and shaking off excess, and dip it in egg. Lastly, dip both sides of each piece in nuts until coated, patting and pressing lightly so nuts adhere. Handle chicken lightly so coating does not come off. Transfer chicken to a plate.

In a large, heavy skillet or in 2 medium skillets heat oil and butter until butter melts. Add chicken and sauté over medium-high heat for 1 minute, then over medium heat for 1½ minutes. Turn chicken over carefully using 2 wide spatulas and sauté on second side for about 2 minutes, or until golden brown. Transfer chicken to paper towels to drain, then to 2 heated plates.

To serve, garnish plates with half-slices of lime, if desired. Pipe a decorative line of nut butter down center of each chicken piece. Serve remaining nut butter separately.

Makes 2 servings

CHICKEN PAILLARDES
WITH PORCINI MUSHROOMS
AND SHALLOTS

An ideal type of entree for summer, when light dinners are most people's preference, is a chicken paillarde (pronounced pie-yard). *Basically a paillarde is a boneless slice of meat that is pounded until thin and then briefly sautéed or grilled.*

In classic cuisine paillardes referred only to beef and veal and were a favorite in Italy and France. Today they are made in more and more places and with several different meats. They are an especially good way to prepare chicken and turkey breasts, because they cook faster than usual and so the lean meat has less chance to become too dry.

Another advantage of paillardes is that they look big! Their area increases as they are pounded, and each portion seems generous in size when in fact it weighs relatively little.

Paillardes are also delicious when grilled. To help control the brief cooking time of the chicken, I find that a ridged stovetop grill pan is better than a broiler or outdoor grill.

For this dish, you can either sauté or grill the chicken, then serve it with the savory Italian-style porcini-onion mixture. If porcini mushrooms are not available, other dried mushrooms can be substituted.

1 ounce dried porcini mushrooms
2 tablespoons (¼ stick) butter
3 to 4 tablespoons vegetable oil
2 medium onions, halved and thinly sliced
2 large shallots, finely chopped
salt and freshly ground pepper
4 boneless and skinless chicken breast halves (6 to 7 ounces each)

2 teaspoons tomato paste
1 teaspoon cornstarch, potato starch, or arrowroot
1 tablespoon plus 1 teaspoon cold water
¼ cup dry white wine
¾ cup chicken stock
1 tablespoon minced fresh parsley

Soak mushrooms in enough hot water to cover them for 30 minutes. Rinse mushrooms and cut any large pieces in half.

Heat butter and 1 tablespoon oil in a large, heavy skillet or sauté pan over medium heat. Add onions and cook, stirring often, until soft, about 15 minutes. Add mushrooms, half the chopped shallots, salt, and pepper. Cover and cook 5 minutes. *Mushroom mixture can be kept, covered, 1 day in refrigerator.*

Trim chicken of fat, cartilage, and tendons. Pound pieces one by one between 2 pieces of plastic wrap or wax paper until ¼ inch thick, using a flat meat pounder or rolling pin. Carefully peel off wrap or paper.

Heat 2 tablespoons oil in another heavy, large skillet over medium-high heat. Add 2 pieces chicken and sprinkle with salt and pepper. Sauté about 2 minutes per side or until chicken's color changes throughout; cut with a small sharp knife to check. Transfer chicken to platter, arrange pieces side by side, and keep them warm in low oven. Sauté remaining chicken, adding more oil if needed. If oil in pan turns brown, reduce heat. Transfer chicken to platter.

In a cup mix tomato paste, cornstarch, and water to a smooth paste. Reheat mushroom mixture. Discard fat from chicken skillet. Add wine and remaining shallots to skillet and bring to a boil, stirring. Add stock and bring to a boil. Add tomato paste mixture, whisking constantly. Simmer 1 or 2 minutes or until thickened. Taste and adjust seasoning.

Serve chicken with mushroom mixture. Coat chicken with sauce and sprinkle with parsley.

Makes 4 servings

SAUTÉED CHICKEN BREASTS WITH HERBED MUSHROOM SAUCE

Poultry is not just a mainstay of home cooking. At every world-famous restaurant I have visited I found poultry specialties an important part of the menu. This chicken in flavorful creamy sauce is a type of dish served in fine European restaurants. It is irresistible with fresh fettuccine or rice and with broccoli, spinach, or other green vegetables.

At the market you will sometimes find skinless boneless chicken breast fillets, or small tender strips; these can also be used for the dish but require only 1 or 2 minutes of sautéing per side.

4 boneless chicken breast halves (1 to 1¼ pounds), skin removed	1 tablespoon butter
salt and freshly ground pepper	¼ cup Madeira (optional)
2 tablespoons vegetable oil	Mushroom Sauce (page 373)
	1 tablespoon snipped fresh chives

Sprinkle chicken with salt and pepper on both sides. Heat oil and butter in a large, heavy skillet over medium-high heat. Add chicken and sauté, pressing on chicken occasionally with slotted spatula, about 4 or 5 minutes per side or until meat feels springy and is no longer pink inside; cut to check. Transfer to a platter, cover, and keep warm.

Discard fat from skillet. Add Madeira and bring to a boil, stirring and scraping in pan juices. Pour into mushroom sauce and heat gently. Taste and adjust seasoning. Transfer chicken to serving plates, discarding juices from platter. Spoon sauce over chicken. Sprinkle with chives.

Makes 4 servings

CHICKEN SALTIMBOCCA

Fresh sage leaves give a burst of flavor in every bite in this chicken adaptation of the Italian classic made with veal and prosciutto. It's very pretty, because you see the sage leaves through the thin slices of smoked chicken. The delicately sweet marsala-sage sauce is a good match for the chicken.

4 boneless chicken breasts (about 1½
   pounds), skin removed
24 to 28 fresh sage leaves
4 thin slices smoked chicken
4 tablespoons olive oil
about ¼ cup all-purpose flour

¼ cup dry white wine
¼ cup marsala or Port
¾ cup chicken stock or broth
1 tablespoon chopped fresh sage
freshly ground pepper

Pound chicken breasts between sheets of wax paper to a thickness of slightly over ¼ inch. Put 6 or 7 fresh sage leaves on the less smooth side of each pounded chicken breast. Cover leaves with thin slice smoked chicken, and pound lightly to make them adhere. Refrigerate 10 minutes.

Divide oil between 2 heavy, large skillets over medium-high heat. Dredge chicken in flour and shake off excess. Sauté chicken about 2 minutes per side or until color changes throughout. Remove chicken. Cover and keep warm.

Divide wine and marsala between skillets and boil, scraping up browned bits, 1 minute. Combine in 1 skillet. Add stock and boil until reduced to ⅓ cup. Add chopped sage. Simmer 1 minute. Add pepper to taste; salt may not be needed. Pour sauce over chicken and serve.

Makes 4 servings

CHICKEN THIGH SAUTÉ WITH RED WINE, BABY ONIONS, AND MUSHROOMS

This is a simpler and lighter variation of Burgundian-style coq au vin, *where bacon is added to the sauce. The taste of the sauce does depend on the quality of the wine. The classic rule of thumb for choosing the right wine for cooking can be applied here too; use a wine that you enjoy drinking. Of course almost nobody cooks with the finest Burgundies, but if you use a fairly inexpensive bottle of Burgundy, Beaujolais, or California Cabernet Sauvignon instead of the cheapest red wine in the store, the sauce will be noticeably superior in flavor.*

Serve the chicken with boiled or steamed new potatoes or just with fresh, crusty French baguette or country bread. For a festive menu à la francaise, serve steamed shrimp or mussels in white wine before the chicken and follow it with green salad, and then with several French cheeses, such as chèvre, Roquefort, or Beaufort (French Gruyère), which also benefit from being served with the wine.

16 baby onions (pearl onions)	2 teaspoons all-purpose flour
1 tablespoon vegetable oil	1 medium garlic clove, minced
3 tablespoons butter	1 cup dry red wine
2½ to 3 pounds chicken thighs, patted dry	1 bay leaf
salt and freshly ground pepper	1 teaspoon dried thyme, crumbled
4 to 6 ounces mushrooms, quartered	⅔ cup chicken stock or broth
	pinch of sugar (optional)

Put onions in a small saucepan, cover with water, and bring to a boil. Boil 1 minute. Drain, rinse under cold water, and drain well. Peel with aid of a paring knife.

Heat 1 tablespoon oil and 1 tablespoon butter in large, heavy skillet over medium-high heat. Add chicken pieces in batches, sprinkle with salt and pepper, and brown on all sides. Set on a plate, using slotted spoon. Add onions and sauté, shaking pan often, until browned on all sides. Transfer to plate. Add mushrooms, salt, and pepper and brown lightly. Transfer to plate.

Return chicken and onions to skillet. Scatter mushrooms over them. Add chicken juices from plate. Cover and cook over low heat about 25 minutes or until chicken is tender when pierced with a knife.

While chicken cooks, mash remaining 2 tablespoons butter in a small bowl with a fork until softened. Mix in flour until mixture becomes a uniform paste.

Transfer chicken to a platter using slotted spoon, cover, and keep warm. With slotted spoon, transfer vegetables to a bowl.

Skim as much fat as possible from juices in skillet. Reheat juices until very hot. Add garlic and stir over low heat for ½ minute. Add wine, bay leaf, and thyme and bring to a boil. Add stock and boil, stirring and skimming fat often, until mixture is reduced to about ¾ cup.

Discard bay leaf. Gradually add butter-flour paste to simmering sauce, a small piece at a time, whisking constantly. Bring to a boil, whisking. Return vegetables to sauce and heat 1 minute over low heat to blend flavors. Taste sauce for seasoning; if it is too tart, add a pinch of sugar. Spoon sauce and vegetables over chicken and serve. *This dish is best if served at once but it can be kept in the sauce, covered, overnight in refrigerator. Reheat in covered skillet.*

Makes 4 servings

SPICY FRIED CHICKEN WITH CAPERS

My favorite way to prepare fried chicken is to give boneless chicken breasts a spicy coating and add a tangy Mediterranean-style topping like the capers and parsley in this recipe, rather than a heavy cream gravy. The lean meat is kept juicy by the rich and crunchy bread crumb coating. To vary the coating, you can substitute whole wheat flour for the white flour, or cornmeal or matzo meal for the bread crumbs. Cooked cauliflower, sautéed zucchini, or fried potatoes are good accompaniments, and so are black-eyed peas.

4 boneless chicken breast halves
  (about 1¼ pounds), skin removed
1½ teaspoons ground cumin
½ teaspoon ground coriander
½ teaspoon salt
¼ teaspoon freshly ground black
  pepper
¼ teaspoon cayenne pepper

⅓ cup all-purpose flour
⅔ cup unseasoned dry bread crumbs
1 egg
⅓ cup vegetable oil
4 teaspoons capers, rinsed and drained
2 tablespoons minced fresh parsley
3 tablespoons butter
lemon wedges, for serving

Arrange chicken in one layer on plate. Mix cumin, coriander, salt, black pepper, and cayenne in a small bowl. Sprinkle 1¼ teaspoons spice mixture evenly over one side of chicken pieces and rub thoroughly into chicken. Turn chicken over, sprinkle with remaining spice mixture, and rub into chicken.

Spread flour in a large plate. Spread bread crumbs in a second plate. Beat egg in shallow bowl. Lightly coat 1 chicken piece with flour on both sides; tap and shake to remove excess flour. Dip piece in egg. Then dip chicken in bread crumbs so both sides are completely coated; pat lightly so crumbs adhere. Repeat with remaining chicken. Set pieces side by side on large plate. Handle chicken lightly.

Heat oil in a heavy, large skillet over medium-high heat. Add enough chicken to make one layer. Sauté until golden brown on both sides, about 3 minutes per side. Turn carefully using 2 wide spatulas. If oil in skillet begins to brown, reduce heat to medium. Set chicken pieces side by side on ovenproof platter and keep them warm in a 275°F. oven while sautéing remaining slices.

Sprinkle chicken with capers and parsley. Heat butter in a heavy medium saucepan (of light-colored interior) over medium-low heat, shaking pan often, just until butter is light brown. Pour immediately over chicken. Serve with lemon wedges.

Makes 4 servings

AUSTRIAN FRIED CHICKEN

Like American fried chicken, this dish is prepared with chicken pieces with the bone in. The bread crumb coating ensures a crisp crust on the pieces. Serve the chicken according to the Austrian custom, with a salad of mixed lettuces or a cucumber salad seasoned with paprika vinaigrette or with sour cream and dill.

4 chicken drumsticks (about 1½ pounds)
4 chicken thighs (about 1½ pounds)
2 eggs
½ teaspoon salt
¼ teaspoon freshly ground black pepper

1¼ cups unseasoned bread crumbs
⅔ cup all-purpose flour
1½ cups vegetable oil
lemon wedges and parsley sprigs, for garnish

Pat chicken dry. In a shallow bowl, beat eggs with salt and pepper. Put bread crumbs on a large plate. Dredge chicken pieces in flour. Dip pieces in beaten egg, then roll in bread crumbs.

Heat oil in a deep, 10-inch skillet to 275°F. Add half the chicken and slowly brown over medium-low heat, turning as needed, about 20 minutes or until juices run clear when a piece is tested; remove from oil to test. Transfer to paper towel-lined baking sheet and keep warm in 250°F. oven. Add oil to pan if needed. Fry remaining chicken. Serve hot, with lemon wedges and parsley.

Makes 4 servings

CHILI-SPICED FRIED CHICKEN

Rubbing the Tex-Mex-style spice mixture over the chicken and refrigerating the chicken overnight before cooking intensifies the spicy flavor of the chicken. Serve the chicken garnished with cilantro or parsley sprigs and lime or lemon wedges.

1 tablespoon plus 1½ teaspoons chili powder
1 tablespoon ground cumin
1 teaspoon turmeric
½ teaspoon cayenne pepper
¼ teaspoon freshly ground black pepper
½ teaspoon salt

8 chicken drumsticks (about 3 pounds), patted dry
2 eggs
¼ teaspoon hot red pepper sauce
1¼ cups unseasoned bread crumbs
⅔ cup all-purpose flour
1½ cups vegetable oil

Mix spices with salt. Rub mixture over chicken pieces. *Spice-rubbed chicken can be refrigerated, covered, overnight.*

In a shallow bowl, beat eggs with hot pepper sauce. Put bread crumbs on a large plate. Dredge chicken pieces in flour. Dip pieces in eggs, then roll in bread crumbs.

Heat oil in a deep, 10-inch skillet to 275°F. Add half the chicken and slowly brown over medium-low heat, turning as needed, about 20 minutes or until juices run clear when a piece is tested; remove from oil to test. Transfer to paper towel-lined baking sheet and keep warm in 250°F. oven. Add oil to pan if needed. Fry remaining chicken. Serve hot.

Makes 4 servings

VARIATION: **Chili Fried Chicken Wings**
Substitute 3 pounds chicken wings or drummettes (largest section of wing) for drumsticks. If using wings, cut off tips, then fold remaining sections of wing backwards to crack the joint and permit them to lie flat. Fry as above, taking about 12 minutes.

STIR-FRIED CHICKEN WITH BABY CORN, SNOW PEAS, AND MUSHROOMS

This is a classic Chinese stir-fry that I learned to make at Wei-Chuan cooking school in Taiwan. It is flavorful, fresh, colorful, and light textured.

The first step, of briefly deep-frying the rice-wine marinated chicken, is designed to seal in the chicken's natural juices and gives a velvety texture to the surface. The chicken is then stir-fried with a variety of vegetables: tender ones like mushrooms; canned Chinese vegetables, which are blanched or rinsed first to remove the taste of the brine; and fresh ones with a longer cooking time, like carrots, which are briefly precooked until nearly tender but still crisp. Finally the chicken and vegetables are moistened with a light sauce flavored with rice wine and soy sauce.

The cooking time of stir-fried chicken dishes is very brief. To cut down on the vegetable preparation time, you can choose two or three vegetables and increase the quantities. SEE PHOTOGRAPH.

1 pound boneless and skinless chicken
   breasts

Rice Wine Marinade

2 teaspoons rice wine or dry sherry
¼ teaspoon freshly ground white
   pepper

⅛ teaspoon salt
1 teaspoon cornstarch

Vegetables

1 large carrot
¼ pound snow peas, strings and ends
   removed
½ cup canned water chestnuts, halved
   crosswise

12 ears canned baby corn
white and light green parts of 3 green
   onions
4 ounces small mushrooms

Soy and Rice Wine Sauce

1 tablespoon rice wine or sherry
2 teaspoons soy sauce
¼ teaspoon salt
¼ teaspoon sugar

freshly ground black pepper to taste
½ teaspoon cornstarch
1 tablespoon water

2 cups vegetable oil, for frying
1 tablespoon plus 1 teaspoon minced
   peeled fresh ginger

2 medium garlic cloves, minced

Cut chicken breasts horizontally in two so pieces are of even thickness. Cut flat pieces in strips of about 1½ × ¾ inch. Mix marinade ingredients in a bowl, add chicken, and toss well. Let stand about 20 minutes while preparing remaining ingredients.

Quarter the thick part of carrot lengthwise. Cut carrot into ¼-inch-thick diagonal slices. Add carrot to a saucepan of boiling water and cook about 3 minutes until barely tender. Add snow peas, water chestnuts, and baby corn and boil ½ minute. Drain, rinse with cold water, and drain well.

Cut thick part of green onion in half lengthwise. Cut green onion in 1-inch diagonal pieces. Quarter the mushrooms.

In a cup, stir together the sauce ingredients until well blended.

Heat a wok or deep, heavy skillet or sauté pan; add oil and heat to 350°F. degrees. Add chicken pieces and cook, stirring often with slotted spoon, about 2½ minutes or until they change color; remove a piece and cut it to check. Remove pieces with a slotted spoon and drain in strainer. Remove oil from pan.

Return 2 tablespoons oil to pan and reheat over high heat. Add ginger, green onions, and garlic and stir-fry 1 or 2 seconds. Add mushrooms and stir-fry 1 minute. Add chicken and remaining vegetables and stir. Stir sauce mixture and add immediately. Stir-fry until thickened, tossing. Serve immediately.

Makes 3 or 4 servings with other dishes, or 2 or 3 servings on its own with rice

SPICY STIR-FRIED CHICKEN WITH PEPPERS AND BROCCOLI

Flavored in the Sichuan tradition with sesame oil and chili paste with garlic, this chicken stir-fry can be quite hot, depending on the strength of the chili paste and how much you add. If chili paste is not available, you can use Oriental chili sauce instead; double the amount specified for chili paste and stir it into the finished dish. For extra heat, you can drizzle a little chili oil over the chicken-vegetable mixture after removing it from the heat.

This is the way stir-fries are often done in home kitchens—there is no marinating and no preliminary deep-frying. In professional kitchens stir-frying is done on very high heat, but at home it's easier to control the cooking if medium-high heat is used.

As with other stir-fried dishes, you can vary the vegetables to your taste; instead of the broccoli, you can add blanched snow peas or sugar-snap peas. For a festive touch, add ½ cup toasted peanuts. Serve this colorful dish with steamed rice.

Soy and Rice Vinegar Sauce

1 tablespoon plus 1 teaspoon soy sauce
1½ teaspoons sugar
2 teaspoons rice vinegar

1 teaspoon cornstarch
1 tablespoon plus 1 teaspoon water

2 cups small broccoli florets
1 to 1¼ pounds boneless chicken
  breast, skin removed
3 tablespoons plus 1 teaspoon
  vegetable oil
1 medium onion, halved, sliced thin
1 red bell pepper, cut in 2 × ½-inch
  strips

2 medium garlic cloves, minced
1 tablespoon minced peeled fresh
  ginger
1½ teaspoons Chinese chili paste with
  garlic
1 teaspoon Oriental sesame oil

Mix sauce ingredients; set aside.

Add broccoli to a pan of boiling water and boil 2 minutes. Rinse gently with cold water and drain. Cut chicken crosswise in slices ¼ inch thick.

Heat 2 tablespoons oil in skillet or wok, add onion and pepper, and sauté over high heat 5 or 6 minutes or until softened. Remove from pan.

Add remaining oil to skillet and heat over medium-high heat. Stir in garlic, ginger, and chili paste. Add chicken and stir-fry 3 minutes or until cooked through; cut a piece to check. Stir sauce mixture and add to skillet. Add all vegetables and stir. Stir 1 or 2 minutes or until thickened. Off the heat, stir in sesame oil. Serve immediately.

Makes 3 or 4 servings

THAI CHICKEN STIR-FRY WITH MINT LEAVES AND CHILIES

Chilies and mint are a wonderful Thai combination, with the mint's freshness slightly balancing the heat of the peppers. The chilies are left in large pieces, so they can flavor and garnish the dish, and can easily be removed by those who do not want to eat them. I like to use boneless chicken thighs in this dish, but if they are not available or if you prefer leaner meat, use boneless breasts. Serve the chicken with steamed rice. SEE PHOTOGRAPH.

4 green onions
8 ounces boneless and skinless
   chicken breasts or thighs
4 tablespoons vegetable oil
1 large onion, halved lengthwise, cut
   in thin slices, separated in half-rings
2 fresh red or green jalapeño or
   serrano peppers, halved lengthwise

4 medium garlic cloves, minced
½ cup chicken stock
2 tablespoons soy sauce
1 cup whole fresh mint leaves
hot cooked rice, for serving

Chop white and light green parts of green onions. Cut dark green part in 3-inch pieces. Cut chicken in 3 × ¼ × ¼-inch strips.

Heat 2 tablespoons oil in a large skillet or wok over medium heat. Add sliced onion and peppers and sauté, stirring, about 7 minutes or until onion browns lightly; it may still be a bit crunchy. Transfer to a bowl.

Add 1 tablespoon oil to skillet and heat over high heat. Add chicken and sauté until it changes color, about 1 minute. Do not overcook. Add to sliced onions.

Add remaining tablespoon oil to skillet and heat over medium-low heat. Add garlic and all the green onions and sauté ½ minute. Add stock and soy sauce and heat through. Add chicken, onion slices, peppers, and mint leaves and toss ½ minute over low heat. Taste, and add more soy sauce if needed. Serve over rice.

Makes 2 or 3 servings

HUNGARIAN-STYLE CHICKEN LIVERS WITH ONIONS

Liver and onions is a popular combination throughout Europe. In this dish the livers are flavored with a typical Hungarian seasoning mixture of sweet and hot paprika and garlic. Serve them with rice or noodles and with carrots, baby onions, mushrooms, or green beans. Since livers are rich, you can serve them instead as an appetizer, inside small puff pastry shells or with crusty bread. If you have a frying screen, use it to cover the livers during sautéing to prevent splatters.

5 tablespoons vegetable oil
2 large onions, thinly sliced
salt and freshly ground pepper
2 medium garlic cloves, chopped
1½ teaspoons sweet paprika

¾ pound chicken livers
¼ teaspoon hot paprika or cayenne
  pepper
½ cup fresh or canned tomato puree

Heat 2 tablespoons oil in a large, heavy skillet over medium heat. Add onions, salt, and pepper and stir until coated. Stir in garlic and 1 teaspoon sweet paprika. Reduce heat to low, cover, and cook, stirring occasionally, until tender, about 20 minutes.

Cut livers in half. Cut out any green spots and discard. Pat livers dry with paper towels. Mix remaining sweet paprika with hot paprika. Sprinkle livers evenly with salt and spice mixture.

Reheat onions if necessary, in skillet over medium heat. Continue sautéing them, uncovered, stirring often, until lightly browned. Stir in tomato puree and bring to a boil. Taste and adjust seasoning. Cover and keep warm.

Heat 3 tablespoons oil in a large, heavy skillet over medium-high heat. Add the livers and sauté until browned, about 3 minutes; turn over and sauté until second side is well browned and tender, about 2½ minutes. To check, cut into a large piece of liver; it should be light pink, not red, inside. Do not overcook, or livers will be dry. Taste, and add salt and pepper if needed. Spoon onion mixture onto plate and serve livers on top.

Makes 4 or 5 appetizer or 2 main-course servings

SAVORY CHICKEN LIVERS WITH ONIONS, MIDDLE EASTERN STYLE

Liver with onions seems to be a universal favorite. In North Africa and the Middle East, cumin is the seasoning of choice, often paired with cayenne and sometimes with garlic, turmeric, or paprika. The chicken livers can be served as a first course, accompanied by pita wedges, or as a main course, served with plain rice or with rice enhanced with raisins or currants. A pleasing vegetable accompaniment is roasted peppers (page 408), sautéed zucchini, or diced Mediterranean salad.

Sautéing is the preferred technique for preparing chicken livers in Europe, but in the Middle East they are also popular threaded on skewers, seasoned as in this recipe, and grilled.

4 to 5 tablespoons olive or vegetable oil	1 pound chicken livers
2 large onions, thinly sliced	1½ teaspoons ground cumin
salt and freshly ground pepper	½ teaspoon turmeric (optional)
2 large garlic cloves, chopped	¼ teaspoon cayenne pepper
	2 tablespoons chopped fresh parsley

Heat 2 tablespoons oil in a large, heavy skillet over medium heat. Add onions, salt, and pepper and sauté, stirring often, about 15 minutes or until tender and lightly browned. Add garlic and sauté over low heat, stirring, 1 minute.

Cut livers in half. Cut out any green spots and discard. Pat livers dry with paper towels. Mix cumin, turmeric, and cayenne pepper. Sprinkle livers evenly with salt, pepper, and spice mixture.

Heat 2 or 3 tablespoons oil in a large, heavy skillet over medium-high heat. Add livers, cover with a splatter screen, and sauté about 3 minutes per side or until well browned and cooked through. To check, cut into a large piece of liver; it should be light pink, not red, inside. Do not overcook, or livers will be dry and tough. Taste and adjust seasoning. Add parsley to pan and toss quickly.

Reheat onions. Spoon livers over onions and serve.

Makes 3 or 4 servings

SAUTÉED TURKEY
WITH SHALLOT PUREE AND BEETS

A creamy puree of braised shallots beautifully complements the lean turkey in this festive fall or winter dish that I learned to make in Paris. Colorful steamed baby beets complete the cool-weather theme and taste wonderful with the shallot puree. Boiled red potatoes and sautéed cabbage, Swiss chard, or spinach also are good accompaniments.

16 to 20 baby beets
½ pound shallots, peeled and cut in
   half
3 tablespoons butter
salt and freshly ground pepper

3 tablespoons heavy cream
3 tablespoons vegetable oil
1 to 1¼ pounds turkey breast slices, ⅜
   inch thick, patted dry

Steam the beets in the top of a covered steamer above boiling water about 15 to 20 minutes or until tender. Rinse lightly, remove tops and root ends, and slip off skins. Return to steamer top with heat turned off, cover, and keep warm.

In a medium saucepan, cover shallots with water, bring to a boil, and cook 2 minutes. Drain thoroughly. In a heavy, medium sauté pan, melt butter over low heat, and add shallots and a pinch of salt and pepper. Cover and cook, stirring often, about 20 minutes, or until shallots are very tender; do not let them burn.

Puree shallots in a food processor. Put puree in a small heavy saucepan and stir over low heat. Add cream and stir until absorbed. Taste and adjust seasoning.

Sprinkle turkey with salt and pepper on both sides. Heat oil in a large heavy skillet over medium-high heat. Add half of turkey slices and sauté about 1½ minutes per side or until they just change color inside; cut to check. Transfer to a plate and keep warm. Repeat with remaining turkey. Transfer to plate. Serve with shallot puree and beets.

Makes 4 servings

TUNISIAN TURKEY SLICES WITH TOMATO SAUCE, OLIVES, AND CAPERS

In this quick, easy dish, the North African seasoning combination of olives and capers in a garlicky tomato sauce does wonders for sautéed turkey slices. Serve them with sautéed zucchini and white rice.

1 pound turkey breast slices (¼ inch thick), patted dry
3 tablespoons olive oil
salt and freshly ground pepper
4 large garlic cloves, chopped
1½ cups Fresh Tomato Sauce (page 369) or packaged

2 tablespoons tomato paste
2 tablespoons water
½ teaspoon dried oregano, crumbled
¾ cup black olives
2 tablespoons capers, rinsed and drained

Cut each turkey slice in 6 or 8 pieces, about 1½- or 2-inch square. Put on paper towel-lined plate. Heat oil in large, heavy skillet over medium-high heat. Add half of turkey, sprinkle with salt and pepper, and sauté, stirring often, about 1 minute per side, just until color changes throughout; cut a piece to check. Transfer turkey to plate and keep warm. Repeat with remaining turkey.

Add garlic to pan and sauté ½ minute over medium heat. Add tomato sauce, tomato paste, and water and bring to a boil, stirring. Add oregano, olives, and 1 tablespoon capers and simmer over low heat 3 minutes. Taste and adjust seasoning. Spoon over turkey and sprinkle with remaining capers.

Makes 4 servings

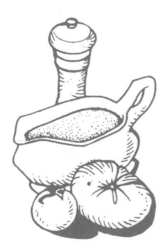

TURKEY BREAST SLICES
WITH HORSERADISH SAUCE

In central Europe horseradish sauce is popular with roast goose. I enjoyed it in Austria, where it is also served with boiled beef, but I prefer this rich creamy sauce with the lean meat of turkey. Serve the turkey with noodles and a green vegetable such as broccoli.

Horseradish Sauce

½ cup chicken stock or broth
½ cup dry white wine
½ cup heavy cream

1 to 1¼ pounds turkey breast slices, ⅜
   inch thick, patted dry
2 tablespoons vegetable oil

¾ cup finely grated peeled fresh
   horseradish (about 4½ ounces)
salt and freshly ground pepper

1 tablespoon butter
parsley sprigs for garnish

Boil stock and wine in a medium saucepan until reduced to about ⅓ cup. Add cream and simmer until thick enough to lightly coat a spoon. Remove from heat. Stir in grated horseradish. Season to taste with salt and pepper.

Sprinkle turkey with salt and pepper on both sides. Heat oil and butter in a large, heavy skillet over medium-high heat. Add half the turkey slices and sauté about 1½ minutes per side or until they just change color inside; cut to check. Transfer to a plate and keep warm. Repeat with remaining turkey. Transfer to plate. Serve with horseradish sauce and garnish with parsley sprigs.

Makes 4 servings

—12—

Braised and Poached Chicken and Turkey

I wonder why cooking chicken and turkey by the two moist-heat methods of braising and poaching is central to so many cuisines throughout the world but not to that of America. We would do well to relearn these valuable techniques, for reasons of flavor and nutrition.

Poaching is a fat-free cooking method that is ideal for those days when we want our meals as lean and healthful as possible. The poaching liquid can be chicken stock, wine, or water flavored with herbs and aromatic vegetables. Red-cooking is a Chinese variation of poaching for which soy sauce is part of the liquid and fresh ginger and star anise provide flavor.

Poaching is, of course, the way chicken and turkey are cooked for soup and stock. But for poaching you can season the liquid more boldly, with plenty of wine and aromatics—more than you would use for seasoning chicken soup. It's best to remove the skin of poached chicken or turkey before serving.

For braising, the chicken is first browned in a small amount of oil or butter so the chicken gains an appealing color. Browning also melts some of the fat under the skin, which can

225

Basquaise Chicken Breasts with Peppers
and Tomatoes
Indian Chicken Breasts
in Fiery Almond Cashew Ginger Sauce
Thai Chicken Curry
Braised Chicken with Morel Sauce
Chicken Braised in Saffron Tomato Sauce
Greek Chicken with Red Wine, Raisins,
and Baby Onions
North African Chicken with Onion Sauce
Brazilian Chicken with Tomatoes, Coconut Milk,
and Cilantro
Moroccan Chicken with Two Heads of Garlic
Iranian Chicken in Walnut-Pomegranate Sauce
(Chicken *Fesanjan*)
Braised Chicken with Watercress Sauce
Moroccan Chicken with Prunes and Almonds
Mediterranean Chicken with Olives
Chicken with Beer and Apples

Philippine Chicken Adobo
Indian Braised Chicken with Ginger, Coriander,
Cumin, and Yogurt
Sri Lankan Chicken Curry
Spicy Ethiopian Chicken (*Doro Wat*)
Red-Cooked Chicken Thighs with Mushrooms
Colombian Chicken
Mexican Chicken with Chilies
and Cilantro-Tomato Sauce
Cumin-Scented Chicken Balls
in Tomato-Basil Sauce
Chicken Gizzards and Wings Cacciatora
Braised Turkey Breast, Hungarian Style
Country Turkey Wings with Cumin
and Tomatoes
Turkey Leg Daube with Cèpes and Red Wine
Turkey Mole
Turkey Chili
Turkey Sausages with Beans and Tomatoes

then be poured off, resulting in a leaner dish. Whole chickens can be braised, and so can chicken pieces, in which case the dish is often called a chicken stew. White or red wine and stock are the most frequently used braising liquids, but there are other options. In Belgium and in northern France, for example, the butter-sautéed chicken may cook in beer or dry cider, while in Mediterranean regions it is typically sautéed in olive oil, then moistened with a fresh tomato sauce, as in Chicken Braised in Saffron Tomato Sauce (page 234). A favorite recipe for braising chicken in Iran requires simmering it in pomegranate juice.

Turkey thighs, drumsticks, and wings deserve to appear more often on our tables, since they, like chicken pieces, are valuable for making delicious stews. Whether braised à la provençale with red wine and mushrooms, or in the Mexican style with a zesty combination of cumin, chilies, and tomatoes, the result of the long, slow simmering is meat that is tender and flavorful.

The advantage of braising is that the chicken or turkey cooks directly in the sauce and gives it an incomparable rich taste. Besides being moist and tender, braised chicken and turkey are convenient: they are easy to prepare, and, like any stew, can be cooked in advance and reheat beautifully. Indeed, braising is the best way to cook poultry for do-ahead dinners.

Chicken and turkey have so much natural flavor that the braising sauce will be tasty even if only a small number of ingredients is added. In Colombian Chicken (page 250), for example, the chicken pieces are braised simply with onions and tomatoes. Many spicy Indian chicken specialties are braised gently with onions, garlic, ginger, cumin, and a variety of other spices. Few dishes are as delicious as French-style chicken braised with wine and mushrooms, or *coq au vin*. The great Moroccan chicken tajines, redolent of saffron, garlic, and herbs, are variations of the poaching technique.

The cooking liquid from poached or braised chicken or turkey can be thickened with a "kneaded butter" (*beurre manié*) of flour mixed with butter or with a classic French roux of flour cooked with butter. A simpler, less rich alternative is a solution of cornstarch and water in the Chinese style, or one of arrowroot or potato starch and water in the French manner. However, the liquid does not necessarily have to be thickened. If you serve the chicken or turkey with couscous or rice, for example, the unthickened sauce is very good with the grain.

Poached chicken is traditionally served with zesty condiments—Italian green sauce, Dijon mustard, Mexican salsa, or Indian chutney, for example. A friend of mine from Romania always has horseradish on the table to accompany poached chicken.

These methods are the easiest to turn into one-pot meals, since you can poach all sorts of vegetables with the poultry—potatoes, carrots, and other root vegetables can be added from the beginning; and quick-cooking ingredients like mushrooms, zucchini, or green beans are added toward the end of the cooking.

Professional chefs often prefer to poach chicken for salads rather than cooking it by other methods because it keeps moist even when refrigerated. For the same reason, it is a good method for preparing chicken at home for mixtures that will be reheated, such as fillings for tortillas or crepes. I find it convenient to poach a chicken every week—I always find a good use for the meat in various dishes, and besides I have great stock to serve as soup or to use for cooking rice.

TIPS

⚔ Professional chefs like to brown chicken in skillets, but I find that a deep casserole is easier to use at home so there is less chance of the oil splattering.

⚔ If you use a good-quality pan, you can use a smaller amount of oil for browning the chicken.

⚔ When browning the chicken, I find it easiest to release it first with a pancake turner, then to turn it with tongs.

⚔ For braised chicken, if you have purchased a cut-up chicken in which the breast is one piece, cut it in half lengthwise along the breastbone. You can add the chicken neck, wing tips, back pieces, and giblets (except liver) to the pan if there is room, to flavor the sauce, and remove them before serving.

⚔ If braised chicken pieces are left over, cut the meat in strips, add them to the heated sauce, and serve it over rice, pasta, or couscous.

BASQUAISE CHICKEN BREASTS WITH PEPPERS AND TOMATOES

When I traveled in the Basque area of France and Spain, I ordered the famous specialty of that region at restaurants and tasted it at charcuteries more than any other dish. At home I like to make a lighter version of the classic by using chicken breasts and omitting the customary ham in the sauce. The glistening pepper strips in the aromatic tomato sauce accented with hot red pepper flakes ensure that this new version will be just as flavorful as the old-fashioned one. A traditional accompaniment is fried cornmeal cakes, but, again in the interest of lightness, I serve it with fresh corn.

2 tablespoons olive or vegetable oil
3 chicken breast halves, with skin and
  bones (total 2¼ pounds)
salt and freshly ground pepper
2 medium onions, sliced (total ½
  pound)
1 red bell pepper, halved crosswise,
  cut in ½-inch strips
1 small green bell pepper, halved
  crosswise, cut in ½-inch strips

4 medium garlic cloves, chopped
1 pound ripe tomatoes, peeled, seeded,
  and chopped; or 1 (28-ounce) can
  plum tomatoes, drained and
  chopped
½ teaspoon dried thyme
1 bay leaf
¼ teaspoon dried red pepper flakes
cayenne pepper to taste (optional)

Heat the oil in a medium sauté pan, add the chicken pieces, sprinkle with salt and pepper, and brown lightly in 2 batches over medium-high heat, taking 5 or 6 minutes for each. Transfer chicken to a plate.

Add onions to pan and sauté over medium heat about 3 minutes. Add peppers and cook, stirring often, for 7 minutes. Stir in garlic, then add tomatoes, thyme, bay leaf, and pepper flakes and bring to a boil. Cook uncovered 5 minutes.

Return chicken pieces to pan, with any juices on plate. Cover and cook over low heat, turning once, about 20 minutes or until meat is no longer pink when cut in thickest part. Remove bay leaf. Taste and adjust seasoning, adding cayenne if needed.

Makes 3 servings

INDIAN CHICKEN BREASTS IN FIERY ALMOND CASHEW GINGER SAUCE

Indian cooking expert Neelam Batra of Santa Monica flavors the sauce for this aromatic chicken dish mostly with fresh seasonings rather than dried spices, then thickens it with ground almonds and cashews. From the list of ingredients, it might not appear hot, but the generous amount of ginger in the seasoning paste contributes to the sauce's fiery and spicy character. Serve this luxurious dish with plenty of rice, and with yogurt to cool the palate.

6 pounds boneless chicken breast
   halves
2-inch piece fresh ginger, peeled and
   cut in 4 pieces
3 medium garlic cloves, peeled
1 small onion, quartered
1 medium tomato, quartered
1 cup cilantro (fresh coriander) sprigs
1 cup plain yogurt
4 to 5 dried red peppers or fresh
   jalapeño peppers

3 tablespoons vegetable oil
20 almonds, ground
20 cashews, ground
½ teaspoon ground cloves
½ teaspoon ground cinnamon
5 whole cardamom pods, pounded
   lightly
salt and freshly ground pepper to taste
cilantro and tomato wedges, for
   garnish

Remove chicken skin. Cut each chicken breast half in 2 pieces.

Process ginger, garlic, onion, tomato, cilantro, and yogurt in a food processor until smooth. Set aside.

If using fresh jalapeño peppers, puncture the skin a few times. Heat oil in a large pan over medium heat and sauté whole peppers for 1 to 2 minutes. Add almonds, cashews, cloves, cinnamon, cardamom, salt, and pepper. Sauté 1 to 2 minutes, stirring; do not let spices burn.

Immediately stir in onion-tomato puree, followed by chicken pieces. Cover and bring to a boil over high heat. Reduce heat to medium-high and cook until chicken is tender and sauce is thick, about 20 to 30 minutes, stirring occasionally. If sauce is not thick enough, uncover pan and cook for a few minutes longer. *Chicken can be kept, covered, 2 days in refrigerator. Add a few tablespoons more yogurt when reheating.*

Garnish with cilantro and tomato wedges, and serve.

Makes 8 servings

THAI CHICKEN CURRY

When I was studying cooking in Paris, one of my best friends was Somchit Singchalee—a student of French cooking by day, chef at a Thai restaurant at night. She practically grew up in a restaurant owned by her mother in northeastern Thailand. On weekends we sometimes cooked together and she taught me many wonderful Thai dishes. First my husband would join us on a visit to the Asian markets of the city, where she explained to us how each of the exotic ingredients was used, and then we'd come back with our purchases and cook all day. These were some of the best weekends I can remember.

For this chicken curry, we bought canned coconut milk and Thai curry paste, which are now carried by fine American supermarkets. (Please see also Mail Order Sources, page 410.) Since Somchit loved the wonderful French cream, she would often finish this Thai curry with a few tablespoons of crème fraîche! Serve this luscious dish with jasmine rice or Basmati rice.

1 or 2 fresh red or green chilies (Thai, serrano, or jalapeño); or ½ red or green bell pepper

1 (14-ounce) can coconut milk

2 teaspoons packaged Thai red or green curry paste

1 pound boneless skinless chicken breasts, cut in 1-inch pieces

1 to 2 tablespoons Thai fish sauce (*nam pla*), or salt to taste

1 medium zucchini, quartered lengthwise, each quarter sliced ½ inch thick

¾ cup fresh shelled (¾ pound unshelled) or frozen peas

½ teaspoon hot red pepper flakes (optional)

1 (6-ounce) can or jar straw mushrooms, drained and rinsed (½ cup)

⅓ cup small basil leaves, or 2 tablespoons coarsely chopped cilantro (fresh coriander)

Cut chilies in thin strips; if using bell pepper, halve crosswise, then cut in thin strips.

Skim the top ⅓ cup from the coconut milk (the slightly thicker part) and put it in a sauté pan, wok, or large saucepan. Heat over medium-low heat, stirring, 3 or 4 minutes or until thickened. Add curry paste and sauté over medium heat about 1 minute. Add chicken and sauté until it changes color at surface, about 3 minutes. Add remaining coconut milk and fish sauce or salt, and bring to a boil, stirring. Simmer uncovered over medium-low heat 5 to 8 minutes or until chicken is tender. Remove chicken with slotted spoon.

Add zucchini, peas, and chilies or bell pepper to pan. If using bell pepper rather than chilies, add hot pepper flakes. Simmer about 5 minutes or until vegetables are just tender. Add mushrooms and heat through. Return chicken and any juices in bowl to sauce and heat gently. Just before serving, stir in basil leaves; or spoon curry into serving dish and sprinkle with cilantro.

Makes 3 or 4 servings

BRAISED CHICKEN
WITH MOREL SAUCE

There is nothing better than chicken with a creamy mushroom sauce, especially when the mushrooms are morels, because their pungent, somewhat smoky taste flavors the sauce throughout. The perfect accompaniment for this French specialty is asparagus and either Basmati rice or the finest fresh pasta. Since the sauce is rich, and the morels are expensive, this is a dish to reserve for special occasions. With this festive chicken, I like to serve a good French white Burgundy or a California Chardonnay.
You can also serve this rich sauce with pan-roasted pheasant, squab, or quail.

¾ to 1 ounce dried morels (about ¾ cup)
2 tablespoons (¼ stick) butter
2 small shallots, minced
½ cup dry white wine
1¼ cups chicken stock or low-salt broth

½ teaspoon dried thyme
salt and freshly ground pepper
1 cup heavy cream
1 tablespoon vegetable oil
3 pounds chicken pieces, patted dry

Soak morels in hot water to cover for about 30 minutes or until soft. Rinse and drain thoroughly. Halve any large morels.

Melt 1 tablespoon butter in medium saucepan over low heat. Add shallots and cook about 2 minutes or until softened. Add ¼ cup wine and bring to a boil, stirring. Add 1 cup stock, thyme, morels, salt, and pepper and bring to a boil. Simmer uncovered over medium heat until liquid is reduced to about 1 cup. Stir in cream and bring to a boil. Simmer, stirring occasionally, over medium heat for 7 minutes, or until sauce is thick enough to coat a spoon. *Sauce can be kept, covered, 1 day in refrigerator.*

Season chicken pieces lightly with salt and pepper. Heat oil and remaining butter in a large, heavy skillet or sauté pan over medium heat. Add leg and thigh pieces and brown lightly. Set on a plate. Add breast and wing pieces to skillet and brown lightly.

Return leg and thigh pieces to skillet. Add chicken juices from plate and remaining wine and stock. Cover and cook over low heat 15 minutes or until breast pieces are tender. Transfer them to a platter, cover, and keep them warm. Cook remaining chicken 10 minutes more or until tender. Add leg and thigh pieces to platter.

Reheat morel sauce in a saucepan. Skim as much fat as possible from chicken cooking liquid. Boil liquid, stirring, until reduced to about ¼ cup. Stir into reheated sauce. If necessary, simmer briefly until thickened. Taste and adjust seasoning. Serve chicken with sauce.

Makes 4 servings

CHICKEN BRAISED IN SAFFRON TOMATO SAUCE

This recipe does not require many ingredients or much work, yet I find it one of the best ways to prepare chicken. Its incomparable flavor is obtained by simmering the bird with saffron, tomatoes, onion, and garlic. In Provence, where this dish originated, a traditional accompaniment is fettuccine or ravioli, which are wonderful with the sauce, but rice, orzo, or couscous are also delightful partners.

3 tablespoons olive oil
2½ pounds chicken pieces, patted dry
salt and freshly ground pepper
½ cup minced onion
6 medium garlic cloves, minced
2 pounds ripe tomatoes, peeled, seeded, and chopped; or 2 (28-ounce) cans whole plum tomatoes, drained and chopped

½ cup chicken stock or broth
1½ teaspoons fresh thyme, or ½ teaspoon dried, crumbled
1 bay leaf
scant ¼ teaspoon crumbled saffron threads

In a heavy skillet large enough to hold the chicken in one layer, heat oil over medium-high heat. Sprinkle chicken with salt and pepper on both sides. Brown it in batches in oil, taking about 3 minutes per side. Transfer browned chicken to a plate.

Discard all but 2 tablespoons fat from skillet. Add onion and cook over medium-low heat, stirring often, until softened, about 7 minutes. Add garlic, tomatoes, stock, thyme, bay leaf, saffron, salt, and pepper and bring to a boil, stirring.

Return chicken to skillet with any juices from plate and bring to a boil. Cover and simmer over low heat 10 minutes. Turn over, cover, and simmer breast pieces about 10 minutes.

Transfer them with tongs or a slotted spoon to a plate. Simmer leg pieces about 10 more minutes or until tender, and remove.

Simmer sauce over medium-high heat, stirring often, about 7 minutes or until thick. Discard bay leaf. Taste and adjust seasoning. Return chicken to sauce. Cover and warm over low heat for 3 minutes. *Chicken can be kept, covered, 1 day in refrigerator.*

Makes 4 servings

GREEK CHICKEN WITH RED WINE, RAISINS, AND BABY ONIONS

This rich-tasting chicken in its deep brown wine sauce bears a certain resemblance to the French coq au vin *and Burgundian chicken, both in technique and in some of the flavorings: the pieces are sautéed, then cooked with red wine, chicken stock, and baby onions. But the raisins and touch of cinnamon give this Greek chicken a different, delicately sweet-and-sour flavor. This Hellenic chicken is lighter than the classic Burgundian chicken too, since it has neither bacon nor butter. Serve it with boiled potatoes or rice.*

1⅓ to 1½ cups baby (pearl) onions (5 ounces)
2 tablespoons olive oil
2½ to 3 pounds chicken pieces, patted dry
salt and freshly ground pepper
2 medium garlic cloves, chopped
1 tablespoon all-purpose flour

1 cup dry red wine
1 tablespoon tomato paste
⅔ cup chicken stock or broth
½ teaspoon ground cinnamon
1 teaspoon cumin seeds
1 bay leaf
⅓ cup raisins
½ teaspoon sugar

Put baby onions in a small saucepan, cover with water, and bring to a boil. Boil 1 minute. Drain in strainer and rinse under cold water. Peel with aid of a paring knife: carefully cut off root, pull off peel gently, then cut off any stringy stems.

Heat oil in large, deep, heavy skillet or Dutch oven over medium heat. Sprinkle chicken lightly with salt and pepper on all sides. Brown on all sides in batches, taking about 7 minutes for leg and thigh pieces, about 5 minutes for breast pieces. Set on a plate, using a slotted spoon.

Add baby onions and sauté about 3 minutes, shaking pan to turn them over, until lightly browned in spots. Remove with slotted spoon. Discard excess fat, leaving 1 tablespoon in pan.

Add garlic to pan and sauté over low heat a few seconds. Stir in flour and cook 30 seconds, stirring, until bubbling. Add wine, stirring until smooth and scraping in brown juices. Bring to a simmer. Stir in tomato paste. Add chicken stock, cinnamon, cumin seeds, bay leaf, and raisins. Mix well.

Return leg and thigh pieces to skillet. Add baby onions. Arrange breast and wing pieces on top. Add chicken juices from plate. Cover and cook over low heat, stirring occasionally, about 20 minutes or until breast pieces are tender when pierced with a knife; turn pieces once to coat with sauce. Transfer them to a platter, cover, and keep warm. Cook remaining chicken and onions about 10 minutes or until all are tender. Add leg and thigh pieces to platter. Remove bay leaf. Skim as much fat as possible from sauce. *Chicken can be kept in sauce, covered, 2 days in refrigerator. Reheat in covered skillet. Remove chicken pieces.*

Add sugar to sauce. Taste sauce and adjust seasoning; if flavor is too acid, add a pinch more sugar, remembering that raisins will give a hint of sweetness. Spoon sauce over chicken.

Makes 4 servings

NORTH AFRICAN CHICKEN WITH ONION SAUCE

From a Moroccan friend in Paris, I learned this easy Moroccan recipe. The slowly cooked onions give the sauce a wonderfully rich flavor, balanced by a hint of cumin and cayenne. Cooked cauliflower is a good accompaniment, and so are rice or couscous and a salad of diced cucumbers, tomatoes, and peppers.

3-pound chicken, cut in pieces, or 2½
   to 3 pounds chicken pieces
salt and freshly ground pepper
½ teaspoon ground cumin
½ teaspoon paprika
¼ teaspoon cayenne pepper, or to taste

2 tablespoons vegetable oil
3 medium onions (1 pound), halved
   and sliced thin
¾ cup chicken stock or low-salt broth
1 large garlic clove, chopped

Pat chicken dry. Sprinkle chicken pieces with salt and pepper on both sides. Mix cumin, paprika, and cayenne and sprinkle over chicken. Rub into pieces.

Heat oil in large, deep skillet or sauté pan over medium heat and lightly brown chicken pieces in 2 batches in oil, about 2 or 3 minutes per side; be careful, as spices burn easily. Remove with tongs to a plate. Add onions and cook over medium-low heat until softened,

10 to 15 minutes. Return chicken to pan and add any juices from plate. Add stock and garlic. Cover and simmer 30 minutes, turning pieces once. Remove breast pieces. Cover and simmer remaining pieces 5 minutes. Skim fat from cooking liquid.

Remove chicken pieces from pan but leave in onion. If desired, boil juices about 3 minutes to thicken. Return chicken to pan. Cover and warm over low heat 2 to 3 minutes. *Chicken can be kept, covered, 1 day in refrigerator. Reheat in covered pan over low heat.* Taste and adjust seasoning. Serve hot.

Makes 3 or 4 servings

BRAZILIAN CHICKEN WITH TOMATOES, COCONUT MILK, AND CILANTRO

In Brazil this chicken in its luscious creamy sauce is served with rice or with cooked manioc meal. Broccoli, spinach, or corn are also good accompaniments, and so is couscous. In fact, Brazil has its own version of couscous, made with cornmeal.

3 pounds chicken pieces
freshly ground pepper
3 tablespoons chopped cilantro (fresh coriander)
2 tablespoons strained fresh lemon juice
2 tablespoons olive oil
1 large onion, halved and sliced thin
1 green bell pepper, cut in strips

2 pounds ripe tomatoes, peeled, seeded, and diced; or 2 (28-ounce) cans plum tomatoes, drained and diced
1 cup canned unsweetened coconut milk
salt
cayenne pepper to taste

Sprinkle chicken with pepper and 1 tablespoon cilantro. Add lemon juice, cover, and marinate 1 hour in refrigerator.

Heat oil in a large casserole, add onion and green pepper and sauté over medium heat about 7 minutes. Add tomatoes and cook about 5 minutes over high heat, stirring often. Stir in coconut milk and bring to a simmer. Add chicken pieces and sprinkle with salt and pepper. Cover and cook over low heat, turning from time to time, until chicken is tender, about 30 minutes for breast pieces and about 45 to 50 minutes for leg pieces.

For a thicker sauce, remove chicken pieces and boil sauce uncovered, stirring, a few minutes to thicken, then return chicken to sauce. Add 1 tablespoon cilantro and a pinch of cayenne pepper. Taste and adjust seasoning. Sprinkle with remaining cilantro when serving.

Makes 4 servings

MOROCCAN CHICKEN
WITH TWO HEADS OF GARLIC

This is the North African cousin of the famous Provençal chicken cooked with 40 cloves of garlic. Like its relative, this dish is not aggressively garlicky because the garlic is mellowed by gentle simmering with the chicken.

In typical Moroccan fashion, a generous amount of Italian parsley completes the dish. I've rarely seen a Moroccan cook who measures parsley by tablespoons—it's always by bunches or handfuls.

2 medium heads garlic
3 pounds chicken pieces
salt and freshly ground pepper
2 tablespoons olive oil

¾ cup chicken stock or low-salt broth
¼ teaspoon hot red pepper flakes
⅓ cup Italian or curly parsley

Peel garlic without crushing it. Sprinkle chicken pieces with salt and pepper. Heat oil in a skillet over medium-high heat, add chicken pieces in batches, and brown them, taking 4 or 5 minutes per side for leg pieces, 3 minutes per side for breast pieces. Pour off all but 1 tablespoon oil.

Add stock and pepper flakes. Return chicken to pan, adding back and neck if available. Bring to simmer. Add garlic; push to bottom of pan. Cook over low heat until tender, removing breast pieces after 25 to 30 minutes, leg pieces after about 35 minutes. Remove chicken and discard neck. Reduce sauce 2 or 3 minutes or until well flavored. Add parsley and cook ½ minute. Return chicken to sauce and heat gently. Serve chicken with sauce and garlic spooned over it.

Makes 4 servings

IRANIAN CHICKEN IN WALNUT-POMEGRANATE SAUCE (CHICKEN *FESANJAN*)

One of the rewards of teaching cooking is learning exciting dishes from my students. That's what happened with this recipe, which I received from Farah Khosrovani, who came to a cooking class I taught in Beverly Hills. She told me that this classic Persian poultry dish is often made with duck, but because of the richness of the sauce, she prefers to make it with chicken. She suggested I use pomegranate juice, because it is sometimes available at the supermarket, but she occasionally uses other forms of pomegranate, which she buys at specialty shops.

My husband and I then searched out the various forms of pomegranate available at our local Iranian specialty shops. We found bottles of pomegranate paste, pomegranate molasses, and pomegranate concentrate, all of which we learned are often used in the dish instead of juice. At the store we met a shopper from formerly Soviet Georgia, who told us that chicken with walnuts and pomegranate juice was a specialty of his region, too. He stressed the importance of having fresh walnuts for the success of the dish.

This is a dish for adventurous eaters—it is very rich and delicious but it is not colorful. The sauce is thick and of a pinkish-beige hue, and, like other nut-based sauces, is not smooth like a sauce made with flour. Cooking with the pomegranate juice reminded me somewhat of preparing chicken in red wine.

This dish should be served with plenty of rice, preferably Basmati, to go with the generous amount of luscious walnut sauce.

2 tablespoons vegetable oil
2½ to 3 pounds chicken pieces, rinsed
  and patted dry
1 large onion, halved and sliced thin
3 cups walnuts (about 10 ounces),
  processed until finely chopped (2⅔
  cups ground)

2 cups pomegranate juice
salt and freshly ground pepper
hot cooked rice, for serving

Heat oil in a wide casserole or Dutch oven. Add chicken in batches and sauté over medium-high heat until brown. Remove chicken to a plate. Discard all but 2 tablespoons oil from pan. Add onion to pan and sauté over medium heat about 10 minutes or until golden. Add walnuts and stir a few seconds over heat. Add pomegranate juice and bring to a simmer. Add chicken and any juices on plate, salt, and pepper. Cover and cook over low heat, turning over occasionally, about 35 minutes or until chicken is tender. Add salt and pepper to taste.

Don't worry that sauce looks separated. *Chicken can be kept, covered, 1 day in refrigerator. Reheat in covered pan over low heat.*

For each serving, make a mound of rice, set a piece of chicken in center, and spoon sauce over chicken.

Makes 4 to 6 servings

NOTE: If using pomegranate concentrate to substitute for pomegranate juice, mix ⅓ to ½ cup with 1½ cups water.

BRAISED CHICKEN
WITH WATERCRESS SAUCE

In the late seventies chefs in France began thickening sauces with vegetable purees instead of flour to give them a lighter texture. These types of nouvelle cuisine *sauces are delicious with chicken. For this dish a puree of watercress gives the sauce a zesty flavor and colors it bright green. Serve the chicken and its luscious sauce with rice, orzo, or couscous, and with glazed or steamed carrots.*

3-pound chicken, cut in pieces
salt and freshly ground pepper
1 tablespoon vegetable oil
1 tablespoon butter
1 shallot, finely chopped

½ cup dry white wine, such as Chablis
½ cup chicken stock or broth
5-ounce bunch watercress
1 cup heavy cream

Season chicken with salt and pepper. Heat oil and butter in a large skillet or sauté pan. Add chicken in batches and brown lightly on all sides. Remove pieces and drain on paper towels. Discard fat from skillet. Return chicken to skillet and add shallot. Add wine and bring to a boil. Add stock and bring to a boil. Cover and simmer over low heat 25 to 30 minutes or until chicken pieces are tender when pierced with a sharp knife. Discard chicken back.

Meanwhile, cut off leafy section of watercress and discard thick stems. Reserve 8 leaves for garnish. Add leafy section of watercress to a large saucepan of boiling salted water. Return to a boil. Drain, rinse with cold water, and drain thoroughly. Squeeze out excess liquid. Puree cooked watercress with ⅓ cup cream in a food processor or blender until mixture turns bright green.

Add reserved watercress leaves to a saucepan of boiling water. Return to a boil. Remove leaves carefully with a small strainer or slotted spoon. Put leaves on paper towels to dry.

Remove cooked chicken from skillet and keep it warm. Boil cooking liquid, stirring occasionally and skimming often, until it is reduced to about ½ cup. Stir in remaining cream and simmer, stirring often, until sauce is thick enough to coat a spoon.

Push watercress puree through a strainer into sauce, pressing hard to make sure as much puree as possible goes through strainer. Simmer 1 minute, stirring. Taste and adjust seasoning. Transfer chicken pieces to a platter and coat with sauce. Decorate with watercress leaves.

Makes 4 servings

MOROCCAN CHICKEN
WITH PRUNES AND ALMONDS

Chicken and prunes are not a familiar match in the American kitchen, but they are common partners in the casseroles of cooks of diverse origins. I have found this combination in several cuisines: Jewish, where it is cooked with sweet potatoes; French, where it features red wine; and in Polish and Russian cooking. When I worked in the kitchen of a Parisian restaurant, this rather hearty pair was turned into a luxurious dish—boned chicken legs stuffed with prunes that were in turn stuffed with foie gras.

In this Moroccan version, the chicken is flavored with honey, saffron, cinnamon, and plenty of onions. The dish is a specialty of the best Moroccan restaurant in Paris, Timgad, where it is also made with lamb. Cooking prunes in the sauce gives it an attractive brown color. The flavor is slightly sweet, exotic, and wonderful and is one of my favorite chicken dishes. Serve the chicken with couscous or rice.

3 pounds chicken pieces, patted dry
2 large onions, minced
salt and freshly ground pepper
2 tablespoons (¼ stick) butter
large pinch of saffron threads (about ⅛ teaspoon)
¼ cup hot water

2-inch cinnamon stick
½ teaspoon ground ginger
¾ cup chicken stock, broth, or water
1 cup moist pitted prunes
2 tablespoons honey
⅓ cup whole blanched almonds, toasted

Combine chicken pieces, onions, salt, pepper, and butter in a heavy, enameled casserole. Cover and cook over low heat, turning chicken pieces over occasionally, 15 minutes. Meanwhile, add saffron to hot water in a cup and let stand 20 minutes.

Add saffron mixture, cinnamon stick, ginger, and water to casserole, pushing cinnamon stick into liquid. Bring to a boil. Cover and simmer over low heat, turning chicken pieces over from time to time, about 25 minutes or until breast pieces are tender when pierced with a knife. Transfer them to a plate. Cook remaining pieces, covered, over low heat, about 10 minutes or until very tender. Transfer remaining pieces to plate, leaving as much of chopped onion as possible in casserole.

Add prunes to chicken cooking liquid and cook, uncovered, over medium heat about 15 minutes or until just tender. Add honey and cook over medium heat, stirring gently to avoid breaking up prunes, about 5 minutes or until sauce thickens. Taste and adjust seasoning. Discard cinnamon stick. With a slotted spoon transfer prunes to a heated bowl, leaving as much of chopped onions as possible in casserole. Cover prunes to keep them warm.

Return chicken pieces to casserole and turn them to coat them with sauce. Cover and reheat over low heat 5 minutes. *Chicken can be kept, covered, 2 days in refrigerator; refrigerate prunes separately. Reheat chicken in sauce over low heat, covered; remove chicken and reheat prunes in sauce.*

Transfer chicken pieces to platter or plates and spoon sauce and prunes over them. Garnish with almonds.

Makes 4 servings

MEDITERRANEAN CHICKEN WITH OLIVES

I always associated chicken and olives with southern French cooking. After all, it is often called Niçoise chicken, for the town of Nice, the capital of the French Riviera. But while I was vacationing in southern France I learned that the dish is also enjoyed on the other side of the Mediterranean, in Morocco, and it might have originated there.

2 tablespoons olive oil
2½ to 3 pounds chicken pieces, patted dry
salt and freshly ground pepper
8 ounces mushrooms, quartered (optional)
3 medium garlic cloves, minced
2 pounds ripe tomatoes, peeled, seeded, and chopped; or 2 (28-ounce) cans whole plum tomatoes, drained and chopped

½ cup dry white wine
⅔ cup pitted black olives
1 teaspoon fresh thyme, or ¼ teaspoon dried, crumbled
few drops of lemon juice
1 tablespoon chopped fresh tarragon, or 1 teaspoon dried, crumbled
1 tablespoon chopped fresh parsley, preferably Italian

In a large skillet, heat oil over medium-high heat. Sprinkle chicken with salt and pepper on both sides and brown it in batches in oil, transferring it as it is browned with tongs to a plate. Discard all but 1 tablespoon oil from skillet. Add mushrooms, salt, and pepper and sauté over medium-high heat until lightly browned. Remove from skillet.

Add garlic to skillet and cook, stirring, ½ minute. Stir in tomatoes and white wine. Return chicken to skillet with any juices from plate and bring to a boil. Partly cover and simmer over low heat 20 minutes. Uncover and cook about 15 minutes or until breast pieces are tender when pierced with a sharp knife. Transfer them to a plate. Continue cooking about 15 minutes or until remaining chicken pieces are tender; transfer them to plate.

Simmer sauce over medium-high heat, stirring often, for 15 minutes, or until thick. Taste sauce and adjust seasoning; do not oversalt because olives will be added.

Return chicken and mushrooms to skillet and add olives, thyme, and lemon juice. Cover and warm over low heat 3 minutes. *Chicken can be kept, covered, 1 day in refrigerator. Reheat chicken in sauce in covered skillet over low heat.* Add tarragon and parsley to sauce. Taste and adjust seasoning. Transfer to a platter or plates and serve.

Makes 4 servings

CHICKEN WITH BEER AND APPLES

Like wine, beer gives good flavor to braised chicken, loses its bitterness, and turns into a tasty sauce, as in this winter recipe from northern France and Belgium. Sautéed apples are a delicious accompaniment for the chicken and its rich sauce. For a cold-weather menu, serve the chicken with mashed potatoes and Brussels sprouts.

2½ to 3 pounds chicken pieces, patted
   dry
salt and freshly ground pepper
2 tablespoons vegetable oil
2 tablespoons (¼ stick) butter
1 medium onion, chopped

1 tablespoon all-purpose flour
1 cup beer
⅔ cup chicken stock or broth
1 bay leaf
3 tart medium apples

Sprinkle chicken with salt and pepper. Heat 1 tablespoon oil and 1 tablespoon butter in a large, heavy skillet over medium heat. Add chicken pieces in batches and brown them on all sides. Transfer to a plate. Add onion to pan and sauté over medium heat about 5 minutes. Sprinkle with flour and stir over low heat 2 minutes. Stir in beer and stock and bring to a simmer, stirring.

Return chicken pieces to pan and add any juices from plate and bay leaf. Reduce heat to low, cover, and cook, stirring often, until pieces are tender when pierced with a knife, about 30 minutes for breast pieces and about 10 more minutes for leg and thigh pieces.

While chicken is cooking, peel apples and cut each into 8 wedges. Heat remaining 1 tablespoon oil and 1 tablespoon butter in a large skillet over medium-high heat. Add apple wedges and sauté them until lightly browned on both sides and just tender, about 7 minutes. Remove from heat.

When chicken is tender, remove to a platter using a slotted spoon. Arrange apple wedges around chicken, cover platter, and keep warm in a 275°F. oven. Discard bay leaf. Skim excess fat from chicken cooking liquid. Cook sauce, stirring often, until thick enough to lightly coat a spoon.

Strain sauce if you like. Taste and adjust seasoning. To serve, spoon sauce over chicken but not over apples.

Makes 4 servings

PHILIPPINE CHICKEN ADOBO

Chicken adobo is the most famous Philippine poultry dish, but adobo *designates a Philippine cooking method—braising with vinegar, garlic, and usually soy sauce—used for meat, fish, and some vegetables. Often the chicken or meat is marinated first.*

Mexico also has a chicken adobo with vinegar and garlic, but it includes chilies and has no soy sauce. Both cuisines are influenced by that of Spain, where adobo *means "marinated" or "pickled."*

For this dish, Filipinos sometimes braise chicken and pork together in the savory sauce. Occasionally the sauce is enriched with coconut milk.

Unlike European-style braising, the chicken is browned after being simmered, rather than before. The traditional way is to brown the cooked chicken in lard, but I prefer to broil the chicken rather than fry it. I find broiling the easiest way and, of course, it has the advantage of not adding fat.

Serve the chicken with rice. I also like to accompany it with sliced papaya, cucumbers, and tomatoes.

3 pounds chicken pieces
8 large garlic cloves, chopped
⅔ cup white vinegar
2 bay leaves

salt and freshly ground pepper
1 cup water
1 teaspoon black peppercorns
3 tablespoons soy sauce

In a shallow dish combine chicken with garlic, vinegar, and bay leaves; turn pieces to coat both sides. Cover and marinate in refrigerator 30 minutes to 1 hour.

Put chicken with its marinade in a saucepan, sprinkle lightly with salt, and add water, peppercorns, and soy sauce. Bring to a boil, cover, and simmer about 40 minutes or until chicken is tender. Remove pieces and pat dry.

Put chicken on a rack above broiler pan and broil about 4 inches from heat about 10 minutes or until browned, turning once.

Skim fat thoroughly from sauce. Boil until reduced to 1 cup. Skim again. Strain and return to pan. Taste and adjust seasoning. Spoon sauce over chicken when serving. *Any leftover chicken can be reheated in the sauce.*

Makes 4 servings

INDIAN BRAISED CHICKEN WITH GINGER, CORIANDER, CUMIN, AND YOGURT

My friend Neelam Batra, a popular Indian cooking teacher in Los Angeles, gave me this recipe for chicken in a delicately spiced yogurt sauce. Along with the coriander and cumin, she adds a teaspoon of the Indian spice mixture called garam masala, *and sprinkles a bit more on the finished dish, but the dish still has plenty of flavor if made without it. The jalapeño peppers can be added whole so they can be removed, or chopped for greater heat. As in most Indian recipes, the chicken pieces are cooked without the skin. Serve the chicken with rice or with Indian bread.*

5 pounds chicken pieces
5 tablespoons vegetable oil
2 cups finely chopped onions
2 tablespoons finely chopped peeled
 fresh ginger
2 jalapeño peppers, whole or chopped
 finely
2 tablespoons ground coriander
1 tablespoon ground cumin
1 teaspoon *garam masala* (optional)

3 black cardamom pods, pounded
 lightly
1 cinnamon stick (about 3 inches)
cayenne pepper to taste
1½ cups yogurt, beaten with a fork
 until smooth
salt to taste
garam masala or freshly ground pepper,
 for sprinkling
chopped cilantro (fresh coriander), for
 garnish

Remove skin from chicken. Heat oil in a large casserole, add onions and ginger, and sauté over medium heat about 10 minutes or until brown.

Add jalapeño peppers and all the spices to casserole. Stir in yogurt in 3 batches over medium heat. Add chicken pieces, sprinkle with salt, and cook over high heat, stirring, about 5 minutes. Reduce heat to medium-low, cover, and cook, turning pieces over a few times, until chicken is tender and sauce is thick, about 30 to 40 minutes. *Chicken can be kept, covered, 1 day in refrigerator. Reheat in covered pan over medium-low heat, stirring occasionally.* Add cayenne pepper. Taste and adjust seasoning.

Serve sprinkled with *garam masala* or freshly ground pepper and cilantro.

Makes 8 servings

SRI LANKAN CHICKEN CURRY

I learned to make this dish from Kusuma Cooray, a Sri Lankan–born chef I met in Paris. Ms. Cooray prepared it at a party she gave at the Sri Lanka ambassador's residence. She seasoned the chicken with cardamom pods, whole cloves, and cinnamon sticks, as well as Sri Lankan curry powder, but you can use any variety of curry you like. The whole spices are left in the dish, and are simply removed by people when they're eating.

At the party Kusuma served this chicken with Basmati rice, which she cooked with cardamom pods and finished with butter and raisins. An additional accompaniment for the spicy chicken was a cooling dish of yogurt mixed with diced tomatoes, cucumbers, chopped mint or cilantro, salt, and pepper, a version of Indian raita. *We ate the chicken and rice the traditional way, with our hands; the Sri Lankans feel you can enjoy the tastes of the rice and sauce together better this way.*

3 tablespoons butter
2 medium onions, chopped
3 medium garlic cloves, chopped
2½ pounds chicken pieces, skin removed
salt
3 fresh medium tomatoes, diced; or 1 (14- to 16-ounce) can plum tomatoes, drained and diced
1 teaspoon curry powder
¼ to ½ teaspoon cayenne pepper
¼ teaspoon turmeric
3 cardamom pods
2 whole cloves
1 cinnamon stick (about 3 inches)
1 tablespoon distilled white vinegar
⅓ cup chicken stock or broth
½ cup canned unsweetened coconut milk (optional)

Heat butter in a casserole, add onions, and cook over medium-low heat until softened. Add garlic, then chicken pieces and brown lightly, stirring. Add salt, tomatoes, curry powder, cayenne pepper, turmeric, cardamom, cloves, cinnamon stick, vinegar, and chicken stock. Bring to a boil. Stir in coconut milk. Cover and simmer until chicken is tender, about 35 minutes for breast pieces, about 50 minutes for leg and thigh pieces. If you would like a thicker sauce, uncover, remove chicken, and simmer sauce until thickened. Return chicken to sauce. Taste sauce and adjust seasoning. Serve hot.

Makes 4 servings

SPICY ETHIOPIAN CHICKEN
(DORO WAT)

This home-style chicken dish is always present on Ethiopian restaurant menus. It is very hot, as the Ethiopians enjoy food with plenty of fiery peppers and spice.

An Ethiopian woman explained to me how she prepares the dish. She buys a toasted spice mixture and clarified butter at an Ethiopian specialty store. Spiced clarified butter is traditionally made at home in Ethiopia and Yemen, so the butter will keep longer without refrigeration. Usually it's made with a pound of butter or more at a time. Since it's not practical to prepare the amount required for a single dish, I have simplified the recipe to include the spices used in the butter and in the toasted spice mixture without taking the extra steps.

This chicken is served with thin sourdough pancakes. Each person takes a piece of pancake, and uses it to scoop up some of the chicken and sauce. You can serve it instead with pita or lavosh bread or with rice. Serve it also with cooked spinach or other greens and with plain yogurt for cooling the fire.

The first time I had an Ethiopian meal, I was surprised at finding a similarity to Yemenite food, with which I was familiar from my Yemen-born in-laws in Israel. After all, the countries were in different continents—Yemen in Asia and Ethiopia in Africa. The large thin Ethiopian sourdough pancakes called injera *served with the main dishes were identical to the Yemenite* lahuh. *And both cuisines use such spices as cumin, cardamom, turmeric, and fenugreek, resulting in food with a similar character.*

Later I realized this was only natural; the countries are divided only by a narrow section of the Red Sea and have had a long history of contacts.

2 tablespoons paprika

1 teaspoon cayenne pepper, or more to taste

seeds of 2 cardamom pods, or ⅛ teaspoon ground cardamom

½ teaspoon ground ginger

½ teaspoon ground cumin

¼ teaspoon ground cinnamon

¼ teaspoon ground cloves

⅛ teaspoon turmeric

pinch of freshly grated nutmeg

4 tablespoons (½ stick) butter; or 2 tablespoons vegetable oil and 2 tablespoons (¼ stick) butter

3 large onions, chopped

2 medium garlic cloves, chopped

2 teaspoons minced peeled fresh ginger

1½ cups water

2 tablespoons tomato paste

3 pounds chicken pieces

salt to taste

4 hard-boiled eggs, shelled

Mix paprika and cayenne pepper in a small dish. In a small, dry skillet toast cardamom, ground ginger, cumin, cinnamon, cloves, turmeric, and nutmeg over low heat, stirring, 2 minutes. Add paprika mixture and toast 2 minutes more. Remove at once to a small bowl.

In a large casserole, melt butter, add onions, and sauté uncovered over medium heat until golden brown, about 30 minutes, stirring often when onions begin to change color. Add garlic, minced ginger, and toasted spice mixture and heat, stirring, about 3 minutes. Stir in water and tomato paste and bring to a simmer. Add chicken, sprinkle with salt, and mix well. Return to a simmer. Cover and cook over low heat about 45 to 50 minutes or until chicken is tender, stirring occasionally. Sauce should be fairly thick. Uncover at this point if sauce is too thin. Add eggs to sauce; cook 5 more minutes. Taste and adjust seasoning.

Makes 4 servings

RED-COOKED CHICKEN THIGHS
WITH MUSHROOMS

Red cooking is a favorite technique in Chinese home kitchens. It is actually a variation of poaching, with soy sauce used in the poaching liquid. The soy sauce flavors and lightly colors the chicken, hence the name, although it isn't really red. Ginger also lends flavor to the liquid. When I studied with Chinese cooking authority Nina Simonds in Taiwan, I learned the trick of adding star anise, which gives the liquid a lovely spicy taste.

Classic formulas often call for deep-frying the chicken first. Chicken thighs have a rich enough flavor anyway, and so I omit this step to cut down the calories, the work, and the expense of the extra oil.

Serve the red-cooked chicken with rice and a green vegetable like asparagus, broccoli, or spinach, or with stir-fried Chinese squash or zucchini. For a refreshing summer dish, it's also good cold, with a green salad.

2 pounds chicken thighs
3 tablespoons soy sauce
2 tablespoons rice wine or dry sherry
2 whole green onions, cut in 2 pieces
3 slices fresh ginger

2 teaspoons sugar
1 whole star anise
1 cup water
½ pound mushrooms, quartered
1 tablespoon cornstarch (optional)

Marinate thighs in soy sauce and wine for 30 minutes, turning pieces over once or twice. Pound green onions and ginger a few times by holding cleaver or knife blade flat, to release flavor.

Put chicken with its marinade in sauté pan. Stir sugar into liquid. Add green onions, ginger, star anise, and water. Bring to a boil. Cover and cook over low heat 20 minutes. Turn pieces over. Add mushrooms, push into liquid, and cook 15 minutes or until chicken is tender. Skim fat from liquid. Remove skin from chicken for serving. Serve hot or cold.

To serve hot, thicken liquid with cornstarch. Dissolve cornstarch in 2 tablespoons water. Remove chicken and mushrooms from liquid. Bring liquid to a simmer over medium heat. Whisk cornstarch mixture into liquid and cook, stirring, until thickened. Return chicken and mushrooms to liquid.

To serve cold, cut meat from bones and slice meat. Spoon liquid (which becomes aspic) and mushrooms on side.

Makes 3 or 4 servings

COLOMBIAN CHICKEN

A former recipe tester of mine learned this dish from her Colombian mother-in-law and shared it with me. It is a very easy, tasty stew that depends for its good flavor on thoroughly browning the onions. In Colombia the chicken is served with hot white rice and usually with fried plantains, which I have included in the recipe.

The plantains, a type of banana used for cooking, can be found in Hispanic markets and in some supermarkets. I have seen them sold in southern California markets as ''macho bananas.'' They're easy to prepare and come out a lovely yellow-orange color with a tasty, delicately sweet banana flavor.

3 tablespoons olive oil
3 medium onions, halved and sliced
5 ripe large tomatoes, diced (2 pounds); or 2 (28-ounce) cans whole tomatoes, drained and diced

salt and freshly ground pepper
6 chicken thighs (about 2 pounds)
1 pound ripe plantains
¼ cup vegetable oil

Heat olive oil in a large, deep skillet or sauté pan. Add onions and cook over medium heat until deep brown but not burnt, about 25 minutes. Stir often, especially during last 10 minutes. Add tomatoes, salt, and pepper. Stir and cook over high heat 3 to 4 minutes, until sauce begins to thicken. Add chicken, salt and pepper generously, cover, and cook over low heat about 25 minutes. Turn over and cook 5 minutes. Uncover and cook 15 minutes or until chicken is tender. *Chicken can be kept, covered, 2 days in refrigerator. Skim fat from sauce and reheat in covered pan over medium-low heat.*

   Peel plantains. Cut in diagonal slices, about ⅜ inch thick. Heat vegetable oil in a large skillet over medium heat. Add plantains, and sauté about 3 or 4 minutes per side or until golden brown and tender. Drain on paper towels. Serve hot, with chicken.

Makes 4 servings

MEXICAN CHICKEN WITH CHILIES AND CILANTRO-TOMATO SAUCE

Jalapeños and roasted green chilies give the sauce for this braised chicken plenty of zip but it's not lip-burning hot. If you like the chicken pieces to be brown, sauté them in the oil and remove them before adding the onion. To make it easier, I usually omit this step and simply remove the skin before serving the chicken. Serve this tasty stew with rice or with heated tortillas, and with lima or pinto beans or sautéed zucchini on the side. The chicken also makes a flavorful filling for enchiladas (see page 27).

Chilies and Cilantro-Tomato Sauce

2 long mild green chilies (Anaheim or California chilies); or 1 green bell pepper, roasted and peeled (page 408)
3 tablespoons vegetable oil
1 large onion, minced
3 jalapeño peppers, chopped (remove seeds if desired)
2 large garlic cloves, minced

1 pound ripe tomatoes, peeled, seeded, and coarsely chopped; or 1 (28-ounce) can tomatoes, drained, halved, squeezed, and chopped
5 tablespoons minced cilantro (fresh coriander)
salt to taste
½ teaspoon dried oregano
½ teaspoon ground cumin
1 cup chicken stock or broth

2¼ pounds chicken thighs (6 thighs)
pure chili powder or cayenne pepper to taste (optional)

Discard seeds from roasted chilies or green pepper. Cut in ¼-inch dice.

Heat oil in a large, wide casserole over medium heat. Add onion and cook about 7 minutes or until softened. Add jalapeño peppers, garlic, tomatoes, diced roasted chili or green pepper, 3 tablespoons cilantro, salt, oregano, cumin, and broth. Bring to a boil. Add chicken thighs. Cover and cook over low heat 20 minutes. Turn pieces over and cook 15 to 20 more minutes, or until meat is no longer pink when cut. *Chicken can be kept, covered, 2 days in refrigerator. Reheat in covered saucepan over low heat.*

If you prefer a thicker sauce, remove chicken pieces and boil sauce uncovered to reduce it slightly. Just before serving, add remaining cilantro. Taste and add chili powder or cayenne, if desired. Remove skin before serving.

Makes 3 to 4 servings

NOTE: You can substitute ¾ to 1 cup diced canned roasted mild green chilies for the Anaheim chili pepper.

CUMIN-SCENTED CHICKEN BALLS IN TOMATO-BASIL SAUCE

These eastern Mediterranean chicken ''meatballs'' can be sautéed first, in the traditional way, or can be simply poached in the sauce, for a low-calorie version. Serve them with rice or noodles and, if you like, with spicy Jalapeño-Garlic Chutney (page 366) on the side.

2 tablespoons unseasoned bread
   crumbs
2 medium garlic cloves, minced
1 teaspoon ground cumin
½ teaspoon ground cinnamon
½ teaspoon freshly ground pepper
¾ teaspoon salt

1¼ pounds ground chicken
Quick Tomato-Basil Sauce (page 371),
   made with dried basil
4 tablespoons olive oil, for sautéing
2 tablespoons chopped fresh basil or
   Italian parsley

For meatballs, mix bread crumbs with garlic, spices, and salt. Add to meat and mix well. Make walnut-size balls, using 1 tablespoon mixture for each. Transfer to a plate. Refrigerate 5 minutes. Heat sauce.

Heat oil in a large, heavy skillet over medium-high heat. Add meatballs in 2 batches and brown them on all sides, taking about 5 minutes; stand back to avoid splatters. With slotted spoon, transfer to paper towels. Add to tomato sauce. Cover and cook over low heat 10 minutes. Just before serving, add chopped fresh basil or parsley. Serve hot with rice or pasta.

Makes 4 to 6 servings

LOW-CALORIE VARIATION:
Omit oil; skip step of frying. Simmer meatballs in 2 batches in tomato sauce, each for 20 minutes.

CHICKEN GIZZARDS AND WINGS CACCIATORA

It's too bad that chicken gizzards are often overlooked in modern cuisine. With their rich flavor and meaty texture, I think they deserve to be better known. In traditional cooking in most parts of the world, from Europe to the Far East, they are often combined with wings, hearts, and necks to make tasty giblet stews.

In this recipe, the gizzards are simmered in a tomato sauce with herbs and mushrooms. The sauce is the same one used to make pollo alla cacciatora *in Italy and* poulet chasseur *in France, both of which mean ''hunter's chicken.'' If you prefer to cook just gizzards or just wings, simply double either of these. Obviously, the sauce can be used to simmer other chicken pieces.*

Good accompaniments are polenta, rice pilaf, or bowtie pasta; and sautéed red, green, and yellow peppers.

2 tablespoons olive oil
2 pounds chicken wings, cut apart at joints, or drummettes (largest section of wing), patted dry
1 medium onion, diced
1 medium carrot, diced
1 medium celery stalk, diced
2 medium garlic cloves, chopped
1½ pounds chicken gizzards, halved
salt and freshly ground pepper

2 tablespoons all-purpose flour
½ cup dry white wine
1 pound ripe tomatoes, peeled, seeded, and chopped; or 1 (14- to 16-ounce) can tomatoes, drained and chopped
1 cup water
2 tablespoons tomato paste
1 teaspoon dried thyme or oregano
8 ounces mushrooms, quartered

Heat the oil in a deep casserole, add wings in batches, and brown lightly over medium-high heat, about 5 minutes. Remove with tongs.

Add onion, carrot, and celery and sauté over medium heat 5 minutes. Stir in garlic, then add gizzards, sprinkle with salt and pepper, and sauté 2 or 3 minutes. Sprinkle with flour and sauté over low heat, stirring, for 2 minutes. Stir in wine and bring to a boil. Stir in tomatoes, water, and tomato paste. Return browned wings to casserole and add salt, pepper, and thyme or oregano. Bring to a simmer. Cover and simmer, stirring occasionally so flour won't stick, about 1¼ hours or until gizzards are tender. Add mushrooms and a pinch of salt and cook 7 minutes or until tender. Taste and adjust seasoning. Serve hot.

Makes 6 servings

NOTE: For extra flavor in the sauce, you can add the wing tips to the casserole after adding the liquid. There is no need to brown them. Discard them before serving.

BRAISED TURKEY BREAST, HUNGARIAN STYLE

Hungarian cooking has the image of being laden with sour cream, but this savory dish is an example of a tasty, low-fat Hungarian-style main course. The accompanying onion-pepper-mushroom sauce has a wonderful, reddish-brown hue from thoroughly browned onions. Be sure to season the sauce well with hot paprika. Serve the turkey with boiled new potatoes or with a pasta—egg barley, bowties, wide noodles, or spaetzle.

The advantage of boneless turkey breasts is that they are lean and easy to carve into neat slices. Braising prevents boneless turkey breasts from becoming too dry. I find this dish even better the next day, after the turkey slices have been in contact with the sauce for some time.

1 boneless turkey breast roast (1½ pounds)
salt and freshly ground pepper
3 tablespoons vegetable oil
3 medium onions, halved and sliced
1 green pepper, diced (¾ to 1 inch cubes)
8 ounces mushrooms, quartered

4 large garlic cloves, chopped
2½ teaspoons sweet paprika
pinch of hot paprika or cayenne pepper
1 cup chicken stock or broth
1 large ripe tomato, peeled, seeded, and chopped
1 bay leaf

Sprinkle turkey with salt and pepper. Heat oil in a large casserole over medium heat. Add turkey breast and brown on all sides, taking about 6 minutes. Remove to a plate.

Add onions to pan and sauté over medium heat about 15 minutes or until browned. Stir in green pepper and mushrooms, and sauté 3 minutes. Stir in garlic, paprika, and hot paprika and sauté a few seconds. Add stock, tomato, and bay leaf and bring to a simmer.

Return turkey to casserole and add juices from plate. Cover and cook over low heat, turning once, about 40 minutes or until thermometer inserted in thickest part of turkey registers 170°F.

Remove turkey to a plate. Boil sauce to reduce until thick and well flavored, about 3 or 4 minutes. Discard bay leaf. Taste and adjust seasoning; add more hot paprika if desired.

Cut turkey into thin slices and serve with sauce. *Turkey can be kept, covered, overnight in refrigerator. To reheat, first remove turkey, reheat sauce to simmer, then heat turkey in sauce gently on both sides.*

Makes 4 servings

COUNTRY TURKEY WINGS
WITH CUMIN AND TOMATOES

In this Mexican-inspired stew, the turkey wings are first poached, then cooked with a chili-garlic-cumin seasoning paste. You can prepare a stew of chicken pieces the same way. Serve the stew with white rice or with tortillas and with lima beans or green beans.

2½ pounds turkey wings
salt and freshly ground pepper
3 small dried hot red peppers
6 medium garlic cloves
½ teaspoon dried oregano, crumbled
1½ teaspoons ground cumin
1½ pounds ripe tomatoes, peeled, seeded, and chopped; or 1 (28-ounce) plus 1 (14-ounce) can whole plum tomatoes, drained and chopped

2 tablespoons vegetable oil
1 medium onion, chopped
1 tablespoon chopped cilantro (fresh coriander) or fresh parsley

Cut each wing into 3 pieces at the joints. Put them in a Dutch oven or heavy casserole. Add enough water just to cover and a pinch of salt and pepper. Bring to a boil, occasionally skimming fat. Reduce heat to low and simmer, covered, for 1 hour, turning the pieces over halfway through cooking time. Remove wings from broth; reserve broth in a bowl.

Meanwhile, soak hot peppers in enough hot water to cover them for 30 minutes. Drain, slit peppers, and remove and discard seeds and membranes, scraping them out with tip of a knife. Cut peppers in a few pieces.

In a food processor or blender, chop peppers with garlic and oregano. Add cumin and 2 tablespoons of the chopped tomatoes, and process together until very fine.

Heat oil in a large skillet, add onion, and cook over low heat, stirring often, for 5 minutes. Add spice mixture and cook 5 minutes, stirring. Add wings and tomatoes and bring to a boil, turning wings over occasionally. Return mixture to Dutch oven.

Pour 1 cup of reserved turkey broth into skillet and bring to a boil, scraping. Add this liquid and another ½ cup turkey broth to wings. Bring to a boil. Cover and simmer over low heat, turning large pieces over occasionally, for 45 minutes.

Uncover and cook, basting occasionally, until sauce is thick and meat is tender and beginning to fall from bones; to check, prick thickest piece with a sharp knife. If sauce becomes thick before meat is tender, add another ¼ cup turkey broth and continue cooking. If turkey becomes very tender but sauce is thin, remove wings with a slotted spoon and boil sauce, stirring, until thick; return meat to sauce.

Taste and adjust seasoning. *Stew can be kept, covered, 2 days in refrigerator. Reheat in a covered pan, adding a few tablespoons water if necessary.* Sprinkle with cilantro or parsley just before serving. Serve either one large piece or the 2 smaller pieces of a wing as one portion.

Makes 4 servings

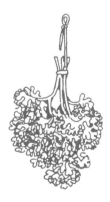

TURKEY LEG DAUBE
WITH CÈPES AND RED WINE

Daube is a wonderful dish from southern France of marinated meats braised gently in wine flavored with onion, garlic, herbs, and often orange peel.

I find the formula for making daube a perfect way to use turkey legs, an inexpensive, flavorful cut that deserves more attention. They come out moist and tender, and gain a rich flavor from the red wine marinade, which turns into a deep brown sauce during the cooking. The dish is easy to make, since there is no need to brown the turkey. I like to use fresh or dried cèpes to flavor the sauce, but you can use shiitake mushrooms also, or simply double the amount of regular mushrooms in the recipe.

Serve the daube with meat- or cheese-filled ravioli, as is the custom in Provence, or with potatoes and green beans. I also like a fresh green salad and seasonal fruit to complete the menu.

Red Wine Marinade

1 tablespoon fresh thyme leaves, or 1 teaspoon dried
1 bay leaf

3 cups dry red wine
1 large onion, halved

3½ pounds turkey drumsticks (2 large)
2 tablespoons olive oil
1 large onion, sliced
1 medium celery stalk, sliced
5 medium garlic cloves, chopped
1 pound carrots, peeled and cut in ½-inch slices
1¾ cups chicken stock or broth
4 whole cloves
2 wide strips of orange zest (peeled from orange, without white part)
¼-inch-thick slice fresh ginger, or ½ teaspoon ground ginger

1 tablespoon fresh thyme leaves, or 1 teaspoon dried
salt and freshly ground pepper
1 ounce dried or ½ pound fresh cèpes, porcini, shiitake, or other exotic mushrooms
cayenne pepper
8 ounces fresh white mushrooms, quartered
3 tablespoons potato starch, arrowroot, or cornstarch
5 tablespoons water
4 tablespoons chopped fresh parsley

Combine marinade ingredients in a large bowl. Add turkey drumsticks and turn so both sides are moistened. Marinate in refrigerator 12 to 24 hours; turn occasionally.

Heat oil in large oval casserole over medium heat. Add sliced onion and sauté 10 minutes or until light golden. Add celery and garlic, and sauté 1 minute. Add turkey, carrots, and stock. Bring to boil, cover, and cook 5 minutes. Stick cloves in onion halves from marinade and add to casserole. Add marinade, orange zest, ginger, thyme, salt, and pepper and bring to a boil. Cover and simmer over low heat, turning turkey over from time to time, for 1½ hours.

If using dried mushrooms, soak them in enough hot water to cover them for 30 minutes. Remove mushrooms and rinse them. If using shiitake mushrooms, discard stems. Cut mushrooms in bite-size pieces.

Add soaked dried mushrooms (but not fresh mushrooms) to casserole and cook about 30 minutes more or until turkey is very tender when pierced in thickest part with a knife. Uncover and cool about 15 minutes.

Remove turkey from liquid. Remove skin with aid of a paring knife. Discard bones, cartilage, and visible fat from turkey. Pull or cut meat into wide strips. Skim fat from liquid. Discard onion halves, fresh ginger, orange rind, and bay leaf. Season liquid to taste with salt, pepper, and cayenne. *If preparing ahead, return turkey to liquid; turkey can be kept, covered, 2 days in refrigerator. Reheat before continuing.*

If using fresh shiitake mushrooms, discard stems. Cut mushrooms in bite-size pieces. Add fresh exotic and white mushrooms to casserole and cook 10 minutes or until tender. Remove ingredients from casserole with slotted spoon.

Mix potato starch with water in small bowl until blended. Bring turkey cooking liquid to a simmer. Gradually whisk in about half the potato starch solution and simmer 1 or 2 minutes or until thickened. For a thicker sauce, whisk in remaining solution and simmer until thickened. Taste and adjust seasoning. Return turkey and vegetables to sauce and heat gently. Stir in 3 tablespoons parsley. Serve sprinkled with remaining parsley.

Makes about 6 servings

TURKEY MOLE

In Mexico, there are many versions of mole (pronounced MO-leh) sauces, and they are usually paired with turkey or chicken. Mole poblano is the most famous because it is one of the few savory recipes that contains chocolate. This is a simplified and lighter version of mole poblano, made with vegetable oil rather than the traditional lard and making use of one type of dried chili pepper rather than three.

Other mole sauces are made by the same basic method used in this recipe, of grinding the chilies and flavorings with nuts or seeds to thicken them, cooking the poultry separately, and finally heating the cooked meat in the sauce to flavor it.

Serve the turkey in its sauce with rice or tortillas and with beans or zucchini.

4 tablespoons vegetable oil
3 pounds turkey thighs or drumsticks
1 quart water
salt and freshly ground pepper
6 ancho chilies (see Note)
½ pound ripe tomatoes, peeled; or 1 (14- to 16-ounce) can plum tomatoes, drained
½ cup almonds, toasted (page 409)
2 tablespoons sesame seeds, toasted (page 409)

1 dry corn tortilla, torn in pieces
½ medium onion, cut in chunks
2 medium garlic cloves, peeled
3 tablespoons raisins
¼ teaspoon ground cinnamon
¼ teaspoon ground coriander
¼ teaspoon anise seed or fennel seed
pinch of ground cloves
1 ounce unsweetened chocolate

Heat 2 tablespoons oil in a heavy casserole over medium heat. Add turkey and brown lightly, in batches if necessary, on all sides. Discard fat from pan. Return all turkey to pan. Add water, salt, and pepper. Bring to a boil. Cover and simmer, turning pieces a few times, 1½ hours or until tender.

Meanwhile, rinse chilies, remove stems and seeds, and tear chilies in pieces. Cover with hot water and soak 1 hour or until softened. Drain chilies, discarding liquid.

When turkey is tender, remove from broth. Pour broth into a bowl and reserve. Skim fat from broth.

Put chilies in blender or food processor. Add tomatoes, toasted almonds, 1 tablespoon toasted sesame seeds, tortilla, onion, garlic, raisins, cinnamon, coriander, anise seed, cloves, and ½ cup turkey broth. Process to a coarse puree.

In casserole from turkey, heat 2 tablespoons oil over medium-high heat. Add chili puree, reduce heat to medium-low, and cook, stirring, for 5 minutes or until thickened. Add 2 cups turkey broth and chocolate; stir over low heat until chocolate melts. Continue cooking over low heat, stirring often, about 15 minutes or until sauce is thick. Season to taste with salt and pepper.

Discard turkey skin and cut meat from bones in large strips. Put in a shallow baking dish. Pour sauce over turkey, making sure all turkey is coated. *Turkey can be kept, covered, overnight in refrigerator.*

Preheat the oven to 350°F. Bake turkey, covered, 30 to 45 minutes or until hot. If sauce is too thick, stir in a few tablespoons heated turkey broth. Sprinkle turkey with remaining toasted sesame seeds and serve.

Makes 4 to 6 servings

NOTE: Ancho chilies are large, wide, reddish brown, wrinkled dried chilies. In some areas they are labeled pasilla chilies, although a true pasilla chili is long and narrow.

TURKEY CHILI

Chili, also known as chile con carne, *is a rich, spicy saucelike meat stew. A specialty of Texas, it is most often made with beef but today leaner chicken and turkey versions are gaining in popularity.*

Like many homey dishes, chili is easy to prepare and to reheat. Some people make it with meat alone, while some stir in cooked dried white or pink beans, or serve beans on the side. It can also include corn, black olives, or mushrooms. The most common way of serving chili is in a bowl, accompanied by tortillas, bread, or crackers, and an assortment of condiments to sprinkle in, such as spicy tomato salsa, chopped onions, cilantro, diced avocado, and grated cheddar cheese.

Chili can be a topping for pasta, rice, corn chips, or pizza; a sauce for poached eggs or hot dogs (to make ''chili dogs''); or a filling rolled with lettuce inside tortillas to make a burrito. It also makes a good, though untraditional, sandwich when spooned inside a pita with lettuce, cheese, and salsa.

For a moderately spicy version I use two jalapeño peppers but if you like it really hot, use four or five, or season the finished chili with hot pepper sauce to taste.

4 tablespoons olive or vegetable oil
1 large onion, chopped
1 pound ground turkey or chicken
6 large garlic cloves, minced
2 to 4 fresh jalapeño peppers
    (optional), seeds discarded, minced
2 to 3 tablespoons chili powder
2 tablespoons ground cumin
1 tablespoon dried oregano, crumbled

½ teaspoon hot red pepper flakes, or ¼
    teaspoon cayenne pepper or to taste
salt and pepper to taste
1 (28-ounce) can whole plum
    tomatoes, with their juice
hot cooked red or white beans, for
    serving (optional)
hot cooked rice or pasta, for serving
    (optional)

Accompaniments

hot tortillas, bread, or pita
sliced or diced avocado
grated cheddar cheese (optional)
sour cream (optional)
Fresh Tomato Salsa (page 362) or
    diced tomato

cilantro (fresh coriander) sprigs
chopped or thinly sliced onion
sliced green onions

Heat 2 tablespoons oil in a large saucepan over medium heat. Add onion and cook, stirring often, about 10 minutes or until tender. Transfer to a bowl.

Add remaining 2 tablespoons oil to saucepan and heat it. Add turkey and cook, stirring often, until it changes color, about 7 minutes. Return onion to pan and add garlic, jalapeños, and seasonings. Cook over low heat, stirring, about 3 minutes to coat meat with spices. Add tomatoes and bring to a boil, stirring and crushing tomatoes. Cook uncovered over low heat about 45 minutes or until thick. Taste and adjust seasoning. If you would like hotter chili, add more cayenne pepper.

Serve chili in a deep bowl, accompanied by beans or rice and tortillas. Surround with small bowls of avocado, cheese, sour cream, salsa, cilantro sprigs, chopped onion, and sliced green onion, for each person to add to his or her portion.

Makes 4 to 6 servings

TURKEY SAUSAGES WITH BEANS AND TOMATOES

Cooks in different countries have recognized that sausages and beans make a fine match, since the mild-flavored satisfying beans are a perfect foil for the rich, often spicy sausages. Turkey and chicken sausages are usually leaner than those made of pork and beef, and if you serve them with beans, a little goes a long way. In this recipe, the sausages and beans are moistened with an Italian-Provençal–style tomato sauce.

1 pound dried white beans, such as
  Great Northern (about 2⅓ cups)
1 bay leaf
2½ quarts water
2 tablespoons olive oil
1 medium onion, chopped
3 medium garlic cloves, minced
2 pounds ripe tomatoes, peeled,
  seeded, and chopped; or 2 (28-
  ounce) cans plum tomatoes, drained
  and chopped

½ teaspoon dried thyme, crumbled
2 teaspoons dried oregano, crumbled
salt and pepper
¾ to 1 pound smoked turkey sausages
1 tablespoon chopped fresh parsley
  (optional)

Sort beans, discarding any broken ones and any stones. In a large bowl soak beans in 7 cups cold water overnight. For a quicker method, cover beans with 7 cups water in a large saucepan, boil 2 minutes, and let stand off heat for 1 hour.

Rinse beans and drain. Put in a large saucepan and add bay leaf and 2½ quarts water. Bring to a boil. Cover and simmer over low heat, adding hot water if necessary so that beans remain covered, until they are tender, about 1½ hours. Discard bay leaf. *Beans can be kept in their cooking liquid, covered, for 1 day in refrigerator.*

Heat oil in a large skillet over low heat. Add onion and cook, stirring occasionally, until soft but not browned, about 7 minutes. Add garlic, tomatoes, thyme, oregano, salt, and pepper. Cook over medium heat, stirring often, about 20 minutes or until tomatoes are soft and mixture is thick.

Cover sausages with water in a medium saucepan and bring just to a simmer. Cover and cook over low heat 7 minutes. Drain well.

Reheat beans, if necessary, and drain well. Gently mix tomatoes with beans. Add sausages, cover, and warm over low heat for 5 minutes to blend flavors. *Dish can be kept, covered, 2 days in refrigerator. Reheat in covered skillet over medium-low heat.* Taste and adjust seasoning. Serve sprinkled with parsley.

Makes 4 to 6 servings

13

Chicken and Turkey in Minutes

 This chapter is for those meals for which you need to get food on the table in record time. Here the recipes are especially quick and easy. Most of the dishes take less than 20 minutes and require a small number of ingredients. They are perfect for a quick lunch or supper. There are plenty of other places to find ideas for quick meals in this book, notably in the chapters on grilled chicken and turkey, sautéed chicken and turkey, chicken and turkey salads, and chicken and turkey sandwiches.

We can take a cue on how to prepare speedy chicken and turkey dishes from cooks all over the globe. By choosing quick versions of such dishes as Oriental stir-fries and curries, chicken burgers with a Middle Eastern flavor, and broiled chicken with a simple Mediterranean-style lemon and olive oil sauce, we can enjoy home-cooked dinners even when we have very little time to devote to their preparation.

Boneless cuts—chicken breasts and thighs and turkey breast slices—are the fastest cooking ones, requiring only a few minutes. Thin chicken breast fillets have the briefest cooking time

Brazilian Chicken and Hearts of Palm Salad
Chicken and Tortellini Salad with Basil
and Roasted Peppers
Chicken Salad with Raspberry Vinaigrette
Ten-Minute Mediterranean Chicken Soup
Chicken Ravioli Soup with Green Vegetables
Chicken Burgers with Pine Nuts
and Fresh Jalapeño-Garlic Chutney
French "Minute" Chicken
Taipei Chicken Curry
Chicken Breasts with Cumin-Tomato Sauce
Grilled Chicken with
Quick Provençal Herb-Lemon Sauce
Almond Chicken with Peppers and Asparagus
Sautéed Chicken with Cabbage
Bulgur Wheat with Smoked Chicken
and Sun-Dried Tomatoes
Turkey Tonnato Salad
Mediterranean Turkey "Schnitzel"
Teriyaki Turkey
Linguine with Smoked Turkey Breast
and Spicy Mushrooms
Turkey Picadillo

of all. The quickest techniques for cooking them are sautéing, stir-frying, broiling, and stovetop grilling.

For a very easy meal, it's useful to take advantage of good-quality packaged foods. I like to keep frozen vegetables on hand for this purpose, the kind without sauce, since I prefer to add my own flavorings. Besides, I want to make sure the vegetables are fat-free. Medleys of several frozen vegetables are especially convenient for preparing fast, colorful menus.

There is a growing selection of poultry products that are helpful for preparing quick meals. Slices of chicken or turkey sausage or small pieces of smoked poultry quickly add flavor and substance to pasta, rice, and vegetable dishes. In any recipe that calls for cooked poultry, you can use roast chicken or turkey from the deli section of the supermarket.

Canned and frozen chicken broth and stock are practical for making quick soups and sauces, as is canned, bottled, or packaged tomato sauce. What other prepared sauces to buy depends on your taste. I like fresh Mexican salsas, pesto, and Chinese plum sauce to quickly add zest to chicken and turkey dishes. For the best flavor, however, I find it a good idea to add at least some fresh ingredients to every dish.

BRAZILIAN CHICKEN AND HEARTS OF PALM SALAD

For this quick and easy salad, chicken is combined with avocado, corn, and sliced hearts of palm in an oregano-scented lime juice dressing with a low proportion of oil. Some versions of this salad feature mayonnaise, but the light lime juice dressing shows off the colors much better and is a perfect complement to the chicken and vegetables.

¼ cup strained fresh lime juice
6 tablespoons extra-virgin olive oil
1½ teaspoons dried oregano, crumbled
1 teaspoon minced garlic
salt and freshly ground pepper
3 cups diced cooked chicken or turkey
1 green bell pepper, diced
⅔ cup chopped green onions

1 (14-ounce) jar hearts of palm, rinsed lightly, drained, and sliced ¼ inch thick
2 large ripe tomatoes, diced
2 cups cooked corn kernels
2 avocados (optional)
lettuce leaves, for serving (optional)

Whisk together lime juice, oil, oregano, garlic, salt, and pepper and set aside. Combine chicken, green pepper, green onion, heart of palm slices, tomato, and corn in another bowl. Add dressing and mix lightly. A short time before serving, peel and dice the avocados and fold into salad. Serve in a bowl or on a lettuce-lined platter.

Makes 7 or 8 servings

CHICKEN AND TORTELLINI SALAD WITH BASIL AND ROASTED PEPPERS

This colorful dish is one of the easiest chicken salads to make, but if you use fresh basil and good olive oil, it is one of the best as well. I always keep a package of cheese tortellini in the freezer ready for this purpose. To prepare the salad in a flash, you can use roasted peppers from a jar, and you can even buy the roast chicken or turkey from a deli. Although the seasonings are of Italian inspiration, chicken and pasta salads like this are actually an American specialty and are rarely prepared in Europe.

Many such chicken and pasta salads do not need a true "dressing," but just enough olive oil to moisten the ingredients. Of course, you can add a tablespoon or two of lemon juice or herb vinegar if you would like a hint of tartness. Serve with freshly grated Parmesan cheese if you like.

1 pound or 2 (9- or 10-ounce)
  packages cheese-filled tortellini,
  fresh or frozen
6 to 8 tablespoons extra-virgin olive oil
1 red and 1 green bell pepper, roasted
  (page 408)

2 cups cooked chicken strips
⅓ cup coarsely chopped oil-packed
  sun-dried tomatoes (optional)
6 plum tomatoes, diced
½ cup chopped fresh basil leaves
salt and freshly ground pepper

Cook pasta uncovered in a large pot of boiling salted water over medium-high heat, stirring occasionally, about 8 minutes or according to package directions or until tender. Drain, rinse gently with cold water, and drain well. Transfer to a large bowl. Add 6 tablespoons oil and toss to combine.

Cut peeled peppers in thin lengthwise strips about ¼ inch wide. Add to pasta. Add chicken, both types of tomatoes, and basil and toss. Season to taste with salt and freshly ground pepper. Add more oil if needed. *Salad can be kept, covered, up to 1 day in refrigerator. Let stand a few minutes at room temperature before serving.*

Makes 8 first-course or 4 main-course servings

VARIATION:
   Substitute thin strips of smoked chicken or turkey for the cooked chicken. Do not add sun-dried tomatoes.

CHICKEN SALAD
WITH RASPBERRY VINAIGRETTE

Chicken fillets are turned quickly into a glamorous but easy entree with the help of raspberry vinaigrette and fresh berries. The pale pink dressing has an appealing fruity aroma and taste that beautifully complement the poultry and is especially popular in California and the Pacific Northwest.

½ small shallot, peeled and halved
3 tablespoons raspberry vinegar
salt and freshly ground pepper
½ cup plus 3 tablespoons vegetable oil
1½ pounds chicken fillets (tender strip
   of boned breast; see page 396) or
   boneless skinless breasts, cut in
   strips

leaves of butter (Boston) lettuce
about 30 fresh raspberries
4 teaspoons chopped chives or
   tarragon

Chop shallot in a food processor by dropping pieces down feed tube one by one, with blade of processor turning. Chop finely. Add vinegar, salt, and pepper and process until combined. With blade turning, gradually pour in ½ cup plus 1 tablespoon oil. Dressing will thicken slightly. Taste and adjust seasoning.
   In a large skillet, heat remaining 2 tablespoons oil over medium-high heat. Add about half the chicken, sprinkle with salt and pepper, and sauté until it changes color throughout, about 3 or 4 minutes. Remove with a slotted spatula and keep warm. Add oil to pan if needed and sauté the remaining chicken.
   Make a bed of lettuce on 6 plates and top with chicken. Whisk dressing, spoon it over chicken, and sprinkle with raspberries and chives or tarragon. Serve warm.

Makes 6 servings

TEN-MINUTE MEDITERRANEAN CHICKEN SOUP

By using boneless chicken breasts, quick-cooking fresh vegetables—red peppers and zucchini—and prepared chicken broth, you can have a colorful, satisfying soup in no time. For a quick meal, prepare a diced salad of cucumbers and tomato while the soup simmers, for serving as a first course. Serve the soup with crusty bread or pita, or with quick-cooking couscous or rice to add to each bowl.

2 boneless and skinless chicken breast halves (about ¾ pound)
1 red bell pepper
2 cups chicken broth, or 1 (14-ounce) can with enough water to make 2 cups
½ cup water
1 teaspoon ground cumin
2 small zucchini, halved lengthwise and sliced

3 tablespoons chopped green or red onion
2 tablespoons chopped cilantro (fresh coriander) or parsley (optional)
salt (optional) and freshly ground pepper
pinch of cayenne pepper

Cut chicken into 1½ × 2-inch strips. Cut pepper in strips of a similar size. Put both in saucepan with chicken broth, ½ cup water, and cumin. Bring to a simmer. Skim foam. Add zucchini and return to simmer. Cover and simmer 10 minutes or until chicken, zucchini, and pepper are tender. Stir in chopped onion and cilantro, and add black pepper and cayenne to taste. Taste before adding salt; it depends on saltiness of broth.

Makes 4 appetizer or 2 main-course servings

CHICKEN RAVIOLI SOUP WITH GREEN VEGETABLES

Ravioli with chicken filling is delicious in this hearty, chunky main-course soup, a simplified version of Italian minestrone made more satisfying with the addition of cooked chicken or turkey. To have the soup ready in no time, use canned broth and frozen vegetables.

1 quart chicken stock or broth
2 cups water
freshly ground pepper to taste
1 small carrot, diced small
1 large garlic clove, chopped
salt
1 (8- to 10-ounce) package fresh
    chicken ravioli, agnolotti, or
    tortellini

½ pound broccoli, divided into small
    florets
½ cup frozen peas
1 cup diced cooked chicken or turkey
2 tablespoons chopped green onion

In a medium saucepan combine stock, water, a pinch of pepper, carrot, and garlic. Add salt if using unsalted homemade stock. Bring to a boil. Cover and cook over medium-low heat 5 minutes.

Add pasta and broccoli and bring to a boil. Cook uncovered over medium heat, stirring occasionally, for 4 minutes. Add peas and cook about 2 minutes or until pasta is tender but firm to the bite; cut off a piece of pasta to check. Add chicken and heat 1 minute. Add green onions and pepper. Taste, adjust seasoning, and serve.

Makes 4 or 5 first-course or 2 or 3 main-course servings

CHICKEN BURGERS WITH PINE NUTS AND FRESH JALAPEÑO-GARLIC CHUTNEY

Nothing is simpler than making chicken burgers, which are lower in fat than those made of beef. Ground coriander and cumin, in addition to the pine nuts, give these burgers an eastern Mediterranean flavor. You can serve them in hamburger rolls, pita breads, or onion rolls. The zesty hot pepper chutney provides quite a punch of flavor, but if you don't have time to prepare it, hot Mexican salsa also makes a good accompaniment.

4 medium garlic cloves, minced
½ teaspoon salt
½ teaspoon freshly ground black
    pepper
2 teaspoons ground coriander

1 teaspoon ground cumin
¼ cup pine nuts
1¼ to 1⅓ pounds ground chicken (2⅔
    to 3 cups)
Jalapeño Garlic-Chutney (page 366)

Mix garlic with salt, pepper, coriander, and cumin. Add spice mixture and pine nuts to chicken and mix lightly to blend. Shape into 6 patties, each about 3 inches in diameter.

Lightly oil the broiler rack and position it about 4 inches from heat source; or prepare a grill with rack about 6 inches above glowing coals. Broil or grill patties, turning once, about 7 or 8 minutes, or until they are springy when pressed. Serve immediately, accompanied by chutney.

Makes 4 to 6 servings

FRENCH "MINUTE" CHICKEN

The fastest French chicken recipe I know is chicken sauté à la minute, *for which the chicken is sautéed in butter, set on a platter, and sprinkled with a little fresh lemon juice, its cooking butter, and chopped parsley. I find it also very tasty with olive oil instead of the butter, and now I often prepare it this way.*

For this recipe you can use boneless chicken breasts with or without the skin. Fastest of all to cook are chicken tenders, the thin fillet strips of the breast, which are sometimes sold separately and take only 1 to 2 minutes per side.

2 boneless chicken breast halves,
   patted dry
salt and freshly ground pepper
1 tablespoon vegetable oil and 1
   tablespoon butter, or 2 tablespoons
   olive oil

1 tablespoon chopped fresh parsley
½ lemon, cut in 2 wedges

Sprinkle chicken with salt and pepper on both sides. Heat oil and butter, or olive oil, in a heavy, medium skillet over medium-high heat. Add chicken and sauté, pressing on chicken occasionally with a flat spatula, about 6 minutes per side, or until chicken has changed color throughout; cut to check. If juices start to brown during sautéing, reduce heat to medium. Transfer to plates and sprinkle with parsley, then with cooking oil. Serve with lemon wedges.

Makes 2 servings

TAIPEI CHICKEN CURRY

Stella Lee, a friend of mine from Taipei, told me how to make this light, easy, meal-in-one-dish of chicken breasts with vegetables flavored with curry powder and soy sauce. It is a typical entree made in Taiwanese home kitchens when a fast dinner is needed, and is a cross between a stir-fry and a quick braise. For best flavor, use imported curry powder. Serve this curry over rice.

3 medium carrots (½ pound)
3 medium boiling potatoes (1 pound)
1 pound boneless and skinless chicken
   breasts
2 tablespoons vegetable oil

1 large onion, diced small
2 teaspoons curry powder
1½ cups water
1 tablespoon plus 1 teaspoon soy sauce
hot cooked rice, for serving

Quarter carrots, then slice ¼ inch thick. Peel potatoes and cut in ½-inch cubes. Cut chicken in cubes of about 1 × ½ × ½ inch.

In a wok, medium sauté pan, or deep skillet heat oil over medium-high heat. Add onion and stir-fry until fragrant, about 2 minutes. Add chicken and stir-fry 1½ minutes. Stir in curry powder, then water, soy sauce, carrots, and potatoes. Simmer covered for 10 minutes. Uncover and simmer 10 minutes more or until chicken and vegetables are tender. Taste and adjust seasoning.

Makes 3 or 4 servings

CHICKEN BREASTS WITH CUMIN-TOMATO SAUCE

If you have tomato sauce on hand, either homemade or packaged, this is one of the quickest ways to prepare a flavorful chicken dish. The Middle Eastern tomato sauce, flavored with cumin, sautéed onions, and garlic, makes a delicious partner for the sautéed chicken. Serve it with rice, couscous, or fettuccine, and with a green or spinach salad.

4 boneless chicken breasts (about 1½
   pounds), patted dry
salt and freshly ground pepper
1½ teaspoons ground cumin

2 tablespoons vegetable or olive oil
1 small onion, chopped
2 large garlic cloves, chopped
1 cup tomato sauce

Sprinkle chicken with salt, pepper, and ¼ teaspoon cumin on each side.

Heat oil in a large skillet over medium heat. Add chicken and sauté until no longer pink inside, about 5 minutes per side; press occasionally with spatula to flatten. Remove with slotted spatula.

Add onion to pan and sauté about 5 minutes or until softened. Add garlic and remaining 1 teaspoon cumin and sauté ½ minute. Stir in tomato sauce and simmer over low heat 2 minutes. Taste and adjust seasoning. Return chicken to sauce, cover, and heat gently about 3 minutes, turning once.

Makes 4 servings

GRILLED CHICKEN WITH QUICK PROVENÇAL HERB-LEMON SAUCE

In Provence chicken is often grilled very simply—sprinkled with a little salt and pepper, lightly brushed with olive oil, and set on the grill. A liberal amount of herbs in the lemon sauce enhances the taste of the grilled chicken. You might like to broil or grill some vegetables—sliced eggplant, zucchini, mushrooms, or peppers—alongside the chicken and moisten them with the sauce, too.

2 tablespoons strained fresh lemon juice
1 small garlic clove, very finely chopped (optional)
salt and freshly ground pepper
about 7 tablespoons extra-virgin olive oil

½ teaspoon dried thyme, crumbled
½ teaspoon dried rosemary
1 tablespoon chopped fresh basil or parsley
4 boneless chicken breast halves, with skin (1¼ to 1½ pounds)
lettuce leaves (optional)

Whisk lemon juice with garlic, salt, and pepper in a small bowl. Whisk in 6 tablespoons oil, thyme, and rosemary. Taste and adjust seasoning.

Prepare a charcoal grill or heat a broiler with rack about 4 inches from heat source; or heat a ridged stovetop grill pan over medium-high heat. Rub chicken with remaining olive oil and sprinkle with salt and pepper on both sides.

Set chicken on an oiled rack above glowing coals, on broiler rack, or on grill, with skin facing down. Grill or broil until meat feels springy, about 5 minutes per side. To check whether chicken is done, cut into thickest part with tip of a sharp knife; color should be white, not pink.

Whisk dressing and add chopped basil. Line 4 plates with lettuce and set chicken on top. Spoon a little dressing over each chicken piece and serve.

Makes 4 servings

ALMOND CHICKEN WITH PEPPERS AND ASPARAGUS

Not much chopping is required for this easy Chinese stir-fry. Toasted almonds provide a pleasing richness and crunch, but you can substitute cashews or peanuts or omit the nuts if you like.

To make preparation even easier, you can use frozen asparagus. In some stores you can buy packages of frozen stir-fry vegetables, which includes such Chinese favorites as snow peas, water chestnuts, bamboo shoots, and mushrooms; they can be stir-fried from the frozen state. You can substitute a 10-ounce package of these stir-fry vegetables for the fresh vegetables here.

Since the dish already contains plenty of vegetables, all you need to add is steamed rice.

½ cup blanched almonds
¾ to 1 pound medium-width asparagus, peeled and cut in 2-inch pieces
¾ cup chicken stock or broth
1 tablespoon soy sauce
1 teaspoon dry sherry
½ teaspoon sugar
salt and freshly ground white pepper

1½ teaspoons cornstarch
4 tablespoons vegetable oil
1 red bell pepper, cored and cut in strips ⅛ inch wide
3 green onions, cut in 1-inch pieces
1 pound boneless and skinless chicken breast fillets (chicken tenders, see page 396 and Note), patted dry
1 tablespoon Oriental sesame oil

Preheat the oven to 350°F. Toast almonds on a baking sheet until lightly browned, about 7 minutes. Transfer to a plate.

In a saucepan cook asparagus in boiling salted water about 3 minutes; it should still be quite crisp. Rinse with cold water and drain well.

In a medium bowl stir together stock, soy sauce, sherry, sugar, salt, white pepper, and cornstarch.

Heat 1 tablespoon oil in a large skillet or wok over medium heat. Add red pepper and green onions and sauté, stirring often, until softened but still crunchy, about 2 minutes. Remove from pan.

Heat remaining 3 tablespoons oil in skillet or wok over medium-high heat until very hot. Add half the chicken pieces and sauté, tossing often, until meat loses its pink color, about 2 minutes. Remove to a plate with slotted spoon. Sauté remaining chicken.

Return all the chicken and vegetables to pan. Stir stock mixture, add to pan, and bring to a boil over medium heat, tossing. Simmer until ingredients are lightly coated with sauce, about 2 minutes. Off the heat, stir in sesame oil. Taste, and add salt and white pepper if needed. Add almonds, toss, and transfer to a serving dish.

Makes 3 or 4 servings

NOTE: If chicken fillets are not available, use chicken breasts, pound them between 2 sheets wax paper until ¼ inch thick, and cut in strips about ½ inch wide and 1½ inches long.

SAUTÉED CHICKEN WITH CABBAGE

Poultry with cabbage is a time-honored combination in much of central, northern, and eastern Europe. Unlike many traditional recipes, however, this recipe calls for a brief cooking time so the cabbage is bright green and slightly crisp. The cabbage is blanched while the chicken breast is sautéed; then the cabbage is heated in the chicken juices and seasoned with garlic and cayenne pepper. Serve the chicken with pumpernickel or rye bread or with noodles sprinkled with caraway seeds.

To quickly cut the cabbage in strips, use a food processor, which can reduce a cabbage to fine shreds in seconds, and can make this inexpensive, nutritionally rich vegetable very quick and easy to prepare.

1 small head green cabbage (about 1 pound), cored, rinsed and shredded
salt and freshly ground pepper
3 boneless chicken breast halves (about 1 pound), patted dry

2 tablespoons vegetable or olive oil
2 medium garlic cloves, minced
⅛ to ¼ teaspoon hot red pepper flakes, or cayenne pepper to taste
½ teaspoon dried thyme, crumbled

In a deep sauté pan boil enough water to cover cabbage. Add a pinch of salt and the cabbage, and boil it for 5 minutes, or until just tender. Drain in a colander, rinse under running cold water, and drain thoroughly. Gently squeeze cabbage by handfuls to remove excess water.

Sprinkle chicken with salt and pepper on both sides. Heat oil in the same pan over medium-high heat. Add chicken and sauté, pressing on chicken occasionally with flat spatula, about 6 minutes per side, or until chicken has changed color throughout; cut to check. If juices start to brown during sautéing, reduce heat to medium. Remove and keep warm.

Add garlic and hot pepper flakes to pan and sauté about 10 seconds. Quickly stir in cabbage and sprinkle with salt, pepper, and thyme. Sauté over medium heat, stirring, for 3 minutes, or until hot. Taste for seasoning. Spoon onto plates, top with chicken, and serve.

Makes 2 or 3 servings

BULGUR WHEAT WITH SMOKED CHICKEN AND SUN-DRIED TOMATOES

For an inexpensive, easy all-in-one-pan lunch or supper, I love to mix diced smoked turkey or chicken with bulgur wheat, a favorite grain in the eastern Mediterranean area. Although they come from farther west, I usually add a few sun-dried tomatoes, which are really a staple of home cooking in some parts of Italy and not just an item on menus of trendy restaurants. If I don't happen to have them, I add diced fresh or bottled red peppers. Any other quick-cooking vegetables such as mushrooms, chopped onions, or zucchini will make a good addition. As an accompaniment to this quick, Mediterranean-style dish, I like to serve sliced tomatoes and cucumbers and a dollop of yogurt.

2 tablespoons vegetable oil
1 medium onion, chopped
4 ounces mushrooms, cut in sixths
1¼ cups bulgur wheat
2½ cups chicken stock, broth, or water
¼ cup dry-pack sun-dried tomatoes,
   cut in bite-size pieces
salt and freshly ground pepper
cayenne pepper to taste

1 tablespoon chopped fresh basil, or 1
   teaspoon dried
1 cup frozen corn kernels
⅔ cup frozen peas
3 ounces thinly sliced smoked chicken
   or turkey pastrami, cut in thin strips
   (about ¾ cup strips)

Heat oil in saucepan, add onion, and sauté over medium heat about 5 minutes. Add mushrooms and sauté about 3 minutes. Add bulgur and sauté lightly. Add stock, sun-dried tomatoes, salt, pepper, cayenne, and dried basil, if using, and bring to a boil. Cover and cook 10 minutes over low heat. Add corn and peas, stir lightly, and cook covered for 5 minutes or until tender and liquid is absorbed. Stir in chicken and let stand briefly to heat through. Add fresh basil, if using. Taste and adjust seasoning.

Makes 3 main-course servings

TURKEY TONNATO SALAD

Turkey tonnato, or turkey with a tangy tuna-caper dressing, is based on an Italian veal recipe but the turkey version has become so popular it has practically become an American classic. Instead of braising the turkey as in many traditional recipes, I like to use roast turkey. I find the tasty dressing is a perfect way to use Thanksgiving leftovers to best advantage. It is also delicious with roast chicken. When you don't have roast turkey or chicken, you can buy some from a deli to make this quick salad.

The dressing can be made with or without mayonnaise. The version with mayonnaise is creamier, and the one without mayonnaise is more piquant.

I like to garnish the salad with chopped parsley, capers, and roasted peppers or sun-dried tomatoes. Rather than serving the turkey as a salad, you can prepare a turkey tonnato sandwich by spreading the tuna dressing on sliced Italian bread and topping it with roast turkey slices and the same garnish ingredients.

Tuna Dressing

1 (3-ounce) can oil-packed tuna, undrained
3 anchovy fillets
2 tablespoons strained fresh lemon juice

2 tablespoons drained capers, rinsed and drained
⅓ cup extra-virgin olive oil
freshly ground pepper
⅔ cup mayonnaise (optional)

leaves of butter (Boston) lettuce, for lining platter
about 16 to 20 thin slices roast turkey (about ¾ pound)
1 tablespoon chopped fresh parsley

1 or 2 tablespoons capers, drained
strips of roasted red peppers, oil-cured sun-dried tomatoes, or fresh tomato wedges, for garnish

For dressing, combine tuna with its oil, anchovies, lemon juice, and capers in food processor and puree until smooth. Scrape mixture down occasionally. With machine running, gradually add oil. Season to taste with pepper. For creamier dressing, put mayonnaise in a bowl and gradually stir in tuna mixture. If dressing is too thick, stir in water by teaspoons until dressing is pourable.

Line platter or plates with lettuce leaves. Arrange turkey slices slightly overlapping on lettuce. Coat turkey lightly with sauce. Sprinkle with parsley and capers. Garnish with peppers or tomatoes.

Makes 4 servings

MEDITERRANEAN TURKEY "SCHNITZEL"

The most delicious and foolproof way to enjoy turkey breast slices is to turn them into turkey schnitzel. As in the Austrian veal specialty, Wiener schnitzel, *a special coating keeps the lean meat juicy. The sautéed turkey slices come out crisp on the outside and moist on the inside. The thin crust, made by dipping the turkey slices successively in flour, egg, and bread crumbs, prevents the turkey from sticking to the pan and protects the meat so it won't become dry.*

Turkey schnitzel is moist enough so that sauce is not needed, but a little sautéed garlic sprinkled on the turkey at the last moment gives it an extra punch of flavor, as in this recipe. Lemon wedges are a standard accompaniment, or you can follow Italian recipes of garnishing the turkey with anchovy fillets rolled around capers, which you can buy at the "gourmet" departments of supermarkets.

1 pound turkey breast slices, about ¼
    inch thick
1 teaspoon dried thyme, crumbled
½ teaspoon dried sage, crumbled
½ teaspoon salt
¼ teaspoon freshly ground black
    pepper

⅓ cup all-purpose flour
¾ cup unseasoned dry bread crumbs
2 eggs
about ⅓ cup vegetable oil
3 medium garlic cloves, minced
1 tablespoon chopped cilantro (fresh
    coriander) or parsley

Arrange turkey in one layer on plate. Mix thyme, sage, salt, and pepper in small bowl. Sprinkle evenly over both sides of turkey.

Preheat oven to 275°F. Spread flour in plate. Spread bread crumbs in second plate. Beat eggs in shallow bowl. Lightly coat a turkey slice with flour on both sides. Tap and shake to remove excess flour. Dip slice in egg. Lastly, dip both sides in bread crumbs so turkey is completely coated; pat and press lightly so crumbs adhere. Repeat with remaining slices. Set pieces side by side on large plate. *Breaded turkey can be kept, uncovered, 2 hours in refrigerator.*

Heat oil in a heavy, large skillet over medium-high heat. Add enough turkey to make one layer. Sauté until golden brown on both sides, about 1 minute per side. Turn carefully using 2 wide spatulas. If oil begins to brown, reduce heat to medium. Set turkey slices side by side on ovenproof platter and keep them warm in oven while sautéing remaining slices.

Discard all but 2 tablespoons oil from pan. Add garlic and cilantro and sauté over low heat about ½ minute; do not let garlic brown. Pour over turkey slices and serve immediately.

Makes 4 servings

TERIYAKI TURKEY

Teriyaki chicken is one of the best-loved entrees at Japanese restaurants and is amazingly easy to make. The basic teriyaki sauce is composed of three ingredients: soy sauce, sugar, and rice wine. It's a delicious mixture for spreading on turkey slices or chicken before cooking, as well as a flavorful marinade. It can be varied with the addition of grated fresh ginger, as in the recipe below, or minced garlic.

This dish makes good use of the lean turkey breast meat with just a minimal amount of added fat. The oil from sautéing is discarded before the teriyaki mixture is added to the pan and so is not part of the sauce.

Serve the turkey with rice, carrots, and a green vegetable—asparagus, sugar-snap peas, peas, or broccoli.

1 pound turkey breast slices (¼ inch thick), patted dry
3 tablespoons vegetable oil
2 tablespoons soy sauce
2 tablespoons mirin (Japanese sweet rice wine)

1 teaspoon sugar
2 teaspoons grated fresh ginger
freshly ground pepper (optional)
1 tablespoon thinly sliced green onion, for garnish

Cut each turkey slice in 6 or 8 pieces, each with about 1½- or 2-inch sides. Put on paper towel-lined plate. Heat oil in a large, heavy skillet over medium-high heat. Add half the turkey and sauté, stirring often, about 1 minute per side, just until color changes throughout; cut a piece to check. Transfer turkey to plate and keep warm. Repeat with remaining turkey. Discard oil if desired.

In a small bowl mix soy sauce, mirin, sugar, and ginger. Add to pan and bring to a boil, stirring. Cook over medium heat 1 minute or until thickened. Return turkey to pan (without adding liquid from plate) and heat gently in sauce, turning pieces over several times, about 2 minutes or until coated. When serving, spoon any remaining sauce in pan over turkey. Sprinkle with pepper and serve.

Makes 3 or 4 servings

NOTE: Mirin can be found in the Oriental section of supermarkets.

LINGUINE WITH SMOKED TURKEY BREAST AND SPICY MUSHROOMS

By using turkey breast cold cuts—either smoked or roasted and cured—and combining them with pasta, sautéed mushrooms, and peppers from a jar, you have a very easy, colorful quick lunch for two. A Moroccan seasoning combination of cumin, cayenne pepper, paprika, and parsley gives it an enticing flavor. To keep the cooking time as brief as possible, use fresh linguine rather than dried.

2 to 3 tablespoons extra-virgin olive oil
4 ounces medium mushrooms,
    quartered
salt and freshly ground pepper
dash of cayenne pepper
½ teaspoon ground cumin
½ teaspoon paprika
½ teaspoon dried thyme, crumbled

8 ounces fresh or dried linguine
1 cup diced smoked or roasted cured
    turkey breast
1 roasted red pepper (page 408 or from
    a jar), cut in thin strips
1 green onion, cut in thin slices (¼
    cup)
2 tablespoons chopped fresh parsley

Heat 2 tablespoons oil in a heavy skillet over medium-high heat. Add mushrooms, salt, pepper, cayenne, cumin, paprika, and thyme. Sauté about 3 minutes or until just tender and well browned. Remove from heat.

Cook linguine in a large pan of boiling salted water about 2 minutes for fresh or 8 minutes for dried, or until just al dente. Drain well.

Add turkey, red pepper, green onion, and parsley to mushroom mixture and heat about 1 minute. Toss with pasta, and add more oil if desired. Taste, adjust seasoning, and serve.

Makes 4 appetizer or 2 main-course servings

TURKEY PICADILLO

Picadillo, a savory and sweet Latin American mixture of ground meat, sautéed onions, peppers, raisins, and olives, is a popular filling for empanadas, tortillas, tamales, and vegetables. Picadillo can also be served on its own, accompanied by tortillas or rice. It is usually made of beef or pork, but it's delicious with turkey or chicken, and of course, it's lower in fat.

2 tablespoons vegetable oil
1 small or ½ large onion, chopped
½ green bell pepper, chopped
½ pound ground turkey or chicken (about 1 cup packed)
2 ripe medium tomatoes, or 4 plum tomatoes, peeled, seeded, and chopped

½ teaspoon dried oregano, crumbled
salt and freshly ground pepper
3 tablespoons raisins
¼ cup diced green olives
1 tablespoon capers, rinsed and chopped
1 chopped hard-boiled egg

Heat oil in skillet, add onion and pepper, and sauté over medium heat 7 minutes or until softened. Add turkey and sauté, stirring, until it changes color, about 3 or 4 minutes. Add tomatoes, oregano, salt, pepper, and raisins; bring to boil and cook over medium heat 5 minutes. Remove from heat. Stir in remaining ingredients. Taste and adjust seasoning. *Picadillo can be kept, covered, 2 days in refrigerator.* Serve hot.

Makes 2 to 4 servings (with tortillas)

14

Chicken and Turkey Sandwiches

Chicken and turkey sandwiches are frequent choices for lunch—not only in lunch boxes, but also on menus of restaurants, both casual and elegant.

All cuts of cooked chicken and poultry make excellent sandwiches. I sometimes find it convenient to roast, braise, or poach an extra chicken so some cooked meat remains for making sandwiches. A friend of mine roasts an extra turkey every Thanksgiving because her husband insists that there be plenty of roast turkey for the sandwiches he takes to work.

Today it's easy to make poultry sandwiches. A variety of prepared meats are made from turkey and chicken—hot, mild, and smoked sausages; thin slices of roasted and smoked chicken and turkey breast; and turkey pastrami, to name a few. Many supermarkets and delis also sell fresh roasted chicken and turkey.

Sandwiches don't have to be served cold. Sautéed chicken or turkey with onions and cumin in a pita makes a delicious hot sandwich with a Middle Eastern accent. Grilled chicken with peppers makes a tasty filling for tortillas, for a Mexican-style "sandwich" called a *fajita*. *Bruschetta*, an Italian open-faced sandwich on toasted country bread, is a restaurant favorite

281

Chicken Bruschetta
Chicken Sandwich in Lavosh
Deli-Style Chicken Salad Sandwich
California Chicken Sandwich
Middle Eastern Chicken in a Pita
Chicken with Tahini in a Pita
Chicken "Sloppy Joe"
Turkey Mushroom Burgers
Turkey Sandwich with Creole Mayonnaise
Turkey Kielbasa Sandwich with Sautéed Onions
Smoked Turkey and
Herbed Cream Cheese Sandwich
Eggplant Pâté Sandwich with Smoked Turkey

that is easy to make at home. Chicken Burgers (page 269) make a delicious hot sandwich *à l'américaine.*

Lately, sandwiches have become chic. Trendy restaurants today offer sandwiches of roast chicken with freshly made pesto or with marinated peppers. At home it's useful to keep a few flavorful items in the kitchen so that, along with chicken or turkey and good bread, you have the makings of a quick and tasty sandwich. I probably wouldn't prepare pesto or marinate peppers especially for a sandwich, but if I had some anyway I would naturally use it. Some ingredients that I find convenient for sandwich making are bottled roasted peppers, oil-packed sun-dried tomatoes, marinated vegetables, capers, olives, and, of course, mayonnaise, mustard, and pickles. It's fun to vary your sandwiches by using spicy mayonnaise or grainy mustard, or to make a quick spread, like Two-Minute Turkey Pâté (page 28), Niçoise Chicken Liver Pâté (page 23), Guacamole (page 365), or Smoked Chicken and Goat Cheese Canapés (page 24).

In the marketplace we're beginning to have an interesting selection of ethnic breads, which make sensational sandwiches possible. More and more bakeries are offering fine-quality French and Italian bread. Good pita is getting easier to find in the average supermarket. Lavosh, the thin, flat soft Armenian bread that looks somewhat like a large square tortilla, is terrific for wrapping chicken or turkey with vegetables and rolling up into a delicious sandwich.

Fresh vegetables are also a great addition to poultry sandwiches. Everyone adds lettuce leaves or sliced tomatoes to sandwiches, but the zesty vegetables shouldn't be ignored; thin red onion rings are a tasty addition, and for real zip, put in a few radish sprouts or a little chopped garlic.

You can easily use poultry to make variations on your favorite sandwiches. Bagel with smoked chicken, tomato, and cream cheese is certainly less expensive than the classic sandwich with lox. Instead of the usual hot dog on a roll, try turkey kielbasa.

Sandwich making is a casual activity, and the ingredient quantities are much more flexible than in most dishes. Look at the following recipes as guides or ideas, and adapt them to ingredients you happen to keep on hand. You can easily turn any chicken or turkey salad that doesn't contain potatoes, rice, or pasta into a sandwich by serving it on bread or rolls or in a pita. (See ''Salads,'' page 47.)

OTHER RECIPES THAT CAN BE SERVED AS SANDWICHES

To adapt these recipes as sandwiches, simply serve them on good fresh or toasted bread or rolls, or in a pita.

Chicken Satays (page 22)
Niçoise Chicken Liver Pâté with Thyme and White Wine
(page 23)
Smoked Chicken and Goat Cheese Canapés (page 24)
Two-Minute Turkey Pâté with Provençal Herbs (page 28)
Creamy Chicken Salad with Jerusalem Artichokes (page 57)
Roast Chicken Salad with Tomato-Garlic Salsa (page 69)
Turkey Salad with Creamy Cilantro Dressing (page 72)
Grilled Chicken Breasts with Easy Barbecue Sauce (page 156)
Chicken Fajitas (page 159)
Grilled Chicken with Italian Green Sauce (page 160)
Turkish Broiled Chicken with Walnut-Garlic Sauce (page 162)
Chicken Burgers with Pine Nuts and Fresh Jalapeño-Garlic
Chutney (page 269)
Turkey Tonnato Salad (page 276)
Teriyaki Turkey (page 278)
Turkey Picadillo (page 280)

In addition, the hot and cold sauces in Chapter 17 (pages 343–381) can be used to moisten cooked poultry or to spread on bread for sandwiches.

CHICKEN BRUSCHETTA

Bruschetta is a fashionable appetizer in Italian restaurants and is easy to prepare at home. Most often bruschetta is made of toasted Italian bread rubbed with garlic and topped with diced tomatoes, basil, and olive oil. Today many variations are prepared, with ingredients from sautéed eggplant to prosciutto. I like to add chicken to make the bruschetta more substantial, so that it makes a hearty appetizer or a light main course for lunch.

The chicken-tomato mixture is also good as a salad, served on a bed of lettuce, or mixed with cooked thin pasta such as linguine or vermicelli.

1 cup diced or thin strips cooked
  chicken or turkey
3 plum tomatoes, diced
3 tablespoons fresh basil strips
3 tablespoons extra-virgin olive oil

salt and freshly ground pepper
4 thick slices Italian or French bread,
  about ¾ inch thick, in about 3- × 5-
  inch slices
1 medium garlic clove, halved

Mix chicken with tomatoes, 2 tablespoons basil, and 2 tablespoons olive oil. Season to taste with salt and pepper. *Mixture can be kept, covered, 2 hours in refrigerator. Bring to room temperature.*

Lightly brush bread with olive oil. Broil it until lightly toasted; turn over, brush with more oil and lightly toast second side. Rub both sides with cut garlic.

Top toast with chicken mixture and let stand 5 minutes to soften slightly. Sprinkle with remaining basil and serve.

Makes 4 appetizer or 2 light main-course servings

CHICKEN SANDWICH IN LAVOSH

Delicate thin bread called lavosh is wonderful for wrapping chicken with fresh vegetables to make a light, tasty sandwich. It can be found in Armenian, Iranian, Lebanese, and Middle Eastern grocery stores and in gourmet stores. Use the soft, flexible lavosh for these sandwiches, not the crisp lavosh crackers. If you can't find lavosh, you can substitute flour tortillas, but you need to heat them first according to the package instructions.

For this Mediterranean-style sandwich, I like to moisten the ingredients with a vinaigrette flavored with harissa, which combines the flavors of hot pepper and garlic. Instead you can sprinkle on your favorite salsa or any light salad dressing. Instead of avocado you can add crumbled Armenian string cheese.

This sandwich is also good as a buffet party dish. You set the ingredients out on platters, and everyone rolls up his or her own sandwich.

Harissa Vinaigrette

1 tablespoon extra-virgin olive oil
¼ teaspoon Harissa (page 366) or
  bottled hot pepper sauce, or to taste

1 teaspoon strained fresh lemon juice
salt to taste

1 green or red pepper, roasted and
  peeled (page 408), or from a jar
1 ripe avocado, sliced
3 sheets lavosh, 8 or 9 inches square
4 to 6 thin slices roast chicken or other
  cooked chicken

1¼ to 1½ cups shredded lettuce,
  preferably romaine
2 small ripe tomatoes, cut in thin slices
  or half slices
2 large fresh mushrooms, sliced thin

Whisk vinaigrette ingredients in a small bowl. Cut roasted pepper in strips. Peel and slice avocado. Put these and remaining ingredients on platters on the table. Each person makes his or her own sandwich.

To make sandwich, put chicken and avocado on lavosh, near the edge nearest you. Top with vegetables. Drizzle with vinaigrette. Roll up and eat.

Makes 2 or 3 servings

DELI-STYLE CHICKEN SALAD SANDWICH

This is the basic American chicken salad sandwich. My mother often prepared one for me to take to school for lunch when I was growing up, with a tomato slice in each sandwich half, and it has remained one of my favorite sandwiches. I like to flavor the creamy salad with Dijon mustard and chopped walnuts, a habit from the time I lived in France.

1⅓ cups finely diced cooked chicken
    or turkey
1 hard-boiled egg, grated or chopped
1 medium celery stalk, finely diced (¼
    to ⅓ cup)
2 to 3 tablespoons chopped walnuts
    (optional)
⅓ cup mayonnaise or light mayonnaise

2 teaspoons Dijon mustard (optional)
freshly ground pepper to taste
mustard or mayonnaise, for spreading
    (optional)
4 large or 8 small slices rye bread with
    caraway seeds
tomato or dill pickle slices (optional)

Combine chicken, egg, celery, and walnuts in a bowl. Add mayonnaise and mustard and mix well. Season to taste with pepper. If desired, spread mustard or mayonnaise on bread slices. Spread chicken salad on half the bread slices, then top with tomato or pickle slices. Top with remaining bread.

Makes 2 servings

CALIFORNIA CHICKEN SANDWICH

A favorite hot chicken sandwich in California is made of grilled chicken breast, fresh vegetables, and avocado slices on toasted sourdough bread, walnut bread, or whole wheat bread. You can spread Pesto (page 363) on the bread for an interesting twist, or you can substitute Guacamole (page 365) and omit the avocado slices. Fresh Tomato Salsa (page 362) is a popular accompaniment.

4 boneless and skinless chicken breast
 halves (about 1¼ pounds)
salt and freshly ground pepper
½ teaspoon dried oregano or thyme
1 tablespoon olive oil
1 tablespoon lemon juice
4 to 8 fairly thick large slices
 sourdough bread
Creamy Cilantro Dressing (page 356)
 or regular or low-fat mayonnaise, for
 spreading

arugula leaves
1 large tomato, sliced; or 1 grilled red
 pepper (page 408), cut in thick
 strips
1 avocado, preferably Haas, sliced
 (optional)
4 thin slices red onion

Pound chicken until about ⅜ inch thick. Put on plate. Sprinkle with salt and pepper. Mix oregano, olive oil, and lemon juice, pour mixture over chicken, and rub on both sides.

Preheat broiler with rack about 4 inches from heat, preheat stovetop grill over medium-high heat, or prepare charcoal grill. Grill or broil chicken 3 to 4 minutes per side, or until it is no longer pink when cut.

Toast bread and spread lightly with dressing or mayonnaise. Top 4 slices with arugula leaves, then with chicken, tomato slices or pepper strips, avocado, and onion. Top with a second slice of bread if desired.

Makes 4 servings

MIDDLE EASTERN CHICKEN IN A PITA

My brother-in-law, Avi Levi, gave me the idea for this recipe. It is his interpretation of the Tex-Mex chicken fajita, but he prefers a pita to a tortilla and uses a popular Middle Eastern seasoning mixture—cumin and turmeric—to flavor the chicken and the sautéed onions. The sandwich makes a quick and delicious lunch or supper.

¾ pound boneless chicken breasts (2 halves), skin removed
1 teaspoon ground cumin
¼ teaspoon turmeric
salt and freshly ground pepper
2 tablespoons vegetable or olive oil

1 large onion, chopped
mayonnaise (optional)
2 pita breads, warmed briefly, halved
2 plum tomatoes, sliced (optional), or
  1 roasted pepper (page 408) or from
  a jar, cut in strips

Cut chicken crosswise in ¼-inch slices. Sprinkle with cumin, turmeric, salt, and pepper.

Heat oil in a large, heavy skillet over medium heat. Add onion and sauté about 7 minutes or until it begins to turn golden. Push onion to side of skillet. Add chicken and sauté about 2 minutes. Stir in onion from side of skillet and sauté about 2 or 3 more minutes or until chicken changes color throughout; cut a thick piece to check for doneness.

Spread mayonnaise lightly in one side of each pita. Spoon chicken mixture inside. Add tomatoes or peppers, or serve them on the side.

Makes 2 servings

VARIATION: **Middle Eastern Turkey in Pita**
  Substitute turkey breast slices for chicken. Cut them in strips about ¼ inch wide. Use 3 tablespoons oil if pan looks dry.

CHICKEN WITH TAHINI IN A PITA

This Middle Eastern sandwich is actually grilled chicken served "falafel style," with hot sauce or chutney, Mediterranean diced vegetable salad, and the famous sesame sauce, tahini, all packed in a pita. Exotic-tasting tahini is great with grilled chicken, and wrapping the two in a pita keeps them in contact, so you enjoy their flavors in every bite.

When I happen to have sautéed or grilled eggplant slices, or roasted red peppers, either homemade or from a jar, I add a few pieces to each sandwich.

½ cup finely shredded red cabbage
1 cup shredded romaine lettuce
½ small cucumber, diced
2 large ripe tomatoes, cut in small dice
4 boneless and skinless chicken breast
   halves

1 or 2 teaspoons vegetable or olive oil
salt and freshly ground pepper
4 fresh or warmed pita breads
Tahini Sauce (page 363)
Jalapeño-Garlic Chutney (page 366) or
   bottled hot sauce

Mix cabbage, lettuce, cucumber, and tomatoes. Prepare a charcoal grill or heat broiler with rack about 4 inches from heat source; or heat a ridged stovetop grill pan over medium-high heat. Rub chicken with oil and sprinkle with salt and pepper on both sides.

Set chicken on an oiled rack above glowing coals, on broiler rack, or on grill, with skin facing down. Grill or broil until meat feels springy, about 5 minutes per side. To check whether chicken is done, cut into thickest part with tip of a sharp knife; color should be white, not pink.

Cut chicken in slices. Cut a strip from top of pita so it opens. Put chicken slices inside and moisten with a spoonful of Tahini Sauce. Add vegetable mixture and spoon more sauce over it. Serve with chutney or hot sauce.

Makes 4 servings

CHICKEN "SLOPPY JOE"

The name of this popular American sandwich gives a more than subtle hint at how impossible it is to eat it neatly. It is basically a thick, hearty, meaty spaghetti sauce served on toasted rolls. If you mix the sauce with spaghetti first, you will get a version of the notorious English ''specialty,'' spaghetti on toast!

3 to 4 tablespoons olive or vegetable
   oil
1 medium onion, minced
½ green bell pepper, diced
1 large celery stalk, diced
1 pound ground chicken or turkey
3 medium garlic cloves, chopped

1 (28-ounce) can plum tomatoes,
   drained and chopped
1 teaspoon dried thyme, crumbled
salt and freshly ground pepper
2 to 4 tablespoons ketchup, or to taste
hot pepper sauce to taste (optional)
6 to 8 hamburger rolls or sesame rolls

Heat oil in a large, heavy skillet over medium heat. Add onion, pepper, and celery and cook, stirring, for 7 minutes or until onion softens. Add chicken and sauté over medium heat, crumbling with a fork, until it changes color. Add garlic, tomatoes, thyme, salt, and pepper and bring to a boil, stirring. Cook uncovered over low heat, stirring occasionally, for 15 minutes. Add ketchup and cook until sauce is thick. Add hot pepper sauce if desired. Taste and adjust seasoning. *Sauce can be kept, covered, 2 days in refrigerator. Reheat before serving.*

   Split rolls and lightly toast them. Spoon chicken sauce on bottom half of rolls and serve immediately.

Makes 6 to 8 servings

TURKEY MUSHROOM BURGERS

A mushroom-topped burger has become a classic American favorite in many of the finer hamburger eateries. This is a leaner version using turkey. The burgers can either be sautéed, as in this recipe, or brushed lightly with oil and broiled 3 or 4 minutes per side. If you like, serve these sandwiches with tomato wedges and thin raw red onion rings, or with cole slaw.

2 medium garlic cloves, minced
½ teaspoon salt
½ teaspoon freshly ground black
   pepper
½ teaspoon paprika
1¼ to 1⅓ pounds ground turkey or
   chicken (2⅔ to 3 cups)
2 tablespoons vegetable or olive oil

6 to 8 ounces mushrooms, sliced
regular or light mayonnaise (optional)
4 onion rolls or hamburger rolls, split
   and lightly toasted
lettuce leaves
Yogurt, Mint, and Garlic Dressing
   (page 359), Jalapeño-Garlic Chutney
   (page 366), or ketchup, for serving

Mix garlic with salt, pepper, and paprika. Add spice mixture to turkey and mix lightly to blend. Shape into 4 patties.

Heat oil in a medium skillet. Add burgers and sauté over medium heat about 3 minutes on each side or until they are springy when pressed. Remove from skillet and keep warm. Add mushrooms to skillet and sauté over medium-high heat until lightly browned, about 3 minutes.

Spread mayonnaise on toasted rolls, if desired. Top with lettuce leaves, then burgers, and spoon mushrooms on top. Serve top half of sandwich separately. Serve immediately, with dressing, chutney, or ketchup.

Makes 4 servings

TURKEY SANDWICH
WITH CREOLE MAYONNAISE

I love the spicy dressings used in New Orleans sandwiches so much, I even came home from a trip to Louisiana carrying a jar of Creole mayonnaise. Actually it's easy to make—you just stir chopped green onion, hot pepper, and other seasonings into mayonnaise. I especially enjoy this type of zesty dressing in turkey sandwiches like this one, for which the turkey is combined with tomatoes and roasted peppers.

Creole Mayonnaise

½ cup mayonnaise
1½ to 2 teaspoons Creole or Dijon
   mustard
2 teaspoons minced green onion

½ teaspoon white wine vinegar
salt and freshly ground pepper
cayenne pepper or Tabasco or other
   hot pepper sauce to taste

8 to 12 thin slices roast turkey
4 or 8 thin slices ripe tomato
pickled hot peppers (optional)

1 green or red bell pepper, roasted and
   peeled (page 408), or roasted pepper
   from a jar (optional)
4 French rolls, split lengthwise, or 8
   thick slices French or Italian bread

For Creole mayonnaise, mix the mayonnaise, mustard, green onion, and vinegar. Season to taste with salt, pepper, and cayenne or Tabasco.

Cut roasted pepper in 8 pieces. Spread Creole mayonnaise lightly on cut sides of rolls or on bread slices. Top each roll or bread slice with turkey, tomatoes, and roasted peppers. Put the 2 sandwich halves together or serve them open-face, whichever you prefer. Serve pickled hot peppers separately.

Makes 4 servings

TURKEY KIELBASA
WITH SAUTÉED ONIONS

Traveling along the ''Romantic Road'' north of Munich, my husband and I thought we would enjoy the picturesque medieval towns but, with our student budget, a delicious meal was not among our expectations. In one small town we had a tasty lunch—it was simply a sandwich of wonderful smoked sausages with a generous amount of sautéed onions, served in a chewy roll. It's easy to reproduce this at home using turkey sausage.

Polish kielbasa sausage is now made with turkey, in a lower fat version than the pork original. When combined with fried onions, sauerkraut, and mustard, the sausage makes a flavorful, satisfying sandwich. The secret to an even better sandwich is having the patience to brown the onions thoroughly to bring out their sweetness. Paprika gives the onions a beautiful reddish-brown color.

The excellent German bread was part of the reason this sandwich was memorable; the better the bread you use, the more you will enjoy the sandwich.

3 or 4 tablespoons vegetable oil
2 large onions, halved and sliced
1 teaspoon sweet paprika
pinch of hot paprika or cayenne
   pepper
salt and freshly ground pepper
1 pound turkey kielbasa sausage, cut
   in 4 pieces

4 long French rolls or hot dog rolls
mustard (any kind you like)
about ⅔ cup bottled sauerkraut, rinsed
   and drained; or 20 to 24 dill pickle
   slices

Heat oil in a large skillet over medium heat. Add onions, sweet and hot paprika, salt, and pepper. Sauté, stirring often, until onions are tender and well browned, about 10 to 15 minutes.

Heat sausage in about ½ cup water in skillet, covered, for 10 minutes or according to package instructions. Drain well.

Warm rolls in oven or toast them lightly if desired. Split in half, and spread with mustard. Top with sauerkraut or pickle slices, sausage, and sautéed onions. Serve hot.

Makes 4 servings

SMOKED TURKEY AND HERBED CREAM CHEESE SANDWICH

Cream cheese flavored with herbs and spices, a popular central European spread, tastes so much better when freshly made, and is a good sandwich partner for smoked turkey or chicken. Serve the sandwiches with dill pickles.

4 ounces regular or light cream cheese, at room temperature
3 to 4 tablespoons regular or light sour cream
½ teaspoon dried thyme
3 tablespoons minced fresh parsley
1 tablespoon snipped chives or finely chopped green onion

½ teaspoon paprika (optional)
salt and freshly ground pepper
8 to 12 thin slices smoked turkey
8 thin slices rye bread or pumpernickel
2 medium tomatoes, sliced

Using a wooden spoon, beat cream cheese with 2 tablespoons sour cream until smooth. Stir in enough of remaining sour cream to obtain a spreading consistency. Stir in thyme, parsley, chives, and paprika. Season to taste with salt and pepper.

Spread on bread and set smoked turkey on half the bread slices. Top with tomato slices and remaining bread.

Makes 4 sandwiches

EGGPLANT PÂTÉ SANDWICH
WITH SMOKED TURKEY

When I lived in Tel Aviv, I used to stop occasionally at a small sandwich shop for my favorite sandwich. The cook would scoop out part of the soft crumb of a long, fresh roll and fill the roll to the brim with a luscious and creamy garlicky eggplant pâté. Finally he would top it with smoked turkey. I find this combination absolutely delightful.

You can buy eggplant pâté with tahini at Middle Eastern delis and other specialty markets and use it to make this sandwich. But I prefer to use Russian-style eggplant pâté enriched with mayonnaise rather than tahini for this sandwich. You can't make it on the spot, because the eggplant takes about an hour to cook, but when you're barbecuing or when you have the oven on for baking potatoes, you can put in some eggplants. Then all you need do is mix the mashed eggplant pulp with garlic and mayonnaise. The pâté keeps well, and together with smoked turkey or chicken, makes sensational sandwiches.

2 long, slender eggplants (about 1 pound each)
1 large garlic clove, minced
6 tablespoons mayonnaise
1 teaspoon strained fresh lemon juice

salt and freshly ground pepper
cayenne pepper
4 crusty French rolls or other long rolls
8 to 12 thin slices smoked turkey breast

Prick eggplant a few times with a fork. Either broil eggplant about 40 minutes, bake it on a foil-lined baking sheet in a preheated 400°F. oven for 1 hour, or grill it above medium-hot coals about 1 hour. Turn eggplant often during cooking; it is done when skin blackens and flesh is tender. Remove eggplant peel. Cut off stem. Drain off any liquid from inside eggplant. Chop flesh very fine with knife; there should still be small chunks. Transfer to a bowl. Add garlic, mayonnaise, lemon juice, salt, pepper, and cayenne pepper to taste. *Pâté can be kept 3 days in refrigerator.*

Halve rolls lengthwise and remove part of crumb from bottom half of each roll. Fill with eggplant pâté. Top with turkey and replace top of roll.

Makes 4 servings

15

Duck, Goose, and Game Birds

 DUCK AND GOOSE

In the Orient and in Europe, duck is a much-esteemed bird. Its tender, flavorful meat and wonderful aroma make roast duck one of the most festive poultry dishes.

Most of us are familiar with the famous European sweet and sour duck-and-fruit dishes, typified by the French *canard à l'orange*, as well as the duck with pineapple served at Oriental restaurants. Both sweetness and tartness are wonderful complements for the rich meat of duck, and this explains the universal appeal of these types of duck dishes.

Yet there are many other ways to season duck. In southern France and in Italy, for example, duck is flavored with garlic, tomatoes, and mushrooms or olives. In Morocco it might have a sweet and savory sauce of saffron, garlic, ginger, and honey, or a spicy sauce of cilantro, hot pepper, and garlic. In the eastern Mediterranean it is served with cinnamon-scented tomato sauce. Lemon and oregano are favored in the Greek kitchen. In Iran, duck is

297

Roast Duck Salad with Papaya
and Citrus Dressing
Roast Duck with Turnips, Carrots, and Ginger
Duck with Cherries
Roast Duck with Cranberries and Red Wine
Vietnamese Duck with Lemongrass
Duck Breast with Sugar-Snap Peas
Duck Breast with Asparagus, Mushrooms,
and Red Wine Sauce
Linguine with Grilled Duck Breast
and Italian Duck Sauce
Rich Man's Cassoulet with Roast Goose
Roast Goose with Sauerkraut
Spicy Roast Cornish Hen with Garlic Stuffing
Baked Cornish Hen with Fennel, Peppers,
and Olives
Cornish Hen with Chestnuts
Quail with Onion Compote and Kiwis
Quail on a Bed of Risotto
Squab with Peppers, Garlic, and Couscous
Pheasant with Orange and Port Sauce

cooked with walnuts and pomegranate juice, as in Iranian Chicken in Walnut-Pomegranate Sauce (page 239).

For all its glory, duck is also loved with humble ingredients like turnips, cabbage, Brussels sprouts, and sauerkraut.

Duck has an image of being difficult to prepare, but it's actually not much more complicated than roasting a chicken. The meat is tasty and moist enough that no sauce is needed. But if you would like one, the duck juices have so much flavor that it is easy to prepare a delicious gravy by adding just a few ingredients.

For an intimate Valentine's Day dinner for two, roast duck is the perfect main course. There probably will be some duck meat left over, which can be enjoyed again in a different form the next day. Either cold or briefly reheated, it makes a delicious addition to salads, whether of baby greens, rice, pasta, or cooked vegetables. Try it, for example, instead of the chicken in Chicken Salad with Raspberry Vinaigrette (page 267) or Chicken, Kiwi, and Rice Salad with Papaya (page 61).

For a holiday main course, roast goose is the meat of choice in many families for Christmas and Hanukkah. In fact, it is one of the few foods that both holidays have in common. The reason for this is that many American customs for both holidays come from Europe, where goose is a popular winter bird. During the colder months, many supermarkets carry goose, and it is available at butcher shops. All of the goose's meat is dark, and it is therefore many people's bird of choice.

For a Christmas menu, a good accompaniment for roast goose is braised chestnuts. For a Hanukkah menu, the preferred side dish is potato pancakes. They can be sautéed in goose fat, according to the custom of Jews from Alsace and Hungary. Other delicious partners for the goose in a celebratory menu are wild rice, sautéed wild mushrooms, sautéed apples, sauerkraut, and glazed winter vegetables—turnips, carrots, and baby onions.

Goose is similar to duck from a culinary point of view except, of course, that it is larger and thus is roasted at a lower temperature so it can cook thoroughly.

The fat on ducks and geese is a mixed blessing. It enables the duck or goose to baste itself and keeps the meat moist. Still, excess fat must be encouraged to leave the bird. A special technique used for ducks and geese, but not for other birds, is to prick the skin in order to help the fat melt and escape as it cooks.

CORNISH HENS AND GAME BIRDS

Cornish hens are quite similar in flavor to chicken and can be prepared as for most chicken recipes. Most often a Cornish hen is roasted and served whole, since this makes an impressive serving. If the hen is cooked with stuffing, it can be served cut in half, for easier eating.

Since the meat of game birds, such as squab, quail, pheasant, and guinea hens, is lean, they are best casserole roasted, sautéed, or braised, rather than roasted in an open pan.

Before game is cooked, it is sometimes marinated in red or white wine with fresh herbs and aromatic vegetables. With hunted game, the purpose of the marinade was mainly to tenderize meat that might be tough. Today a marinade serves a different purpose—to help keep the meat moist and add flavor to it. The marinade then becomes part of the sauce, as in quail on a bed of risotto, for which the bird is marinated in white wine.

Wild game birds have a distinct taste, which is more assertive than that of other poultry. They are, therefore, traditionally complemented by aggressive flavors such as vinegar and spices. The game birds available in our markets are farm raised and are milder in taste, but highly seasoned sauces are in tune with today's tastes and so these time-honored partners are still appropriate with game.

The most famous classic sauce for game in Europe is *sauce poivrade*. Its name comes from the French word *poivre*, meaning pepper, because a liberal amount of pepper is added to the brown sauce. Strong spirits, such as Cognac, Armagnac, and Calvados, are added generously to game sauces. Red and white wines, as well as port and Madeira, are also used abundantly.

Throughout much of Europe, sweet and sour sauces are favorite accompaniments for game. Red currant or other fruit jelly or jam provides the sweetness, which is balanced by the tartness of wine vinegar or lemon juice or sometimes by the heat of horseradish. Often fruit, especially apples, pears, cherries, oranges, or dried fruit, is simmered in the sauce and served with the game. In a similar spirit, Moroccan cooks complement the taste of game birds in sweet tajines by pairing them with honey and a hint of cinnamon; but they also prepare them as spicy tajines with plenty of hot pepper and garlic.

To impart additional flavor and richness to a sauce for game, the pan is deglazed. To do this, a small amount of liquid—stock, wine, Cognac, fruit or vegetable juice, or even water—is added to the hot casserole or sauté pan. It is heated in the pan and stirred well so that the game juices adhering to the pan will dissolve. The resulting game-flavored essence is strained if necessary and stirred into the sauce.

Game has a traditional image as an autumn specialty, and so it is frequently accompanied by that other fall treat, wild mushrooms. Italian chefs favor porcini mushrooms, the French love chanterelles, and Oriental cooks prefer shiitake mushrooms. But even regular button mushrooms can be the basis of flavorful sauces for game. Other beloved European accompaniments are chestnuts and celery root puree.

TIPS

✂ A heavy roasting pan is best for roasting ducks so it can withstand the high oven temperature and can be used on top of the stove for deglazing.

✂ For browner skin of roast duck, transfer whole duck to broiler pan and broil about 5 inches from heat source until skin is deep brown.

✂ Be careful when removing the hot fat from the roasting pan of ducks and geese. The easiest way is to use a bulb baster to transfer the fat to a bowl.

✂ Turn the roasting pan around once or twice in the oven to brown ducks and geese evenly.

✂ After carving a duck, you can reheat the pieces briefly in the oven or broiler. To broil, arrange the duck pieces skin side up in the broiler pan and broil them until the skin is brown.

ROAST DUCK SALAD
WITH PAPAYA AND CITRUS DRESSING

Roast duck, paired with the orange and lemon dressing, diced papaya, and crisp sweet sugar-snap peas, makes a refreshing and elegant salad in the California style. The rich meat of duck is best with a tart dressing that contains less oil than in the classic vinaigrette proportions.

2 (4½- to 5-pound) ducks, thawed if frozen, patted dry
salt and freshly ground pepper
½ pound sugar-snap peas, stem ends removed

2 small papayas (total about 2 pounds)
Citrus Dressing (page 358)
⅓ cup finely chopped red onion
4 large green leaf or "salad bowl" lettuce leaves

Heat the oven to 450°F. Remove fat from inside ducks. Sprinkle ducks inside and out with salt and pepper. Prick duck skin all over with skewer at intervals of about ½ inch; do not pierce meat.

Set each duck on its breast on a rack in a heavy roasting pan. Roast 30 minutes. Remove fat from pan. Set ducks on their backs, reduce oven temperature to 400°F. and roast ducks 45 to 50 minutes or until done to taste. To check, use skewer to prick thigh meat in plumpest part: if juices that escape are red, duck is not done; if they are clear, duck is well done. Remove ducks from pan. Let cool.

Cook sugar-snap peas in a medium saucepan of boiling salted water, uncovered, over high heat for 2 minutes or until crisp-tender. Drain, rinse with cold water, and drain thoroughly.

Cut off duck legs. Remove each duck breast half in 1 piece, moving point of knife against breast bone to avoid cutting into meat. Gently pull skin off breast, legs, and body and discard. Using a long thin sharp knife, cut duck breasts in crosswise slices on diagonal, slightly less than ½ inch thick. Reserve 12 slices for garnish. Remove remaining meat from bones and cut it and remaining duck breast in strips about 2 × ½ × ¼ inch.

Halve the papayas, discard seeds, and cut off peel. Cut 12 thin lengthwise papaya slices and reserve for garnish. Cut remaining papaya in ½-inch dice.

Spoon a little dressing over reserved duck breast slices. In a medium bowl mix duck strips, diced papaya, and onion with ⅔ cup dressing and let stand about 30 minutes. Reserve 12 sugar-snap peas for garnish. Halve remaining peas diagonally. *Salad can be kept, covered, 1 day in refrigerator; keep remaining dressing, sugar peas, and garnish ingredients separately.*

Add cut peas to duck salad. Taste and adjust seasoning, adding more dressing if desired. Set a lettuce leaf on each plate, off center. Spoon enough duck salad on lettuce to make an attractive mound. On each plate (not on lettuce) set 3 papaya slices, 3 overlapping duck breast slices and 3 sugar-snap peas. Serve remaining duck salad separately.

Makes 4 servings

ROAST DUCK WITH TURNIPS, CARROTS, AND GINGER

Today's trend of serving a luxurious ingredient, such as duck, with humble ones, such as root vegetables, to create a dish with rustic appeal, is not new. It has been a standard way of preparing poultry in European country cooking for ages. Roast duck with turnips is an old-fashioned favorite. I find that fresh ginger adds a pleasing zip to the sauce.

4 medium, thin carrots of uniform size and shape (about ¾ pound)
3 small turnips of uniform size and shape (about ¾ pound)
1½ cups duck stock, chicken stock, or chicken broth
4 tablespoons minced peeled fresh ginger
4½- to 5-pound duck, thawed if frozen, patted dry

salt and freshly ground pepper
2½ cups water
1½ teaspoons sugar
3 tablespoons butter
¾ teaspoon potato starch or arrowroot dissolved in 1½ teaspoons water
¼ teaspoon finely grated lemon peel
1 teaspoon strained fresh lemon juice

Cut carrots in 1½-inch lengths. Using paring knife, trim each piece to oval shape. Quarter turnips from top to bottom and trim each piece to oval shape.

Bring stock to boil with 2 tablespoons ginger. Simmer, uncovered, over medium-low heat for 30 minutes. Strain, pressing on ginger.

Preheat the oven to 450°F. Remove fat from inside duck. Sprinkle duck inside and out with salt and pepper. Using a skewer, pierce skin all over, at intervals of about ½ inch; do not pierce meat. Truss duck, if desired.

Set duck on its breast on rack in heavy, medium roasting pan. Roast 30 minutes. Using a bulb baster, remove fat from pan. Turn duck on its back and roast 10 minutes. Reduce oven temperature to 400°F. Roast duck 20 to 40 more minutes. To check, prick thigh meat in plumpest part with skewer: if juices are red, duck is not done; if they are pink, duck is rare; if they are clear, duck is well done.

Meanwhile, put carrots in small saucepan in which they fit in one layer and add 1¼ cups water, pinch of salt, 1 teaspoon sugar, 2 tablespoons butter, and remaining 2 tablespoons ginger. Bring to boil. Simmer, uncovered, over medium heat until carrots are tender, about 15 minutes. Remove carrots, leaving ginger in liquid. Boil liquid until reduced to ⅓ cup. Strain liquid, pressing on ginger. Cool to room temperature. Return liquid and carrots to saucepan.

Put turnips in another small saucepan in which they fit in one layer and add 1¼ cups water, salt, remaining ½ teaspoon sugar, and remaining tablespoon butter. Bring to boil.

Simmer, uncovered, over medium heat until turnips are barely tender, about 7 minutes. Remove gently with slotted spoon. Boil liquid until reduced to ¼ cup. Cool to room temperature. Return turnips to saucepan.

When duck is done, transfer it to platter, draining juices from inside duck into roasting pan. Discard any trussing strings. Cover duck loosely and keep warm.

Pour off fat from roasting pan but leave in darker colored duck juices. Reheat juices over medium-high heat. Add ½ cup ginger-flavored stock and bring to boil, stirring and scraping up browned bits. Strain into medium saucepan. Add remaining stock and boil, skimming occasionally, until mixture is reduced to ¾ cup, about 5 minutes. Remove from heat. Skim fat from sauce.

Bring sauce to a simmer over medium heat. Whisk potato starch solution until blended and gradually whisk it into simmering sauce. Return to boil, whisking. Add grated lemon peel, lemon juice, and salt and pepper to taste. Reheat each vegetable in its liquid, uncovered, over medium-high heat, tossing often. Add 1 tablespoon sauce to each pan of vegetables, and heat over medium-low heat, tossing, until sauce blends with vegetable cooking liquid.

Serve duck with vegetables. Serve remaining sauce separately.

Makes 2 to 4 servings

DUCK WITH CHERRIES

To enjoy the rich meat of duck with spiced cherries and deep, reddish brown port sauce, it's even worth roasting a duck in summer. Anyway, roasted the French way at high heat, a duck takes only a little longer to roast than a chicken. Of course, you can buy out-of-season cherries from South America in December and prepare this for the holidays, or you could use frozen ones.

This festive recipe is a new, easier version of the classic duck with cherries. Traditional versions have sugar or jam added to sweeten the cherries, but I find that if you use sweet dark cherries, you don't need any sweetener. For an elegant menu, serve the duck with wild rice and lightly cooked crookneck squash, peas, or green beans.

2 cups sweet cherries, stems removed
1 cup port
1 slice fresh ginger (¼ inch thick), or a
    pinch of powdered ginger
¼ teaspoon ground cinnamon
dash of ground cloves
4 ½- to 5-pound duck, thawed if
    frozen, patted dry
salt and freshly ground pepper

1 medium onion, quartered
1 carrot, quartered
1½ cups duck stock (page 391),
    chicken stock, or chicken broth
2 teaspoons potato starch, arrowroot,
    or cornstarch dissolved in 4
    teaspoons water
a few drops lemon juice (optional)

Cut halfway around each cherry at stem end. Press the 2 halves apart, leaving 1 end joined, and pull out pit. Bring port to a simmer with ginger, cinnamon, and cloves. Add cherries, cover, and simmer over low heat 5 minutes or until just tender. *Cherries can be kept, covered, 2 days in refrigerator.*

Preheat the oven to 450°F. Remove fat from inside duck. Sprinkle duck inside and out with salt and pepper. Using a skewer, pierce skin all over, at intervals of about ½ inch; do not pierce meat. Truss duck, if desired.

Put onion, carrot, and duck giblets (except liver) and neck in a heavy, medium roasting pan. Set duck on its breast on rack in pan. Roast 30 minutes. Using a bulb baster, remove fat from pan. Turn duck on its back and roast 10 minutes. Reduce oven temperature to 400°F. Roast duck 20 to 40 more minutes. To check, prick thigh meat in plumpest part with skewer: if juices are red, duck is not done; if they are clear, duck is well done.

Transfer duck to a platter, draining juices from inside duck into roasting pan. Discard any trussing strings. Cover duck loosely and keep warm. *Duck can be prepared 30 minutes ahead, covered loosely and kept warm in oven with heat turned off and door ajar.*

Gently reheat cherries in a covered pan over low heat. Discard ginger. Pour off fat from roasting pan but leave in darker duck juices. Reheat juices in pan over medium heat. Add ¾ cup stock and bring to boil, stirring and scraping up any browned bits. Strain into medium saucepan. Add remaining stock and bring to a boil, skimming occasionally. Remove from heat. Skim excess fat from surface of sauce.

Bring sauce to a simmer over medium heat. Add all but 1 or 2 tablespoons of liquid from cherries. Rewhisk potato starch mixture. Gradually whisk mixture into simmering sauce. Return to boil, whisking. Remove from heat. Taste and adjust seasoning. Add a few drops lemon juice if desired.

Carve duck; if meat becomes cold during carving, cover platter with foil and reheat briefly in 350°F. oven. Reheat sauce gently. Spoon sauce over duck pieces, with cherries alongside.

Makes 2 to 4 servings

ROAST DUCK
WITH CRANBERRIES AND RED WINE

Roast duck garnished with bright red cranberries makes a festive and very attractive platter for celebrating Thanksgiving in a small group. The bittersweet taste of the sauce, which is a French-style red wine sauce made with an American ingredient—cranberries—is a good complement for the rich duck meat. I like to serve it with rice, mashed potatoes, or sweet potatoes and with glazed baby onions. SEE PHOTOGRAPH.

4½-pound duck, thawed if frozen,
   patted dry
salt and freshly ground pepper
1½ cups dry red wine
½ cup water
½ cup plus 2 tablespoons sugar
1 cinnamon stick (about 3 inches)

12 ounces (3 cups) fresh or frozen
   cranberries, rinsed
few drops of lemon juice
1 teaspoon potato starch, arrowroot, or
   cornstarch
1 tablespoon water

Preheat the oven to 425°F. Season duck with salt and pepper. Prick duck skin all over with a skewer. Truss duck if desired. Set duck on its side in roasting pan. Roast it for 15 minutes and turn it onto its other side. Spoon out excess fat from pan. Roast duck 15 minutes longer. Reduce heat to 375°F. Set duck on its back and continue roasting 45 to 60 minutes. As fat collects in roasting pan, spoon most of it out and discard it. To check whether duck is done, prick thigh: if juices that escape are pink, duck is rare; if juices are clear, duck is well done.

Meanwhile, prepare cranberries. Combine wine, water, ½ cup sugar, and cinnamon stick in a medium saucepan. Bring to a boil, stirring. Add cranberries, cover, and simmer over low heat 6 to 7 minutes or until tender. Discard cinnamon stick. Set aside 1 cup of cranberry cooking liquid. Leave cranberries in remaining liquid.

When duck is tender, transfer it to a platter, discard any trussing strings, and keep duck warm. Discard fat from roasting pan but leave in layer of darker colored duck juices underneath. Add reserved cranberry liquid to roasting pan. Bring to a boil, scraping up brown pieces from pan. Strain into a saucepan. Add a few drops of lemon juice and season to taste with salt and pepper. Return to a simmer.

Whisk potato starch with water until smooth. Gradually whisk mixture into simmering sauce. Bring back to a simmer and remove from heat.

Add remaining sugar to whole cranberries and reheat. Carve duck and set pieces on a platter. Garnish platter with a few spoonfuls of whole cranberries, one in center and a few more between pieces of duck. Serve remaining cranberries in a bowl and sauce in a sauceboat.

Makes 2 generous or 4 small servings

VIETNAMESE DUCK WITH LEMONGRASS

For this recipe, the duck is cut in pieces before being roasted, which makes for easier serving since there is no need to carve a hot duck. To crisp the skin, the duck is finished in the broiler or on the grill.

Lemongrass, a favorite seasoning for poultry in Vietnam and Thailand, has a pleasant flavor and aroma reminiscent of lemon peel. You can find it in Oriental markets and in some supermarkets. In this Vietnamese dish, the lemongrass is combined with garlic, soy sauce, and onion as an easy marinade and flavoring for the duck. Sometimes the marinade is made with Vietnamese fish sauce (nuoc mam) replacing half the soy sauce.

Serve the duck with rice and with stir-fried vegetables such as asparagus, mushrooms, zucchini, or bok choy; or for a tasty American-style accompaniment, serve it with baked winter squash.

3 fresh lemongrass stalks
½ medium onion, quartered
3 medium garlic cloves, peeled
4 tablespoons soy sauce

3 tablespoons white wine
cayenne pepper to taste
4½- to 5-pound duck, quartered (page 404)

Discard outer leaves, upper half, and tough base (about 1 inch from bottom) of each lemongrass stalk. Cut stalks in thin slices, then chop in food processor; you should have about ¾ cup chopped. Remove to a bowl. Add onion and garlic to processor and chop them. Return lemongrass to processor, add 2 tablespoons soy sauce, and process to blend ingredients. Transfer to a bowl. Stir in remaining soy sauce, wine, and cayenne pepper.

Prick skin of quartered duck without piercing meat. Separate skin from meat at edges of each piece. Put duck on platter or in shallow baking dish and add marinade. Rub marinade into duck pieces and under skin. Cover and refrigerate 2 to 6 hours; turn pieces from time to time. Remove duck from marinade, removing excess pieces of onion mixture but leaving on mixture adhering to duck; reserve marinade.

Preheat the oven to 400°F. Put duck pieces, skin side up, on a rack set in a roasting dish. Roast uncovered for 30 minutes. Turn pieces over, spoon marinade mixture generously over them, and roast about 20 to 30 more minutes or until duck is tender; juices that run from leg when pricked should be clear.

Just before serving, transfer duck pieces to broiler or grill. Broil or grill 3 to 4 minutes per side or until deep brown. Serve immediately.

Makes 4 servings

DUCK BREAST WITH SUGAR-SNAP PEAS

This is a new, quick and easy twist on the old-fashioned European spring specialty, duck with peas. Instead of roasting or braising a whole duck with green peas, I use duck breasts, which I broil or grill on top of the stove and serve with lightly cooked sugar-snap peas. This makes an elegant main course in a few minutes. See more on duck breasts in the next recipe.

1 pound sugar-snap peas, trimmed
salt and freshly ground pepper
boneless breast of 2 ducks (about 1¾
    to 2 pounds total), thawed if frozen
a few drops vegetable oil

2 tablespoons (¼ stick) butter
1 medium shallot, minced
1 teaspoon finely grated peeled fresh
    ginger

Cook peas in a large pan of boiling salted water until just tender, about 3 minutes. Rinse with cold water and drain well.

Preheat broiler or prepare grill. Lightly rub meat side of duck breast with a few drops oil. Season both sides with salt and pepper. Broil duck breast, or grill it above glowing coals, about 5 inches from heat source, turning once, 5 to 6 minutes per side or until just tender but still slightly pink; duck should be springy to touch. Cover and keep warm.

Melt butter in a medium skillet, add shallot, and sauté about 1 minute. Stir in ginger, then add peas. Sprinkle with salt and pepper. Cook until heated through.

Remove skin from duck breast. Carve breast in thin diagonal crosswise slices. Serve sugar-snap peas alongside duck.

Makes 4 servings

DUCK BREAST WITH ASPARAGUS, MUSHROOMS, AND RED WINE SAUCE

Duck breast is not an easy cut to find, but some specialty butchers and excellent supermarkets do carry it. When you find it, grab it! It is delicious, like a steak with duck flavor. And it's as fast and easy to cook as a steak. In this French recipe, the duck's pan juices are used to enrich a red wine sauce, but to save time, you can skip the sauce and simply serve the duck with the asparagus and sautéed mushrooms.

Red Wine Sauce (page 374)
2 tablespoons (¼ stick) butter or olive
  oil
½ pound mushrooms, quartered
salt and freshly ground pepper
1 pound medium-width asparagus,
  peeled

boneless breast of 2 ducks (about 1¾
  to 2 pounds total), thawed if frozen
2 tablespoons vegetable oil
¼ cup dry red wine
pinch of sugar (optional)

Heat the sauce and set aside. Heat butter or olive oil in a large skillet, add mushrooms, salt, and pepper and sauté about 5 minutes or until tender.

Trim asparagus and cut off tough ends. Cut each spear in 2 equal pieces crosswise. Cut the stems again in half crosswise. Reserve tips. Cook asparagus in a pan of boiling salted water until crisp-tender, about 4 minutes. Rinse with cold water and drain well. Add to pan of mushrooms; set aside.

Remove skin and fat from duck, using paring knife. Pat duck dry. Season duck with salt and pepper. Heat vegetable oil in a heavy skillet over medium-high heat. Add duck and sauté about 3 minutes per side or until tender but still slightly pink when cut. Remove duck, cover, and let stand 5 minutes.

Pour off fat from skillet. Add wine to skillet. Boil, stirring, until reduced to about 2 tablespoons. Add to Red Wine Sauce. Taste and adjust seasoning; if sauce is too tart, add a pinch of sugar. Reheat asparagus and mushrooms.

To serve, cut duck in thin slices. Add carving juices to sauce. Spoon sauce onto plate and set duck slices on top, fanning out from center. Serve asparagus and mushrooms alongside.

Makes 4 servings

LINGUINE WITH GRILLED DUCK BREAST AND ITALIAN DUCK SAUCE

For this Italian-style duck and pasta feast, the duck legs are braised with mushrooms, tomatoes, and red wine to make a rich sauce for the linguine. The breast is grilled separately and its tender slices top the pasta.

4½- to 5-pound duck, thawed if frozen
2 tablespoons olive oil
4 ounces mushrooms, quartered
½ cup minced onion
½ small carrot, finely diced
½ medium celery stalk, finely diced
⅓ cup dry red wine
1 bay leaf
freshly grated nutmeg to taste
2 tablespoons chopped fresh marjoram, or ¾ teaspoon dried, crumbled
small pinch ground cloves
salt and freshly ground pepper to taste

2 pounds ripe tomatoes, peeled, seeded, and chopped; or 2 (28-ounce) cans whole plum tomatoes, drained and chopped
1 large garlic clove, minced
1½ cups duck stock, chicken stock, or chicken broth
2 tablespoons chopped fresh sage leaves
cayenne pepper to taste
9 to 10 ounces fresh linguine or 8 ounces dried

Cut each leg and thigh from body of duck at thigh joint by cutting between thigh bone and body. Cut off wings. Using a boning knife, slit breast meat along 1 side of breastbone. Remove breast half from bone in 1 piece by scraping carefully with knife, keeping its point against bone, and pulling meat gently. When meat is released from bone, cut skin to free breast half. Repeat with other side. Reserve duck breasts in refrigerator.

Prick skin of duck thigh pieces all over with a skewer, without piercing meat. Heat oil in a medium sauté pan or deep skillet over medium-high heat. Add thigh pieces and brown them, taking about 15 minutes on skin side and about 5 minutes on meat side. Brown wings about 5 minutes per side. Remove duck. Pour off fat into a bowl.

Return 2 tablespoons fat to pan. Add mushrooms and sauté over medium-high heat until lightly browned, about 5 minutes. Remove with slotted spoon. Add 1 tablespoon fat to skillet and heat over medium-low heat. Add onion, carrot, and celery and cook, stirring occasionally, about 10 minutes or until softened.

Return duck legs to pan and add wine, bay leaf, nutmeg, marjoram, cloves, salt, and pepper. Bring to a boil, stirring. Add tomatoes and garlic, and bring to a boil. Simmer uncovered over medium heat, turning duck pieces often, 15 minutes. Add ½ cup stock and simmer 20 minutes. Return mushrooms to sauce and add remaining stock. Continue cooking about 5 minutes, until duck is tender. Remove duck. Discard bay leaf. If necessary, cook sauce a few more minutes or until it is thick. Add sage and cook 1 minute.

Remove duck skin, then remove meat from bones. Cut meat in thin strips and stir into sauce. Add a pinch of cayenne pepper. Taste and adjust seasoning. *Sauce can be kept, covered, 2 days in refrigerator; reheat in covered saucepan over medium-low heat.*

Preheat broiler or prepare grill. Lightly rub meat side of duck breast with a few drops oil. Season both sides with salt and pepper. Grill duck breast about 5 inches from heat source, turning once, 5 to 6 minutes per side or until just tender but still slightly pink; duck should be springy to touch. Cover and keep warm.

Cook pasta uncovered in a large pot of boiling salted water over high heat, about 2 minutes for fresh or about 8 minutes for dried or until tender but firm to the bite. Drain well. Transfer to a large heated bowl. Toss with duck sauce.

Remove skin from duck breast. Carve breast in crosswise slices. Divide pasta among 3 or 4 heated plates. Set slices of duck breast, slightly overlapping, on top of or next to pasta and serve.

Makes 3 or 4 servings

RICH MAN'S CASSOULET WITH ROAST GOOSE

There is an on-going debate in France about whose traditional cassoulet is best. The three most famous versions are from three towns in the Languedoc region in southern France: Castelnaudary, Toulouse, and the beautiful walled city of Carcassonne. In Castelnaudary, the beans are layered with pork, ham, and sausages; in Carcassonne, with lamb and partridge; and in Toulouse, with pork, lamb, and pork sausages.

In all three towns, pieces of confit, or salted poultry or pork cooked in fat, are sometimes added. Duck confit can be purchased at some gourmet food stores, and one small piece per person can be added to the cassoulet.

Many gastronomes consider the Castelnaudary version of cassoulet to be the best. Cassoulet is definitely what put this village on the map. Huge signs advertise the town's specialty, so the visitor has no doubt that he's in cassoulet country.

Still, the other towns are not to be outdone, and restaurants boast their own special recipes, with various embellishments. When I visited Carcassonne, I noticed that menus featured many variations, such as pork cassoulet with goose fat, with duck breast, or with confit of duck neck and gizzards. A chef in Toulouse told me he finds that the more valid distinction today is cassoulet des riches, *or rich man's cassoulet (with duck or goose) and* cassoulet des pauvres, *or poor man's cassoulet (with sausages as the only meat), rather than the location at which it was prepared. With good products, delicious cassoulet can be prepared anywhere.*

1 pound dried white beans, such as
   Great Northern (about 2⅓ cups)
2 bay leaves
2 teaspoons dried thyme, crumbled
1 young 8- to 9-pound) goose, thawed
   if frozen, patted dry
2 tablespoons olive oil (optional)
2 to 2½ pounds chicken drumsticks
1 large onion, chopped
4 large garlic cloves, chopped

2 pounds ripe tomatoes, peeled,
   seeded, and chopped; or 2 (28-
   ounce) cans whole plum tomatoes,
   drained and chopped
½ cup chicken stock, broth, or water
salt and freshly ground pepper
½ pound smoked chicken sausages or
   other sausages
¼ cup unseasoned bread crumbs

Sort beans, discarding any broken ones and any stones. In a large bowl soak beans in 7 cups cold water overnight. For a quicker method, cover beans with 7 cups water in a large saucepan, boil 2 minutes, and let stand off heat for 1 hour.

Rinse and drain beans and put them in a large saucepan. Add enough water to cover them by at least 2 inches. Add 1 bay leaf and ½ teaspoon thyme. Cover and bring to a boil over medium heat. Simmer over low heat for 1½ hours or until just tender, adding hot water if necessary so beans remain covered. Keep beans in their cooking liquid. Discard bay leaf. *Beans can be cooked 1 day ahead and refrigerated.*

Preheat the oven to 450°F. Pull out fat from inside goose. Sprinkle goose inside and out with salt and pepper. Using a skewer, pierce skin several times without piercing meat. Roast goose on a rack in a roasting pan for 30 minutes. Reduce oven temperature to 350°F. Roast 1 hour, basting and removing fat occasionally. Cover goose and roast 30 minutes more or until drumstick meat no longer looks pink when pierced deeply with thin knife. Transfer goose to a board. Cut off goose legs and breast pieces. Cut meat in slices.

Heat oil or 2 tablespoons roasting fat from goose in a large, heavy casserole over medium-high heat. Add chicken pieces, brown them lightly, and remove them. Add onion and sauté about 7 minutes. Add garlic and tomatoes, and cook 2 minutes. Return chicken to pan; add stock, remaining thyme, and remaining bay leaf. Cover and simmer, turning pieces once, about 35 minutes or until chicken is tender. Discard bay leaf. Taste sauce and adjust seasoning. Skim off excess fat.

Meanwhile, put sausage in a pan, cover with water, and bring just to a simmer. Cook over low heat for 15 minutes. Drain and slice.

With a slotted spoon, put half the beans in a 10-cup gratin dish in an even layer. Arrange chicken and goose pieces and sausage slices on beans. Spoon remaining beans on top. Reserve remaining bean liquid. Ladle chicken sauce over beans; add enough of reserved bean cooking liquid to come nearly to top of beans. *Cassoulet can be kept, covered, 2 days in refrigerator.*

Preheat the oven to 375°F. Sprinkle cassoulet with bread crumbs and bake for about 35 minutes (*or 50 minutes if it was cold*) or until hot and golden brown. Serve from baking dish.

Makes about 8 servings

ROAST GOOSE WITH SAUERKRAUT

For a hearty winter dinner, there's nothing better than rich roast goose served with gently braised sauerkraut. The rich meat and the sour cabbage complement each other beautifully. The combination is a favorite throughout much of central Europe; the cuisines of Alsace, Germany, Czechoslovakia, and Hungary all proudly claim it as theirs.

This dish is easy to make ahead for a party. To reheat it, you can cut the roast goose in portions and heat it in the oven in a covered casserole on top of the sauerkraut. Serve it with hot boiled potatoes and Dijon mustard.

1 young (8- to 9-pound) goose,
   thawed if frozen
salt and freshly ground pepper
1 medium onion, quartered, and 2
   medium onions, sliced
4 pounds uncooked sauerkraut
3 tablespoons vegetable oil (optional)
1 bay leaf
3 whole cloves

6 coriander seeds
6 peppercorns
6 medium garlic cloves, peeled
2¼ cups Riesling or dry white wine
1½ cups goose or chicken stock
1 tablespoon potato starch, arrowroot,
   or cornstarch, dissolved in 2
   tablespoons water

Preheat the oven to 450°F. Remove excess fat from goose. Cut off fatty flap of skin near tail. Prick goose skin several times with a skewer; do not pierce meat. Season goose inside and out with salt and pepper. Put quartered onion inside goose. Put goose on its back on a rack in a roasting pan.

Roast goose 30 minutes or until beginning to brown. Baste occasionally. Remove fat with a bulb baster as it accumulates. Reserve 3 tablespoons, if desired, for sauerkraut.

Reduce oven temperature to 350°F. Turn goose over onto its breast. Roast 1 hour and 15 minutes. Cover goose with foil and continue roasting, removing fat from time to time and basting once or twice, about 45 more minutes. To check, pierce thickest part of drumstick deeply with thin knife; meat should no longer look pink.

Meanwhile, rinse sauerkraut thoroughly under cold running water. Drain and squeeze out excess liquid. Heat 3 tablespoons goose fat or oil in a large casserole, add sliced onions, and cook over low heat, stirring, until soft but not brown. Tie bay leaf, cloves, coriander seeds, peppercorns, and garlic in cheesecloth. Add sauerkraut, cheesecloth bag, and 2 cups wine to casserole. Cover and simmer for 1 hour and 30 minutes or until sauerkraut is tender, adding water if pan becomes dry. Discard cheesecloth bag. Taste sauerkraut and adjust seasoning. If mixture is soupy, simmer uncovered for a few minutes to evaporate excess liquid.

When goose is cooked, discard fat from pan. Add remaining wine and ½ cup stock to pan, place over 2 burners, and bring to a boil, stirring and scraping.

Strain wine mixture into a medium saucepan. Add remaining stock and bring to a boil. Season it lightly with salt and pepper, then reduce heat to low. Whisk potato starch mixture to blend. Gradually whisk half the potato starch mixture into the simmering stock mixture. Return to boil, whisking. For thicker sauce, whisk in remaining potato starch mixture and return to boil. Taste and adjust seasoning.

To carve goose, cut off breast and legs; discard onion. Carve breast in thin slices. Serve goose with sauerkraut. Spoon sauce over portions of goose.

Makes 6 to 8 servings

SPICY ROAST CORNISH HEN
WITH GARLIC STUFFING

I love the Middle Eastern spice mixture of coriander, cumin, and turmeric with roast Cornish hens and chickens, because it gives the birds and their juices a wonderful aroma and flavor and a lovely color. And the spiced meat is a perfect match for the tasty garlic-scented bread stuffing.

Garlic Stuffing (page 336)
4 medium (1¼- to 1½-pound) Cornish
  hens
¼ teaspoon salt
¼ teaspoon freshly ground pepper
1 teaspoon ground cumin

1 teaspoon ground coriander
¼ teaspoon turmeric
1 tablespoon olive or vegetable oil
¼ to ½ cup chicken stock or broth
  (page 389)
1 to 2 tablespoons butter

Prepare stuffing. Preheat oven to 400°F. Discard excess fat from hens. Mix salt, pepper, cumin, coriander, turmeric, and oil. Rub hens all over with mixture. Spoon stuffing lightly into hens.

Add a little stock to remaining stuffing so that most of bread is very lightly moistened. Butter a casserole of same or slightly larger volume than extra stuffing and spoon stuffing into it. Dot with butter. Cover casserole.

Set hens in a roasting pan or shallow baking dish just large enough to contain them. Put hens and extra stuffing in oven. Every 15 minutes, baste hens with pan juices and baste stuffing with 2 tablespoons stock. Add 1 or 2 tablespoons hot water to pan juices if they brown. Bake stuffing 30 minutes, uncover and bake 5 minutes more. Roast hens for a total of about 45 minutes or until juices that run from thigh, when pierced in thickest part with a skewer, are clear. If juices are pink, roast a few more minutes and check again. Check stuffing in birds also; skewer inserted in it should come out hot.

Serve hens whole; or spoon stuffing from hens onto plates, cut hens in half lengthwise with poultry shears, and arrange pieces over stuffing on plates. Spoon a little of pan juices over each hen, if desired.

Makes 4 servings

BAKED CORNISH HEN WITH FENNEL, PEPPERS, AND OLIVES

Flavors of Provence enhance these casserole-roasted birds. Serve the hens whole or halved, with pasta, such as spirals or bowties, and with a Mediterranean vegetable such as zucchini or eggplant.

2 medium Cornish hens (each about
   1½ pounds), patted dry
salt and freshly ground pepper
5 tablespoons olive oil
2 medium fennel bulbs (total about 1¼
   pounds)
2 red bell peppers, cored

½ cup dry white wine
½ teaspoon dried thyme, crumbled
1 teaspoon tomato paste
½ cup pitted black olives, drained well
½ cup pitted green olives, drained well
2 tablespoons Pernod

Preheat the oven to 400°F. Sprinkle hens evenly with salt and pepper. Heat 3 tablespoons oil in a heavy, oval, enamel-lined casserole over medium-high heat. Set hens in hot oil on their sides. Cover with large splatter screen and brown side of hens. Using 2 wooden spoons and standing back to avoid splatters, turn hens onto their breasts and brown them. Brown other side, then brown backs of hens. If oil begins to turn dark brown, reduce heat to medium.

Leave hens on their backs. Baste hens with pan juices. Cover and bake until juices run clear when thickest part of leg is pierced with thin skewer, about 35 minutes; if juices are still pink, bake a few more minutes and test again. *Hens can be kept warm in casserole, covered, for 15 minutes.*

Meanwhile, remove stalks and any browned outer leaves from fennel. Quarter fennel bulbs. Cut off and discard core from each piece. Holding layers together, cut each piece in ¼-inch slices lengthwise, to obtain long strips. Halve peppers crosswise and cut each half in lengthwise strips about ¼ inch wide.

Heat remaining oil in a large skillet over low heat. Add fennel, salt, and pepper and stir. Cover and cook, stirring occasionally, 15 minutes. Add peppers, cover, and cook until tender, about 10 minutes.

Transfer hens to platter, reserving juices in casserole. Cover hens with foil and keep warm. Reheat vegetables if necessary. Add 1 tablespoon of hen juices. Taste vegetables and adjust seasoning. Discard any juices that escaped from hens onto platter. Spoon vegetables around hens on platter. Cover and keep warm.

Skim as much fat as possible from juices in casserole. Bring juices to boil. Add wine and bring to boil, skimming fat. Add thyme and tomato paste and whisk until blended. Boil, stirring and scraping up any browned bits from casserole, until sauce is slightly thickened, about 1 minute. Reduce heat to low, add olives and simmer 2 minutes. Stir in Pernod and bring to boil. Taste and adjust seasoning. Using slotted spoon, scatter olives over vegetables on platter. Serve sauce separately.

Makes 4 servings

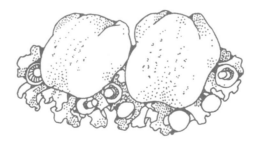

CORNISH HEN WITH CHESTNUTS

Chestnuts with poultry, especially duck and turkey, is a traditional holiday pair in Europe. The problem is that peeling chestnuts for a large crowd is time-consuming. For a festive treat for a small group, I love this dish. Each person is served his or her own golden brown bird, and the roasting juices of the hens are wonderful with the braised chestnuts. Although a whole bird on each plate makes an impressive portion, the hens are much easier to eat if you cut them in half in the kitchen with poultry shears. SEE PHOTOGRAPH.

¾ pound fresh chestnuts
2½ cups chicken stock or broth
1 small celery stalk, broken in 2 pieces
salt and freshly ground pepper
4 medium Cornish hens (each 1¼ to
    1½ pounds), patted dry
¾ cup dry white wine

2 medium shallots, minced
½ teaspoon dried thyme, crumbled
¾ teaspoon potato starch, arrowroot, or
    cornstarch dissolved in 1½
    teaspoons water
1 tablespoon tomato paste (optional)

Put chestnuts in a medium saucepan and add water to cover them by about 1 inch. Boil over high heat 1 minute. Remove from heat. Remove 1 chestnut with slotted spoon; cover pan. Cut into chestnut peel at base and pull off outer skin. Scrape off inner skin with paring knife. Repeat with remaining chestnuts, removing them from water one by one.

Put peeled chestnuts in a medium saucepan with 1½ cups of stock, celery, salt, and pepper. Bring to boil. Cover and simmer over low heat until chestnuts are just tender when pierced with point of sharp knife, about 15 minutes; do not overcook or they may fall apart. Uncover and leave in liquid until ready to use. *Chestnuts can be kept in their liquid, covered, up to 2 days in refrigerator.*

Preheat the oven to 400°F. Sprinkle hens with salt and pepper. Roast hens in a shallow roasting pan for about 45 minutes or until juices that run from thigh, when pierced in thickest part with a skewer, are clear.

When hens are nearly done, cover chestnuts and reheat in their cooking liquid over low heat. Discard celery. Drain chestnut liquid and reserve. Cover chestnuts and keep them warm.

Pour off fat from roasting pan but leave in darker colored juices. Reheat juices in pan over medium-high heat. Add wine and bring to boil, stirring and scraping up any browned bits. Strain into a medium saucepan, add shallots and thyme, and boil over medium-high heat until reduced to ⅓ cup. Add remaining 1 cup stock and chestnut cooking liquid and bring to a boil. Remove from heat. Skim fat from sauce.

Bring sauce to simmer over medium heat. Whisk potato starch mixture to blend. Gradually whisk half the potato starch mixture into simmering sauce. Return to boil, whisking. For thicker sauce, gradually whisk in remaining potato starch mixture and return to boil. Taste and adjust seasoning. Whisk in tomato paste if desired.

Add ¼ cup sauce to hot chestnuts and mix gently. Transfer hens to plates and spoon chestnuts around them. Serve sauce separately.

Makes 4 servings

QUAIL WITH ONION COMPOTE AND KIWIS

The flavorful meat of quail is delicious with delicate sweet-and-sour tastes, as in this modern French-style dish, in which the bird is accompanied by sweet onion compote, fresh kiwis, and a richly flavored tarragon vinegar sauce.

4 tablespoons vegetable oil
2 tablespoons (¼ stick) butter
2 pounds onions, halved and cut in
   thin slices
salt and freshly ground pepper
3 kiwis, peeled
8 quail (each about ¼ pound), thawed
   if frozen, patted dry

2 shallots, minced
1 cup chicken stock or low-salt broth
2 tablespoons tarragon vinegar
6 tablespoons (¾ stick) cold butter, cut
   in 6 pieces

For onion compote, heat 2 tablespoons oil and 1 tablespoon butter in a large, heavy casserole over low heat. Add onions, salt, and pepper. Cover and cook, stirring often, 45 minutes. Uncover and cook, stirring very often, about 15 minutes or until onions can be crushed easily with a wooden spoon; do not let them burn. *Compote can be kept, covered, 1 day in refrigerator.*

Cut kiwis in half lengthwise and slice them. Cut about half the slices in half again, making quarter slices.

Heat remaining oil and 1 tablespoon butter in a large sauté pan over medium-high heat. Sprinkle 4 quail with salt and pepper and add to pan. Brown birds on all sides for 7 minutes, turning with tongs and covering with a splatter screen. If juices darken, reduce heat to low; do not let them burn. Repeat with remaining quail.

Pour off all but a thin film of fat from pan. Reduce heat to low. Stir in shallots. Add quail with liquid from plate and ⅓ cup stock. Cover and cook about 5 minutes on each side or until quail legs are tender. To check, make a slit in plump part of leg—meat should be pink, not red. Transfer to a platter and keep warm.

Reheat onions in saucepan over low heat. Keep warm.

Add vinegar and remaining ⅔ cup stock to pan from quail and bring to a boil, stirring and scraping to dissolve pan juices. Boil until reduced to about ¾ cup. Strain, return to pan, and heat. With pan over low heat, add pieces of cold butter, one by one, shaking pan to swirl butter into sauce. Remove from heat. Taste and adjust seasoning.

Add kiwi quarter-slices to onions and stir a few seconds over low heat. Remove from heat. Taste and adjust seasoning.

Spoon onion compote on center of each plate. Set 2 quail on opposite sides of compote and spoon some sauce over quail. Garnish each plate with kiwi half-slices. Serve any remaining sauce separately.

Makes 4 servings

QUAIL ON A BED OF RISOTTO

This is a re-creation of a dish I feasted on recently at a new Italian restaurant in Los Angeles. One quail was served per person on a plateful of risotto as a substantial first course, but for serving at home I prefer it as a main course, with two quail for each portion.

You can use this recipe as a basic guide to cooking quail for serving in other ways, too. Quail are great with couscous or pasta, or with mushrooms cooked along with the birds. If you can find quail that is boneless, buy it; it's much easier to eat.

⅔ cup dry white wine
½ teaspoon dried thyme, crumbled
8 quail (each about ¼ pound), thawed
   if frozen, patted dry
4 tablespoons olive or vegetable oil
1 tablespoon butter
salt and freshly ground pepper

1 cup chopped onion
4 cups chicken stock or broth
2 large garlic cloves, minced
1½ cups Arborio or other round risotto
   rice
¼ cup grated Parmesan cheese

Combine ⅓ cup wine and thyme in a bowl. Add quail and turn to moisten all sides. Cover and marinate in the refrigerator 2 hours or up to overnight.

Pat quail dry, reserving marinade. Heat 2 tablespoons oil and 1 tablespoon butter in a large sauté pan over medium-high heat. Sprinkle 4 quail with salt and pepper and add to pan. Brown birds on all sides for 7 minutes, turning with tongs and covering with a splatter screen. If juices darken, reduce heat to low; do not let them burn. Repeat with remaining quail.

Pour off all but 1 tablespoon oil from pan. Reduce heat to low. Stir in ½ cup onion and sauté about 5 minutes. Add quail with liquid from plate, marinade, and ⅓ cup stock. Cover and cook about 5 minutes on each side or until quail legs are tender. To check, make a slit in plump part of leg—meat should be pink, not red. Remove quail to a platter. Boil sauce about 2 or 3 minutes to reduce slightly. Taste and adjust seasoning.

Meanwhile, prepare risotto. Heat remaining chicken stock; cover and keep warm. Heat remaining oil in a heavy, medium saucepan over medium heat. Add remaining onion and sauté 5 minutes or until soft but not brown. Add garlic and rice and stir 2 minutes until coated. Add remaining ⅓ cup wine and stir. Simmer over medium heat 1 or 2 minutes until wine evaporates.

Add 2 cups hot chicken stock and stir. Simmer uncovered, stirring occasionally, 9 to 10 minutes or until liquid is absorbed. Add remaining stock, stir, and cook 8 minutes or until rice is al dente. Remove from heat. Add pepper to taste. Let stand 2 or 3 minutes.

Meanwhile, reheat quail in sauce. Add cheese to risotto. Taste and adjust seasoning. Serve risotto in deep dishes, top with quail, and spoon sauce over quail and rice.

Makes 4 servings

SQUAB WITH PEPPERS, GARLIC, AND COUSCOUS

The flavorful dark meat of squab is popular in many Mediterranean countries. In Morocco it is either grilled or prepared in a savory sauce, as in this recipe. Garnish it with cilantro and serve it with green beans or sautéed zucchini, in addition to the couscous.

4 squabs (each about 12 to 14 ounces), thawed if frozen
salt and freshly ground pepper
3 tablespoons olive oil
1 large onion, chopped
1 red bell pepper, diced
2 pounds ripe tomatoes, peeled, seeded, and chopped; or 2 (28-ounce) cans whole plum tomatoes, drained and chopped

6 medium garlic cloves, minced
1 jalapeño pepper, minced (optional)
½ cup chicken stock or broth
cayenne pepper to taste
2 tablespoons chopped cilantro (fresh coriander) or parsley
Quick Couscous (page 110)

Pull out fat from inside of squabs. Pat squab dry. Sprinkle squabs evenly on all sides with salt and pepper. Heat 2 tablespoons oil in a heavy, enamel-lined casserole over medium-high heat. Add squabs and brown lightly on all sides, taking about 2 minutes per side. Remove to a plate.

Add onion and pepper to casserole and cook over medium-low heat, stirring often, until softened, about 7 minutes. Add tomatoes, garlic, jalapeño pepper, stock, salt, and pepper and bring to a boil, stirring. Reduce heat to low, cover, and simmer 30 minutes.

Return squabs to pan and add any juices from plate. Cover and simmer over low heat 8 minutes. Turn over and simmer 7 minutes or until just tender; when thickest part of leg is pierced with a knife, meat should look pink.

If sauce is too thin, boil uncovered, stirring often, until thickened. Add cayenne pepper and cilantro. Taste and adjust seasoning.

Prepare Quick Couscous. Reheat squab in sauce. Serve with couscous.

Makes 4 servings

PHEASANT
WITH ORANGE AND PORT SAUCE

The meat of pheasant is lean, and so it is best when casserole-roasted to prevent it from being dry. Here it is complemented by a savory European-style port sauce with orange segments, orange rind julienne, and a touch of Cognac. Instead of the orange sections, other fruit such as poached cherries, poached apricot halves, or raw grapes can be added to the sauce. If pheasant is not available, this sauce is also good with quail and duck.

1 large navel orange
1 cup chicken stock or low-salt broth
1 teaspoon tomato paste
1 tablespoon potato starch, arrowroot, or cornstarch
2 tablespoons water
2 young pheasants (each about 2½ pounds), thawed if frozen

salt and freshly ground pepper
3 tablespoons vegetable oil
3 tablespoons port
2 teaspoons Cognac
¼ cup fresh orange juice, strained
1 tablespoon red currant jelly or other red jelly (optional)
a few drops of lemon juice (optional)

Using a vegetable peeler, remove zest of orange without bitter white pith. Cut zest in thin, needlelike strips. Put them in a saucepan and cover with water. Boil 5 minutes. Rinse with cold water and drain. Remove pith from peeled orange. Cut orange carefully in segments, removing as much as possible of membrane between them.

Bring stock to a simmer and whisk in tomato paste. Stir in orange zest. Whisk potato starch with water until smooth. Gradually whisk mixture into simmering sauce. Remove from heat.

Preheat the oven to 400°F. Pull out fat from inside pheasants. Pat pheasants dry. Sprinkle them inside and out with salt and pepper. Heat oil in heavy, oval, enamel-lined casserole over medium-high heat. Set pheasants in casserole on their sides. Cover with large splatter screen if desired. Brown pheasants on all sides, taking about 2 minutes per side. (If fat begins to turn dark brown, reduce heat to medium.) Leave pheasants on their backs.

Baste pheasants with pan juices. Using a bulb baster, remove most of fat from pan. Cover and bake about 20 minutes or until meat is white with just a touch of pink near bone; check by piercing breast meat with a knife. Do not overcook or pheasant will be dry. *Pheasant can be kept warm in casserole, covered, for 15 minutes.*

Pour cooking juices into a glass measuring cup. Pour off lighter layer of fat, leaving dark juices (at bottom) behind. Return dark juices to casserole and bring to simmer. Meanwhile, reheat sauce in separate saucepan. Add port and Cognac to juices in casserole and bring to a simmer, stirring. Pour into sauce, whisking. Add orange juice and heat gently. Add jelly and lemon juice and taste for seasoning. Add orange segments and heat very gently. Remove from heat.

Carve pheasant, removing excess fat. Serve breast and thigh meat. Drumsticks are full of sinews; their meat can be reserved and used like diced cooked chicken. Spoon sauce with oranges over pheasant.

Makes 4 to 6 servings

16

Stuffings

Stuffing is a symbol of home cooking. Our memories of wonderful stuffing are seldom associated with fancy restaurants or famous chefs, but rather with dinners prepared with love at home and shared with family or close friends.

Like other favorites of home cooking, stuffing is easy to prepare. It can be made from a variety of ingredients, but by far the most popular type of stuffing in America is one based on bread. When tossed with gently cooked onions and seasonings, bread is magically turned into moist, flavorful stuffing.

In Mediterranean countries, stuffings of rice, couscous, and bulgur wheat are more common than bread stuffing. Stuffings based on ground meat are well loved in most of Europe. These stuffings are flavored with herbs, spices, dried fruit, or occasionally wine. Often toasted nuts or chestnuts are added for contrasting texture.

Stuffing lends itself to numerous flavoring variations because the bread or grain is a neutral base that tastes good with almost any food. Traditional American seasonings for stuffing the Thanksgiving turkey are thyme and sage, while time-honored additions are oysters, sausage, pecans, or apples.

Pepper, Corn, and Cilantro Stuffing
Apple, Apricot, and Walnut Stuffing
Herbed Onion Stuffing
Hazelnut-Mushroom Stuffing
Spicy Sausage Stuffing
Brazil Nut and Thyme Stuffing
Bacon Stuffing
Dill Stuffing
Rosemary Stuffing
Aromatic Rice Stuffing with Pistachios,
Almonds, and Raisins
South American Orange-Scented Rice Stuffing
Orzo, Garlic, and Walnut Stuffing
Bulgur Wheat Stuffing
Couscous, Almond, and Date Stuffing
Chestnut Stuffing

Lighter stuffings are made of sautéed vegetables, such as carrots, mushrooms, and onions, or of peeled and quartered apples, a common central European stuffing for goose.

In the Far East, stuffings are less important, but flavors of the East can be used to create terrific bread or rice stuffing.

Originally developed as an economical way to stretch meat, stuffing has become for many people the best part of a roast poultry dinner, especially one planned around turkey. In fact, in America a roast turkey menu without stuffing is almost unthinkable. Yet stuffing has other uses—it can be baked in a separate dish and served as a delicious accompaniment for any roast or grilled poultry.

As a stuffing bakes in a turkey, chicken, or Cornish hen, it gains good taste from the roasting juices. Most people prefer to roast ducks and geese without stuffing, because so much fat drips out of the skin and makes the stuffing too greasy.

It is a pleasure to try exotic seasonings in stuffing sometimes. This might sound like heresy, but for Thanksgiving I have enjoyed fruity stuffing spiked with spirits and even spicy stuffing flavored with cilantro, cumin, and jalapeño peppers.

TIPS

✂ About ½ cup stuffing per pound of poultry is enough to fill the bird, but I like to allow about ¾ to 1 cup stuffing per pound of poultry and to bake the extra stuffing separately, so there will be enough for good-size servings.

✂ Although stuffing mixtures can be prepared ahead, for reasons of hygiene stuffing should never be spooned into the poultry ahead of time. Put stuffing in the bird just before roasting.

✂ Remove all stuffing from the bird before carving. Always refrigerate stuffing in a container, never in the bird.

✂ To save time, remember that an unstuffed bird roasts faster. Bake the stuffing in a separate dish and baste it occasionally with the roasting juices or with stock.

✂ Day-old or slightly dry bread is best for stuffing because it is easiest to cut in cubes. Since the bread is dried in the oven for many stuffing recipes, there is no advantage to using fresh bread.

✂ To cut bread in cubes, use a serrated knife to first slice the bread, then cut the slices in strips, and last in small cubes.

✂ Baking the bread cubes in the oven gives a slightly crisper stuffing, and the bread retains its texture more than if it is not baked. This type of stuffing becomes softer if made ahead and refrigerated.

✂ When baked separately, bread stuffing is dryer and crisper than when baked inside a bird.

✂ Leftover stuffing can be reheated in a buttered shallow baking dish or buttered ramekins. Sprinkle it with a little stock, cover and bake at 350°F. about 35 to 45 minutes or until hot. Uncover for the last 10 minutes.

PEPPER, CORN, AND CILANTRO STUFFING

In this American bread stuffing with Mexican-inspired flavors, jalapeño peppers, bell peppers, cilantro, corn, and smoked turkey turn toasted bread cubes into a lively and colorful mixture. If you want the roast turkey or chicken to cook more quickly, simply spoon the stuffing into a greased baking dish and bake it separately.

about 8 to 10 ounces day-old or stale white bread (preferably good-quality French or Italian bread)
7 tablespoons olive oil
2 medium onions, finely chopped
1 red bell pepper, diced (about ½-inch cubes)
1 green bell pepper, diced (about ½-inch cubes)
2 jalapeño peppers, ribs and seeds removed, minced

salt and freshly ground pepper
¾ teaspoon dried thyme, crumbled
1 cup corn kernels, fresh or frozen, cooked
⅓ cup chopped cilantro (fresh coriander)
3 tablespoons chopped green onion
½ cup finely diced (¼-inch cubes) smoked turkey (2 ounces)
4 to 6 tablespoons chicken or turkey stock or broth

Preheat the oven to 275°F. Cut bread in ½-inch cubes; you will need 2 quarts. Put bread cubes on a large baking sheet. Bake until crisp and dry, stirring frequently, about 20 minutes. Cool and transfer to a large bowl.

Heat oil in a large skillet over medium heat. Add onions, bell peppers, jalapeño peppers, and a pinch of salt and ground pepper. Cook, stirring occasionally, until onions are soft but not brown and peppers are tender, about 12 minutes. Stir in thyme. Remove from heat.

Add onion mixture, corn, cilantro, green onion, and smoked turkey to bread and toss lightly until blended. Gradually add 4 tablespoons stock, tossing lightly. Mixture may appear dry, but will become much moister from juices in bird. For baking separately, most of bread should be very lightly moistened; if most of it is still dry, gradually add more stock by tablespoons. Taste and adjust seasoning. *Stuffing can be refrigerated up to 1 day in covered container.*

To stuff chickens, spoon stuffing lightly into body cavity; for turkey, spoon stuffing lightly into neck and body cavities. Do not pack stuffing in tightly. Fold skin over stuffing; truss or skewer closed. Roast as desired.

Makes 8 to 9 cups, about 6 to 8 servings; enough for one 10- to 12-pound turkey or two 4-pound chickens

NOTES:

a. *If there is extra stuffing,* add a little more stock, if necessary, so most of bread is very lightly moistened. Butter casserole of same or slightly larger volume than amount of extra mixture and spoon stuffing into it. Dot with butter. Cover and refrigerate until about 1 hour before roast is done. If roasting poultry or meat at 375°F. or lower, bake stuffing during last hour of roasting, basting stuffing with 2 or 3 tablespoons stock every 15 or 20 minutes. If baking less than 4 cups stuffing, bake only 45 minutes. If roasting poultry at higher temperature, bake extra stuffing separately at 325°F.

b. *To bake all of stuffing separately,* preheat oven to 325°F. Butter a 2½-quart casserole and spoon stuffing into it. Dot stuffing with butter and cover casserole. Bake 20 minutes. Baste stuffing by pouring ¼ cup stock evenly over top. Bake 20 more minutes and repeat with another ¼ cup stock. Bake 20 minutes more; uncover for last 10 minutes for crisper top. Serve hot.

APPLE, APRICOT, AND WALNUT STUFFING

Fruit stuffings like this are popular in much of Europe as well as America. They are wonderful with the Thanksgiving turkey but for other occasions also make delicious stuffing for roast chicken. For a special flavor, the fruit is simmered in Calvados, the famous French apple brandy.

1 cup walnuts
1 cup finely diced (¼-inch cubes) dried apricots (about 5 ounces)
¼ cup dark raisins
½ cup Calvados
about 8 to 10 ounces day-old or stale white bread (preferably good-quality French or Italian bread)
6 tablespoons (¾ stick) butter
1 large onion, finely chopped
1 cup chopped celery

2½ cups peeled, finely chopped tart green apples (about 1¼ pounds or 3 medium apples)
salt and freshly ground pepper
⅛ teaspoon ground cloves
1 teaspoon minced fresh thyme, or ¼ teaspoon dried, crumbled
1 teaspoon minced fresh sage, or ¼ teaspoon dried, crumbled
4 to 6 tablespoons chicken or turkey stock or broth

Preheat the oven to 350°F. Toast nuts until lightly browned, about 5 minutes. Cool nuts and coarsely chop.

Combine apricots, raisins, and Calvados in a small saucepan and mix well. Bring to a simmer. Cover, remove from heat, and let stand 30 minutes, stirring occasionally.

Reduce oven temperature to 275°F. Cut bread in ½-inch cubes; you will need 2 quarts. Put bread cubes on a large baking sheet. Bake until crisp and dry, stirring frequently, about 20 minutes. Cool and transfer to a large bowl.

Melt butter in large skillet over medium heat. Add onion, celery, apples, and a pinch of salt and pepper. Cook, stirring occasionally, until onion is soft but not brown, about 10 minutes. Add cloves, thyme, and sage and stir until blended. Remove from heat.

Add onion mixture, nuts, and apricot mixture with its liquid to bread and toss lightly until blended. Gradually add 2 tablespoons stock, tossing lightly. Mixture may appear dry, but will become much moister from juices in bird. Taste and adjust seasoning. *Stuffing can be refrigerated up to 1 day in covered container.*

To stuff chickens, spoon stuffing lightly into body cavity; for turkey, spoon stuffing lightly into neck and body cavities. Do not pack stuffing in tightly. Fold skin over stuffing; truss or skewer closed. Roast as desired.

To bake extra stuffing or to bake all of stuffing separately, follow notes after Pepper, Corn, and Cilantro Stuffing, page 327, using remaining stock as needed.

Makes 8 to 9 cups, about 6 to 8 servings; enough for one 10- to 12-pound turkey or two 4-pound chickens

HERBED ONION STUFFING

This Italian-inspired stuffing is good baked inside a chicken or turkey, or baked separately to accompany Roast Turkey Breast with Sage and Thyme (page 198).

about 8 to 10 ounces day-old or stale white bread (preferably good-quality French or Italian bread)
6 tablespoons olive oil
3 medium onions, finely chopped (about 3 cups)
¼ cup chopped celery
salt and freshly ground pepper

4 teaspoons minced fresh rosemary, or 1½ teaspoons dried
1 teaspoon dried oregano, crumbled
2 teaspoons minced fresh sage, or ¾ teaspoon dried, crumbled
½ cup chopped Italian or curly parsley
¼ to ½ cup chicken or turkey stock or broth

Preheat the oven to 275°F. Cut bread in ½-inch cubes; you will need 2 quarts. Put bread cubes on 1 large or 2 small baking sheets. Bake until crisp and dry, stirring frequently, about 20 minutes. Cool and transfer to a large bowl.

Heat oil in large skillet over medium heat. Add onions, celery, and a pinch of salt and pepper. Cook, stirring occasionally, until onion is soft but not brown, about 10 minutes. Add rosemary, oregano, and sage and stir until blended.

Add onion mixture and parsley to bread and toss lightly until blended. Gradually add ¼ cup stock, tossing lightly. Mixture may appear dry, but will become much moister from juices in bird. For baking separately, most of bread should be very lightly moistened; if most of it is still dry, gradually add more stock by tablespoons. Taste and adjust seasoning. *Stuffing can be refrigerated up to 1 day in covered container.*

To stuff chickens, spoon stuffing lightly into body cavity; for turkey, spoon stuffing lightly into neck and body cavities. Do not pack stuffing in tightly. Fold skin over stuffing; truss or skewer closed. Roast as desired.

To bake extra stuffing or to bake all of stuffing separately, follow notes after Pepper, Corn, and Cilantro Stuffing, page 327.

Makes 8 to 9 cups; about 6 to 8 servings

NOTE: This recipe makes enough stuffing for one 10- to 12-pound turkey or two 4-pound chickens. Double recipe for a large (16- to 20-pound) turkey. If roasting only 1 chicken, prepare half a recipe, using a medium skillet, and bake extra stuffing in a baking dish.

HAZELNUT-MUSHROOM STUFFING

Toasted hazelnuts, sautéed mushrooms, and herbs make this a luscious stuffing with a European flavor. SEE PHOTOGRAPH.

1½ cups hazelnuts
2 tablespoons vegetable oil
½ pound mushrooms, halved and cut in thin slices
salt and freshly ground pepper
½ cup (1 stick) butter
2 large onions, chopped

1 cup chopped celery
3 medium garlic cloves, chopped
½ pound zucchini, coarsely grated
½ pound day-old French or Italian bread, cut in ½-inch cubes
¼ cup chopped fresh parsley
1½ teaspoons dried thyme, crumbled

Preheat the oven to 400°F. Toast hazelnuts in a baking dish in oven for 7 minutes. Put nuts in strainer and rub with terry cloth towel to remove skins. Transfer to a bowl and let cool. Chop coarsely.

Heat oil in a large skillet over medium-high heat. Add mushrooms, salt, and pepper and sauté until lightly browned, about 3 minutes. Transfer to a bowl.

Melt butter in a very large skillet over medium-low heat. Add onions and celery and cook, stirring, until softened, about 7 minutes. Add garlic and cook ½ minute. Remove from heat.

Put grated zucchini in a colander and squeeze out excess liquid. Stir zucchini into onion mixture.

In a large bowl combine bread cubes, vegetable mixture, mushrooms, hazelnuts, parsley, thyme, and a pinch of salt and pepper. Toss using 2 tablespoons until ingredients are mixed thoroughly and bread is moistened. Taste, and add salt and pepper if needed.

To bake extra stuffing or to bake all of stuffing separately, follow notes after Pepper, Corn, and Cilantro Stuffing, page 327.

Makes 9 to 10 cups, enough for one 12- to 14-pound turkey

SPICY SAUSAGE STUFFING

Indian flavors—chilies, fresh ginger, cumin, and turmeric—lend a Far Eastern character to this hot and spicy stuffing. I prefer to use turkey sausage when making it, so it will be rich but not heavy. This stuffing is also good inside bell peppers instead of in a bird.

about 8 to 10 ounces day-old or stale white bread (preferably good-quality French or Italian bread)
¾ pound hot Italian sausage or other fresh sausage (1½ cups)
5 tablespoons butter or vegetable oil
2 medium onions, finely chopped (about 2 cups)
1 cup chopped celery
2 serrano or jalapeño peppers, cored, ribs and seeds removed, and minced

salt and freshly ground pepper
2 tablespoons minced peeled fresh ginger
4 medium garlic cloves, minced
1 tablespoon ground cumin
1 teaspoon turmeric
¼ cup chopped fresh parsley
3 tablespoons chopped green onion
2 to 4 tablespoons chicken or turkey stock or broth

Preheat the oven to 275°F. Using a serrated knife, cut bread in ½-inch cubes; you will need 2 quarts. Put bread cubes on 1 large or 2 small baking sheets. Bake until crisp and dry, stirring frequently, about 20 minutes. Cool and transfer to a large bowl.

Cook sausage in a large, heavy skillet over medium-high heat, breaking up meat with wooden spoon, until it is no longer pink, about 10 minutes. Transfer to a strainer above a bowl and drain, reserving drippings.

Transfer 1 tablespoon drippings to skillet. Add butter and melt over medium heat. Add onions, celery, peppers, and a pinch of salt and ground pepper. Cook, stirring occasionally, until onions are soft but not brown, about 10 minutes. Add ginger and cook 2 minutes. Add cooked sausage, garlic, cumin, and turmeric and cook, stirring, 1 minute. Remove from heat.

Add sausage mixture, parsley, and green onion to bread and toss lightly until blended. Gradually add 2 tablespoons stock, tossing lightly. Mixture may appear dry, but will become much moister from juices in bird. Taste and adjust seasoning. *Stuffing can be refrigerated up to 1 day in covered container.*

To stuff chickens, spoon stuffing lightly into body cavity; for turkey, spoon stuffing lightly into neck and body cavities. Do not pack stuffing in tightly. Fold skin over stuffing; truss or skewer closed. Roast as desired.

To bake extra stuffing or to bake all of stuffing separately, follow notes after Pepper, Corn, and Cilantro Stuffing, page 327, using remaining stock as needed.

Makes about 9 cups, about 6 to 8 servings; enough for one 10- to 12-pound turkey or two 4-pound chickens

BRAZIL NUT AND THYME STUFFING

The usual American bread stuffing is transformed into a holiday treat with the addition of Brazil nuts and a generous amount of herbs. This stuffing is delicate in flavor and is good with any type of bird.

1 cup Brazil nuts
about 8 to 10 ounces day-old or stale
    white bread (preferably good-quality
    French or Italian bread)
6 tablespoons (¾ stick) butter or olive
    oil
2 medium onions, finely chopped
    (about 2 cups)

1 cup chopped celery
1 bay leaf
salt and freshly ground pepper
4 teaspoons minced fresh thyme, or 1½
    teaspoons dried, crumbled
½ cup chopped fresh parsley
⅓ to ⅔ cup chicken or turkey stock or
    broth

Preheat the oven to 350°F. Toast nuts until lightly browned, about 7 minutes. Transfer nuts to large strainer and rub with terry cloth towel to remove most of skin. Cool nuts and coarsely chop.

Reduce oven temperature to 275°F. Using a serrated knife, cut bread in ½-inch cubes; you will need 2 quarts. Put bread cubes on 1 large or 2 small baking sheets. Bake until crisp and dry, stirring frequently, about 20 minutes. Cool and transfer to a large bowl.

Melt butter in large skillet over medium heat. Add onions, celery, bay leaf, and a pinch of salt and pepper. Cook, stirring occasionally, until onion is soft but not brown, about 10 minutes. Stir in thyme. Discard bay leaf.

Add onion mixture, parsley, and nuts to bread and toss lightly until blended. Gradually add ⅓ cup stock, tossing lightly. Mixture may appear dry, but will become much moister from juices in bird. For baking separately, most of bread should be very lightly moistened; if most of it is still dry, gradually add more stock by tablespoons. Taste and adjust seasoning. *Stuffing can be refrigerated up to 1 day in covered container.*

To stuff chickens, spoon stuffing lightly into body cavity; for turkey, spoon stuffing lightly into neck and body cavities. Do not pack stuffing in tightly. Fold skin over stuffing; truss or skewer closed. Roast as desired.

To bake extra stuffing or to bake all of stuffing separately, follow notes after Pepper, Corn, and Cilantro Stuffing, page 327.

Makes 8 to 9 cups; about 6 to 8 servings

BACON STUFFING

A favorite in eastern Europe, this stuffing is a rich and tasty complement to the lean meat of turkey. If you like, use turkey bacon, following the variation.

about 8 to 10 ounces day-old or stale
   white bread (preferably good-quality
   French or Italian bread)
6 ounces bacon, cut in ¼-inch dice
¼ cup (½ stick) butter or vegetable oil
2 medium onions, finely chopped
   (about 2 cups)
1 cup chopped celery

1 bay leaf
freshly grated nutmeg to taste
salt and freshly ground pepper
¾ teaspoon dried marjoram or thyme,
   crumbled
½ cup chopped fresh parsley
¼ to ½ cup chicken or turkey stock or
   broth

Preheat the oven to 275°F. Using a serrated knife, cut bread in ½-inch cubes; you will need 2 quarts. Put bread cubes on a large baking sheet. Bake until crisp and dry, stirring frequently, about 20 minutes. Cool and transfer to a large bowl.

Put bacon in a cold, heavy, large skillet. Sauté over medium heat, stirring occasionally, until fat is rendered and bacon is just beginning to brown, about 7 minutes. Pour into strainer above bowl and let fat drain through. Reserve 2 tablespoons fat. Transfer bacon to paper towels.

Heat butter or oil with reserved bacon fat in large heavy skillet over medium heat. Add onions, celery, bay leaf, nutmeg, and a pinch of salt and pepper. Cook, stirring occasionally, until onion is soft but not brown, about 10 minutes. Stir in marjoram or thyme. Discard bay leaf.

Add onion mixture, bacon, and parsley to bread and toss lightly until blended. Gradually add ¼ cup stock, tossing lightly. Mixture may appear dry, but will become much moister from juices in bird. For baking separately, most of bread should be very lightly moistened; if most of it is still dry, gradually add more stock by tablespoons. Taste and adjust seasoning. *Stuffing can be refrigerated up to 1 day in covered container.*

To stuff chickens, spoon stuffing lightly into body cavity; for turkey, spoon stuffing lightly into neck and body cavities. Do not pack stuffing in tightly. Fold skin over stuffing; truss or skewer closed. Roast as desired.

To bake extra stuffing or to bake all of stuffing separately, follow notes after Pepper, Corn, and Cilantro Stuffing, page 327.

Makes 8 to 9 cups, about 6 to 8 servings; enough for one 10- to 12-pound turkey or two 4-pound chickens

NOTE: You can substitute turkey bacon for regular bacon. Cook as above. Practically no fat will come out, so there is no need to drain or put bacon on paper towels. Add 2 tablespoons oil when sautéing vegetables.

DILL STUFFING

Bread stuffing flavored with fresh dill is loved in central and eastern Europe. My mother, who was born in Poland, adds vegetables to make the stuffing lighter—in addition to sautéed onions and celery, she adds grated carrot, as in the recipe below, and sometimes a grated zucchini as well. Some cooks also add ½ cup chopped ham, but when I'm adding meat, I prefer smoked turkey.

about 4 to 5 ounces day-old or stale
   French, Italian, or European white
   bread
4 to 5 tablespoons vegetable oil or
   butter
1 medium onion, finely chopped
½ cup chopped celery

1 teaspoon paprika
salt and freshly ground pepper
1 medium carrot, coarsely grated
3 to 4 tablespoons snipped fresh dill
1 egg, beaten
2 to 4 tablespoons chicken stock or
   broth

Cut bread in ½-inch cubes; you will need 4 cups. Put in a large bowl. Heat 3 tablespoons oil or butter in medium skillet over medium heat. Add onion, celery, paprika, and a pinch of salt and pepper. Cook, stirring occasionally, until onion is softened, about 10 minutes. Stir in carrot and remaining oil and remove from heat. Add onion mixture, dill, and egg to bread and toss lightly until blended. Gradually add stock, tossing lightly. Mixture may appear dry, but will become much moister from juices in bird. Taste and adjust seasoning. *Stuffing can be refrigerated 1 day in covered container.*

Makes 4 to 5 cups, about 4 servings; enough for 1 chicken

ROSEMARY STUFFING

Along with thyme and garlic, rosemary gives a Mediterranean flavor to this bread stuffing. To further heighten the flavor, rub the chicken with rosemary and olive oil before roasting it.

about 4 to 5 ounces day-old or stale
  white bread (preferably good-quality
  French or Italian bread)
3 to 4 tablespoons (½ stick) butter or
  olive oil
1 medium onion, finely chopped
  (about 1 cup)
salt and freshly ground pepper
1 large garlic clove, minced

2 teaspoons minced fresh rosemary, or
  ¾ teaspoon dried
1 teaspoon minced fresh thyme, or ½
  teaspoon dried, crumbled
¾ cup finely diced ham, turkey ham,
  or smoked turkey
¼ cup chopped fresh parsley
2 to 4 tablespoons chicken stock or
  broth

Preheat the oven to 275°F. Cut bread in ½-inch cubes; you will need 1 quart. Put bread cubes on a baking sheet. Bake until crisp and dry, stirring frequently, about 20 minutes. Cool and transfer to a medium bowl.

Heat butter or oil in medium skillet over medium heat. Add onion and a pinch of salt and pepper. Cook, stirring occasionally, until onion is soft but not brown, about 10 minutes. Add garlic and cook, stirring, ½ minute. Stir in rosemary and thyme.

Add onion mixture, ham, and parsley to bread and toss lightly until blended. Gradually add 2 tablespoons stock, tossing lightly. Mixture may appear dry, but will become moister from juices in bird. Taste and adjust seasoning. *Stuffing can be refrigerated up to 1 day in covered container.*

Makes 4 to 5 cups, about 4 servings; enough for 1 chicken

VARIATION: **Garlic Stuffing**
Increase garlic to 3 cloves. Sauté ½ cup chopped celery along with the onion. Increase fresh thyme to 1½ teaspoons. Omit rosemary and ham.

AROMATIC RICE STUFFING WITH PISTACHIOS, ALMONDS, AND RAISINS

Saffron, nuts, and raisins give this flavorful rice stuffing an exotic Persian touch. I like to prepare generous quantities of this pretty stuffing for serving some alongside the chicken as well.

3 cups boiling water
¼ teaspoon crushed saffron threads (2 pinches)
4 tablespoons vegetable oil
1 cup minced onion

1½ cups long-grain white rice
salt and freshly ground pepper
½ cup dark raisins
½ cup slivered almonds, toasted
½ cup toasted shelled pistachios

Combine boiling water and saffron in a small saucepan. Cover and keep warm over low heat. In a sauté pan or deep skillet, heat oil over low heat, add onion, and cook, stirring, about 7 minutes, or until soft but not brown. Raise heat to medium, add rice, and sauté, stirring, about 4 minutes, or until grains begin to turn milky white.

While rice is sautéing, bring saffron water to boil over high heat. Pour over rice and stir once. Add ½ teaspoon salt and pinch of pepper. Bring to boil. Cover and cook without stirring 10 minutes. Add raisins, cover, and cook 8 minutes or until rice is just tender. *Stuffing can be prepared 2 days ahead and refrigerated.* Lightly mix in almonds and pistachios. Taste and adjust seasoning.

Makes about 4½ cups, enough for 1 chicken with extra to serve separately

SOUTH AMERICAN ORANGE-SCENTED RICE STUFFING

Serve this savory rice pilaf, flavored with orange juice, orange zest, and sautéed onions, to stuff chickens or Cornish hens before roasting them, or as a side dish for roast or grilled turkey. To turn the rice into a main course, you can gently stir in 1 or 2 cups diced or shredded roast turkey or chicken.

3 tablespoons butter or vegetable oil
1 small or ½ large onion, minced
1 cup long-grain rice
1½ cups hot water

½ cup orange juice
salt and freshly ground pepper
finely grated rind of 1 orange

Heat butter or oil in a deep skillet or sauté pan, add onion, and cook over low heat about 5 minutes or until tender. Add rice and sauté over medium heat about 2 minutes. Add water, orange juice, salt, and pepper and bring to a boil. Cover and cook over low heat 15 minutes or until rice is nearly tender. Stir in orange rind and taste for seasoning. Let cool before using as stuffing.

NOTE: If serving this as a side dish rather than to stuff a bird, cook it 18 to 20 minutes or until rice is just tender.

Makes about 3 cups, enough to stuff 1 chicken

ORZO, GARLIC, AND WALNUT STUFFING

I find the Greek rice-shaped orzo an ideal pasta to use as stuffing, because it holds its shape well and doesn't become crushed or soggy. Like rice, the orzo is prepared as a pilaf by being sautéed before liquid is added. Onions, garlic, and hot pepper flakes give this stuffing lots of flavor, while toasted walnuts add a slightly crunchy texture. SEE PHOTOGRAPH.

¾ cup walnut pieces
6 tablespoons (¾ stick) butter or olive
    oil
1 medium onion, minced
3 medium garlic cloves, minced
1½ cups orzo or riso (rice-shaped
    pasta) (about 12 ounces)

3 cups hot chicken stock or broth
¼ teaspoon hot red pepper flakes, or to
    taste
1 teaspoon dried oregano, crumbled
¼ cup chopped fresh parsley

Preheat the oven to 350°F. Toast walnut pieces in oven about 4 minutes or until lightly browned. Transfer to a plate and let cool.

Set aside 2 tablespoons butter at room temperature. Melt remaining 4 tablespoons butter in a medium saucepan over medium heat. Add onion and sauté, stirring often, 7 minutes. Add garlic and orzo, and cook over low heat, stirring, 3 minutes. Add stock or broth, pepper flakes, and oregano and bring to a boil. Cover and cook over low heat about 14 minutes or until barely tender.

Fluff mixture with a fork to break up any lumps in orzo. Add reserved 2 tablespoons butter, walnuts, and parsley and toss mixture to combine it. Taste and adjust seasoning. Let stuffing cool.

Makes about 4 cups, enough for 1 chicken, with extra for serving separately

VARIATION: **Orzo Pilaf with Garlic and Walnuts**
Reduce butter or oil amount to 4 tablespoons. Omit the butter added at the end. Serve hot as a side dish.

BULGUR WHEAT STUFFING

Nutty-tasting bulgur wheat, a Middle Eastern staple, makes a flavorful stuffing for chicken, especially when embellished with toasted pine nuts and accented with cilantro, garlic, and sautéed vegetables.

3 tablespoons olive or vegetable oil
½ medium onion, minced
½ medium carrot, cut in small dice
1 medium celery stalk, cut in small
 dice
3 medium garlic cloves, minced
1 cup medium bulgur wheat

2 cups water
salt and freshly ground pepper
3 or 4 tablespoons chopped cilantro
 (fresh coriander) or parsley
⅓ cup pine nuts or slivered almonds,
 toasted

Heat oil in a heavy, medium saucepan over medium heat. Add onion, carrot, and celery and cook, stirring often, about 7 minutes or until softened. Add garlic and cook 1 minute. Add bulgur and sauté, stirring, 2 minutes. Add water, salt, and pepper and bring to boil. Reduce heat to low, cover, and cook about 15 minutes or until water is absorbed. Gently stir in cilantro and pine nuts. Taste and adjust seasoning.

Makes about 3½ cups, enough for 1 chicken

COUSCOUS, ALMOND, AND DATE STUFFING

In Moroccan cuisine, couscous is a popular poultry stuffing. I like this savory fruity stuffing in chickens or Cornish hens.

2 pinches of saffron threads (about ¼
 teaspoon)
1¼ cups hot chicken stock or broth
4 tablespoons (½ stick) butter, at room
 temperature
1 medium onion, chopped
1 teaspoon ground ginger

¼ teaspoon ground cinnamon
1¼ cups couscous
salt and freshly ground pepper
½ cup chopped dates
½ cup slivered almonds, toasted
pinch of freshly grated nutmeg

Crush saffron between your fingers. In a small saucepan combine saffron and hot chicken stock; cover and let stand 20 minutes.

In a large skillet melt 2 tablespoons butter. Add onion, ginger, and cinnamon and sauté over medium heat, stirring, for 7 minutes or until soft but not brown. Add couscous, salt, and pepper and stir mixture with a fork to blend. Scatter chopped dates on top. Remove skillet from heat and shake it to spread couscous in an even layer. Bring saffron-flavored stock to a boil, pour it evenly over couscous, immediately cover skillet tightly, and let mixture stand 3 minutes. Fluff couscous with a fork. Cut remaining butter in small pieces and add them. Add almonds and toss mixture to combine it. Season with nutmeg. Taste and adjust seasoning. Let stuffing cool completely.

Makes about 3 cups stuffing, enough for 1 chicken or 4 Cornish hens

CHESTNUT STUFFING

Chestnut stuffing is a favorite for the French dinde de Noël, *or Christmas turkey. For the classic stuffing the chestnuts are mixed with ground pork, but I prefer a lighter stuffing of ground turkey seasoned with the traditional shallots, brandy, and herbs. If you don't feel like peeling and cooking chestnuts, you can use canned ones.*

¾ pound chestnuts
2 cups turkey or chicken stock or
  broth
1 celery stalk
salt and freshly ground pepper
about 8 to 10 ounces day-old or stale
  white bread (preferably good-quality
  French or Italian bread)

6 or 7 tablespoons butter
¾ pound ground turkey (1½ cups)
2 medium onions, chopped (about 2
  cups)
2 teaspoons minced fresh thyme, or ½
  teaspoon dried, crumbled
2 tablespoons Cognac
2 tablespoons chopped fresh parsley

Put chestnuts in a medium saucepan and add enough water to cover them by about 1 inch. Boil over high heat 1 minute. Remove from heat. Remove 1 chestnut with slotted spoon and cover pan. Cut into chestnut peel at base and pull off outer skin. Scrape off inner skin using paring knife. Repeat with remaining chestnuts, removing from water one by one.

Put peeled chestnuts in medium saucepan with 1½ cups of stock, celery, salt, and pepper. Bring to boil. Cover and simmer over low heat until chestnuts are just tender when pierced with point of sharp knife, about 15 minutes. Discard celery.

Slice bread and put it, a few slices at a time, in food processor to make crumbs. You will need 4 cups crumbs; transfer to a large bowl.

Melt 2 tablespoons butter in a large, heavy skillet over medium heat. Add turkey and sauté, breaking up meat with wooden spoon, until it is no longer pink, about 7 minutes. Transfer to a bowl.

Add remaining butter to skillet and melt over medium heat. Add onions, and a pinch of salt and pepper. Cook, stirring occasionally, until onions are soft but not brown, about 10 minutes. Add turkey and thyme and cook, stirring, 1 minute. Remove from heat. Let cool and add Cognac.

Add turkey mixture, chestnuts, and parsley to bread, and toss lightly until blended. Add ½ cup stock and toss again. Mixture should be lightly moistened; if very dry, add a little of chestnut cooking liquid. Taste and adjust seasoning. *Stuffing can be refrigerated up to 1 day in covered container.*

Makes about 8 cups, about 6 to 8 servings; enough for one 10- to 12-pound turkey or two chickens

17

Marinades and Sauces

MARINADES

Marinades are a special type of seasoning, used to introduce flavor to poultry before it is cooked. In addition, marinades help keep poultry moist during cooking. A traditional function of marinades is to tenderize meats, but poultry sold today is young and tender and so this is no longer a purpose of marinating.

Marinades can be used for poultry cooked by any technique, but are most often used for poultry to be grilled or broiled, to help prevent it from becoming dry. Oil-based marinades are best for this purpose, especially in the case of lean cuts such as boneless skinless chicken or turkey breast meat. Less oil can be used if the skin is left on, or if you are using dark meat like leg or thigh meat or wings.

Most marinades also contain a tart or acid element, which might be lemon, lime, or orange juice, vinegar, wine, or yogurt. These provide a pleasant zip.

343

MARINADES

Indonesian Satay Marinade
Ginger-Lime Marinade
Orange Marinade/Vinaigrette
Herb Marinade/Vinaigrette
Provençal Garlic and Herb Marinade
Lemon and Thyme Marinade
Mexican Marinade
Mediterranean Marinade
Middle Eastern Marinade
Wine and Rosemary Marinade
Moroccan Cilantro Pesto Marinade
Classic Red Wine Marinade

SAUCES

Fresh Rosemary-Sage Vinaigrette
Creamy Cilantro Dressing
Mustard-Caper Vinaigrette
Citrus Dressing
Shallot-Herb Vinaigrette
Yogurt, Mint, and Garlic Dressing
Sesame-Soy Dressing
Mustard-Wine Vinaigrette
Tapenade Dressing
Garlic Oil
Fresh Tomato Salsa
Tahini Sauce
Pesto
Bajan "Pesto"
Walnut-Garlic Sauce
Guacamole
Jalapeño-Garlic Chutney
Harissa
Macadamia Nut Butter
Cilantro Butter

Roquefort Butter
Fresh Tomato Sauce
Creole Sauce
Spanish Pepper and Tomato Sauce
Quick Tomato-Basil Sauce
Chinese Sweet-and-Sour Sauce
Easy Barbecue Sauce
Mushroom Sauce
Red Wine Sauce
Velouté Sauce
Raspberry Beurre Blanc
Cilantro Beurre Blanc
Vegetable Julienne Sauce
Curry Cream
Madeira Sauce
Mustard Cream
Red Wine Marinade Sauce

Vinaigrette, best known as a salad dressing, can also be a dual-purpose marinade. Like other marinades, it can be used to season poultry before cooking. For salads, vinaigrette can be mixed with already cooked poultry, which can be left to marinate in it before the salads are served, thus absorbing more flavor.

There is nothing mysterious about marinades. As with vinaigrette, you can flavor them with the seasonings you like best—herbs and garlic in the Provençal manner, spices in the Middle Eastern and Indian fashion, or soy sauce and rice wine in the Chinese style.

I love poultry prepared with a simple Mediterranean marinade of olive oil, lemon juice, and either rosemary and thyme or coriander and cumin. The aromatic Indian-style yogurt marinade for Easy Tandoori Chicken (page 188), redolent of fresh ginger, garlic, and a mixture of spices, is another favorite of mine, and so are lemon and orange-flavored marinades, as in Citrus Marinated Chicken (page 163).

Some marinades are simply mixtures of spices that are rubbed into the meat of the chicken. These are sometimes called dry marinades and serve purely as seasonings. This type of marinade can be used with chicken that will be fried or sautéed, such as Chili-Spiced Fried Chicken (page 215), and is best marinated without oil or other liquids. Dry marinades are also good with rich meats like duck or goose.

The longer you let poultry stand with a marinade, the more it flavors the meat, but even a brief marinating will impart some flavor. You can marinate poultry for as long as is convenient for you—for about half an hour while the coals or the oven are heating, or up to 4 hours for boneless meats or overnight for chicken or turkey pieces with bones. Thin boneless cuts could become too soft if the marinade contains a generous amount of lemon or lime juice or vinegar. It is safest to marinate poultry in the refrigerator.

TIPS

✕ Since the acid in marinades can react with metal, choose a glass or plastic container for marinating poultry. Cover the poultry so it won't dry out.

✕ If you wish to use a marinade for basting poultry as it cooks, set aside some of the marinade for this purpose. For reasons of hygiene, it is best not to baste with the marinade in which the poultry was sitting.

✕ A marinade should not be reused for an additional batch of poultry.

✕ A marinade can be used as the basis for a sauce, but should be brought to a boil before being served.

SAUCES

Sauces lend excitement and elegance to poultry dishes of all types. It's almost unthinkable to serve roast turkey without gravy, since it not only imparts good flavor but moistens the lean meat. A tangy or fruit-flavored sauce balances the rich meat of duck or goose.

Chicken is wonderful with sauces of every style, from delicate to spicy, from sharp and thin to rich and creamy. A sauce can accompany chicken merely to make the meal festive. Although sauce can be served with chicken cooked by any technique, it is most often used to lend zest to poached chicken.

Chicken appetizers go well with dipping sauces. The charm of Indonesian satays lies in the luscious peanut dipping sauce that comes with these chicken "kabobs." Dunking grilled chicken wings in a lively garlic oil gives them an additional punch of flavor that makes you sit up and notice them.

The beauty of sauces is their versatility. If you like a sauce that goes with one recipe, such as the ginger-scented Chinese sauce in Sweet-and-Sour Wings (page 20), you can use it another time with other poultry, like roast duck, grilled turkey, or braised quail.

A good sauce does wonders for poultry leftovers. The next time you have extra cooked chicken or turkey, try serving it with Cumin-Tomato Sauce (page 271), Mushroom Sauce (page 373), Italian Green Sauce (page 160), Horseradish Sauce (page 224), Mexican fresh salsa (page 362) or Chilies and Cilantro-Tomato Sauce (page 251). If you have just a little meat, cut it in strips or dice, mix it with the sauce, and serve it over or mixed with pasta or grains. Any of these sauces will turn extra poultry into a glamorous entree.

Many poultry dishes form their own sauce during the cooking process. Because chicken lends good flavor to its cooking liquid or sauce, in many cuisines it is cooked with a generous amount of sauce, so that even if there is a small piece of meat for each person, it will still be satisfying to eat the flavorful sauce with rice.

If a sauce is left over from a braised poultry dish or stew, I put it in small containers and save it like a precious treasure in the refrigerator or the freezer. I can always use it to create new dishes with cooked vegetables, pasta, or grains.

MARINADES

INDONESIAN SATAY MARINADE

This aromatic, delicately sweet and sour marinade, traditional for Indonesian-style kabobs known as satays (as on page 22), is also good for perking up plain grilled or broiled chicken breasts.

1 tablespoon vegetable oil
1 tablespoon strained fresh lemon juice
1 medium garlic clove, minced
1 tablespoon soy sauce

1 teaspoon brown sugar
1 teaspoon ground coriander
½ teaspoon ground cumin
pinch of cayenne pepper

Mix ingredients in a bowl. Pour over poultry and mix well. Cover and marinate in refrigerator 1 to 2 hours.

Makes about 3 tablespoons, enough for 1 to 1½ pounds poultry

GINGER-LIME MARINADE

Marinate chicken or turkey in this zesty Caribbean mixture before grilling or broiling it, or use the marinade as the basis for a dressing. For example, you can combine it with chopped mangoes to prepare a ginger-mango dressing, as in Mango, Chicken, and Pasta Salad with Ginger (page 58).

6 tablespoons vegetable oil
3 tablespoons strained fresh lime juice
1 tablespoon grated peeled fresh
   ginger

5 teaspoons soy sauce
¾ teaspoon bottled hot pepper sauce,
   or more to taste

Combine oil, lime juice, ginger, soy sauce, and hot sauce in a large bowl and whisk until blended.

Makes about ½ cup, enough for 2½ to 3 pounds poultry

ORANGE MARINADE/VINAIGRETTE

Pairing orange juice with poultry is a custom in many cuisines. Chicken with orange is loved in Spain, the Caribbean, Mexico, and Israel, and duck with orange sauce is one of the best-known French specialties. This marinade gives a good flavor to any poultry that is to be grilled, broiled, or roasted. As a dressing, it is more tangy than classic vinaigrette and is ideal for rich meat like duck, goose, or the dark meat of chicken. You can also add a minced garlic clove, for a variation that I enjoyed with roast chicken at a Cuban restaurant.

2 tablespoons extra-virgin olive oil
2 tablespoons vegetable oil
1 tablespoon strained fresh orange
   juice

1 tablespoon strained fresh lemon juice
1 teaspoon finely grated orange rind
salt and freshly ground pepper
cayenne pepper to taste

Combine olive oil, vegetable oil, orange juice, lemon juice, orange rind, salt, pepper, and cayenne in a bowl. Whisk to combine. Taste and adjust seasoning.

Makes about ⅓ cup, enough for about 2 pounds poultry

HERB MARINADE/VINAIGRETTE

You can make this Mediterranean vinaigrette with red, white, or Balsamic wine vinegar or with lime or lemon juice. The oil can be olive oil or vegetable oil. For use as a marinade, it's best to choose herbs that have plenty of character, like thyme, oregano, or cilantro. For a dressing for poultry salads, the more delicate herbs, like tarragon, chives, and chervil, can also be used.

6 tablespoons olive or vegetable oil
2 tablespoons strained fresh lemon or
   lime juice or wine vinegar
1 teaspoon dried oregano, crumbled

salt and freshly ground pepper
cayenne pepper to taste
1 tablespoon chopped cilantro (fresh
   coriander) or parsley

In a small bowl, whisk oil, lemon juice, oregano, salt, pepper, and cayenne. Stir in cilantro. Taste and adjust seasoning.

Makes ½ cup, enough for 2½ to 3 pounds poultry

PROVENÇAL GARLIC AND HERB MARINADE

Olive oil, lemon juice, garlic, and a mixture of herbs give this marinade a Provençal character. Use it to lend flavor and richness to lean poultry, such as chicken or turkey breasts and pheasant.

2 tablespoons strained fresh lemon
   juice
¼ cup olive oil
1 medium garlic clove, minced
½ teaspoon salt

1 teaspoon freshly ground black
   pepper
½ teaspoon dried thyme, crumbled
½ teaspoon dried basil, crumbled
½ teaspoon dried rosemary, crumbled

In a small bowl combine lemon juice, oil, garlic, salt, pepper, and herbs.

Makes about ⅓ cup, enough for about 2 pounds poultry

LEMON AND THYME MARINADE

This is a tangy marinade, containing equal amounts of lemon juice and oil, and is good for rich meats like chicken thighs. It can be used for chicken breasts too, but their skin should be on for additional protection during grilling or broiling. Thyme gives this marinade a flavor loved in France, but you can substitute oregano for an Italian or Greek accent, or mint or cilantro for a Lebanese touch.

2 tablespoons strained, fresh lemon
   juice
2 teaspoons chopped fresh thyme, or ¾
   teaspoons dried, crumbled

2 tablespoons olive or vegetable oil

Mix ingredients in a small bowl.

Makes about ¼ cup, enough for about 1½ to 2 pounds poultry

MEXICAN MARINADE

Lime juice, garlic, cayenne pepper, and cumin give this marinade a lively flavor. Because the marinade contains a generous proportion of oil, it is perfect for moistening lean skinless chicken breasts, as in Chicken Fajitas (page 159). It is also good for turkey breast slices.

4 teaspoons strained fresh lime juice
¼ cup vegetable oil
a few dashes of pure chili powder or
   cayenne pepper

2 medium garlic cloves, minced
½ teaspoon ground cumin

Combine ingredients in a bowl.

Makes about ¼ cup, enough for about 1½ to 2 pounds poultry

MEDITERRANEAN MARINADE

This lemony, slightly spicy marinade is ideal for kabobs, or for chicken pieces that will be broiled or roasted.

2 tablespoons strained fresh lemon
   juice
2 tablespoons extra-virgin olive oil
½ teaspoon freshly ground white
   pepper

¾ teaspoon dried oregano, crumbled
a few shakes of cayenne pepper

Mix ingredients in a bowl.

Makes about ¼ cup, enough for about 1½ pounds poultry

My mother-in-law, who is from Yemen, frequently uses this marinade on poultry, and it is a favorite in our house. It gives a wonderful flavor reminiscent of curry to any poultry that will be grilled, broiled, roasted, or braised. For the best possible flavor, grind cumin seeds in a spice grinder just before making the marinade.

2 tablespoons olive oil
4 teaspoons ground cumin
1 teaspoon turmeric

½ teaspoon freshly ground black
   pepper

Mix all ingredients.

Makes about 2 tablespoons, enough for 1 chicken or 2½ to 3 pounds chicken pieces

WINE AND ROSEMARY MARINADE

This Italian marinade is often used for roast veal. I like to use it on turkey breasts or whole chickens before roasting them, or on turkey breast slices or chicken pieces before broiling them.

2 tablespoons chopped fresh or 2
    teaspoons dried rosemary
½ cup olive oil

¼ cup dry white wine

Mix ingredients in a bowl.

Makes ¾ cup, enough for 3 pounds chicken pieces, 1 medium chicken, a 2- to 3-pound turkey roast, or 2 pounds turkey breast slices

MOROCCAN CILANTRO PESTO MARINADE

This marinade is made quickly in the food processor like pesto, but makes use of cilantro and parsley rather than basil. It might sound like a new culinary creation but is actually a traditional marinade loved in Moroccan cuisine. I like it as a marinade for whole chickens, chicken pieces, or Cornish hens that will be roasted or braised. The garlicky cilantro mixture is also delicious mixed with pasta as you would the usual basil pesto.

4 medium garlic cloves
1 (1¼-ounce) bunch cilantro (fresh
    coriander), leaves and very fine
    stems only
¾ cup loosely packed parsley sprigs,
    without large stems

3 tablespoons vegetable oil
¼ teaspoon salt
½ teaspoon paprika
freshly ground black pepper

Finely chop garlic in food processor. Add cilantro and parsley and chop fine. Transfer to a bowl. Add oil, salt, paprika, and pepper to taste; mix well.

Makes about ⅓ cup, enough for 1 chicken

CLASSIC RED WINE MARINADE

European chefs traditionally use this flavorful marinade of wine, herbs, spices, and aromatic vegetables for game such as venison and hare, but it's also excellent with game birds, turkey parts, and chicken. If you're braising the bird, you can use the marinade as part of the braising liquid, but add an equal amount of stock to balance the wine's acidity. If you're roasting or grilling the bird, use the marinade to prepare a Red Wine Marinade Sauce (page 381).

As a variation, the marinade can be made with white wine and white wine vinegar instead of red. Its uses are the same, and it's generally made into a creamy sauce. For example, it would be substituted for the wine and vinegar in Shallot Cream (page 377).

2 cups dry red wine
1 tablespoon red wine vinegar
1 tablespoon vegetable oil
½ medium onion, diced
1 small carrot, diced
1 large sprig fresh thyme, or ½
    teaspoon dried

1 sprig fresh rosemary, or pinch of
    dried leaves
1 bay leaf
1 whole clove
6 juniper berries (optional)

Mix ingredients in a bowl.

Makes 2 cups, enough for 3 to 4 pounds poultry

SAUCES

FRESH ROSEMARY-SAGE VINAIGRETTE

This is a favorite dressing for Italian, Provençal, or California-style chicken salads, both hot and cold. It is also delicious as a marinade for chicken before grilling, or a sauce for grilled or broiled chicken or turkey.

2 tablespoons white wine vinegar
salt and freshly ground pepper
6 tablespoons extra-virgin olive oil

1½ tablespoons chopped fresh sage
1 tablespoon chopped fresh rosemary

Whisk vinegar with salt and pepper in a medium bowl. Whisk in oil. Stir in sage and rosemary. Taste and adjust seasoning.

Makes ½ cup; about 4 servings

CREAMY CILANTRO DRESSING

Mexican flavors—jalapeño peppers, cilantro, and lime juice—transform the familiar American mayonnaise and sour cream dressing into a spirited sauce, perfect for adding zip to poached chicken or turkey. Use it in salads or to make terrific turkey sandwiches.

2 large garlic cloves, peeled
1 fresh jalapeño pepper, cut in 4 pieces
⅓ cup packed cilantro (fresh
  coriander) leaves, patted dry
¼ cup packed small parsley sprigs,
  patted dry

salt and freshly ground pepper
1 tablespoon strained fresh lime juice
1 tablespoon olive oil
¾ cup mayonnaise
½ cup sour cream or yogurt

With blade of food processor turning, drop garlic cloves, then pepper pieces, through feed tube and process until finely chopped. Add cilantro, parsley, and pinch of salt and process until finely chopped. Add lime juice and olive oil and process until thoroughly blended; scrape bottom and sides of processor container several times. Add mayonnaise and process until blended. Transfer to bowl and stir in sour cream. Taste and adjust seasoning, adding ground pepper if desired. *Dressing can be kept, covered, 1 day in refrigerator.*

Makes about 1¼ cups; 6 to 8 servings

MUSTARD-CAPER VINAIGRETTE

The zesty dressing of mustard and capers is loved in France for beef salads. I love it with roast chicken or turkey salads as well, combined with vegetables and either potatoes or pasta. In fact, the tangy dressing is also a great partner for hot grilled chicken.

3 tablespoons plus 2 teaspoons Dijon
   mustard
¼ cup plus 1 teaspoon white wine
   vinegar
salt and freshly ground pepper
¾ cup vegetable oil

¼ cup minced green onions
¼ cup minced fresh parsley leaves
3 tablespoons finely chopped rinsed
   and drained capers
2 medium garlic cloves, minced

Whisk mustard in a medium bowl with vinegar, salt, and pepper. Gradually whisk in oil. Stir in green onions, parsley, capers, and garlic. Taste and adjust seasoning.

Makes about 1 cup; 4 to 8 servings

CITRUS DRESSING

This type of orange and lemon dressing is popular along the west coast of the United States, where Pacific Rim cooking is in style, and in Hawaii. Soy sauce lends depth of flavor, and hot pepper sauce adds punch. The dressing is especially good with duck or with the dark meat of chicken.

¼ cup strained fresh lemon juice
½ cup plus 2 tablespoons vegetable oil
½ cup strained fresh orange juice
2 teaspoons finely grated orange zest

2 teaspoons soy sauce
a few drops Tabasco or other hot
  pepper sauce
salt and freshly ground pepper

Pour lemon juice into a medium bowl and gradually whisk in oil. Gradually whisk in orange juice, grated orange zest, soy sauce, and Tabasco. Add salt and pepper to taste.

Makes about 1¼ cups; about 6 servings

SHALLOT-HERB VINAIGRETTE

Serve this French dressing with poached or grilled chicken, or use it to flavor chicken salads.

3 tablespoons white or red wine
  vinegar or tarragon vinegar
½ small shallot, minced
salt and freshly ground pepper

½ cup plus 1 tablespoon vegetable or
  olive oil
1 tablespoon chopped fresh parsley,
  chives, basil, or tarragon

Whisk vinegar with shallot, salt, and pepper in a small bowl. Whisk in oil. Taste and adjust seasoning. Just before using, whisk again and add fresh herbs.

Makes about ½ cup dressing; 3 or 4 servings

YOGURT, MINT, AND GARLIC DRESSING

Yogurt is a common accompaniment in the Middle East for rice and lentils, and in Ethiopia and India for spicy dishes. I love this cool, refreshing Greek dressing as a topping for salads or chicken burgers or a partner for hot dishes of pasta or grains with poultry, such as bulgur pilafs or rice and chicken casseroles.

¾ cup plain yogurt
1 tablespoon chopped fresh mint

½ medium garlic clove, finely minced
salt and freshly ground pepper

Mix yogurt with mint and garlic. Season to taste with salt and pepper.

Makes ¾ cup; about 4 servings

SESAME-SOY DRESSING

This Oriental dressing is good on salads of poultry and pasta, such as Hawaiian Chicken and Somen Salad with Seafood (page 60). It also can be used as a dipping sauce for grilled or broiled chicken wings.

2 tablespoons sesame seeds
⅓ cup rice vinegar
3 to 4 tablespoons sugar, or to taste

1 tablespoon vegetable oil
1 tablespoon Oriental sesame oil
½ cup soy sauce

Toast sesame seeds in a small skillet over medium heat, shaking pan often, about 4 minutes or until golden brown. Transfer immediately to a plate and let cool.

Whisk vinegar, 3 tablespoons sugar, and both oils in a medium bowl. Whisk in soy sauce. Taste, and whisk in more sugar if desired. Whisk in sesame seeds.

Makes about ¾ cup; 4 servings

MUSTARD-WINE VINAIGRETTE

For a tasty salad, toss this French dressing with grilled, poached, or roasted chicken or turkey, then refrigerate it for an hour or two to marinate before adding vegetables or greens. Instead of regular Dijon mustard, you can use any flavored mustard, like herb mustard or green peppercorn mustard.

2 tablespoons white wine vinegar
2 tablespoons dry white wine
4 teaspoons Dijon mustard, or more to
   taste

salt and freshly ground pepper
6 tablespoons vegetable oil

Whisk vinegar with wine, mustard, salt, and pepper in a medium bowl; whisk in oil. Taste and adjust seasoning.

Makes about ⅔ cup; 4 servings

TAPENADE DRESSING

Based on the Provençal olive spread known as tapenade, this dressing is a delicious way to add zest to cooked chicken or turkey. Simply mix the dressing with the diced poultry and diced tomatoes, and serve the salad on a bed of lettuce, or use it in Turkey Tapenade Salad (page 71).

3 to 4 tablespoons extra-virgin olive oil
3½ to 4½ teaspoons strained fresh
   lemon juice
½ teaspoon dried thyme, crumbled
1 medium garlic clove, minced
1½ teaspoons Cognac or brandy

salt and freshly ground pepper
1 tablespoon water
4 anchovy fillets, minced
2 tablespoons capers, rinsed and
   minced
½ cup pitted chopped black olives

Whisk 3 tablespoons oil with 3½ teaspoons lemon juice, thyme, garlic, Cognac, pepper, and water in a medium bowl. Stir in anchovies, chopped capers, and chopped olives. Taste, and add more olive oil or lemon juice if desired.

Makes about ⅓ cup; 2 or 3 servings

GARLIC OIL

This assertive-tasting garlic oil resembles aïoli in flavor but is much lighter and thinner in consistency. Use it as a dipping sauce for grilled chicken or turkey, or add 2 tablespoons lemon juice and use it as a marinade. Unlike other recipes for garlic oil, which require several days for the garlic flavor to enter the oil, this Middle Eastern version is ready instantly because the garlic is minced.

4 medium garlic cloves
¼ teaspoon salt

¼ cup extra-virgin olive oil

In a food processor, mince garlic very fine. Add salt. Gradually add olive oil, stopping processor often and scraping mixture inward. *Can be kept, covered, 5 days in refrigerator. Return to room temperature before serving.*

Makes ¼ cup; 2 to 4 servings

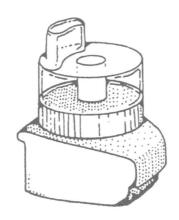

FRESH TOMATO SALSA

Salsas may have been the greatest contribution of Mexican cuisine to modern American cooking. Americans use the word salsa *to denote a Mexican-style* salsa cruda, *or uncooked salsa, and it would not be an exaggeration to say that we are in the midst of a salsa craze. Part of the reason for the popularity of salsas is that they are not as rich as most traditional sauces; in fact, many contain no oil at all, and so are perfect for light cooking. With a variety of chilies and herbs, you can produce an array of salsas of fresh flavors. For dishes for which many people would ordinarily reach for a bottle of ketchup, why not serve fresh salsa instead? It even does wonders for burgers (for example, Chicken Burgers with Pine Nuts, page 269).*

Adjust the hotness of this Mexican salsa cruda *to your taste by leaving some or all of the seeds in the jalapeño peppers—the more you leave in, the hotter it is. If fresh jalapeño peppers are not available, you can use other fresh hot peppers or diced canned jalapeños.*

¾ pound ripe tomatoes, chopped
2 jalapeño peppers, seeds removed,
  minced
½ cup chopped cilantro (fresh
  coriander)
2 large green onions, chopped (scant ⅔
  cup)

¼ teaspoon salt
ground red pepper or freshly ground
  black pepper
3 to 4 tablespoons water (if using
  plum tomatoes)

Combine tomatoes, jalapeño peppers, cilantro, and green onions in a bowl. Season to taste with salt and pepper. Add a little water if mixture is dry; it should have a chunky, sauce-like consistency. *Can be kept 2 days in refrigerator.* Serve at room temperature.

Makes about 2½ cups; 4 to 6 servings

NOTE: To make thick salsa (for serving with fajitas), omit water.

TAHINI SAUCE

Use this rich Middle Eastern sauce in sandwiches made with pita and grilled chicken, or toss a small amount with cooked chicken and diced vegetables to create a change-of-pace chicken salad.

½ cup tahini (sesame paste)
½ cup plus 1 tablespoon water
½ teaspoon ground cumin
¼ teaspoon salt, or to taste

2 tablespoons strained fresh lemon
   juice
3 large garlic cloves, minced
pinch of cayenne (optional)

In a medium bowl, stir tahini to blend in its oil. Stir in ½ cup water. Add cumin, salt, lemon juice, garlic, and cayenne. If sauce is too thick, gradually stir in more water. Taste, and add more salt or lemon juice if desired. *Tahini thickens on standing, and may need a little water mixed in before serving.*

Makes about 1 cup; about 6 servings

PESTO

This light, flavorful version of the famous Genoese sauce contains modest amounts of olive oil and Parmesan cheese. If you like, omit the cheese, and you will have the related French pistou. You can even substitute chicken stock for half the oil. Use pesto as a dressing for chicken salads, or combine it with vinaigrette or mayonnaise for a more delicate flavor. Of course, pesto is also wonderful in poultry-and-pasta dishes.

2 large garlic cloves, peeled
2 tablespoons pine nuts or walnuts
1 cup packed basil leaves (1 bunch of
   about 1 ounce)

¼ cup freshly grated Parmesan cheese
¼ cup extra-virgin olive oil

With blade of food processor turning, drop garlic cloves, 1 at a time, through feed tube and process until finely chopped. Add nuts, basil, and cheese and process until basil is chopped. With blade turning, gradually add olive oil. Scrape down sides and process until mixture is well blended. Transfer to a small bowl and set aside. *Pesto can be kept, covered, 2 days in refrigerator. Bring to room temperature before using.*

Makes about ½ cup; about 4 servings

BAJAN "PESTO"

This aromatic herb paste from Barbados is based on a Bajan spice mixture used in everything from fried chicken to grilled fish. It is especially good spread under the skin of a chicken before roasting. I received this recipe from Steven Raichlen, whose popular Caribbean cooking course on St. Barthélemy island, "Cooking in Paradise," has been called the "Club Med of cooking classes." He suggests making slits in chicken to be grilled and placing a spoonful of this spicy pesto in each.

3 medium garlic cloves
½-inch fresh ginger, peeled (about 1 teaspoon chopped)
2 shallots
1 Scotch bonnet chili pepper (or jalapeño pepper for a milder taste)
1 cup loosely packed fresh parsley
½ cup loosely packed cilantro (fresh coriander)
4 green onions, coarsely chopped

1 bunch chives, chopped
1 teaspoon fresh thyme leaves
½ teaspoon salt (or to taste)
½ teaspoon ground cumin
¼ teaspoon freshly ground black pepper
¼ teaspoon ground allspice
the juice of 1 lime, or to taste
about 4 tablespoons olive oil or softened butter

Coarsely chop the garlic, ginger, and shallots. Seed and chop the pepper. (If you like your food really spicy, leave the seeds in.) Stem and chop parsley and cilantro.

Combine all the ingredients, except the lime juice and olive oil, in a food processor and finely chop. Work in the lime juice and enough oil or butter to obtain a thick paste. Taste and adjust seasoning, adding salt or lime juice to taste.

Makes about 1 cup; 8 servings

WALNUT-GARLIC SAUCE

As in aïoli, the uncooked garlic in this Mediterranean sauce packs quite a punch, and so it stands up beautifully to the smoky taste of grilled chicken, turkey, or duck.

3 large garlic cloves, peeled and halved
¼ cup parsley sprigs
⅔ cup walnuts

salt and freshly ground pepper
2 tablespoons cold water
⅔ cup vegetable oil

Drop garlic cloves into a food processor one at a time, with blades turning, and puree until finely chopped. Add parsley sprigs and chop together. Add walnuts, salt, and pepper and puree until walnuts are finely ground. Add water and puree to a smooth paste. With blades turning, add oil in a very fine stream. Stop occasionally and scrape down sides and bottom of work bowl. Transfer to a bowl and taste for seasoning. *Sauce can be kept, covered, 2 days in refrigerator.* Serve at room temperature. Stir before serving.

Makes about 1 cup; about 6 servings

GUACAMOLE

Best known as a dip, guacamole also makes a good sauce for broiled chicken or turkey breasts. Serve this Mexican classic with burritos or fajitas, or use it to make delicious chicken sandwiches. For a good fresh flavor, prepare it a short time before serving.

3 large ripe avocados (each 9 or 10 ounces), preferably Haas
½ cup minced green onions
3 tablespoon minced cilantro (fresh coriander) leaves
3 fresh serrano chilies, seeded and minced, or hot pepper sauce to taste

2 tablespoons fresh lime or lemon juice, or to taste
1½ cups finely diced tomato (optional)
salt to taste

Halve and pit avocados, spoon pulp into a bowl, and mash pulp with a fork. Stir in green onions, cilantro, chilies or hot pepper sauce, lime juice, tomato, and salt. *The guacamole may be made 2 hours in advance, covered with plastic wrap pressed directly on its surface, and chilled.*

Makes 6 servings

JALAPEÑO-GARLIC CHUTNEY

Serve this Middle Eastern chutney/salsa with grilled poultry as a fresh and zesty alternative to ketchup. Remove the seeds and ribs from the jalapeño peppers if you wish the chutney to be less hot.

¼ cup garlic cloves, peeled
2 medium jalapeño peppers, seeds and
   ribs removed, if desired
¼ cup small cilantro sprigs (fresh
   coriander)

¼ teaspoon salt
1½ teaspoons ground cumin
1 pound ripe plum tomatoes

Puree garlic and peppers in blender or mini food processor until finely chopped. If necessary, add 1 or 1½ tablespoons water, just enough to enable mixture to be chopped. Add cilantro and process until blended. Add salt and cumin. Transfer to a bowl.

   For a smooth-textured sauce, puree tomatoes in blender or food processor. For a chunky chutney, chop tomatoes with a knife. Stir 3 tablespoons garlic mixture into tomatoes. Taste chutney; if desired, add remaining garlic mixture and more salt.

Makes 6 servings

HARISSA

This brick red, fiery North African hot sauce is very potent. It is served as a condiment or is sometimes mixed with a little water as a sauce to be used sparingly with couscous. Harissa is also used in cooking, adding its sharp accent to Moroccan and Tunisian stews, such as Mediterranean Chicken with Okra, Jalapeño Peppers, and Tomatoes (page 134). It can be used like any hot sauce—to add a touch of heat to salad dressings and to pasta and rice dishes, for example.

   If you use a blender or mini chopper, the ingredients will blend to a more uniform paste than in a food processor, but with repeated processing the food processor will give an acceptable paste also. Avert your face when you open the processor or blender—the fumes can be overpowering!

   To grind the caraway seeds, use a spice grinder.

15 small dried red chilies, such as *chiles
   japones* (scant ¼ cup)
2 large garlic cloves

1 teaspoon ground caraway seeds
1 teaspoon ground coriander
olive oil (for keeping)

Put dried chilies in small bowl and cover with hot water. Soak 1 hour. Remove chilies, reserving soaking water. Put chilies and 3 tablespoons soaking water in blender or food processor with garlic, caraway, and coriander. Process until blended to a paste. Some pepper pieces will remain. If processor blades won't blend mixture, add another tablespoon soaking water. Keep in a small container in the refrigerator for several weeks, covered with a thin layer olive oil and a cover.

Makes scant ¼ cup; 4 to 6 servings

MACADAMIA NUT BUTTER

Like almonds, macadamia nuts are as good in savory dishes as in desserts, and Hawaiian cooks are using them to great advantage. It takes only a small amount of nuts to prepare a seasoned butter such as this one, which is gently flavored with lime juice. To add an elegant note to broiled or sautéed chicken or turkey breasts, pipe or spoon a little of this flavored butter onto each portion at serving time.

¼ cup (about 1 ounce) lightly salted
   macadamia nuts
6 tablespoons (¾ stick) butter, slightly
   softened, cut into bits

1 teaspoon fresh lime juice
1 tablespoon plus 1 teaspoon minced
   fresh parsley leaves
salt and freshly ground pepper

Grind nuts in food processor until very fine. Add butter and process to blend. Scrape down mixture, add lime juice, and process until blended. Transfer to a small bowl, stir in parsley, and season to taste with salt and pepper. *Nut butter keeps, covered, 2 days in refrigerator.* Serve at room temperature.

Makes about ½ cup; 3 to 5 servings

CILANTRO BUTTER

A new twist to the classic European herb butter, this version, popular in California cooking, gains zest from cilantro and lime juice. Put a spoonful of this on a sizzling hot grilled chicken breast, and as it melts into the meat and forms a savory sauce, it will give the chicken a wonderful taste.

6 tablespoons (¾ stick) butter,
  softened
1 teaspoon strained fresh lime juice
2 to 3 tablespoons chopped cilantro
  (fresh coriander)

salt and freshly ground pepper
cayenne pepper to taste

Beat butter until soft. Beat in lime juice. Stir in cilantro. Season to taste with salt, pepper, and cayenne pepper. *Butter keeps, covered, 1 day in refrigerator.* Serve at room temperature.

Makes about ⅓ cup; 2 to 4 servings

ROQUEFORT BUTTER

The French use this seasoned butter to give pizzazz to grilled steak, but it also is wonderful with grilled or broiled chicken breasts.

6 tablespoons (¾ stick) unsalted
  butter, softened
¼ cup crumbled Roquefort cheese

2 teaspoons dry white wine
1 tablespoon chopped green onions
freshly ground pepper

Beat butter with Roquefort and wine. Stir in green onions. Season with pepper to taste. Cover and refrigerate for 1 hour to blend flavors. Serve at room temperature.

Makes about ½ cup; 3 to 5 servings

FRESH TOMATO SAUCE

When tomatoes are plentiful, it is a good idea to make plenty of this sauce and freeze it. Of Italian origin, the sauce has been adopted by cooks throughout Europe, the Mediterranean countries, the Middle East, and the New World. The sauce reheats easily and is wonderful with poultry cooked by any technique. If you wish to add chopped fresh basil, do it just before serving.

1 to 3 tablespoons olive or vegetable
  oil
½ cup minced onion
2 medium garlic cloves, minced
2 pounds ripe tomatoes, peeled,
  seeded, finely chopped; or 2 (28-
  ounce) cans plum tomatoes, drained
  and chopped

1½ teaspoons fresh thyme leaves, or ½
  teaspoon dried, crumbled
½ teaspoon dried oregano, crumbled
  (optional)
1 bay leaf
salt and freshly ground pepper to taste

Heat oil in a large, heavy skillet over medium-low heat. Add onion and cook, stirring, until very soft but not browned, about 10 minutes. Add garlic and cook ½ minute. Add tomatoes, thyme, oregano, bay leaf, salt, and pepper and bring to boil. Cook, uncovered, over medium-high heat, stirring often, 10 to 15 minutes or until tomatoes are very soft and sauce is thick; reduce heat if necessary as sauce begins to thicken—it burns easily. Discard bay leaf. Taste and adjust seasoning. *Sauce can be kept, covered, up to 3 days in refrigerator; or it can be frozen.*

Makes about 2 cups; 4 to 8 servings

VARIATION: **Smooth Tomato Sauce**
  Puree finished sauce in food processor or blender.

CREOLE SAUCE

This Louisiana favorite is a zesty version of tomato sauce. It contains plenty of aromatic vegetables—onions, garlic, bell peppers, and celery—as well as hot sauce and Worcestershire sauce for a spicy character. Herbs are added to taste; in addition to or instead of the rosemary and thyme used here, you can add oregano or fresh basil. Serve Creole sauce with grilled, broiled, roasted, or poached chicken or turkey.

2 tablespoons (¼ stick) butter or
    vegetable oil
1 small onion, chopped (about ½ cup)
½ green bell pepper, cut in thin strips
2 celery stalks, cut in small dice
1 large garlic clove, chopped
2 pounds ripe tomatoes, peeled,
    seeded, and chopped; or 2 (28-
    ounce) cans plum tomatoes, drained
    and chopped

2 teaspoons chopped fresh thyme, or ¾
    teaspoon dried, crumbled
½ teaspoon dried rosemary
1 teaspoon paprika
1 bay leaf
salt and freshly ground pepper
1 to 2 teaspoons Worcestershire sauce,
    or to taste (optional)
1 teaspoon Louisiana or other hot
    pepper sauce, or more to taste

Heat butter or oil in a large, heavy skillet over medium-low heat. Add onion, pepper, and celery and cook, stirring, until onion is soft but not browned, about 7 minutes. Add garlic and cook ½ minute. Add tomatoes, thyme, rosemary, paprika, bay leaf, salt, and pepper and bring to boil. Cook, uncovered, over medium-high heat, stirring often, 10 to 15 minutes or until tomatoes are very soft and sauce is thick; reduce heat if necessary as sauce begins to thicken—it burns easily. Discard bay leaf. Add Worcestershire sauce and hot sauce to taste. Taste and adjust seasoning. *Sauce can be kept, covered, up to 3 days in refrigerator; or it can be frozen.*

Makes about 2½ cups; 4 to 8 servings

SPANISH PEPPER AND TOMATO SAUCE

Hot and sweet peppers accent this tomato sauce, a specialty of northern Spain and southern France. Serve it with grilled, broiled, or sautéed chicken or turkey.

2 tablespoons vegetable or olive oil
1 large onion, chopped
2 red bell peppers, or 1 green and 1 red pepper, chopped
2 medium garlic cloves, chopped
1 fresh jalapeño pepper, seeds discarded, chopped

1½ pounds ripe tomatoes, peeled, seeded, and chopped; or 1 (28-ounce) and 1 (14-ounce) can plum tomatoes, drained and chopped
salt and pepper

Heat oil in a deep skillet over medium-low heat. Add onion and cook, stirring often, until soft but not brown, about 5 minutes. Add bell peppers, garlic, and hot pepper and cook, stirring often, until peppers soften, about 5 minutes.

Add tomatoes, salt, and pepper and raise heat to medium. Cook, uncovered, stirring often, until sauce is thick, about 30 minutes. Taste and adjust seasoning. *Sauce can be kept for about 4 days in the refrigerator; or it can be frozen.*

Makes about 1½ cups; 4 to 6 servings

QUICK TOMATO-BASIL SAUCE

This version of Mediterranean tomato sauce is faster to prepare than most because there is no need to chop or sauté any onions. Use it for cooking chicken balls (as on page 252), mix it with chicken strips and your favorite pasta shapes, or serve it with grilled or sautéed chicken or turkey breasts.

2 pounds ripe tomatoes, peeled, seeded, and chopped; or 2 (28-ounce) cans plum tomatoes, halved, drained well, and chopped
2 tablespoons olive oil
2 medium garlic cloves, chopped

2 teaspoons tomato paste (optional)
salt and freshly ground pepper
3 tablespoons chopped fresh basil, or 2 to 3 teaspoons dried
¼ to ½ teaspoon sugar (optional)

In a large saucepan combine tomatoes with olive oil, garlic, and tomato paste. Bring to boil. Add salt and pepper (and dried basil, if using). Cook uncovered over low heat about 15 minutes or until softened. Taste and adjust seasoning. Add sugar if needed. *Sauce can be kept, covered, 3 days in refrigerator. Reheat sauce over low heat.* Add fresh basil just before serving.

Makes about 1¼ cups; 4 to 6 servings

CHINESE SWEET-AND-SOUR SAUCE

Fresh ginger gives this quick and easy sweet-and-sour sauce a pleasant zip. Serve it as a dipping sauce for grilled or broiled poultry or use it to baste chicken pieces during their last few minutes of roasting. I love to use the sauce to make Sweet-and-Sour Wings (page 20), or to add it to sautéed chicken, along with sliced fruit such as pineapple or kiwi. It might seem surprising to include ketchup as an ingredient in a Chinese dish, but in fact the word ketchup *comes from the Chinese, and the sweet and sour taste of ketchup gives a good flavor balance to the sauce.*

2 tablespoons rice vinegar
2 tablespoons soy sauce
¼ cup ketchup
2 tablespoons sugar
2 teaspoons minced peeled fresh
  ginger

2 medium garlic cloves, minced
⅓ cup chicken broth or water
1 teaspoon cornstarch
a few drops chili oil or hot pepper
  sauce, or cayenne pepper to taste

Combine vinegar, soy sauce, ketchup, sugar, ginger, garlic, broth, and cornstarch in a small saucepan and mix well. Cook over medium-high heat, stirring constantly, until sauce thickens and comes to a simmer. Add chili oil or hot pepper to taste.

Makes about ⅔ cup; about 4 servings

EASY BARBECUE SAUCE

This bright red American barbecue sauce gives chicken a slightly spicy, sweet and sour taste. If you would like it spicier, add ¼ to 1 teaspoon cayenne pepper or Mexican chili powder.

1 tablespoon vegetable oil
½ small onion, finely chopped
½ cup ketchup
1 tablespoon brown sugar

1 tablespoon white or red wine
  vinegar
1 teaspoon chili powder
1 tablespoon Dijon mustard

Heat oil in a medium saucepan over low heat. Add onion and cook, stirring, until soft, about 7 minutes. Stir in ketchup, brown sugar, vinegar, and chili powder and bring to a simmer. Remove from heat and stir in mustard. Taste, and add salt and pepper if needed. Cool to room temperature.

Makes about ½ cup; 3 or 4 servings

MUSHROOM SAUCE

This rich French sauce is one of the most delicious partners imaginable for sautéed or poached chicken or turkey. The cream gains a terrific flavor from being simmered with sautéed mushrooms. When exotic mushrooms such as morels or cèpes are available, use them instead, for a luxurious variation.

1 tablespoon vegetable oil
1 tablespoon butter
6 ounces small mushrooms, halved and
  thinly sliced
salt and freshly ground pepper

1 large shallot, minced
¾ cup dry white wine
¾ cup chicken stock or broth
3 medium garlic cloves, minced
1 cup heavy cream

Heat oil and butter in a large skillet over medium heat. Add mushrooms, salt, and pepper and sauté about 7 minutes or until lightly browned. Transfer to a bowl. Add shallot and wine to skillet and bring to a boil. Add stock and boil 2 minutes. Add garlic and cream and bring to a boil. Return mushrooms to pan and simmer over medium heat, stirring, until sauce is thick enough to coat a spoon, about 7 minutes. Taste and adjust seasoning. *Sauce can be kept, covered, 1 day in refrigerator. Reheat over low heat before serving.*

Makes about ¾ cup; about 4 servings

RED WINE SAUCE

Serve this easy-to-make, rich flavored sauce, which is popular throughout much of Europe, with sautéed or grilled duck breast, or with roast duck, chicken, or turkey. It's also delicious with roasted pheasant or quail. For best flavor, use a good red wine. Enrich the sauce with butter for the leaner birds—turkey or pheasant, and for chicken if you like—but not when serving the sauce with the rich meat of duck.

½ cup dry red wine
1 shallot, minced
½ teaspoon dried thyme, crumbled
1 cup duck, turkey, or chicken stock or
    broth
1 teaspoon potato starch, arrowroot, or
    cornstarch, dissolved in 2
    tablespoons cold water

salt and freshly ground pepper
pinch of sugar (optional)
2 tablespoons (¼ stick) cold butter
    (optional)

In a medium saucepan boil wine with shallot and thyme until wine is reduced to about ¼ cup. Add stock and bring to boil. Boil 1 or 2 minutes to reduce slightly. Whisk potato starch mixture and gradually pour into simmering sauce, whisking constantly. Bring to a boil, whisking constantly. Simmer 1 or 2 minutes until thickened. Remove from heat. Season to taste with salt and pepper. If sauce is too tart, add a pinch of sugar. *Sauce can be kept, covered, 2 days in refrigerator. Reheat over low heat.* Stir in butter just before serving.

Makes about 1 cup; about 4 servings

VELOUTÉ SAUCE

Americans love this French sauce so much as a partner for chicken that they have made it an integral part of an American classic, chicken pot pie. It is good with poached poultry, or for moistening leftover roast chicken or turkey. If you simmer a few sliced mushrooms in the sauce and enrich it with ¼ to ⅓ cup cream, you will have sauce suprême. *Either version can be accented at the last moment with 2 or 3 tablespoons chopped herbs, such as tarragon, parsley, chives, dill, or cilantro; with a pinch of a spice like paprika, curry powder, or cayenne pepper; with 2 to 3 teaspoons Dijon mustard; or with ½ cup diced tomatoes.*

1½ tablespoons butter
1½ tablespoons all-purpose flour
1 cup chicken poaching liquid (page
    391), chicken or turkey stock (page
    389), or prepared broth

salt and freshly ground white pepper
a few drops lemon juice (optional)
cayenne pepper (optional)

Melt butter in a small, heavy saucepan over low heat. Whisk in flour. Cook, whisking constantly, about 3 minutes or until mixture turns light beige. Remove from heat. Add liquid, whisking. Bring to a boil over medium-high heat, whisking. Add pinch of salt and white pepper. Simmer uncovered over medium-low heat, whisking often, for 5 minutes. Taste and adjust seasoning, adding lemon juice and cayenne pepper if desired. If not using sauce at once, dab top with butter to prevent a skin from forming. *Sauce can be kept, covered, up to 1 day in refrigerator; or it can be frozen.*

Makes 1 cup; about 4 servings

RASPBERRY BEURRE BLANC

This pink, raspberry vinegar–flavored variation of the French nouvelle favorite, beurre blanc, *is characteristic of California cuisine. Serve this luscious sauce with poached chicken breasts or turkey or with braised quail or pheasant, for a rich and fabulous treat.*

1 cup (2 sticks) cold unsalted butter,
    cut in 16 pieces
2 tablespoons minced shallots
¼ cup raspberry vinegar
3 tablespoons chicken stock or broth
    or water

¼ cup heavy cream
salt and freshly ground white pepper
    to taste

Melt 1 tablespoon butter in a small, heavy saucepan over low heat. Add shallots and cook about 2 minutes or until soft but not brown. Add vinegar and stock and simmer over medium heat until liquid is reduced to about 3 tablespoons. Stir in cream and a pinch of salt and white pepper and simmer, whisking occasionally, until mixture is reduced to about 4 or 5 tablespoons. Keep remaining butter in refrigerator until ready to use. *Sauce can be prepared to this point 4 hours ahead and kept, covered, at room temperature.*

A short time before serving, finish sauce. Bring shallot mixture to simmer in its small saucepan over low heat, whisking. Add 2 pieces of chilled butter and whisk until just blended in. Whisk in remaining butter a piece at a time, lifting pan from heat occasionally to cool mixture and adding each new piece of butter before previous one is completely blended in. Butter should soften as it is added but sauce should not get hot enough to liquefy. Remove from heat as soon as last butter piece is incorporated. Taste and adjust seasoning. Keep sauce warm if necessary in a bowl set on a rack over hot but not simmering water over low heat, or in a thermos; serve it as soon as possible.

Makes 1 cup; about 5 or 6 servings

CILANTRO BEURRE BLANC

Cilantro, a customary element of Mexican salsa, has become so much a part of the American produce selection that many people have forgotten the name for it in English, fresh coriander. We consider it a ''south of the border'' ingredient although it is central to many cuisines, from Middle Eastern to Chinese. In recent years it has been used more and more in European cuisines as well. The first time I tasted cilantro in Western-style food was fifteen years ago in Paris, when French chef Fernand Chambrette made a fabulous cilantro beurre blanc that I now love to serve with chicken breasts. This was a great use of the ''south of the border'' ingredient—south of the French border, that is! In Paris cilantro is considered a Moroccan ingredient.

3 tablespoons minced shallots
¼ cup dry white wine
2 tablespoons white wine vinegar
3 tablespoons heavy cream
salt and freshly ground white pepper
   to taste

1 cup (2 sticks) cold unsalted butter,
   cut in 16 pieces
2 to 3 tablespoons chopped cilantro
   (fresh coriander)

Combine shallots, wine, and vinegar in a small, heavy saucepan and cook over medium heat until liquid is reduced to about 3 tablespoons. Stir in cream and a pinch of salt and white pepper and simmer, whisking occasionally, until mixture is reduced to about 3 tablespoons. *Sauce can be prepared to this point 4 hours ahead and kept, covered, in refrigerator.*

A short time before serving, finish sauce. Bring shallot mixture to a simmer in its small saucepan over low heat, whisking. Add 2 pieces of chilled butter and whisk until just blended in. Whisk in remaining butter a piece at a time, lifting pan from heat occasionally to cool mixture and adding each new piece of butter before previous one is completely blended in.

Butter should soften as it is added but sauce should not get hot enough to liquefy. Remove from heat as soon as last butter piece is incorporated. Stir in cilantro. Taste and adjust seasoning. Keep sauce warm if necessary in a bowl set on a rack over hot but not simmering water over low heat, or in a thermos; serve it as soon as possible.

Makes 1 cup; about 5 or 6 servings

VEGETABLE JULIENNE SAUCE

Thin strips of leeks, carrots, and mushrooms add color and flavor to this rich and delicate French sauce of white wine, shallots, and reduced cream. Serve the sauce or its simpler variation, Shallot Cream, with poached chicken breasts or turkey.

1 medium carrot, peeled
½ small celery stalk
1 small leek, white and 2 inches of
   deep green, cleaned (page 238)
6 large white mushroom caps
¼ cup dry white wine
1 tablespoon white wine vinegar

2 tablespoons minced shallots
salt and freshly ground white pepper
1 cup heavy cream
cayenne pepper to taste
2 teaspoons snipped chives or minced
   parsley (optional)

Cut carrot, celery, and leek in thin strips about 1½ inches long. Slice mushroom caps crosswise in rounds. Cut rounds in thin strips.

Combine wine, vinegar, and shallots in a heavy, medium saucepan and bring to a simmer over medium heat. Simmer until liquid is reduced to about 3 tablespoons, stirring occasionally. Add mushroom strips and pinch of salt and pepper, and bring to a boil. Stir in cream and simmer over medium heat, stirring occasionally, about 6 minutes, or until mushrooms are tender and sauce is thick enough to coat back of a spoon lightly. Remove from heat.

Boil carrot, leek, and celery in a medium saucepan of boiling water for 3 minutes. Drain well. *Sauce and vegetables can be kept overnight in separate containers in refrigerator.*

Just before serving, reheat sauce, stir in vegetables, and bring to simmer. Remove from heat. Add a pinch of cayenne pepper. Taste and adjust seasoning. Stir in chives or parsley. May be served hot or cold.

Makes about 1 cup; about 4 or 5 servings

VARIATION: **Shallot Cream**
   Omit carrot, celery, leek, and mushrooms.

CURRY CREAM

This quick, simple to prepare sauce is both spicy and creamy and lends zip to chicken or Cornish hens cooked by any method. The next time you have turkey leftovers, be sure to try them with this luscious sauce. A typical nouvelle French sauce, it belongs to a modern category of creamy reduction sauces, which have been enthusiastically adopted by chefs at the forefront of new American cuisine.

1 tablespoon butter
2 tablespoons finely chopped onion
1 medium garlic clove, minced
1 jalapeño pepper, minced (optional)
1½ teaspoons curry powder
3 tablespoons dry white wine

1 tablespoon white wine vinegar
3 tablespoons chicken stock or broth
  or water
1 cup heavy cream
salt and freshly ground pepper

Melt butter in a heavy, medium saucepan over low heat. Add onion and cook, stirring, until soft but not browned, about 5 minutes. Add garlic and jalapeño pepper and cook, stirring, ½ minute. Add curry powder and cook, stirring, ½ minute. Add wine, vinegar, and stock, and simmer over medium heat until liquid is reduced to about 3 tablespoons.

Stir in cream, salt, and pepper and bring to a boil, stirring. Cook over medium heat, stirring often, until sauce is thick enough to coat a spoon, about 4 minutes. Taste and adjust seasoning. *Sauce can be kept, covered, 1 day in refrigerator.*

Makes about ¾ cup; about 4 servings

MADEIRA SAUCE

A traditional partner in Europe and North America for beef and lamb, Madeira sauce is also delicious with roast chicken, turkey, or duck. It is rich in flavor but relatively low in fat.

1 tablespoon vegetable oil
1 medium onion, diced
1 medium carrot, diced
1 medium garlic clove, chopped
4 fresh or canned plum tomatoes, diced
2 cups chicken poaching liquid (page 391), chicken, turkey, or duck stock or canned broth

½ teaspoon dried thyme
1 bay leaf
1 tablespoon tomato paste
2 tablespoons cold water
1 tablespoon potato starch, arrowroot, or cornstarch
salt and freshly ground pepper
¼ cup Madeira
1 tablespoon butter (optional)

Heat oil in a heavy, medium saucepan over medium-high heat. Add onion and carrot and sauté, stirring often, until well browned. Stir in garlic, then tomatoes, poaching liquid or stock, thyme, and bay leaf. Bring to a boil, stirring. Cover and cook over very low heat for 30 minutes. Whisk in tomato paste.

Whisk water into potato starch in a small bowl. Gradually pour mixture into simmering sauce, whisking constantly. Bring back to a boil, whisking. Season lightly with salt and pepper. Strain sauce, pressing on vegetables. *If not using immediately, dab surface of sauce with a small piece of butter to prevent a skin from forming. Sauce can be kept, covered, up to 3 days in refrigerator; or it can be frozen.*

Bring sauce to a boil in a heavy, medium saucepan over medium heat, stirring often. Stir in 2 tablespoons Madeira and simmer uncovered over medium-low heat for 10 minutes. Add remaining 2 tablespoons Madeira and bring just to a simmer. Remove from heat and stir in butter if desired. Taste and adjust seasoning. Serve hot.

Makes about 1½ cups sauce; about 6 servings

MUSTARD CREAM

Serve this quick and easy sauce hot or cold, with poached or roasted chicken or turkey. Originally a French sauce, it has become a favorite in California, where it is often made with a larger quantity of mustard to suit the local love of assertive tastes. If you have flavored mustards, you can use them in the sauce. For extra zip, stir in 2 to 3 teaspoons green peppercorns at the last minute.

1 tablespoon butter
2 shallots or white part of 2 green
  onions, minced
¼ cup dry white wine
½ cup chicken or turkey stock or
  chicken broth

salt and freshly ground pepper
1 cup heavy cream
4 to 6 teaspoons Dijon mustard

Melt butter in a heavy, medium saucepan over low heat. Add shallots and cook, stirring, until softened, about 2 minutes. Add wine, stock, salt, and pepper and simmer, stirring, until liquid is reduced to about 2 tablespoons. Stir in cream and bring to a boil, stirring. Cook over medium heat, stirring often, until sauce is thick enough to coat a spoon, about 7 minutes. *Sauce can be kept, covered, up to 1 day in refrigerator.*

Reheat sauce if necessary, whisking. Reduce heat to low and whisk in 4 teaspoons mustard. Taste, and add salt, pepper, and more mustard if needed. Serve hot or cold.

Makes about ¾ cup sauce; about 4 servings

RED WINE MARINADE SAUCE

This rich sauce of complex flavors, loved in much of Europe, is based on a red wine marinade. After the poultry has been marinated in the mixture, the flavors of the wine, herbs, and spices in the marinade are intensified by the technique of reduction, or boiling until the volume is decreased considerably, before being used in the sauce. The sauce's flavor is rounded out by the addition of stock, and the wine's acidity is balanced by a touch of jelly. Serve the sauce with roasted or broiled game birds, chicken, or turkey.

Classic Red Wine Marinade (page 355)
1 tablespoon butter or vegetable oil
¾ cup chicken or turkey poaching
    liquid (page 391), stock, or broth
1 tablespoon tomato paste

salt and freshly ground pepper
2 tablespoons Cognac or brandy
¼ to ½ cup heavy cream
1 to 2 teaspoons red currant jelly

Using a strainer, separate onions, carrots, and herbs from wine of marinade; reserve both.

Melt butter in a large, heavy saucepan. Add onion and carrot from marinade and cook over medium heat, stirring often, until they begin to brown, about 10 minutes. Add remaining marinade (liquid portion) and bring to a boil. Simmer uncovered, over medium heat, skimming occasionally, for 30 minutes. Add stock, tomato paste, and a small pinch of salt and pepper and bring to a boil. Simmer 10 minutes. Strain sauce into a medium saucepan, pressing on vegetables.

Bring sauce to a boil. Stir in Cognac. Whisk in cream and bring to a boil. If sauce is too thin, simmer it, whisking often, until it is thick enough to lightly coat a spoon. Whisk in jelly. Taste and adjust seasoning. *Sauce can be kept, covered, 1 day in refrigerator; reheat over low heat.*

Makes about ¾ cup; about 4 servings

18

Recipes Using Cooked Chicken or Turkey

Cooked chicken and turkey are treasures in the kitchen. They enable you to quickly and easily make a delicious and satisfying dish. If you have roasted, poached, or braised poultry on hand, you can toss it with cooked pasta and vegetables, stir it into rice pilaf or risotto, or add it to a colorful minestrone for a hearty main course. Moisten cooked chicken or turkey with a zesty vinaigrette for a light salad or top it with pastry for an elegant main-course pie. Combine cooked poultry with sautéed onions, mushrooms, peppers, or other vegetables and wrap the mixture in crepes, or mix chicken or turkey with a spicy cilantro-tomato sauce as a tasty enchilada filling.

Cooked chicken and turkey are interchangeable in most recipes, so use whichever you have.

APPETIZERS AND PASTRIES

SALADS

SOUPS

PASTA AND GRAIN DISHES

OTHER DISHES

Chicken and Vegetables with Korean Sesame Sauce
(page 142)
Turkey Hash with Vegetables and Rosemary (page 146)

SANDWICHES

Chicken Bruschetta (page 285)
Chicken Sandwich in Lavosh (page 286)
Deli-Style Chicken Salad Sandwich (page 287)
Turkey Sandwich with Creole Mayonnaise (page 293)

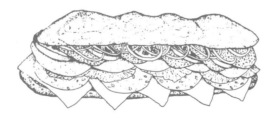

Chicken Stock
Turkey Stock
Basic Poached Chicken
Chinese Omelet Strips
Crepes
Pie Dough

19

Basic Recipes

CHICKEN STOCK

Chicken stock is simply a well-flavored, concentrated chicken soup. It enriches poultry dishes in the world's best cuisines. From Far Eastern to European cooking, stock constitutes the main ingredient of many sauces and soups, and adds flavor to poached and braised chicken dishes. Homemade stock gives an unmistakable fullness of flavor to foods prepared with it.

Chicken stock is the most popular basic stock in the world because its taste harmonizes beautifully with most ingredients and it is much quicker to make than meat stock. In the Chinese kitchen chicken stock is flavored with ginger and green onions and serves as the principal broth. Chicken stock is important in European and American cuisines as well, but in the West it is flavored with onion, carrot, bay leaves, and sometimes thyme or celery.

The most difficult aspect of preparing chicken stock as a basis for other dishes is making enough of it—it disappears quickly because it's so easy to heat up for a satisfying snack. Strained chicken stock, with perhaps just a sprinkling of parsley, cilantro, or green onion, makes a light, comforting first course.

What cut to use in making stock is up to you. Except for breast pieces, almost any part of the chicken is fine. A whole chicken is perfect, and is usually more economical than chicken pieces. Sometimes backs and necks are sold at a low price for making stock, but if they are used alone, I find that the stock's flavor is not as fine. They also give off a large amount of fat. Occasionally I combine veal bones with chicken pieces for a veal-chicken stock, which is very good in sauces, but this requires 6 hours of cooking for the veal bones to give off their flavor.

3 pounds chicken pieces, including
   backs, necks, wing tips, and giblets
   (except livers)
2 medium onions, quartered
green part of 1 leek (optional), cleaned
   (page 408)
2 medium carrots, quartered

2 bay leaves
5 stems of parsley without leaves
   (optional)
about 4 quarts water
2 fresh thyme sprigs, or ½ teaspoon
   dried leaves, crumbled
½ teaspoon black peppercorns

Combine chicken, onions, leek, carrots, bay leaves, and parsley in a stock pot or other large pot. Add enough water to cover ingredients. Bring to a boil, skimming foam from top. Add thyme and peppercorns.

Reduce heat to very low so that stock bubbles very gently. Partly cover and cook, skimming foam and fat occasionally, for 2 to 3 hours.

Strain stock into large bowls; discard mixture in strainer. If not using immediately, cool to lukewarm. Refrigerate or freeze stock. *Stock can be kept, covered, 3 days in refrigerator; or it can be frozen several months.* Before using, skim solidified fat off top.

Makes about 10 cups

NOTE: If you wish to substitute canned chicken broth for homemade stock, I find the low-salt varieties are best.

TURKEY STOCK

This is an easy stock that can be prepared while the turkey is roasting, and used to enrich the sauce or gravy. Duck or goose stock are made the same way.

turkey neck and giblets (except liver)
1 medium onion, diced
1 medium carrot, diced
1 celery stalk, diced (optional)

1 bay leaf
½ teaspoon dried thyme, crumbled
2 cups water
2 cups chicken stock

In a medium saucepan combine turkey neck and giblets (except liver), onion, carrot, celery, bay leaf, thyme, water and chicken stock. Bring to a boil. Cover and simmer over low heat for 1 to 1½ hours. Strain stock. Use at once, refrigerate, or freeze. *Stock can be kept, covered, 3 days in refrigerator; or it can be frozen several months.*

Makes about 3 cups

NOTE: For a darker colored stock, sauté the giblets in 2 tablespoons vegetable oil over medium-high heat until browned. Add the vegetables and sauté until beginning to brown. Continue as above.

VARIATION: **Duck or Goose Stock**
   Substitute duck or goose neck and giblets for those of turkey.

BASIC POACHED CHICKEN

When you need cooked chicken for salads or any recipe that calls for poached chicken, here is an easy and fairly quick European-American way to prepare it. You can poach light or dark meat, whichever you prefer; the light meat cooks faster. Chicken for poaching is added to hot liquid rather than cold, because you're not trying to draw its flavor out into the liquid as you are when making soup. Generally chicken cooked on the bone is more moist and flavorful but to save time you can poach boneless chicken, as in the variation.

As soon as the chicken is tender, it is removed from the liquid, which can be used as a light stock or soup. If you want a more concentrated stock or soup, you can return the chicken bones to the liquid to cook for another hour, or cook the broth uncovered until it is reduced by one-fourth to one-half.

1 medium onion, sliced
2 small carrots, sliced
2 bay leaves
½ teaspoon dried thyme

salt and freshly ground pepper
3 or 4 cups water
6 chicken thighs, drumsticks, or breast
 halves, with skin and bones

Combine onion, carrots, bay leaves, thyme, salt, and pepper in a sauté pan with 3 cups water. Bring to a simmer. Add chicken and more water if needed so chicken is just covered. Return to a simmer. Cover and cook over low heat until chicken is tender, about 25 minutes for breasts, 35 minutes for drumsticks and 45 to 50 minutes for thighs.

If using for salad, remove skin, bones and any visible fat.

Makes about 3 to 6 servings; or 2½ to 3 cups diced chicken for salads.

VARIATION: **Poached Boneless Chicken**
Poach 1½ pounds boneless breasts or thighs about 15 to 20 minutes, or until meat changes color throughout.

CHINESE OMELET STRIPS

Bright yellow omelet strips are traditional additions to Oriental noodle-and-chicken dishes and salads.

2 teaspoons vegetable oil
2 large eggs

salt and freshly ground pepper

Heat oil in a 10-inch skillet, preferably nonstick, over medium heat. Tilt pan to coat it with oil. Beat eggs with salt and pepper to taste. Add egg mixture to hot oil and cook it, loosening sides often with a pancake turner to allow the uncooked egg mixture to flow to edge of pan, for 2 minutes, or until it is set. Slide pancake turner carefully underneath to release omelet. Cut omelet in half with pancake turner. Turn each half omelet over and cook it for ½ minute longer. Transfer omelet halves carefully to a plate and let them cool to room temperature. Cut each omelet half in half lengthwise, then in crosswise strips about ¼-inch wide.

Makes 4 servings

CREPES

Crepes are wonderful for turning small amounts of chicken into tasty treats. Melted butter in the batter gives these crepes a delicious flavor and makes them easy to cook, as little or no additional butter is needed for greasing the crepe pan.

3 large eggs
1¼ cups milk, or a little more if
   needed

¾ cup all-purpose flour
¾ teaspoon salt
4 tablespoons (½ stick) unsalted butter

Combine eggs, ¼ cup of milk, flour, and salt in food processor and mix using several on/off turns; batter will be lumpy. Scrape down sides and bottom of processor container. With machine running, pour 1 cup milk through feed tube and process batter about 15 seconds. Scrape down sides and bottom again. Blend batter about 15 seconds.

Strain batter if it is lumpy. Cover and refrigerate about 1 hour. *Batter can be refrigerated, covered, up to 1 day. Bring to room temperature before continuing.*

Melt butter in a small saucepan over low heat. Gradually whisk 2 tablespoons melted butter into crepe batter. Pour remaining butter into small cup. Skim off foam to clarify. Batter should have consistency of whipping cream. If it is too thick, gradually whisk in more milk, about 1 teaspoon at a time.

Heat crepe pan or skillet with 6- to 6½-inch base over medium-high heat. Sprinkle with few drops of water. If water immediately sizzles, pan is hot enough. Brush pan lightly with some of clarified butter; if using nonstick pan, no butter is needed. Remove pan from heat and hold it near bowl of batter. Working quickly, fill a quarter-cup measure half-full of batter (to easily measure 2 tablespoons) and add batter to one edge of pan, tilting and swirling pan until its base is covered with thin layer of batter. Immediately pour any excess batter back into bowl.

Return pan to medium-high heat. Loosen edges of crepe with metal spatula, discarding any pieces of crepe clinging to sides of pan. Cook crepe until its bottom browns lightly. Turn crepe carefully over by sliding spatula under it. Cook until second side browns lightly in spots. Slide crepe out onto plate. Reheat pan a few seconds. Make crepes with remaining batter, stirring it occasionally with whisk. Adjust heat and add more clarified butter to pan if necessary. If batter thickens, gradually whisk in a little more milk, about 1 teaspoon at a time. Pile crepes on plate as they are done. *Crepes can be kept, wrapped tightly, up to 3 days in refrigerator; or they can be frozen. Bring them to room temperature before using, to avoid tearing them.*

Makes about 20 crepes; 6 to 8 servings

NOTE: To prepare batter in blender, combine eggs, 1¼ cups milk, flour, and salt in blender. Mix on high speed until batter is smooth, about 1 minute.

PIE DOUGH

Use this to make Chicken Pot Pie (page 37) or other chicken pies.

2 cups all-purpose flour
½ teaspoon salt
½ cup (1 stick) cold unsalted butter,
   cut in bits

3 tablespoons cold vegetable
   shortening
5 to 6 tablespoons ice water

Combine flour and salt in a food processor fitted with metal blade. Process briefly to blend. Scatter butter pieces and shortening over mixture. Mix, using on/off turns, until mixture resembles coarse meal. Pour 5 tablespoons water evenly over mixture in processor. Process with on/off turns, scraping down occasionally, until dough forms sticky crumbs that can easily be pressed together but do not come together in a ball. If crumbs are dry, sprinkle ½ teaspoon water, and process with on/off turns until dough forms sticky crumbs. Add more water in same way, ½ teaspoon at a time, if crumbs are still dry. Using a rubber spatula, transfer dough to a sheet of plastic wrap, wrap it, and push it together. Shape dough in a flat disk and refrigerate 1 hour or up to overnight.

Makes enough for a 9½- to 10-inch square pie

20

Buying and Storing Poultry

Most of the chickens at the store are broiler-fryers, which weigh on the average 3 to 3½ pounds and make four portions. This is an all-purpose chicken, and can be used for all cooking techniques—broiling, grilling, frying, roasting, braising, and poaching.

Roasting chickens and capons are larger and usually more flavorful than broiler-fryers. They are perfect for roasting, but I find that roasting chickens are also delicious braised and poached.

Stewing chickens, sometimes called stewing hens, can occasionally be found at some markets. They are best for making soup. Because they are more mature than broiler-fryers and roasting chickens, they require longer simmering, but the result is tastier soup.

Cut-up chickens are readily available in most supermarkets. Sometimes the packages of assorted chicken pieces vary in price, depending on whether it's a whole chicken that is simply cut in pieces, or whether only the meaty parts—the legs, thighs, breasts, and wings, but not the backs—are included.

You can buy separately packaged chicken drumsticks, thighs, or legs, the latter being thighs with drumsticks attached. At fine markets, thighs are also available boneless. Chicken breasts can be purchased as half breasts with skin and bones or as boneless half breasts with or without skin. The tender strip of meat at the bottom of the breast is sold as "chicken tenders" or "fillets," but labeling is not standard, and sometimes the word *fillets* refers simply to boneless breasts. Wings are available whole and as drummettes—the meaty section of the wing, which looks like a small drumstick. Chicken backs and necks are packaged for making stock or soup.

Turkeys are available at a great range of weights. Their size does not determine their tenderness or flavor, so what size to buy depends on how many portions you want it to serve. Allow ¾ to 1 pound of turkey per serving.

Turkey is also sold in parts. You can buy a whole or half breast, either with bones or as a boneless roast. For quick cooking, there are long boneless breast "tenderloins" or "steaks," which are a muscle from the breast, and thin turkey breast slices or cutlets, which are cut crosswise. Turkey thighs, drumsticks, and wings are also sold separately, for braising or poaching.

Ground chicken and turkey are readily available and can be substituted for ground beef in many recipes, for a dish that is lower in fat. Leanest of all is ground turkey breast, which is offered at upscale markets.

Chicken and turkey, both whole and in parts, are marketed fresh or frozen.

Most other poultry and game birds—geese, Cornish hens, pheasant, quail, and squab—are available only whole and usually frozen. Occasionally boneless duck breasts can be purchased separately.

Some markets carry two additional types of poultry: free range and kosher. Free-range poultry, sometimes called organic or natural, is raised with more living space in which to roam than other poultry and little or no chemicals, and the poultry are fed a natural grain diet that they supplement with what they catch. The most commonly available free-range poultry is chicken and turkey. Kosher poultry is prepared under rabbinical supervision. It is slaughtered by a special method and often koshered, or salted, according to Jewish dietary law. Some kosher poultry is raised in a way similar to free-range poultry. Kosher chickens, turkeys, Cornish hens, ducks, and geese are available often in the frozen foods section of supermarkets. Some people find that these higher-priced birds taste better. Others buy them for philosophical or religious reasons.

When choosing packaged poultry, select packages with little or no liquid. Whole birds should be plump and should have smooth, tight skin. The color of a chicken's skin varies from white to deep yellow, depending on diet, and does not indicate a difference in quality. If the poultry is not packaged, it should have no unpleasant odor. Packages of frozen poultry should not be torn and should not have frozen liquid.

If you purchase packaged poultry, store it in its original packaging. Fresh poultry should be used within 1 or 2 days of purchase, or of the "sell-by" date, if there is one. Frozen whole chickens or turkeys keep for 1 year in the freezer, chicken parts keep for 9 months, and turkey parts for 6 months.

21

Guidelines for Handling Poultry

Today's standards of hygiene are stricter than in the past. Whereas older recipes advised us to bring chickens to room temperature before roasting them, or to marinate them at room temperature, today this is discouraged. Instead, poultry should be kept in the refrigerator until you are ready to cook it. It should be cooked until well done and served hot or cold, but not at room temperature. Once the poultry is cooked, it should not be left at room temperature for longer than 2 hours.

Some recipes recommend rinsing poultry before cooking. According to the latest information from the U.S. Department of Agriculture, this is optional and is a question of esthetics, but is not necessary from a microbiological standpoint.

It is very important, however, to wash your hands with hot water and soap before and after you handle poultry. Also, the cutting board and any utensils that were in contact with raw poultry should be thoroughly washed before being used on any other foods.

397

STORING AND THAWING POULTRY

Fresh poultry keeps only 1 or 2 days in the refrigerator, according to the USDA, and so it can be convenient to use frozen poultry. It should be thawed in the refrigerator, never on the counter.

Defrosting poultry pieces and small birds takes overnight. A frozen chicken or duck requires at least 24 hours and sometimes more to thaw in the refrigerator.

An 8- to 12-pound turkey or goose takes 1 to 2 days to thaw in the refrigerator; a 12- to 16-pound turkey takes 2 to 3 days.

If you forgot to take the bird out of the freezer, you can thaw it more quickly by putting the bird in its unopened bag in a sinkful of cold water. A duck or chicken will take several hours, an 8- to 12-pound bird will take 4 to 6 hours, and a 12- to 16-pound bird will require 6 to 9 hours. The water should be changed often, about every 30 minutes.

If you have questions about storing or handling poultry, you can call the USDA Meat and Poultry Hotline's toll-free number: 1-800-535-4555.

PREPARING POULTRY FOR COOKING

1. Whole birds usually come with giblets inside, either loose or in a packet. Remove them before cooking the bird. The liver can be sautéed or grilled; the other giblets can be used to flavor sauces or stocks.

2. Lift the two flaps of skin near the bird's tail. Often they have a pad of fat on each side. This fat should be pulled out.

3. If a bird has pinfeathers, singe them for a few seconds over a direct flame and pull them out before roasting.

CHECKING POULTRY FOR DONENESS

If the poultry is large enough so a thermometer can be inserted about 2 inches into it, use a meat thermometer or instant-read thermometer to check its temperature. Insert the thermometer in the thickest part of the thigh. Boneless turkey should be 170°F. when it is done. Poultry with a bone should reach 180°F.

To check smaller cuts of poultry, pierce it with a skewer in the thickest part of the thigh. The juices that come out should run clear.

If cooking a boneless breast or other small piece of meat, check the color of the meat at the thickest part; for chickens or turkey, it should be white rather than pink. With other birds, the color varies depending on the variety of the bird. Consult individual recipes for direction.

STORING AND REHEATING COOKED POULTRY

Cooked poultry should not be left at room temperature for longer than 2 hours. The meat should be refrigerated or frozen in several shallow, covered containers. If covered with broth or gravy, poultry keeps 1 or 2 days in the refrigerator; other cooked poultry dishes keep 3 to 4 days in the refrigerator.

Do not try to reheat leftover roast poultry on the carcass. The heat will take too long to reach the bird's interior and the meat will dry out. The best way is to remove the meat from the bones, cut it in pieces and either broil or sauté it in a skillet, or heat it gently but thoroughly in chicken stock.

TIP

✗ To shred chicken, pull it apart or cut it in thin pieces, following the natural grain of the meat.

HOW TO TRUSS POULTRY

Chefs insist on trussing poultry before roating it. Trussing keeps a bird in a neat, compact shape for roasting, holds the neck skin over the breast meat to protect this meat, and prevents the legs and wings from drying out. In home kitchens trussing is an optional step; it can be skipped to save time.

This method can be used for chickens, ducks, and turkeys. For an easier way to truss a turkey, see the instructions on "turkey," below.

1. Thread a trussing needle with string and tie a knot at the eye. Put the bird on its back and hold the legs close to the body. Stick the needle into one leg between the thigh and the drumstick and push it through the body and then out through the other leg.

2. Turn the bird over. Push the needle through the closer wing, then through the neck skin and under the backbone, then through the other wing, securing the wings and neck skin to the back. Turn the bird on its back and tie the ends of the string tightly.

3. Push the tail well into the bird's cavity. Using a new piece of string, insert the needle through the lower part of the drumstick, then through the fold of the tail, through the lower part of the other drumstick, and back over this drumstick, through the flaps of skin above the tail. Tie the ends of the string tightly.

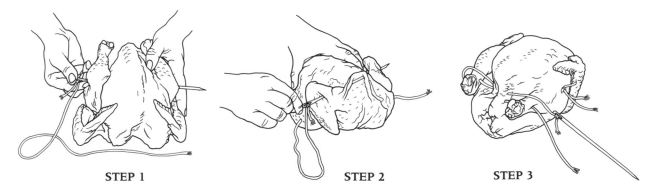

STEP 1   STEP 2   STEP 3

Here is a simpler way to truss that does not require a trussing needle:

Push the bird's tail into the body. Tie two pieces of kitchen string around the bird crosswise, so that one holds the neck skin over the breast meat and the wings tightly to the body and the other holds the legs to the body and the tail inside.

TRUSSING TURKEY: An easy way to truss a turkey or other bird, in order to keep a soft stuffing from coming out, is to close the skin flaps with small skewers.

HOW TO CARVE A ROAST CHICKEN OR DUCK

1. Slit the skin between one thigh and the body with a boning knife or thin sharp knife, and pull the leg back to expose the joint attaching it to the body. Cut at the joint and remove the leg and thigh piece; repeat with the second leg. If desired, cut each leg in two at the joint between the leg and the thigh, using a heavy knife.

2. With the boning knife, cut lengthwise along each side of the breastbone, slitting the breast meat. Carefully slip the knife under each breast half to separate it from the breastbone and remove the meat in one piece, pulling it back and scraping with the knife. For a duck or large chicken, you might like to slice the breast meat in lengthwise or in diagonal slices.

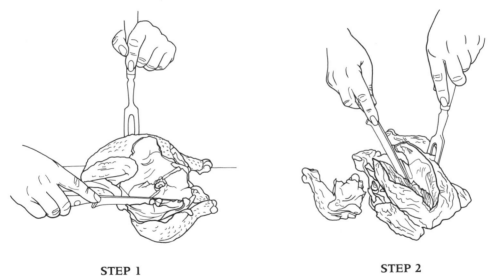

STEP 1   STEP 2

HOW TO CARVE A ROAST TURKEY

There are two basic ways to carve a turkey, the "kitchen method" and the "table method." In both methods, the drumstick and thigh meat are carved the same way.

The two methods differ in the way to carve the breast meat: For the "kitchen method," each breast is removed in one piece, placed on the cutting board and sliced. The advantage is that you can carve thin, even slices. For the "table method" the breast is cut in slices while it is still on the turkey. This method is more convenient for large turkeys because removing a heavy turkey breast in one piece from a hot turkey can be awkward.

CARVING DARK MEAT:

1. Remove drumstick and thigh as in carving a chicken: Slit skin between leg and body, pull leg away from body, and cut through joint connecting leg to body. Cut off any dark meat remaining on body.

2. Place leg on cutting boad and cut through joint connecting drumstick to thigh.

3. To carve drumstick meat, hold bone and slice meat downward. Cut thigh meat in thin slices parallel to bone.

4. To carve breast meat, follow either kitchen method or table method below.

CARVING BREAST MEAT—KITCHEN METHOD:

5. With a sharp knife, cut lengthwise along one side of the breastbone, slitting the breast meat. Carefully cut the breast half away from the breastbone and rib cage. Remove the beast half in one piece.

6. Place breast meat on cutting board and cut in thin, even slices. Repeat with other breast.

CARVING BREAST MEAT—TABLE METHOD:

5. With carving fork placed in one side of turkey breast, hold turkey firmly on cutting board. With knife close to wing on opposite side of bird, make a deep cut horizontally into breast meat, cutting toward ribs. This will make it easier to carve neat slices, as each slice will end at this cut.

6. With a sharp, thin-bladed knife, carve breast on one side in thin even slices by carving downward. Repeat with other side.

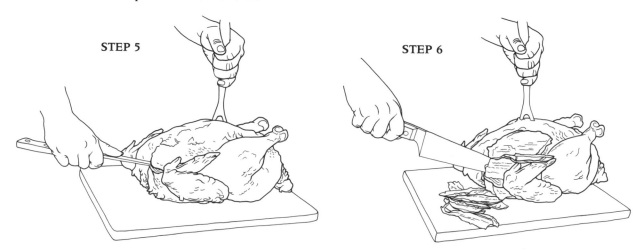

STEP 5   STEP 6

HOW TO CUT A CHICKEN IN PIECES

This method of cutting chicken produces 8 small pieces or 4 servings, each of which includes both light and dark meat, plus 2 back pieces for flavoring the sauce.

1. Pull out and discard fat from chicken. Using a large knife, cut off wing tips. Reserve wing tips and neck for adding flavor to sauce or for chicken stock.

2. Using a boning knife or medium-sized sharp knife, cut skin between leg and body. Outline the small round piece of meat (the "oyster") in center of back behind each leg, so this piece will remain attached to leg meat. Pull leg back until joint attaching it to body is visible. Cut through joint, then along body to separate rest of leg meat. Repeat with other leg.

3. Move drumstick until you feel joint between it and thigh. Separate each leg piece in two by cutting through this joint.

4. Holding chicken with neck side down, divide back half from breast half by cutting along edge of rib cage with knife, so that rib bones remain attached to back section. Use a heavy knife or poultry shears to separate back from breast section at neck end.

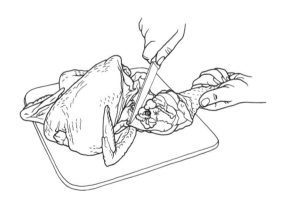

STEP 2

STEP 4

5. Move wing to feel joint attaching it to body. With boning knife, cut through joint and cut off a lengthwise strip from the edge of the breast meat along with wing, so this strip remains attached to wing. Repeat with other wing.

6. Use heavy knife or poultry shears to cut breast section in half lengthwise. If any small sharp bones protrude from breast meat, cut them off with poultry shears and discard them.

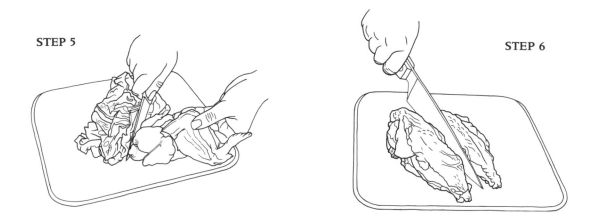

STEP 5   STEP 6

HOW TO QUARTER A CHICKEN OR DUCK

For roasting chicken or duck in pieces rather than whole, it can be convenient to quarter them, to avoid having to carve the hot bird before serving. The technique is similar to cutting a chicken in pieces.

1. Pull out and discard fat from bird. Using a large knife, cut off wing tips if desired.

2. Using a boning knife or medium-sized sharp knife, cut skin between leg and body. Outline the small round piece of meat (the "oyster") in center of back behind each leg, so this piece will remain attached to leg meat. Pull leg back until joint attaching it to body is visible. Cut through joint, then along body to separate rest of leg meat. Repeat with other leg.

3. Cut along backbone of bird with heavy knife or poultry shears to split bird in half. Open bird flat. Cut off backbone. Then cut breast in half along breastbone. Cut off neck skin with excess fat.

4. Reserve wing tips, neck, and back for making stock.

HOW TO BONE A CHICKEN BREAST

In most markets boneless chicken breasts are easy to find, but preparing your own saves money. You can prepare boneless chicken breast halves from whole or half breasts.

1. If wings are attached to breasts, cut them off at the joint.

2. If you would like skinless chicken breasts, remove the skin by pulling it off. Hold the skin with a paper towel to get a good grip on it. Cut off any pieces of skin that remain attached to meat with the aid of a paring knife.

3. If you have a whole chicken breast, use a sharp boning knife or thin sharp knife to slit breast meat lengthwise along one side of breastbone. Keeping knife close to bone and gently pulling meat away from bone, cut and pull breast meat off bone. Cut to release meat. Repeat with other side of breast.

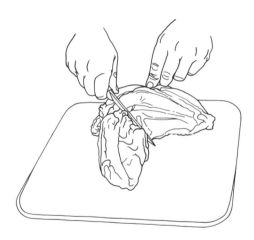

STEP 3

If you have chicken breast halves, follow step 3 above for each one. Begin to remove meat near cut side of breast, which will be the longest side of the piece.
Save the bones for stock.

22

Cooking Techniques

PEELING AND SEEDING TOMATOES

To peel, cut cores from tomatoes. Turn tomatoes over and slit skin in an X-shaped cut. Fill a large bowl with cold water. Put tomatoes in a saucepan of enough boiling water to cover them generously and boil them 10 to 15 seconds or until skin begins to pull away from flesh. Remove tomatoes with a slotted spoon and put them in the bowl of cold water. Leave for a few seconds. Remove tomatoes and pull off skins.

To seed, cut tomatoes in half horizontally. Hold each half over a bowl, cut side down, and squeeze to remove the seeds and juice.

ROASTING AND PEELING
PEPPERS AND CHILIES

Bell peppers: Put boiler rack about 4 inches from heat. Preheat broiler. Broil peppers turning every 4 or 5 minutes with tongs, until pepper skin is blistered and charred, 15 to 20 minutes. Transfer to a bowl and cover, or put in a bag and close bag. Let stand 10 minutes. Peel using paring knife. Discard top, seeds, and ribs. Be careful; there may be hot liquid inside pepper. Drain well and pat dry.

Anaheim chilies (mild green chilies): Put broiler rack 2 inches from heat. Roast chilies, turning often, until skin is blackened on all sides, about 7 to 10 minutes. Continue as for bell peppers.

Jalapeño peppers: Roast as for Anaheim chilies, for about 5 minutes.

CLEANING LEEKS

Discard very dark green parts of leeks. Split leeks lengthwise twice by cutting with a sharp knife, beginning about 1 inch from root end and cutting toward green end, leaving root end attached. Dip leeks repeatedly in a sinkful of cold water. Check the layers to be sure no sand is left. Rinse well. Cut off root ends.

PREPARING ARTICHOKE HEARTS

Squeeze juice of ½ lemon into a medium bowl of cold water. Break off stem of 1 artichoke and largest leaves at bottom. Put artichoke on its side on board. Holding a very sharp knife or small serrated knife against side of artichoke (parallel to leaves), cut lower circle of leaves off, up to edge of artichoke heart; turn artichoke slightly after each cut. Rub cut edges of artichoke with cut lemon. Cut off leaves under base. Trim base, removing all dark green areas. Rub again with lemon. Cut off central cone of leaves just above heart. Put artichoke in bowl of lemon water. Repeat with remaining artichokes. Keep artichokes in lemon water until ready to cook them.

To cook artichoke hearts, squeeze any juice remaining in lemon into a medium saucepan of boiling salted water. Add artichoke hearts. Cover and simmer over low heat until tender when pierced with knife, 15 to 20 minutes. Cool to lukewarm in liquid. Using a teaspoon, scoop out hairlike "choke" from center of each artichoke heart.

HOW TO TOAST NUTS

Preheat oven or toaster oven to 350°F. Toast nuts on a small cookie sheet in oven until aromatic and lightly browned; almonds and hazelnuts take about 10 minutes, walnuts and pecans take about 5 minutes, and diced nuts or pine nuts take about 3 minutes. Transfer nuts to a plate and let cool.

HOW TO TOAST SESAME SEEDS

Toast sesame seeds in small dry skillet over medium heat, shaking pan often, about 4 minutes or until golden brown. Transfer immediately to a plate.

MAIL ORDER SOURCES

I purchase all of the ingredients for these recipes in local supermarkets. However, if you can't find an ingredient, here are sources for ordering them by mail:

SPECIALTY POULTRY, SUCH AS PHEASANT, SQUAB, AND QUAIL

CAVANAUGH LAKEVIEW FARMS LTD.
821 Lowery Road
P.O. Box 580
Chelsea, MI 48118-0580
800-243-4438

HOT PEPPER SAUCES, CURRY PASTES, DRIED CHILIES

MO HOTTA—MO BETTA
P.O. Box 4136
San Luis Obispo, CA 93403
800-462-3220

SPICES AND INGREDIENTS FOR INDIAN COOKING

HOUSE OF SPICES
76-17 Broadway
Jackson Heights, NY 11373
718-476-1577

SPICES AND INGREDIENTS FOR CENTRAL EUROPEAN COOKING

PAPRIKAS WEISS IMPORTERS
1546 Second Avenue
New York, NY 10028
212-288-6117

ORIENTAL INGREDIENTS

CHINA BOWL TRADING COMPANY
169 Lackawanna Avenue
Parsippany, NJ 07054
800-526-5051
201-335-1000

SPECIALTY GRAINS AND INGREDIENTS FROM EUROPE, ASIA, AFRICA, AND SOUTH AMERICA

G.B. RATTO & CO. INTERNATIONAL
  GROCERS
821 Washington Street
Oakland, CA 94607
800-228-3515 (in CA, 800-325-3483)
415-836-2250

SPECIALTY OILS AND VINEGARS

WILLIAMS-SONOMA
Mail Order Department
P.O. Box 7456
San Francisco, CA 94120-7456
800-541-2233
415-421-4242

DEAN AND DELUCA
560 Broadway
New York, NY 10012
212-431-1691
800-221-7714

CONVERSION CHART

LIQUID MEASURES

Fluid Ounces	U.S. Measures	Imperial Measures	Milliliters
	1 tsp.	1 tsp.	5
¼	2 tsp.	1 dessert spoon	7
½	1 T.	1 T.	15
1	2 T.	2 T.	28
2	¼ cup	4 T.	56
4	½ cup or ¼ pint		110
5		¼ pint or 1 gill	140
6	¾ cup		170
8	1 cup or ½ pint		225
9			250 (¼ liter)
10	1¼ cups	½ pint	280
12	1½ cups or ¾ pint		340
15		¾ pint	420
16	2 cups or 1 pint		450
18	2¼ cups		500 (½ liter)
20	2½ cups	1 pint	560
24	3 cups or 1½ pints		675
25		1¼ pints	700
27	3½ cups		750
30	3¾ cups	1½ pints	840
32	4 cups or 2 pints or 1 quart		900
35		1¾ pints	980
36	4½ cups		1000 (1 liter)

SOLID MEASURES

U.S. and Imperial Measures		Metric Measures	
Ounces	Pounds	Grams	Kilos
1		28	
2		56	
3½		100	
4	¼	112	
5		140	
6		168	
8	½	225	
9		250	¼
12	¾	340	
16	1	450	
18		500	½
20	1¼	560	
24	1½	675	
27		750	¾
28	1¾	780	
32	2	900	
36	2¼	1000	1
40		1100	
48	3	1350	
54		1500	1½

OVEN TEMPERATURE EQUIVALENTS

Fahrenheit	Gas Mark	Celsius	Heat of Oven
225	¼	107	Very Cool
250	½	121	Very Cool
275	1	135	Cool
300	2	148	Cool
325	3	163	Moderate
350	4	177	Moderate
375	5	190	Fairly Hot
400	6	204	Fairly Hot
425	7	218	Hot
450	8	232	Very Hot
475	9	246	Very Hot

INDEX

413